Hey Ho Let's Go
The Story Of The
Ramones

EVERETT TRUE

OMNIBUS PRESS
London/New York/Paris/Sydney/Copenhagen/Berlin/Madrid/Tokyo

Jacket designed by Chloë Alexander
Picture research by Steve Behan

ISBN: 0.7119.9108.1
Order No: OP 48686

Exclusive Distributors:
Music Sales Limited,
8/9 Frith Street,
London W1D 3JB, UK.

Music Sales Corporation,
257 Park Avenue South,
New York, NY 10010, USA.

Macmillan Distribution Services,
53 Park West Drive,
Derrimut, Vic 3030,
Australia.

To the Music Trade only:
Music Sales Limited,
8/9 Frith Street,
London W1D 3JB, UK.

Every effort has been made to trace the copyright holders of the photographs in this book but one or two were unreachable. We would be grateful if the photographers concerned would contact us.

Typeset by Galleon Typesetting, Ipswich.
Printed in Great Britain by Creative Print & Design (Wales) Limited

A catalogue record for this book is available from the British Library.

www.omnibuspress.com

Contents

Acknowledgements

All of the following people gave freely of their time to be interviewed for this book, and have my heartfelt thanks:

Joey Ramone (singer), Tommy Ramone (drummer and producer), Marky Ramone (drummer), CJ Ramone (bass player), Arturo Vega (creative director), Monte Melnick (tour manager), Daniel Rey (guitarist and producer), Andy Shernoff (bass player), Ed Stasium (producer), Craig Leon (producer), Ida Langsam (PR), John Holmstrom (editor and cartoonist), George Seminara (video director), George DuBose (photographer), Roberta Bayley (photographer), Donna Gaines (doctor and sociologist), George Tabb (writer, guitarist and fan), David Fricke (writer), Linda Stein (manager), Janis Schacht (PR), Jaan Uhelszki (writer), Joan Tarshis (writer), Kevin Patrick (record executive), Rachel Felder (writer), Michael Hill (writer and record executive), Rodney Bingenheimer (Mr LA himself), Handsome Dick Manitoba (The Dictators), Captain Sensible (The Damned), Gary Valentine (ex-Blondie), Helen Love (Helen Love), Brijitte West (ex-NY Loose), Kim Thayil (ex-Soundgarden), Carla Olla (ex-Spikey Tops), Cynth Sley (ex-Bush Tetras), Don Fleming (guitarist and producer), Nicole Spector (student), David Kessel (producer), Andy Paley (ex-Paley Brothers), Victor Bockris (writer), Slim Moon (record executive), Pete Gofton (ex-Kenickie), Harvey Kubernik (writer), Mark Bannister (fan), Lindsay Hutton (fan), Roy Carr (writer), Chris Charlesworth (writer), Scott Rowley (writer), Mark Spivey (writer), Leigh Marklew (Terrorvision), Gloria Nicholl (PR and manager), Eric Erlandson (ex-Hole), Carol Clerk (writer), Lisa Gottheil (PR), Marty Thau (manager), Carrie Brownstein (Sleater-Kinney), Mark Perry (fanzine writer), David Keegan (ex-Shop Assistants), Seymour Stein (record executive) and Danny Fields (manager).

Many thanks to http://www.ramones-club.de/ for additional background information on solo material and tour dates, and also to Arturo Vega's official Ramones site www.officialramones.com.

The following people also helped, in one form or another – Risa (for her efforts in helping me set up the Stein interviews), Mickey Leigh, Grace

Fox (for all those hours of transcription, and unpaid research), my fiancée Charlotte Snazell (for her love and support under testing circumstances), my editor Chris Charlesworth (for his unflagging good humour), Andy Neill and Penny Brignell.

I would also like to single out Mark Bannister, Daniel Rey and Ida Langsam, and those members of the Ramones I was able to speak to, for help above and beyond. I was particularly touched by the obvious love and affection in which all those around the Ramones still clearly hold them. Daniel, CJ, Arturo, Monte, Tommy . . . these are some fine people indeed.

This book is dedicated to my brother Mick Thackray.

Introduction

Willesden 1984. I saved up for weeks to buy *Too Tough To Die* on import, and was so excited when I took it back home. The first time I took it out of its sleeve to play on my Dansette mono record player, my tiny white kitten – who was also excited – jumped up onto the vinyl as it spun round on the turntable. The cat and I then embarked on an exciting game of hide and seek round the house while Joey's voice sounded out, poignant and raw and scratched.

That same year, I formed a New Wave a cappella group, The Legend! And His Swinging Soul Sisters with my brother and Dave Smith from work, for the sole purpose of singing Ramones and Sixties soul covers in front of a live audience. We'd learnt the first rule of punk: that it didn't matter how proficient you were at playing guitar – indeed, we'd taken the "less is more" maxim of the Ramones to its logical conclusion. We'd dispensed with instruments altogether.

London Electric Ballroom, 29/2/80. One of the first times I saw Ramones was also one of only two times I took my shirt off while dancing. I was so hot, and the whole venue was going berserk, jumping up and down. In the distance, I spied one other person with his shirt off. So I thought I'd pogo my way over to him. It was my brother Michael, the one who turned me onto the Ramones and pop music back in 1976, the same brother I once mistook for Joey in a photograph in *Punk* magazine – that famous shot of Joey cuddling up in bed with Debbie Harry. I didn't even know he was at the show.

On the way back down the underground, I led the chants of "Hey ho let's go!"

Seattle, April 1999. After a nine-month residence as the music editor of grungetown USA's iconoclastic *The Stranger* weekly paper, I fulfil a lifelong ambition by performing a set of Ramones covers at my farewell party with local scum rock band The Promise Keepers as back-up. It was the first time (aside from with a brief college band) that I'd ever sung a Ramones song with guitars behind me. Man, it felt sweet as I hugged and leant over the microphone stand, like a slightly more rotund Joey – savouring every last drawled-out vowel, the drums churning up blue thunder.

Of course, we only chose songs from the first three albums.

New York, 1989. I'm recording a single for Sub Pop. More importantly, I'm interviewing Joey Ramone for *Melody Maker*. (This, after I've had several dreams where I've been watching the Ramones down the front of a tiny pub venue: myself and no one else. They're incredible, of course – but Dee Dee, pissed off with the lack of attention, announces he's had enough and he's out of here! Two weeks before I interview Joey, Dee Dee leaves the band.) Joey is like the tallest, sweetest man I've ever met. He shows me his stack of Sixties psychedelic art posters, and plays me tracks from a projected solo (country) album. I ask him if he'd like to come down to the studio and sing backing harmonies on an a cappella version of 'Rockaway Beach'. He agrees, but never shows. Instead, he phones the studio and spends 15 minutes making up some lame apology . . .

"Hey Jerry? It's Joey here. I'm real sorry, but I can't make it down to the studio today."

Lollapalooza, 1996. I'm passed out drunk on the ground, among the sand and dirt, 115 in the shade. Screaming Trees singer Mark Lanegan is pouring water over me, in a desperate attempt to keep me alive. Joey Ramone walks by and tells me, "Hey man! Don't rock the ground!"

Later, I can be seen dancing wildly down the front, banging the heads of kids half my age together, and screaming, "This is the Ramones, you assholes! Dance! DANCE!"

London Lyceum Ballroom, February 1985. The Ramones are having equipment difficulties. The sound keeps cutting in and out. During one of the breaks, buzzing and perspiring freely from the manic dancing, I yell at Dee Dee, "Give us a solo." The Ramones weren't known for their spontaneity – indeed, it was anathema to their creed – but the bassist obliged, by playing his teeth for a few seconds, creating a tuneful noise with his finger inside his cheek, the way some people are able to.

For months afterwards, I would tell people how Dee Dee had played a "tooth solo" for me.

Chelmsford, 1976. I've sneaked the first Ramones album down from my brother's stash and am listening to it on the family radiogram. It sounds strange, oddly tuneful in a buzzsaw way. My mother comes into the room, and utters the immortal words "but where are the *tunes*?" The tunes? There were bloody millions of them, not only that, but the Ramones had thoughtfully left spaces where you could fill in your own on the top. I knew right then that anyone able to create a generation gap was good, decent and proper.

I'll miss you, Joey and Dee Dee.

everett_true@hotmail.com

"THEY WERE ALWAYS there. They were always there. Even after they'd split up – they were still always there. It wasn't like they'd gone away. And I think that's probably why the waves of shock hit the entire music community across the world. It's like one of the things that had become permanent touchstones in their lives had suddenly been taken away from them and they weren't expecting it. I don't think actually that many people knew Joey was ill.

"Those of us who knew him, who were friends with him, we knew he was ill. Many of us knew that he'd been in the hospital since his fall that December night. And I knew in the last week that things had gotten worse. I didn't realise how much worse they'd gotten but I knew he was doing much worse in the last week than he had previously. But the general public didn't know. Joey never went out and made any kind of general announcement about his condition – why would he?

"The Ramones always kept their troubles to themselves. That was part of being a family unit. They never took the stance that they were stars. People who view themselves as celebrities, often have this demeanour that everything they do is newsworthy – and therefore many of them air their dirty laundry in public. You never knew personal things about the Ramones. You didn't know who was married, who wasn't married, if any of them were going out with someone, if they had children. You didn't know any of that."

(Author's interview with Ida Langsam, Ramones PR, 2002)

1

Hills Street Blues

THE TIME YOU discover there's life outside school, outside your family, outside your immediate environs, that's the real important time in life. It's when your tastes, your sense of being, your ideals and morals and sexual preferences coalesce and become real: adolescence shapes your future life. Yet it's also a period that is rarefied to the extreme – and that's why rock'n'roll bands always refer back to it, however old they become. Rock bands utilise the teen ideal in their lyrical imagery: see a girl, walk in the park and hang out – Carbona or soda pop, it's your drug of choice. Ramones songs, too, hark back to that time.

"Wait," says Joey Ramone, confused. "Can you repeat that again? When you're young and you're in a structured situation and you want to break away . . . which song in particular are you talking about?"

Your band's oeuvre is shot through with classic teen angst in the style of the doomed Sixties girl groups – 'My-My Kind Of A Girl', 'I Wanna Be Your Boyfriend', 'All Screwed Up' . . .

"That last one is basically about . . . it's about life." Joey laughs. "It's about fucking up. It's also about how you've got to live it the way you learn it, even though you might never really learn it." The singer pauses, considers the question. "It's the story of my life. You never really know and you might never really ever learn. Relationships are the hardest to figure out. I don't believe in giving up.

"When you're about 15, 16, that's when you start to learn how to live and stay alive," he continues. "You learn the ways of the street or else you get fucked. What they teach you in school doesn't prepare you for life. Textbooks don't compare to living in the real world. Rock'n'roll teaches you how to live. When it's your money, and it affects you directly, that's when you wake up. If you don't know how to count and spell or read and write, you'll get fucked with."

(Interview with author, 1989)

"BRIGHT, CHEERFUL HOUSES, well-arranged, well-trimmed lawns, hedging carefully cut . . . distinctly joyous," wrote architectural critic Herbert Croly in 1914 about the Forest Hills Gardens community in Queens, New

York. *The New York Tribune* agreed, reporting the area was a "modern Garden of Eden, a fairy tale too good to be true".

Forest Hills was once a dry riverbed called Whiteput ("pit") by the Dutch. In 1664, English settlers renamed it New Towne. In 1906, sugar-refining heir Cord Meyer built a community on 600 acres that he named Forest Hills because it bordered Forest Park and was on high rolling ground. The Sage Foundation purchased 142 acres in 1909, constructing a Tudor-style community called Forest Hills Gardens, conceived as an experiment that would apply the new science of city planning to a suburban setting and provide alternate housing for the cramped apartment dwellers of New York City.

The middle-class, mostly Jewish, neighbourhood of Forest Hills was known for a couple of reasons by the time the Ramones started attending the local high school.* Its local tennis arena (and part-time rock emporium) was home to the US Tennis Open before the tournament moved to Shea Stadium in 1978. Nearby Flushing Meadow park served as a venue for many a Sixties rock hippie-fest.

According to local websites, Forest Hills is a "piece of small town America smack dab in New York City", wonderful to grow up in during the Fifties and Sixties, with its wide ethnic diversity, and Witts, the early twentieth-century soda fountain on Metropolitan Avenue. It's perfect for commuting to Manhattan, too – 30 minutes on the F train and G local to 8th Street and Sixth Avenue.

Drummer and founder member of the Ramones, Tommy Erdelyi has fond memories of his hometown: "It was a pleasant place to grow up. I liked living there. It had trees and nice streets. It had a good high school, supposedly one of the top 25 in the nation."

Bassist Dee Dee Ramone found it pleasing, too. "It is a nicely groomed neighbourhood with lots of Coupes de Ville and Lincoln's parked on the street," he wrote in his 1997 book *Poison Heart: Surviving The Ramones*. "All the buildings are the same red brick colour, and chewing gum coloured sidewalks snake through the area. In the mornings, the janitors would burn the trash in incinerators and a thick grey smoke would pour out of the chimneys."

Flushing Meadow was also the site of both the 1939 and 1964 World's Fairs. And in much the same way that the 1893 World's Columbian Exposition in Chicago inspired the creation of Coney Island, the 1939 New

* Fellow alumni include Simon & Garfunkel, *Little House On The Prairie*'s Michael Landon, Burt Bacharach and Jerry Seinfeld.

York World's Fair with its amusement parks and vernacular architecture helped inspire the creation of Disney World. Appropriate perhaps for the hometown of a band whose image was so rooted in the cartoons and trash culture of their youth. It was nowhere special, basically – a precursor of the Edge Cities that now take precedence in (lack of) town planning across America.

What better place for four bored teenagers to grow up?

JOEY RAMONE WAS born Jeffrey Hyman to a reasonably well-off Jewish family on May 19, 1951 – the only Ramone actually born in Forest Hills.

Joey's upbringing fell into the classic pattern of the dysfunctional baby-boomer American family – his parents divorced in the early Sixties and he had three different fathers. Biological father Noel Hyman owned a Manhattan trucking company, but Joey didn't get along too well with him when he was younger. Noel made him cut off his hair in Junior High when it got too long, even though Joey considered it his defence mechanism against an uncaring outside world. Mother Charlotte (Lesher: an accomplished artist and art collector) owned a gallery next door to Trylon Cinema on Queens Boulevard, where Joey would later practise his drums in the basement alongside younger brother Mickey Leigh – first having saved up for a snare drum using King Korn trading stamps.

"I rented a hi-hat," he said, "and I'd play along with The Beatles and Gary Lewis & The Playboys on my record player."

His grandmother Fanny (who used to sing for Macy's department store – they would send her out to parties along with a rented piano) gave him a full set when he was 13. It was a nice change from Joey's beloved accordion, a present from his dad some years earlier, which he squeezed until there was no sound left. Charlotte chipped in with lessons a year later, plus guitar lessons for 11-year-old Mickey – who was later to join rock critic Lester Bangs' band Birdland as guitarist. Eventually, Joey bought a "dream" kit modelled on the one used by Keith Moon from The Who, his drumming idol, alongside Cream's Ginger Baker, and Ringo Starr.

"Forest Hills is a very conservative, conventional place. I think we were the black-sheep household of our street," Joey's mother told *Rolling Stone* in 1979. "It was a meeting place for both of my boys' friends because we also had the basement there open to them, and there was always a lot of music going on. They taught me how to smoke pot when they were about 13. I realised they were doing something down there, and I didn't want them to do it outside where they could be busted."

She wasn't sure if the basement was ever a haven for glue sniffing (as later immortalised in songs like 'Now I Wanna Sniff Some Glue' and 'Carbona Not Glue') but, as she added, "I'm sure there were things that they did that I didn't know about. It's very possible. The little devils tried everything."

As a kid, Joey would seek escape from the outside world via his transistor. "I was spending a lot of time by myself. Rock'n'roll was my salvation," he declared in a 1999 interview, "listening to the WMCA Good Guys and Murray the K," an experience he later immortalised on 'Do You Remember Rock'N'Roll Radio?' on *End Of The Century*. His earliest musical heroes included Del Shannon, Phil Spector, The Rolling Stones, The Shangri-Las, The Kinks, The Beach Boys, Buddy Holly and Gene Vincent.

"The first record I bought may have been Del Shannon's 'Runaway'," Joey told amazon.com in 1999. "My early life, I went through a lot of crap with divorce and my mom remarrying and getting a new family. I remember being turned on to The Beach Boys, hearing 'Surfin' U.S.A.', I guess, in 1960.* But The Beatles really did it to me. Later on, The Stooges were a band that helped me in those dark periods – just get out the aggression. Nobody picked up guns in those days. You put on music and it made you feel great."

Joey wasn't too happy at school, either – even with The Jetsons and The Beatles on his lunchbox.

"The thing about school is that if you're forced into learning stuff, you're not going to be into it," he told this writer in '89. "Let's just say I wasn't the best student. If it intrigued or fascinated me, then I was into it. I liked English and biology. I would read about English art schools with their bands like The Kinks and Bowie. They didn't have anything like that in Queens. Philosophy and psychology excited me."

Were you bullied?

"At one point, when the segregation and bussing started it was weird because there were a lot of junkies and stuff, but not really. Later on, I would get into trouble because of the way I dressed. I used to wear sunglasses to school and messed-up jeans. I started to spend a lot of time in the dean's office. I wasn't a conformist."

Charlotte wanted her son to go to college, but Joey refused and quit his studies to concentrate on music. "I knew they all had that little anger in them," she told *Rolling Stone*, "and I thought it was a great release for him to get it all out of his system."

* Surfin' U.S.A.' was released in 1963.

Although it's underplayed in Ramones lore, the fact that Joey was Jewish is important: for that sense of alienation that occurs when cultures clash in adopted countries. (It also heightens the surreal dark sense of humour of the gawky freakish Semite singing lines like "I'm a Nazi baby/I'm a Nazi, yes I am".) Certainly, Handsome Dick Manitoba – Dictators singer and Joey's friend – thinks so.

"I grew up in this wonderful time in New York in the Sixties and Seventies where there was a lot of Jewish culture around – delis, candy stores, Brooklyn, the Bronx. There's a closeness between us New York Jews. It's the same heart, the same experiences, the same type of mother. You're from a certain type of small town neighbourhood. Joey and the Ramones come from that same rich time and place and culture."

So Joey would travel into Manhattan, handing out fliers for massage parlours in the West Village in the winter: at 17 he was earning $50 a week, paid by the hour – and like anyone with any sense, he'd dump the fliers somewhere and go get a beer instead. He experimented with LSD, ended up in the psychiatric ward a couple of times, painted with vegetables and fruit as his tools, recorded the sound of thunderstorms and a bouncing basketball: basically, the singer didn't fit in.

"I never liked Queens," he told me. "I still don't. I felt alienated. It's middle class. It's not wealthy. The kids were, for the most part, more normal than me. I got kicked out of my own bed so I moved to the Village. I tried doing a lot of odd jobs. I had to go on welfare for a while.* I used to work at an art gallery, selling sculptures and modern art stuff on commission."

His mother also recalls the period: "A couple of times we went into the store in the morning, and found Joey asleep on the floor," she recalled in a 1998 interview. Joey built little houses out of the paintings so the police couldn't see him through the window. "So we bought him some pants and a shirt, and he worked at the Art Garden [her gallery]. The old ladies would come in to have their pictures of the Wailing Wall framed, and Joey would be there with his dark glasses. But they got used to him, and he was really good with them."

Joey wasn't as successful with the girls, however.

In the 1979 *Rolling Stone* interview, he revealed that he would get drunk and hang around institutions because, "the girls are all loose and . . . fun, you know? I kind of fell in love with this girl, and every week they took her upstairs to the fifth floor to have shock treatments. They would strap her into a wheelchair. Before they took her up she was fine. Then

* Joey signed off the day the Ramones appeared on the first *Village Voice* cover.

she came down and she was like a zombie. That's what happens to you when you have a lobotomy."

"I knew Joey had been in a mental hospital," Dee Dee told NYC author Legs McNeil for his hilarious oral history of punk, *Please Kill Me*. "I thought he was clever, because a lot of people go in there and never come out. What's more, he always had these girlfriends that he met in the nuthouse."

It was while Joey was working as a sales person – and playing with his glam rock band Sniper – that he met his fellow Ramones. "I liked lyrics about violence and sexual perversion," he explained to Charles Young about his Alice Cooper-influenced first band, for which he would wear a black satin-like jumpsuit with a bullet chain hanging around the groin, "but I wanted take the antics a step further. I wanted more realism – humping the bass player's leg like a dog." Dee Dee lived with Joey in the art shop for a while when he too was kicked out by his mother – and it was the future bassist who re-christened Jeff as Joe (he added a "y" to his name when he became a Ramone). Joey stuck with it: the girls seemed to like it.

Was Dee Dee a delinquent then?

"Yeah," Joey laughed. "He was a little more . . . I can remember him saying he was in that band, Neon Boys or something, with Richard Hell. It was a little after that we started the Ramones. We all lived close by, and we'd go over to John's house and write songs. I'd written some stuff even before the band – 'I Don't Care' and 'Here Today, Gone Tomorrow'. We shared similar musical tastes: New York Dolls, Alice Cooper, The Stooges . . . Actually, this was before the Dolls, so it was MC5, The Stooges, back to the early Seventies."

"Each Ramones Show that Johnny would turn up to, he'd have this little radio, a little red, portable AM radio, and he'd be listening to the Yankee games. If it got too loud in the dressing room, he'd just snap on a little earpiece and keep listening. If the game got really exciting, he'd wave his arm, his hand, waving it back and forth towards Monte [Melnick, tour manager]. And then Monte would go, 'OK, everybody out of the room, we're getting ready to play now' – but half the time it was just because Johnny wanted to hear the game. OK, so Johnny was more into the baseball. But I would talk to John about his guitar playing. I think he's the greatest guitar player that ever was.

"I asked him once, 'Johnny, do you practice a lot at home? What do you do?' and John said, 'George, a carpenter has his hammer, the musician has his guitar. The carpenter doesn't bring his hammer home. He's not going to work at home, he's going to relax at home. So I don't have a guitar at my house. This is my job. I bring my tools to work. I leave them at work.' I thought that was a really interesting insight.

"Probably, early on, Johnny was really into it. But as his career went on, he was the business guy. He left his hammer at work – he was Johnny Ramone, which I thought was the coolest shit in the world. You're not pretending to be some great fucking artist . . . you are what you are, which is pretty neat. I asked him why he never brought his girlfriends to the gigs, and this was even before the Joey thing [with Linda, Joey's former girlfriend who Johnny later married]. He would say, 'George – does a carpenter bring his wife to work with him? She can meet me for a couple of days but this is my job. I go do my job, I go home.'

"Every time I would see Johnny backstage, it would be like, 'When's our next job?' It was never a gig or a date or a show. In Johnny's own words, he was the businessman. But he'd created something that hadn't been done before, the buzzsaw guitar sound that was so amazing everybody copied it. The whole world – now, popular music is the Ramones.

"I've heard him play leads, I've jammed with him before. Johnny can't play lead? Sure he can, he's a great lead player. But why should he play lead when he's so good at what he does, not even trying to compete with the Jimmy Pages and Jeff Becks of the world. This guy created his own genre – why go beyond that?"

(Author's interview with George Tabb, Ramones fan)

JOHNNY RAMONE WAS born John Cummings on October 8, 1948 in Long Island, the only son of a mechanical constructor.

A lifetime Yankees fan, he wanted to be a baseball-player from the age of five but wasn't prepared to make the necessary compromises: he didn't want to cut his hair. So he bought a guitar instead.

As he explained on the 1990 video compilation, *Lifestyles Of The Ramones*, "All [my] life as a kid growing up, I either wanted to be in a rock band or I wanted to be a baseball player. [I] never thought [I'd] ever succeed at doing that."

Johnny was a self-confessed teenage reprobate who drifted from one military school* to another during his formative years – occasionally ending up on the wrong side of the law.

* Former Ramones fanzine contributor Mark Bannister writes: Like other elements of the Ramones myth, Johnny's military school background invites closer scrutiny. Did Johnny ever attend a military school?

Pupils tend to enter the military school system either as cadets at the age of 11 or 12, or much later after graduating from high school. It seems unlikely that Johnny went as a cadet because as he later said himself, "To be on the high school [baseball] team you had to get a haircut, and even then I couldn't take any form of discipline. Then I went to military school for two years, and looking back, I did learn discipline."

"I guess we were sort of juvenile delinquents," he told *Sounds* magazine, "but Forest Hills ain't the South Bronx; it's a nice neighbourhood. So if you walk around like this [he indicates his leather jacket, T-shirt, jeans] you're already looked upon as a hoodlum. We were general *nogoodnicks*."

A firm believer in enforced discipline – he once stated he believed that everyone should do military service for two years, mandatory – he didn't turn bad until he got out of high school: "Sniffing glue was probably the start of my downfall," he stated. "We tried it and then moved on to Carbona. We once tried robbing a drug store on Queens Boulevard – unsuccessfully. It was in a whole row of stores and we broke into the laundromat by mistake. The next time, we tried robbing a bakery on 63rd Drive. The police came to my house and asked somebody to identify me."

Johnny became interested in music after seeing Elvis Presley on *The Ed Sullivan Show* in 1957, and still cites his favourite artists as Elvis and The Beatles. When the early Sixties British Invasion hit America he started practising guitar but couldn't figure out how to play it like his heroes, so he gave up – until The New York Dolls came along in the early Seventies to show there was another way. But to this day, Johnny contends he has no influences as a guitarist.

In fact, Johnny loved Bo Diddley, Dick Dale, Cream-period Eric Clapton, Mountain's Leslie West (who back then was in a local band called The Vagrants), and Jimi Hendrix, among others.*

However, Johnny also claimed that after high school he went through a delinquent phase, itself an even more important element of the Ramones myth. He was quite specific about it, saying, "I didn't become bad until I got out of high school" and "I used to do that stuff from ages 18 to 21, then I stopped" so it seems even more unlikely that the two years Johnny said he spent in military schools were between 1966 and 1969 either.

Attending a military school and throwing TV sets off rooftops are not necessarily mutually exclusive activities but for Johnny Ramone they are chronologically incompatible. Either the military schooling or the juvenile delinquency must have been a figment of Johnny's imagination. Readers must draw their own conclusions, although Dee Dee offered a clue as to which element of the Ramones myth Johnny may have fabricated. Dee Dee reported that in 1969 Johnny had waist length hair. Presumably, it would have taken Johnny the two or three years since graduating from high school to have grown hair that long. At military school, he would still have been growing out of a crew cut.

* "Leslie West never gets any recognition," he said later. "I've always been a big fan of his, since back when he was a fat kid dropping out of high school in Forest Hills. He was, to me, one of the top five guitar players of his era. His playing is so soulful and tasteful. His break in 'Theme For An Imaginary Western' is the best thing I've ever heard. It builds so melodically. The last note in the break – he hits [a] note that just shoots up the octave, this harmonic jump. The whole solo is a thing of beauty."

Johnny chose to shut out his musical past and start all over again when inventing the Ramones sound: sucking out the extraneous soloing and virtuosity with a belligerent force. One of his favourite bands was LA's Love; and the clipped brilliance of their 1966 debut album's rhythm guitars can be detected in Johnny's brutal harmonic minimalism.

Dictators bassist Andy Shernoff, meanwhile, thinks the blueprint for the Ramones sound comes directly from two songs – 'Paranoid' from the second Black Sabbath record, and 'Communication Breakdown' from the first Led Zeppelin album. "But," as he adds, "when they made their first record everything else was overblown drum solos and classical rock and explosions and it was like – what happened to 'Wop Bop A Loo Bop'?"

As part of his musical apprenticeship, Johnny played bass in Tommy Erdelyi's high school band Tangerine Puppets: "We were like the *Nuggets* album, that era," Tommy says, "a conglomeration of that sort of music. Mostly covers. It was songs like 'I Just Want To Make Love To You' by the Stones, 'I Ain't Gonna Eat Out My Heart Any More' by the Rascals, 'Gloria', the hipper songs from that era. We lived within a couple of blocks of each other, in the same area of Forest Hills, so we hung out like teenagers do. Johnny was really good at stickball, a form of baseball, and we'd play a lot of that."

"Once we all went to see The Beatles at Shea Stadium and John brought a bag of rocks, and threw them at The Beatles all night," fellow Puppet Richard Adler told Finnish writer Jari-Pekka Laitio. "It's amazing nobody got hurt. These were rocks as big as baseballs."

Johnny wore his guitar high, and dived around on stage. He could get carried away in his exuberance. In Rego Park 1966, he beat up the band's singer right in front of an audience. Another time, he shoved Adler right through the drum kit. Yet another time, he ran into a girl and she fell and cut herself – an incident that, according to Ramones video director George Seminara, led to the Puppets being banned from playing colleges. Consequently the band, unable to find work, split in the summer of 1967.*

"Johnny has a wicked sense of humour, coming from Queens," explains journalist Joan Tarshis. "It was like Beatles humour, sarcastic. The Ramones all shared a similar sense of humour – on the dark side. Joey's

* Adler claims that both Randy California – the future Spirit front man who played with Jimi Hendrix when he was just 15 – and Steely Dan's Walter Becker were also in the band, although not necessarily all at the same time.

was more acceptable, not so many people know about Johnny's because he's more private."

Johnny became known for his cartoon T-shirts, and like his fellow future band mates, cited *The Texas Chainsaw Massacre* as a favourite film.

Several years of welfare cheques and building work followed. According to *Poison Heart*, Dee Dee and Johnny first met when the latter was delivering dry cleaning at the top of the hill on 66th in Queens. Johnny's hair was down to his arse, and he was wearing tie-dyed jeans and a headband. The pair discovered a shared love of The Stooges and mischief, and began chatting about amps and guitars.

The two hung around during evenings and weekends after that, being near neighbours, and after Johnny got a construction job at a 50-storey building at 1633 Broadway (on 50th St) they were able to meet up at lunchtime as well – Dee Dee worked as a mail clerk at the same place. It was during the lunch sessions that the pair talked of starting a band together.

"John and I used to sit on rooftops and sniff glue and drop television sets on people," Dee Dee told *Rolling Stone* writer Charles M. Young in '83. "Actually, John used to drop the television sets. I only threw firecrackers. We didn't receive proper guidance from our parents."

Johnny had actually grown past his delinquent phase by the time the two future Ramones met, along with any usage of hard drugs – Dee Dee was guilty of embellishing the past to suit his own present. It wouldn't be the first or last time, either.

"DEE DEE WOULD write three or four songs in a sitting. Two of them were bad but one of them would be genius. And he wasn't precious about it neither – he'd be like, 'You don't like that one?' and he'd tear it up."

He was the punk, wasn't he?

"He was the punk before there was punk – and Joey was the soul of the Ramones, the voice, he tied it all together. He encompassed the great singing styles that went before him. With two words he could sum up any situation. He knew that music saved his life and he knew that the Ramones had saved other people's lives and I think that was something he was really proud of."

(Author's interview with Daniel Rey,
Ramones producer and songwriter)

DEE DEE RAMONE was born Douglas Glenn Colvin on September 18, 1952 in Virginia – and spent the next 14 years moving between different towns in Germany.

Although he went to army school in Munich, Dee Dee mostly grew up in Berlin where he would lie awake at night listening to his parents' drunken brawling (his parents divorced when he was 15: another classic dysfunctional American family). In a preview of his own second marriage, his mother was only 17 when she met her 38-year-old future husband – a Master Sergeant who fought in the Battle Of The Bulge and the Korean War.

For recreation, Dee Dee would scour the old war fields for Nazi paraphernalia to sell to visiting American soldiers – bullets, gas masks, bayonets, helmets. One time he claimed to have found an unexploded bomb. He started experimenting with drugs barely into his teens: found tubes of morphine in a garbage dump – the experimentation escalated and turned into a 14-year heroin addiction. A divided Germany, still licking its wounds from the war, later became a rich metaphorical source for Dee Dee's lyrics – darkly humorous slices of barely restrained anger and cartoon violence.

"People who join a band like the Ramones don't come from stable backgrounds, because it's not that civilised an art form," Dee Dee explained later.

In the early Sixties, his family – father, mother and sister Beverly – were stationed in Atlanta, Georgia for a while, and Dee Dee recalls hearing rock'n'roll blaring from the PX snack bar, and at the swimming pool ("with the sun, the comic books and the potato chips"). Back in Pirmasons, Germany, aged 12, he heard The Beatles, and got himself a Beatles haircut and suit. A couple of years later, he bought a cheap Italian electric guitar. It was after reading an article about a wrestler called Gorgeous George discovered in a pile of discarded *Playboys* that he decided to change his name to Dee Dee, and – inspired by The Beatles movie *A Hard Day's Night* – changed his last name to Ramone, after Paul McCartney had called himself Paul Ramon.*

From there, it was a typical Sixties rock'n'roll upbringing for this alienated youth – shoplifting in Berlin, dope, Levi's jackets, LSD, Hush Puppies, and concerts by British groups like The Troggs, The Kinks, The Small Faces, The Rolling Stones, The Who and The Walker Brothers . . . His favourite TV viewing in the Seventies was archetypal good-time rock'n'roll sitcom *Happy Days* and old war movies: which makes a lot of sense.

* McCartney called himself Paul Ramon in 1960 when the Silver Beatles (as they were known then) undertook a Scottish tour as backing group for singer Johnny Gentle.

"I hung out in Lefrak City, Queens," Dee Dee told *Spin* in 1989, "and I'd do glue and Tuinals and Seconals. We used to call up numbers on the phone, and it would go beep-beep-beep-beep-beep and we'd listen to that for hours. Then sniff some more glue."

"Dee Dee was lovely, a big dangly puppy," says Gloria Nicholl, future Sire regional PR. "He even had this lovely Frankfurter-type dog called Kessie. He was my first boyfriend, straight out of convent school. I was 15. He was 16. We all went to school together in Forest Hills. Joey was always hanging around outside the flagpole. We dressed in the fashions of the day: bell-bottoms, long hair. We wore matching pink aviator shades. He shocked the life out of me because once he shot up right in front of me. We used to go to the pizza den and listen to the jukebox and eat pizza for 15 cents a slice – ha! 15 cents a slice. We were into all that *Nuggets* stuff. I liked him because he wasn't going to grow up to be a dentist. That's why we all became punks – we didn't want to be dentists or dentists' wives."

In one of his final interviews, conducted by Harvey Kubernik in the spring of 2002 for use in the authorised liner notes to the reissued *End Of The Century*, Dee Dee also revealed that he had lived in a suburb of Culver City, California in 1970: "I hitchhiked out here and when I got to LA, first stop was Newport Beach. I met some guys, service men, jarheads, who drove me into LA. I stayed in LA for five minutes, hitched up the Pacific Coast Highway to Big Sur for a month. Then I came back, and stayed in Culver City in the Washington Hotel. MGM Studios right down the street. Worked as a maintenance man. Helms Bakery. I might have been 18, and started at midnight, and hosed all the garbage dumps. I listened to the radio, AM and FM dial. I used to go to all the thrift shops and look for 45s."

Back in Forest Hills, Dee Dee would take the F train to New York City, and cop heroin, sometimes by the fountain in Central Park. In 1969 he accepted a job in an insurance company, delivering the mail. He later became a hairdresser – a good one, too.* When he first met Joey, the singer was sporting a red Afro hairstyle, a yellow suede fringed jacket, moccasins and round, tinted glasses. The pair became drinking buddies – wine on stoops on summer evenings.

* Bannister casts doubts on this widely reported version of history. "If you look at the chronology, Dee Dee worked in a supermarket after dropping out of high school," he writes. "He left the supermarket to take up the mail room job. Dee Dee was still working in the mail room when they formed the band so if he was ever a hairdresser it would have to have been sometime after that. Not impossible but I just don't buy it. I know Deborah Harry said he was a hairdresser but I'm pretty sure that was just a euphemism for all the 53rd and 3rd stuff. Knowing what we know about Dee Dee, could he even have mastered a skill like hairdressing?"

All four future Ramones attended early Seventies glam rock clubs in Manhattan, and dabbled in the look of the time. It was a small scene where everybody sort of knew each other and hung out at the Mercer Arts Center, the original Max's Kansas City, and Nobody's on Bleecker Street. The Mercer was to glam what CBGBs would be to punk: the crucial centre, where the New York Dolls would frequently play.

"They were great, those times," the bassist told *Mojo* in 2001. "The people in [the Mercer] really lit up the place. There would be bands there like Eric Emerson [a Warhol Factory fixture who died in 1976], Magic Tramps, Teenage Lust, who had these really cute dancers who everyone wanted to go out with but nobody ever saw except on stage. Too bad."

Dee Dee was a fan of the Bay City Rollers (the Ramones' famous "Hey ho, let's go" chant was an attempt to emulate the Rollers' 'Saturday Night' 1976 chart-topper), and had an autographed biography of the Scots teen idols. In one interview, he even claimed the Ramones were as influenced by Shaun Cassidy and The Wombles* and the Rollers as they were by Iggy, the Dolls and Alice Cooper.

Of course, all they were trying to do was to recapture the innocence of rock'n'roll as fans.

LET'S TALK ABOUT the New York Dolls.

David Johansen, Sylvain Sylvain, Arthur 'Killer' Kane, Jerry Nolan (replacing the late, OD'd Billy Murcia) and Johnny Thunders brought a trash aesthetic back to rock music in the early Seventies that had previously been the preserve of female pop artists like The Ronettes and The Crystals. Like early Aerosmith (only 4 Real), like a revolver concealed in lingerie, this troublesome trans-gender New York five-piece fucked, flirted and flounced their way across just two gloriously throwaway albums before self-destructing in a downward spiral of drugs, alcohol and recriminations. It's been well documented how their lippy loudmouthed behaviour and police siren guitars helped serve as the blueprint for the Sex Pistols and, through them, British punk. The Dolls understood that what was important in rock music wasn't the ability to play three fret-boards simultaneously, but to have FUN.

It took a little while before others caught on.

Tommy, for one, was initially taken aback by their lack of musicianship: "Here were the New York Dolls, and they could hardly play," he told *Mojo*

* Strange rotund creatures who would clear London's Wimbledon Common of litter and sing odes to their "Uncle Bulgaria".

writer Michael Hill. "Yet they were much more exciting and entertaining than any of those virtuosos. Why was that? What was going on? Everyone was having a great time. It was like a party atmosphere. And I realised we were basically tired of what was going on. Everything was being rehashed and reformulated. It was getting to be like fifth generation Led Zeppelin clones. Subconsciously, it struck me, if there's going to be a new direction in music it's not going to be through virtuosity, but through ideas."

"TOMMY RECOGNISED SOMETHING in the other Ramones they definitely didn't recognise in themselves. That was his genius – they had the heart and the idea, but not the cohesion. Tommy was able to unite the others over his backbeat, which you'd think anybody could've done . . . but then you'd think anybody could be Ringo Starr. It's not possible because most drummers can't sit still long enough to play a simple beat."

Yeah, well it's the old joke about how do you tell when the drummer's knocking on your door? He speeds up at the third knock.

"Tommy plays at the same speed, the same beat, the same patterns all the way through. Most drummers are genetically incapable of doing that. He knew that simplicity was king. Simplicity was . . ."

Yeah, he's fascinating. I spoke to him the other day on the phone – he's so unassuming.

"They all are. I would sit and interview Joey and, considering his height and the way he was recognisable everywhere he went, he did not carry that overbearing aura about him, you know? He had a quiet, shy nature that suited the celebrity he had. The Ramones were the normal guys everybody loved to love."

(Author's interview with David Fricke,
Rolling Stone writer/editor, 2002)

TOMMY RAMONE WAS born Tommy Erdelyi on January 29, 1949 in Budapest, Hungary.

The future drummer came to the US with his family in 1956: "I was six or seven when it happened," he told me. "It was a very restrictive regime, you didn't hear too much Western music. I remember the early stages of rock'n'roll, how much it excited me – even as a young kid I was into dressing cool, into wearing a certain type of shoes. It was nice there, except for the political regime. One of the first records I had was a score to a Hungarian movie, with a rock beat to it, making fun of America. I'd go to playgrounds in the city, but I also used to spend some time in the country – I have some rural memories of rolling hills and stacks of hay, dug wells with stone casings, very pastoral. I had a regular childhood."

At school, Tommy was into The Beatles, playing his guitar and listening to music – a good guy, but quiet.

After he graduated in 1967, Tommy became a recording engineer at Manhattan's Record Plant, where he worked with Hendrix on his *Band Of Gypsies* sessions, Leslie West (pre-Mountain), and on John McLaughlin's *Devotion* album.

"You won't find my name on any albums," he told *NME* in 1978. "The only group that gave me credit was 30 Days Out. I was very young and working with Hendrix was a thrilling experience. He'd come back in the studio and play back the stuff, and say, 'Oh, that's awful,' and I'd thought it was great. He'd put down a guitar track and say he wanted to do it over. And he'd do it over and over and over . . ."

Tommy then took a job at a film company near the Museum of Modern Art and would take long lunch breaks so he could see avant-garde films by directors like Spanish surrealist Luis Buñuel that showed there.

At this point, the drummer was also going under the name Scotty: "I was using the name Scott Thomas," he explains. "It was a stage name I had. I had a group after Tangerine Puppets called Butch, alongside Monte Melnick [future Ramones tour manager]. I was lead singer and guitar player. We dressed in the rock'n'roll fashions of the times. We were part of the glitter scene but didn't wear make-up or anything. My most outlandish outfit would have been a silver Mylar plastic *Granny Takes A Trip* shirt jacket, with no shirt, suspenders and a tie."

It was during this period he encountered The Stooges: "I heard them on late night radio when they first came out, and I thought they sounded interesting, like an avant-garde version of The Rolling Stones. Next time I saw Johnny, I mentioned he should check them out."

"WHEN I HAD MY dark room," begins Roberta Bayley, photographer of the first Ramones album cover, "I would put a Ramones record on and I could use the length of the songs to time the print.

"I'm from California, but I'd been living in London. In April '74, I got a one-way ticket to New York. I wanted to see the New York Dolls because I'd heard a lot about them. It turned out one of the people on my list to look up was the Dolls' sound guy. So we went to see them at Club 82 on East 4th Street, a former drag club. The first time I ever saw the Dolls, David Johansen was wearing a strapless dress and heels and a wig. Of course, I just assumed that was their regular look because everyone always said they wore make-up. From there, over that summer, I saw many different bands. I remember hearing about the Ramones and thinking they were probably a Spanish group, or Puerto Rican, from the name.

"Through the trajectory of my New York experience, I ended up falling in love with Richard Hell. My first memory of seeing the Ramones was going along with Richard to the Performance Studio at 23 East 20th Street where they were doing little showcases. It was a tiny place, no stage. It was very strange, seeing them for the first time, because you didn't have any precedent for the look or the sound or the really short songs, even. They played a really short set. It was almost like conceptual art, thinking about it. It was weird but great. Like, 'Wow, who would have thought of this?' It seemed so funny but it wasn't like you were laughing at them, more because it was so wacky.

"Other people said they would stop and start between songs and have arguments. But the framework was all there. I'd seen all these different musical things from San Francisco to London. I'd observed the different crazes. Before the San Francisco thing, I'd been into the British Invasion bands, The Rolling Stones and The Beatles. There was a feeling that the Ramones could be something like that, that you really were in on something different and interesting and fun."

(Interview with author, 2001)

BY COMMON ASSENT, the music scene sucked in 1974.

Sure, there were bright spots. There always are, if you look hard enough. The New York Dolls in NYC, Iggy and The Stooges in Detroit, the bare-ass metal minimalism of Black Sabbath, and the glam rockers like Slade, Sweet and T.Rex in Britain . . . hell, there was plenty going on if you cared. Still, it was in the mainstream and in the pages of the music press that rock bands' self-indulgence was really getting out of hand: rock'n'roll had been through its bratty childhood and even early teens – and now, it felt, it was time it grew up, shocked by the loss of innocence following Vietnam and the student riots of the Sixties.

Hence, musicians who really should have known better – The Who ("hope I die before I get old"), some of the old Stax stable, The Rolling Stones, Paul McCartney and his loose bland of musicians in Wings, Neil Young – and some who didn't – ELP, Yes, Genesis, Jethro Tull – began taking over the scene with their six-minute-long drum solos and tuneless keyboard noodles.

Rock was initially indistinguishable from pop: both Elvis and The Beatles appealed to precisely the same audience as Del Shannon and Helen Shapiro, but as popularity and riches and fawning press praise grew, so did the self-importance . . . by the start of the Seventies, rock and pop had become two entirely different entities, the former having almost completely lost sight of its initial *raison d'être* – to have fun.

Rock is a young person's music. It's that simple.

The reason why rock historians use the New York Dolls as an example of a great rock band is because they matched the full-on lipstick swagger of the Stones to a keen sense of pop, as evinced by the presence of Shadow Morton – the mastermind behind The Shangri-Las – as producer of the Dolls' prophetically titled second album *Too Much Too Soon* (1974).

New York, being a thriving metropolis, felt rock's betrayal of its youth keener than most. "Fun disappeared in 1974," Joey Ramone told journalist Jaan Uhelszki in 1999. "There were too many serious people out there at that time. Rock'n'roll is about fun, and fun didn't exist in rock for a long period of time. Everybody took themselves too seriously. When we came along there was Foreigner, Boston and Toto . . . all that shit. And then there was disco, with 'Disco Duck' and CW McCall. It was us and them. It was like the big corporations, the big machine didn't want us to succeed. We were shaking things up, and they fought against us, as far as not being able to get radio play, throwing any obstacle they could in our path. We were like aliens."

The week the Ramones played their first show at Performance Studio, Paper Lace had the Number One song on *Billboard* with 'The Night Chicago Died'. Other chart toppers that year included 'Billy Don't Be A Hero', 'Seasons In The Sun' and (the actually rather fine) 'Kung Fu Fighting'. Still, whenever the mainstream becomes too complacent, there's always something right around the corner waiting to stick two fingers right up its cocaine-addled nose. Right?

THE DATE JOHNNY RAMONE bought his first guitar is well documented, mainly because Johnny – the consummate professional – kept records about everything concerning his band. It was on January 23, 1974 that he and Dee Dee wandered into Manny's Guitar Centre on 156 West 48th & Broadway. Johnny was looking for a guitar that no one else was using, a cheap one too. He bought a blue Mosrite for $50, plus $4.55 tax. The asking price was initially $69.55 (including tax). Johnny bartered them down after pretending 55 bucks was all the money he had with him at the time. The store receipt stated, 'Must be picked up 1/24/74'. (It also showed that Johnny lived at 6758 108th Street, Forest Hills.) Mosrite, with its distinctive twang, had been used on The Ventures' surf instrumentals in the early Sixties, but the make didn't bother him too much – Johnny (correctly) figured all guitars sound the same when turned up loud enough. The original was stolen in 1977, although at least one interviewee for this book claims to know its whereabouts.

In an interview with Lester Bangs, conducted for a guitar magazine,

Johnny stated: "I bought it because it was the cheapest guitar in the store. Now I've gotten used to it and I like it. I also didn't wanna get a guitar that everybody else was using – I wanted something that could be identified with me.

"I bought a guitar in 1965," he continued, "fiddled around for about a year and didn't learn how to play anything. I just more or less gave it up. So when we started the group, I didn't know how to play it too well. I knew a couple of chords from when I'd bought these guitar chord books in 1965, but I didn't know how to play a song or anything."

After that, Johnny used Mosrites exclusively because, as he explained to David Fricke when being interviewed for the Ramones *Anthology* sleeve notes in 1999, he'd "found something to be identified with. It was a good guitar for me: lightweight, very thin neck, easy to bar chord. It had a sound of its own. I was happy with it."

Johnny forgot his previous aspirations to be Hendrix, and just learnt what he deemed necessary for the Ramones sound: "Pure, white rock'n'roll, with no blues influence. I wanted our sound to be as original as possible. I stopped listening to everything."

On the same visit Dee Dee claimed to have picked up a Danelectro bass for 50 bucks, which he later smashed. He then bought and broke a Gibson Firebird, before buying his first Fender Precision from Fred Smith of Television. He soon sold that, against Smith's advice, and to his lasting regret.

In the Bangs article, Dee Dee stated that when he first bought a guitar, at age 13, it was "immediately too complicated for me. I just kept it in my room and when kids'd come over I'd show it off to 'em but I never learned how to play it. By the time I was 21 and the Ramones started, uh, even a halfwit would know those three chords, y'know that D, E and G? So I know them. I just always wanted to be a bass-player."

Four days after the visit to Manny's, the pair held their first rehearsal.*

* Bannister also queries this version of events. "Are we supposed to believe that Dee Dee bought his first bass just a few days before the Ramones' first rehearsal when, in fact, records show he only switched to bass after not working out on rhythm guitar? The Ramones Myth says it was a bass, but I'm not so sure."

An interesting point: if Ritchie Ramone existed – see later – then why was Dee Dee buying himself a bass? Could he have afforded an instrument he didn't even intend to play? Or maybe Ritchie himself was a figment of the imagination that helped create the early Ramones Myth (Tommy's, probably) – a tragic Stu Sutcliffe-style figure for the Forest Hills boys so in love with the image and style of early Beatles. Certainly, early elements of the Ramones story seem a little too perfect with hindsight – Joey's girlfriend from the mental hospital, Johnny's previous career as a juvenile delinquent. Dee Dee does describe the missing Ramone quite vividly in his book, however, as a "crazy supermarket clerk dope-fiend type".

"We wrote two songs the very first day we were a band," Johnny told *Rolling Stone*. "One was called 'I Don't Wanna Walk Around With You' and the other was called 'I Don't Wanna Get Involved With You'. It was very much like 'I Don't Wanna Walk Around With You', almost the same song."

"That was just before I hooked up with them," remembers Tommy. "The Ramones was a slow involving process. I was on the New York scene, seeing groups like the Dolls and the Glitter scene, the local bands, and I had this group of friends I grew up with in Forest Hills that I thought were much more colourful and charismatic and I thought it would be great to get a group together. I was on the phone with Johnny for a year and a half, telling him this. It didn't matter to me whether he was the singer or guitarist.

"So one day he calls me up and says that him and Dee Dee have bought guitars and I said, 'Great, let's get together.' We got together at his apartment, and there was Dee Dee and Joey and a fellow named Ritchie Stern – Ritchie was going to be the bass player but he couldn't master the instrument. They came in with songs at that first rehearsal and we worked on them. We were always working on songs, formulate them, arrange them, track them. We were doing all originals straight from the start. My take on that was that the songs were so good we had no interest in doing covers. They're going to tell you the reason we didn't do covers is 'cos they couldn't play them, but that's nothing to do with it. I don't think they could have played ELP, but they could have done The Who or Little Richard."

Dee Dee did indeed disagree: "It was risky and nervy what we were doing," he told Michael Hill in 2001. "We started trying to figure out songs from records and we couldn't, maybe 'Yummy, Yummy, Yummy' by The Ohio Express, or 'Can't You Hear My Heartbeat' by Herman's Hermits . . . It sounds absurd because we had such advanced and maybe even narrow-minded taste at the same time."

Frustrated, Joey started writing his own ideas for songs on scraps of paper and the backs of shopping bags, "really weird songs," his mother recalls.

Charlotte let the Ramones hold their early practices in the basement of her Art Garden gallery in Forest Hills: "I remember going down there once with a business partner and seeing all of these overhead lights and plants," she told littlecrackedegg.com. "My partner thought it nice that the boys were such ambitious horticulturalists. She was a bit naïve about the proclivities of rock musicians."

It was decided who would play what by who wanted to play what. Dee Dee chose rhythm guitar and to be lead singer, Johnny – lead guitar, Joey

– drums, Ritchie – bass – but he dropped out straight away. (The band later delighted in telling British music journalists it was because he'd gone into a mental institution.) So the Ramones became a trio, but Dee Dee would go hoarse after a couple of songs because he sang so hard, so they passed the microphone over to Joey.

"As a drummer, Joey was a basher, a choppy kind of guy, a lot of cymbals and stuff," Tommy reminisces. "A little bit like The White Stripes. I got them together for artistic reasons, thinking this would be a great thing to do. Money didn't even enter our minds. No one was making money back then."

What made you think Joey would make a better singer than Dee Dee?

"He had a nice sound to his voice, and he wouldn't go hoarse, he had a strong voice. So we began auditioning drummers and I was trying to explain to them the style we wanted – eighth-notes across, with the 'one' on the bass and the 'two' on the snare, fast and consistent. At the time everyone wanted to do heavy metal drumming, putting in the rolls. No one could do it, so I tried it and it worked. I'd never played drums before. I was more the mentor at the time, I always was. Once I got behind the drums, all the elements clicked together."

"John and I weren't vocal musicians," Dee Dee told Harvey Kubernik. "We're like a machine. We used to say horrible things about Joey. 'We could have made it if we had Billy Idol.' [Laughs] We were nasty."

Tommy knows the exact moment when he realised how good the Ramones were. It was in '74, in the Art Garden. Dee Dee and Joey were going over one of Joey's songs, 'Judy Is A Punk'.

"The whole thing clicked in my head," Tommy says. "Before that, I thought the band was good and interesting. 'Judy' made the difference. It was beyond good. There was brilliance there."

Choosing the name was easy. They lifted it from Dee Dee's Sixties alias. Other stories have appeared as to its origin, however. It was chosen in homage to the street tough image of the Fifties greaser rockers. Joey told a journalist that they thought it had a ring to it – like "Eli Wallach".

"We made a list of 40 names on a piece of paper," Tommy recalls. "That was the one we all agreed upon. Also, it sounded ridiculous. We immediately decided to call each other Ramone, probably because of The Walker Brothers, 10 years before. We thought it would be hilarious."

DO YOU KNOW anything about how they met?

"It was via Mickey, and Mickey told me the story, but I don't remember it verbatim. I know it had something to do with dirty laundry in a room and sharing a

room with some mob pals or something like that. John being some guy and Jeff being some other guy – whatever, I don't really know all the details. I can say that Joey's family is really nice though. Mickey and Charlotte are two of the nicest people in the world."

Yeah, I've been told that.

"They're really great. Joey's mum was so great because she loved them both equally. She has scrapbooks on both of them. Great."

(Author's interview with George Tabb, Ramones fan)

2

Hey Ho, We're The Ramones

"I WAS ATTRACTED TO the Ramones because I grew up reading Spiderman comics, in a very dysfunctional family like the Ramones. My parents were divorced early and I got stuck with my dad who was a dick and it was awful. And the Ramones had this family imagery.

"Four brothers – I believed at first they were brothers. They all had leather jackets, they all looked the same and they sang songs like 'We're A Happy Family' and 'Blitzkrieg Bop' and I thought, 'Whoa, this is great.' The imagery, with the uniforms and leather jackets, was something I could actually do. I could go out and buy a leather jacket, even though they cost a lot of money. I liked the whole ripped jeans thing and sneakers – I had those anyway. I thought I could fit into it, you know? They were like the New York Beatles. I got so into it. I wore the uniform 24 hours a day and I still do, 25 years later. The music was original. The lyrics are so clever. I've always played Ramones-type songs in my bands. It was only in the last six or seven years I realised their lyrics really were that dumb and really were that clever. I thought the Ramones were so smart they knew that what they were doing was a joke, and maybe Joey did know and John did know. But Dee Dee would write these lyrics that . . .

"I loved the fact the Ramones were able to use really sick twisted humour, and play rock'n'roll at the same time. Rock'n'roll to me is, 'Hey baby, let's get laid, I got a rocket in my pocket' – bullshit, bullshit, bullshit – AC/DC stupid. Writing songs about getting laid or giving a dog a bone, a piece of your pie, whatever – that's not even clever stupid, that's just stupid stupid. The Ramones are so clever stupid about the whole thing. They weren't singing about getting laid or working for the man or waiting for the weekend. It was about sniffing glue, fucking Carbona, cretin families, teenage lobotomies. It was like, 'God this is genius! It's funny!' It was so funny but you could also relate to it because, when you're a teenager, the angst is so real. You're so angry and then you hear this and it's like, 'Wow – this rings true.' I am a teenage lobotomy – my parents fucking hated me. They really hit on something there.

"The lyrics stopped them from getting a hit because they were way ahead of their

time. Right now, the Ramones would be huge. You have Andrew WK with his 'Party on, party hard' – this is big music? Obviously you missed a few steps there. Occasionally, the Ramones would try doing a few straight songs with Joey-penned lyrics and the love songs . . . but they came at the weirdest time possible in '77. They weren't gorgeous guys like all the others. All the New Romantics and New Wave bands got picked up by MTV. But the Ramones were these strange, tough-looking guys and Middle America did not understand that.

"Back when I was a teenager, and even in my early twenties, 'The Ramones suck' were fighting words. We'd go to war. We'd beat up people for 'Johnny looks like a dog' . . . 'Yeah, I'll fucking kick your ass' – you know? The Ramones were like a family and you wanted to defend them to the death. That's why I think the Ramones got so big in the end: everyone was on their side, every outsider, every geek, every kid, every freak, every nerd, everybody was on the Ramones' side because the Ramones were a happy family and . . . 'Gabba Gabba Hey! We accept you/One of us'. They accepted everybody in."

(Author's interview with George Tabb, Ramones fan)

"THE RAMONES WERE as much guys like Monte and Arturo [Vega]," explains Scottish writer Lindsay Hutton. "In many ways they were more Ramones than John (Ramone) – these guys lived by the code, they were 100 per cent behind it. The Ramones were a workhorse and never fucking stopped playing. I'm sure Joe's health could have been better if he hadn't been on the road so much, but he liked being on the road. The Ramones couldn't have been the Ramones without Monte. He was absolute salt of the earth. He should get a special award."

The debut Ramones show took place at Performance, on March 30, 1974 – with Joey on drums, in front of 30 people. The set comprised seven songs: 'I Don't Wanna Go Down To The Basement', 'I Don't Wanna Walk Around With You', 'Now I Wanna Sniff Some Glue', 'I Don't Wanna Be Learned, I Don't Wanna Be Tamed', 'I Don't Wanna Get Involved With You', 'I Don't Like Nobody That Don't Like Me' and 'Succubus'. It was, by all accounts, appalling – perhaps unsurprisingly. According to *Please Kill Me*, at the first rehearsal, Joey couldn't even set up the stool on the drum stand: he sat on the point.

"It was hilarious," Blondie singer Debbie Harry recalled. "Joey kept falling over. [He] couldn't see very well, plus he had his shades on . . . all of a sudden, WHHHOMP, and he was lying facedown on this flight of stairs."

"I wasn't there," admits Tommy. "I was on the road doing sound for Buzzy Linhart. They did just one show as a trio with Joey playing drums."

"We were terrible," Johnny told *Punk* magazine in 1976. "Dee Dee was so nervous he stepped on his bass guitar and broke its neck."

Performance was a loft on East 20th Street that Tommy and Monte Melnick had converted into a rehearsal and showcase space, and recording facility. Local bands would play and rehearse there because it had a good atmosphere – Blondie, New York Dolls, The Fast, Tuff Darts. It would have been a major success, except for the old lady upstairs who complained all the time.

"Monte was the first person I met when I moved to Forest Hills," Tommy says. "We were in the same class in Junior High. He's a dedicated hard worker, he sees the world differently – he reminds me of Jay Leno. He's about 5′ 11″, brown hair, brown eyes, slim, has a moustache, curly hair."

Monte played bass in Butch, and later joined 30 Days Out, a country rock band that released two albums on Reprise. After that finished, the Ramones' future tour manager did some commercial work, helped with a rock opera symphony, and came back to New York where his cousin introduced him to a woman who wanted him to design her a studio. So he called up Tommy and together they built Performance.

"He had his projects and I had my projects," recalls Monte. "One of his projects was the Ramones, so we started doing two dollar showcases for them and other groups. I ran the sounds and the lights. Eventually, we had to shut the studio down because the neighbours were suing us over the noise."

Monte hated the Ramones when he first saw them: "Forget it. I came from a musical background. I was a bass player. My groups had three part harmonies, you know? I helped them out – Tommy was my friend. It was rawer than raw. Unbearable."

TELL ME ABOUT Monte Melnick. He seems rather quiet.

"He's quiet? He speaks quietly."

For a tour manager.

"He can raise his voice. I've seen him get angry."

I'm sure you have.

"But he's a sweet person."

(Author's interview with Ida Langsam, former Ramones PR, 2002)

BACK IN 1974 when The Dictators were playing regularly at the Coventry on Queens Blvd, opening for bands like the New York Dolls and The Harlots of 42nd Street, there would always be a tall, skinny, odd-looking guy hanging out at the bar. "Who is that guy?" Handsome Dick

Manitoba, The Dictators singer wanted to know. "That's Jeff Starship," he was told. "He's got a band called Sniper!"

The Dictators were an early New York band. The loud, obnoxious, fun, five-piece brought the wrestling mentality to rock – *Fuck 'Em If They Can't Take A Joke*, as one title put it. Handsome Dick was The Wrestler, the lead singer, backed up with great pop songs that later got called punk rock, fast and aggressive, outside of normal rock'n'roll – like MC5, or The Stooges, but with a pop sensibility. Bassist Andy Shernoff was the mastermind: he called the shots and wrote about bands like Blue Oyster Cult and The Velvet Underground in his fanzine, alongside legendary rock critics Richard Meltzer and Lester Bangs.

"I was raised in New York City," begins Andy. "I moved to Whitestone, which is about 10 minutes from Forest Hills, same general area of the city where the Ramones grew up. Society was divided back then between 'hip' and straight. Rock'n'roll encompassed all I found fascinating about American and British culture – I'm a big Kinks fan, The Who, Beatles, Stones. College didn't work out, so I formed a band. We made a punk rock record in '74 that came out in 1975.

"In the early Seventies, glam rock was the toast of New York. The Dictators didn't look good in satin – it wasn't us. High heels? We dressed on stage with what we always wore, which was jeans, T-shirts, denim, leather jackets and sneakers – that became our look. Joey Ramone came to see us play live. He looked a little like Freddie Mercury. We never really spoke. He didn't look healthy. He certainly didn't look like one of the Dolls. It was the singer in his band Sniper who did.

"One day, I saw a poster on a lamppost saying Joey was the singer of the Ramones. I'd been to CBGBs to see Patti Smith – she was getting very popular – so I went along to see the Ramones. There were maybe 20 people in the audience. Blondie were opening up – they were sloppy and still developing. The Ramones did 15 songs in 15 minutes, and it was great. They cut all the fat out. It was surf music, it was pop, it was hard rock – with a big beat. We obviously had the same influences but they sharply focused them and cut out all the fat."

"Listen to The Dictators singing 'C'mon boys, let's go' from 'Master Race Rock'," suggests John Holmstrom, founder of *Punk* magazine. "And then tell me it's not where Joey or Dee Dee got the Ramones' 'Let's go' from."

ON AUGUST 16, 1974, the Ramones made their debut at CBGBs – a seedy Bowery bar that would soon become synonymous with the burgeoning explosion of new music happening in NYC. Talking Heads, Patti Smith, Suicide, Blondie, The Heartbreakers, and thousands of lesser-known names like Milk 'n' Cookies, The Marbles and The Mumps honed their stagecraft there with its tiny stage and legendarily foul toilets. It was cheap. The bands were cheap. The beer was cheap. The punters were cheap. The groupies were plentiful.

"Did the Ramones piss in other people's drinks?" asks founder Blondie member Gary Valentine, referring to a famous, possibly apocryphal story. "It was impossible to tell at CBGBs. All the beer there tasted like piss."

Stepping into CBGBs in '74 was a sobering experience. "It was very homey," recalls Tommy Ramone. "There was a little bookstore so you could browse while you were soundchecking. Very few people went there initially. I think the Hell's Angels used to hang there before us. The local marines would come in. It had a pool table. It was small but intimate. It was never clean – and the bathrooms got worse and worse."

The nervy, wired Television had taken a Sunday night residency earlier that year when founders Richard Hell and Tom Verlaine – who had briefly tried out Dee Dee for the bass slot in the short-lived Neon Boys before discovering he could barely play – had lied barefaced to owner Hilly Kristal about their music.

"Hilly was like, 'What kinda music you play?' " fellow Television member Richard Lloyd told *Please Kill Me*, "and we said, 'What does CBGB-OMFUG [the sign outside the club] stand for?' " It stood for Country, Bluegrass, Blues, and Other Music for Uplifting Gourmandizers. So Television told him that's exactly what they played.

The Ramones debuted at CBGBs on August 16 – a show that has been listed by *Entertainment Weekly* as one of the greatest moments in rock. Not according to cbgb.com: "They were the most un-together band I'd ever heard," Hilly wrote. "They kept starting and stopping – equipment breaking down – and yelling at each other. They were a mess." The Ramones played CBGBs another 22 times that year alone.

"I don't know if the Ramones picked up a crowd immediately," thinks photographer Roberta Bayley. "I used to do the door when Richard Hell was in Television. On a very good night, they'd take about $50, you know? Most of the people coming in were their friends so they didn't pay. The whole door taking would go to the band theoretically, but it was never more than $100. The big night was when Patti Smith played with Television and they made $300. Three hundred dollars means there were a hundred people paying. But then the legal capacity of CBGBs is only about 115 or 150, I think. Not that they haven't packed in 1,000 people."

"Until I saw the Ramones play, I thought the Dolls were the loudest band ever," offers Valentine. "They were fantastic, 20 songs in 15 minutes, one after the other, one minute, two minute songs. There was this tacit, pent-up notion of violence in the background, but on stage they were a lot of fun, in a Saturday morning cartoon, 'Hey hey we're the Ramones' way. Even though all the songs were different they all sounded the same – it was like Beethoven over one-and-a-half minutes, with Joey Ramone mumbling over the top."

"When I first saw them at CBs," says Marc Bell, aka Marky Ramone, "I thought they sucked because there were no fills, no drum rolls because that's what I'd been doing all my life. When the first album came out I kept listening and listening to it. It was the most stripped-down version of rock I'd heard, and that's what I admired because I was so young. It was such a wall of sound. The image with the leather jackets wasn't developed yet in '74, John would wear the gold lamé pants from the glam days. The image wasn't planned. They grew into it. The bickering was all part of it."

"Dee Dee would shout '1-2-3-4' and everybody would start playing a different song," Tommy admitted in an interview with *NME* in 1978. "Then we'd throw the instruments around and walk off, and that wasn't a put-on either."

"They'd play for 40 minutes," recalls Hilly. "And 20 of them would just be the band yelling at each other."

JUST AROUND THE corner from CBGBs, on East 2nd Street, was (and still is) the loft dwelling space of Arturo Vega. Vega was an immaculately dressed Mexican painter and impresario who'd first seen the Ramones at Performance, and went on to become their lighting and artistic director. He was responsible for the Ramones' logo – a parody of the presidential seal with an eagle holding a baseball bat and gripping the "Hey Ho, Let's Go" banner in its beak. The loft itself was fairly large, kitsch, decorated with goldfish bowls full of old Mexican cigarettes, Day-Glo swastikas and Mexican hats. It served as both rehearsal and living quarters to various Ramones over the years, as well as temporary practice space to Blondie in early '76.

"I wanted to give them an all-American powerful presence," the artist says, in reference to the logo. "The first time we went to Washington, I was very impressed with all the officialdom, the flags and eagles everywhere. I was creating it up here with Joey, and he wanted me to put something in, instead of the arrows. I had no idea Johnny was such a baseball fanatic. I think Joey knew. The other major decision was 'Whose name goes first?' Joey sounds too Italian, Dee Dee is like a cartoon, Tommy was too sweet so, Johnny got to go on top."

Joey lived with Arturo in the loft for many years. "But I had to kick Dee Dee out right away," Vega says, "because of the fights with girls, and the drugs." The band would wait "like puppies" for Arturo to come home from his job in a restaurant to bring them food – mostly sugary desserts.

"The first one I met was Dee Dee," Arturo recalls. "He used to come and see a girl who lived right above me, Sweet Pam. I thought he was very friendly and shy and vulnerable. He told me he was forming a rock'n'roll band. I couldn't even imagine what kind of a band he would be in. This was in late '73, early '74."

Sweet Pam was with The Cockettes, a transvestite acid theatre troupe from San Francisco – a little girl with a big vaudeville voice who sang Twenties torch songs.

"It took them about a year to solidify the image," he continues. "At the beginning, Dee Dee would look . . . prep school, like a rich kid or something. He would wear nice clothes, nice sweaters – slacks, even. He looked like a guy that had a nice job. Joey was always absolutely the same. Johnny was more into portraying a rock'n'roll image – the silver lamé pants. Then they got the leather jackets."

"I lived on Bowery with a lighting guy so I'd know where to come to," Joey told me in 1989. "It was a crazy house. People went in and out all the time. I had a really great record collection at one time. I had, like, my *Nuggets* album. Somebody was painting the house with a roller, and one side of the record turned white. All my good stuff got ripped off, like the first Sex Pistols single, my Charles Manson album . . ."

After CBGBs, everybody would go to Lady Astor with its mirrored bar and Billie Holiday on the jukebox. It wasn't that posh, but to the Ramones coterie it was. It was there Roberta Bayley first met Dee Dee. "He sat next to me," she says, "and talked about how German was his first language. He was fixated that he'd seen me in porn films. Well, that wasn't me, but he was like, 'That's alright, Roberta. It's not like I'm judging you.' Dee Dee and Richard [Hell] had this period where they were shooting drugs, so there would always be little dramas about that. It wasn't like buying drugs nowadays where everything's so organised – back then you went down Avenue D and took a chance.

"Dee Dee was very charming and handsome but also very odd," she adds. "Not evil or anything, his impulses were directed towards himself but that's part of the brilliance of the Ramones that they would have these weird sick songs like '53rd And 3rd'."

'53rd And 3rd' was a perversely upbeat anthem with an almost cross-eyed funk that appeared on the debut Ramones album.* It was written by Dee Dee about a notorious pick-up spot for male prostitutes. "They'd get in cars with businessmen and give them a blow job for 30 dollars," Roberta recalls. "I guess if you need heroin, that seems like a small price to pay.

"I remember with Dee Dee and Pam, he was always pawning the TV set and you'd get 20 dollars for that. She'd get some money and then they'd get it out, then it'd go back in. What a way to live. But god forbid anyone would get jobs. Dee Dee did work at a high-end beauty salon, cutting hair. It wasn't until I read his book I realised he had all these resentments about the bowl haircut. Dee Dee joining the Ramones must have been like joining the army: 'Here's your uniform, your regulation haircut' and that was it."

Was Dee Dee a male prostitute?

"Sure he was," replies Victor Bockris, co-writer of *Making Tracks*, the official Blondie biography. "It's true. It wasn't that unusual in those days . . . every year, around September, there would be a big influx of young people starting their lives in the city, and a number of them who were able to be gay used that the same way a lot of women would use their sex to get ahead. There was nothing particularly frowned upon."

In *Please Kill Me*, Joey's brother Mickey Leigh recollects seeing Dee Dee standing on the corner of 53rd and 3rd in a black leather jacket (later to feature on the sleeve of the debut Ramones album), waiting for some action. "I was kind of shocked to see somebody I knew doing it," he says. "It was like, 'Holy shit. That's Doug standing there. He's really doing it.' "

The stories of Dee Dee's salacious, heroin-spiked past are legion. Foremost is the one about Dee Dee shredding all of Johnny Thunders' clothes when they were both staying at [Dead Boys' singer] Stiv Bators' place in Paris, working on a group together after the bassist had left the Ramones. Thunders was stealing stuff from Dee Dee to buy drugs, so Dee Dee went to Thunders' place and got a suitcase of all his silk stage clothes, and poured bleach all over them and ripped them up. Next time they saw each other they were standing in line waiting to score on the Lower East Side.

And then there was Connie . . .

* It later gave its name to an Eighties Scots record label, home of the Ramones-inspired, female-led Shop Assistants, and minimalist Olympian Nirvana influence Beat Happening.

WHAT KIND OF mischief did Dee Dee get up to when you first met him?

"Uh, Dee Dee was always into drugs," excplains Arturo, "from his childhood in Germany. The girls that he got involved with, they were always the dangerous kind. I recently found some photographs from the day the band was leaving for London in '76, taken here in the loft. Connie appears in one of them – Connie is the famous 'Bitch, I should have been rich'* . . . Bad girls and drugs: that was the trouble Dee Dee got himself into, very easily."

Connie Gripp was a very tall, statuesque junkie/hooker/dancer with long blonde hair. She'd previously sliced open the hand of New York Dolls' bassist Arthur Kane in a jealous rage – and climbed out onto the fire escape naked to avoid him. *Poison Heart* details many of her (and Dee Dee's) excesses: how she set Arturo's loft alight after a wine and Thorazine-fuelled threesome: how she once came at a love rival with a brick in her handbag: how she shared a *ménage à trois* with Nancy Spungen and Dee Dee: how she sliced up Dee Dee's arse with a bottle. Dee Dee was actually very fond of her.

"Connie was a nut," says Marky succinctly.

"Connie was psychotic. She once lamped Dee Dee over the head with his guitar when he was sleeping," shudders Janis Schacht, Sire Records PR between August 1975 and January '79. "She had that dangerous, self-destructive Nancy Spungen personality. I often wonder whether she wasn't Nancy's hero, the same way Dee Dee was Sid's – it certainly would have made sense."

"Connie was a crazy groupie," laughs Holmstrom. "There were always a lot of groupies at CBGBs – she was in the upper echelon. They were together a long time, breaking up and fighting. It was a very tempestuous relationship. She dressed really well. She probably worked as a stripper and earned a lot of money. I seem to remember her wearing furs. A lot of people didn't like Connie so they'll think I'm nuts for saying anything nice – but she reminded me of Nancy Sinatra. Nancy was a role model for a lot of punk rock girls."

" 'Glad To See You Go' was written the day Connie left," divulges Arturo. "Joey and I were trying to stay out of her way. She would walk this way and we would walk that way, because we were afraid she was going to grab something and throw it at us. We knew that she'd stabbed Dee Dee a couple of times so we were afraid, especially when she came

* The line is actually "It's hard as a bitch, I should have been rich" from the Heartbreakers harrowing drug anthem 'Chinese Rocks' which Dee Dee helped to co-write.

around the kitchen. Dee Dee's trying to calm her down, but nothing is working. Finally, she walks out the door, and the three of us go to the window to make sure she's really gone, and we're all looking down like this . . . [Arturo pulls up the blinds in his loft apartment where this interview is being conducted, and looks down onto the sidewalk outside] . . . and she comes out and starts cursing, so Dee Dee goes, 'Oh, I'm glad you're leaving, glad to see you go, goodbye.' "

BEFORE THE RAMONES crashed at Arturo's pad, Tommy shared an apartment on 2nd and 9th Street with Chris Stein, songwriter with Blondie.

Blondie are an underrated band. An early NYC scene report by *NME* writer Charles Shaar Murray in 1975 patronisingly described them as "this cute little bundle of platinum hair with a voice like a squeaky bath toy and quite the cruddiest garage-type garage band". He then went on to write "Blondie will never be a star," proving music critics do not possess the gift of prescience (among other things). If songs like the genre-crossing 'Heart Of Glass', 'Call Me', and 'Atomic' hadn't achieved such success, Blondie's first three albums would be held up today as prime examples of post-Sixties girl group garage pop – sultry, smart and filled with enough hooklines to mortgage your Shirelles collection for. As much a part of the art-punk New York scene as more critically acclaimed peers like Talking Heads and Television (and indeed the Ramones), Blondie were perfect musical pin-ups for an entire generation. No wonder the "Blondie is a singer, not a band" tag used to annoy them.

"Blondie and the Ramones were much more closely associated than the other punk groups," says Victor Bockris, "because in '72 and '73 Chris Stein was sharing an apartment with Tommy. Dee Dee would stay a lot, and the crazies would stay there too. That's where the early punk craziness – all-night activities, druggies, junkies, sexual partners – would happen with these young guys, crawling onto the edge of the scene. When the Ramones started playing at CBs, one of the first groups they played with was Blondie. Both groups created a cartoon image around them – not in a putdown sense, but iconic like Superman – that resonated equally with people in Japan and Germany, and created a much bigger thing."

When Blondie became ultra-successful in '79, there was some jealousy; like the Ramones saying Debbie would always fall over on stage so people could see her panties. That antagonism soon disappeared, though.

"Chris Stein was one of the first Goths I ever saw," recollects Tommy. "The apartment looked like a Goth museum. It had a life-sized painted statue of the Madonna that used to terrify Dee Dee. He was hardly ever there because he was so scared of it. There were crucifixes, monster movie stills, a tapestry, things in jars, old furniture he'd picked up. It was like a hippie pad. It was a real nice apartment, and it was real nice of him to let us sublet it."

"The first one I met was Tommy," says Gary Valentine, "because he was living in Chris Stein's old welfare flat. He was gnome-like with his dark shades and long hair with the fringe. I was 18, and had just been introduced to this weird community in East Village – oh, look, that's a Ramone! Things would get destroyed there – they had a party and the wall was missing. The flat itself had a long history. Eric Emerson [of Warhol's Factory entourage, famed for stripping on the tables at Max's Kansas City] had lived there, and he'd already been killed before I was on the scene."

AT THE END of 1974, the Ramones were reported to have put up $1,000 for eight hours of recording time in a small Long Island studio to make a demo of 15 songs.

"I don't think it cost that much," Tommy says now. "It was a lot of fun. I did a lot of pre-planning for that. Set up, laid the tracks down. Came back a week later and mixed it. It went pretty smooth. It felt like we were making important music. We knew we didn't sound like anyone else. It was funny and smart and good. We listened to old Beatles records – and because they were mono, and then stereo, the vocals would go on one side, and the guitars on the other. So that's what we did."

Many folk felt the brevity of their songs was a gimmick. Wrongly. For, as Johnny explained back then – perhaps disingenuously – it was because they were new at writing songs, "So we couldn't write anything too complicated. It was nothing intentional."

When pressed to describe their own music, the differences of response between the two guitarists was telling.

Dee Dee: "We're playing at our level of ability."

Johnny: "We're playing pure rock'n'roll with no blues or folk or any of that stuff in it. And we try to be entertaining and bring back the feeling of kids coming and having a good time – united with us."

3

Definition Of Punk

"No rules. Aggression in music and clothing and cultural outlook aimed at progressive, not negative, change." – David Kessel, producer

"When the word punk was put in the dictionary it was meant for the Ramones." – Rodney Bingenheimer, DJ

"Garage bands, street based, snotty, unmediated – that's a joke, but I'm trying – unmediated, wink, wink. Loud, snotty, angry and smart. The dividing line is mediation, gloss, melody . . . and pretty. The Ramones had beautiful ballads, though. Prettified is a better word. We love the Ramones and consider them our brothers. There are people who found them scary because of the paramilitary and the adrenalin. They should get out more." – Donna Gaines, professor of punk

"Punk was stupid. I didn't like when it became so self-conscious. What was interesting about it was early poetry/rock fusion. I didn't like *Punk* magazine or any of that stuff. When certain aspects of what was happening were given precedence over others, especially by *Punk*, it wasn't a real insight into what was happening. If you want to go back, punk is Rimbaud." – Gary Valentine, bassist

"Punk is this steadfast denial of the real world. I don't mean that in a smarmy way. For me, anyway, it has that in common with the hippie notion, as repulsive as that is. The hippies, though, thought they could do something. The punks never thought they could and didn't care. They were just going to do what they were going to do, and it didn't matter what." – George Seminara, video director

"I don't think the Ramones were punk. Punk for me is the Sex Pistols, with safety pins and spitting at people and walking off interviews and being nasty and rude. The Ramones were never like that. And of course they're credited with starting punk and being the godfathers of punk, but not punk as it became known. A leather jacket in America has always been a red flag. It's always been a sign of rebellion – up until recently when designers have been making them and charging $3,000 for the same leather jacket you can buy in a second-hand store for 20 bucks. But it's always had that James Dean defiance about it. Blue jeans and a leather jacket? Forget it. And then there was the hair, which was unruly and wasn't fashionable. And then you've got the fact that the jeans were torn and they didn't bother buying new ones. People didn't know what to do with that." – Ida Langsam, publicist

"We published the definition in the third issue of *Punk*. Anybody can be a rock star regardless of, or because of, any lack of talent or ability. That's the attitude. That is what rock'n'roll is all about. It's not about this is shit, or connections. The life of Dee Dee is almost the definition of punk. He can't help it. He's Dee Dee. With most rock'n'roll bands, the first record is called punk rock because they don't know what they're doing yet. As they progress they get more and more boring. Some of that early Elvis stuff sounds like punk rock to me." – John Holmstrom, publisher

"There wasn't punk without the Ramones. They were held back the same way every band on Sire was held back – even Renaissance and The Paley Brothers – because radio people believed everything on Sire was punk. When a new Sire record came out, you could trust it. It was reasonably amusing when Seymour [Stein, Sire boss] lost Fleetwood Mac because he forgot to sign the contract, but it was kind of sad because if he'd had the money from *Rumours* it's possible Ramones would have cracked it – there's a reason for everything." – Janis Schacht, publicist

"I think [the establishment] associated punk with animals. It was distrusted. On American TV if they wanted to use villains it'd be a punk because they couldn't use minorities anymore. It took 20 years for punk to break in the States because of the fear that people would lose their jobs. When grunge happened, the music industry rushed to jettison the whole thing and bring in the boy bands and Britney Spears. They found the whole grunge thing distasteful. They were happy to see it die. Now they're trying to bring back hard rock, but industry controlled. Very few executives are from the music world, they're from accounting and attorneys." – Tommy Ramone, drummer

"Fast. Energetic. Short, to the point. Songs that don't necessarily have to have meaning but have to get you excited and moving and going – if you have something to say, say it quick, and to the point, keep the song within two-and-a-half minutes. Image wise, it doesn't matter what you look like, as long as you're not a fucking asshole. If you have to act punk then you're not a punk. It's not an act. You either are or you're not." – Marky Ramone, drummer

"The first line reads 'Punk rock exists because so many bands assumed it was easy to imitate the Ramones.' I mean – hello? What more needs to be said? So that may answer the question of Pearl Jam or Soundgarden or any other number of bands, who clearly love the Ramones – why don't you show any influences in your music? Well, it's not fucking that easy to be that special, to have that magic the Ramones have. First of all, one of the things it was based on was no guitar solos, instead of hideously long ones. If you're not going to have guitar solos then in the space that's left in the song, you really have to say something, progression-wise, melody-wise and every other way. And these people don't have that kind of talent, do they?" – Kevin Patrick, (cool) A&R executive

"They can label it how they want to label it. I don't care. I never resented it, but, if anything, when punk started getting this bad reputation, we started getting lumped in with the stuff and being excluded – you know, 'We're not going to play punk on the radio.' Now we are being included, where other times we weren't being included. There'd be an article on punk in a magazine and they'd exclude the Ramones and make it about British bands. We got shafted both ways by punk. But as far as being labelled, it's fine. If you're a heavy metal group, you're a heavy metal group. You're a speed metal group, hardcore punk band, British Mersey-beat sound, whatever it is, rockabilly. There's always labels." – Johnny Ramone, guitarist

4

The Year Punk Broke

"MAN, THEY WERE so New York. They were so New York that there was also something irreducibly American about them. They could have not existed in any other country, or in any other city, or been born in any other borough than Queens. There was just something very . . . not working class . . . but almost the labour of the fantasy of being a rock star. They were committed to the work that it takes to be a rock star. Most people, they form bands because they want to be rock stars. They don't think of the labour that goes into it.

"If nothing else, they ensured their legacy by doing it for 22 years – two more than Johnny wanted to do. He really thought of it as a job, and come 20 years, he was ready to quit. It was a prolonged ending, of course, but there was no question he thought of it as his life's work. Joey, in a different way, thought of it as his life's calling. There was nothing else he could do. Being this tall gawky guy who didn't look like every other Average Joe at school, he was forced to a certain marginal point of his adolescence where what he discovered about himself was that, if he was going to do anything, he was going to be a rock star. He loved music enough that he was going to stick with it for as long as it took, to the point where he was recording that solo record, literally as he was dying. That's the mark of a guy who really believes that this is his life, that it's not a fantasy, it is not just something to get girls, but that it's something that you do with your heart, and soul, and intellect, as God gave you. And they did it.

"Johnny, though, is retired. He's got his gold watch.

"It's not the most obvious choice, picking up the guitar for your trade, but Johnny worked in the construction industry. The guitar's a tool, and he used it like a jackhammer. He told me about seeing bands like Mountain and the MC5 at the Fillmore, and he was committed to that kind of rock'n'roll – hard guitars, used as weapons. Used as something to break down and build. He played the guitar with all of the crap taken out of it. He played guitar with the absolute essence of the force – it wasn't even sound any more, it was just the force of what the instrument could do – and his guitar playing was a marvel 22 years later. Everyone tried to do it, but nobody could do it with the concentration that he could muster because he decided that

he was going to play guitar with all of the extra stuff removed. No solos, because that's for jerking off; no blues licks, because he wasn't black and from Mississippi; he's a white guy from Queens and this is what you do when this is all you're given.

"In doing so, he reduced a music that had gotten so florid and over-reaching to such bare essence, you couldn't argue with it. You either loved it or you hated it. That was the genius of what he, and they, did. They created a sound in which you could take no middle ground. You couldn't simply accept it: you had to either embrace it; or you had to say it was the worst shit you'd ever heard in your life. And there were a lot of people that took the second position. And they were wrong.

"Johnny and Joey were made for each other, and to be in contention with each other. You know Johnny believed he should've been a star. Because that's what you do, you get paid for your labour, you get respected for the work that you do. And that bothers him still. So the Ramones finally got into the Rock'N'Roll Hall of Fame after how many years, and how many tours, and how many shows, and people saying, 'Yeah, they were the greatest, they started it all.' Pearl Jam, Green Day, everyone worships at their altar, and yet the established music industry took forever to understand them. It can really bum a guy out. A lot of bands have broken up over a lot less, a lot sooner. The estrangement between Johnny and Joey for the last 10, 15 years of the group is no secret, but they still didn't break up, they still refused not to do it."

(Author's interview with David Fricke, *Rolling Stone*)

I NEVER TRUSTED the punks.

Alienation, I could relate to. Maybe the originals wanted to map out new paths for themselves, new ways of seeing. I don't know. By the time I'd caught up with modern music – 1978, or thereabouts, at the aggravatingly ancient age of 17 – all it seemed the (male) punks were interested in was creating a new hierarchy. Furthermore, it was one that was visibly based on the old hierarchy: The Rolling Stones' template for destruction and mistreatment of others. Leather jackets, torn jeans, macho revelry and chords ripped off from The Kinks and The Troggs and The Who's back catalogues. I never wanted to relive the dreams of my parents' generation. Never saw the point.

If pressed, I'd admit to a fondness for the show tunes of *South Pacific* and Abba and *Grease*, life amplified and reduced to teen angst: words that mirrored the heart-stopping importance of the way her eyes wouldn't catch yours across the floor. Romance. Romance. Repetition. I didn't want those dreams either, even more hackneyed and useless than the last, but there was no let out for a teenage loser seeking teenage kicks dressed up in confusion. At that point, I wasn't too conversant with The Shangri-Las' traumatic side ('Dressed In Black', 'I Can Never Go Home Anymore') nor was I aware of the shimmering, eternal brilliance of the entire Spector/ Ronettes *oeuvre* – and it wouldn't have mattered if I was. Those sounds belonged to another generation. The only songs I enjoyed were ones belonging to totally alienated voices like [early British punk fanzine] *Sniffin' Glue* founder Mark Perry's ATV and those on the debut Fall album. Fall singer Mark E. Smith's voice seemed to crack and fold its way through a thousand diverse melodies, but even then I was aware I was projecting, that this made me separate from the crowd, not part of it.

If you wanted to join the crowd in 1978, you needed to be a punk – join the punks, and you had a ready-made crowd of like-minded disaffected and dysfunctional peers ready to enfold and encircle you in their freshly created layers of tradition.

I didn't discover the Ramones till late on.

The first time I recall truly enjoying "da bruddas" was their double 1979 live album *It's Alive* – a bunch of great melodies, reminiscent of Sixties girl groups, raced through at terrifying speed: with lyrics borrowed heavily from the faux-diseased imagery of Seventies horror B-movies and the cartoon slapstick of my beloved *Spiderman* and Fifties horror EC comics. The sheer pace, the strangeness of Joey's almost English drawl coupled with the amphetamine blast of Johnny's chainsaw guitar, did it for me. I couldn't give two craps for their image, being brought up to hate regimentation and artifice – although even I could see it was as near to perfection as rock would ever allow: the essence of the Stones' street-tough image stripped down to a bunch of ripped jeans and sneakers. Who needs more? The leather jackets seemed extraneous. It wasn't until a good decade later I understood the complete necessity of looking cool. Still, I've always had a healthy distrust of pretension: it was perfect, the way the Ramones shed rock of its trappings, back to the essentials: melody, noise, a great voice. Their lyrics were funny and moving and said as much as was needed, no more.

'I Don't Wanna Walk Around With You', Joey complained on one of the first songs the Ramones ever wrote. The line was sung three times, fast, before the killer punch, "So why you wanna walk around with me?" Twenty-five seconds of pop, brutally shorn of all colour. This was pure *West Side Story* grit and heartbreak. Even now, I believe it to be a perfectly encapsulated break-up song – what more needs to be said? "I don't wanna walk around with you. I don't wanna walk around with you. I don't wanna walk around with you. So why do you wanna walk around with me?"

Why indeed?

The fact that *It's Alive* was the first Ramones record I experienced led to a surreal experience. (It appeared after their fourth album, 1978's *Road To Ruin*, the one on yellow vinyl with the great Holmstrom cover illustration, the one that featured the yearning country-esque 'Questioningly', the one that should have spawned a thousand Monster Number One hits.) The first time I heard the studio version of 'Sheena Is A Punk Rocker', I thought it was a spoof, a joke band like Albertos Y Los Trios Paranoias covering the Ramones, slowing them down to take the piss. What was this sludge guitar sound, I wondered? It took me a long time to readjust.

Now, of course, I understand.

The debut Ramones album was so minimalist, so basic, there was a delicious rumour flying round back in those days that their management couldn't get the songs published: "These aren't real songs," they were supposed to have been told, "these are fragments." Not real songs? Next you'll be telling me The Beach Boys had no harmonies. The strength of an idea can often be measured by its simplicity. Rock groups spend years and millions of pounds in studios, trying to come up with a song with even a hundredth of the power of the Ramones' debutante 'Blitzkrieg Bop' (its "Hey ho, Let's go" chant now appropriately used as a between innings warm-up in the New York Yankees stadium). The debut Ramones album was recorded in four days, and mixed on the fifth: why spend longer? It provides a direct link between The Ronettes, the straight-edge pop purity of Jonathan Richman, the much underrated punk melodies of Ireland's Undertones, Edinburgh's Shop Assistants, Olympia's Nirvana and . . . (insert your own favourite here). There has always been a strong strain of regression in the greatest rock music. The Ramones were living proof of this, and never stopped being vital because they – or at least Joey and Dee Dee – resolutely refused to grow up. Their final album even contains a version of Tom Waits' 'I Don't Want To Grow Up'.

The 14 songs on 1976's *Ramones* are a blueprint for everything that followed: relationship songs ('Judy Is A Punk'), horror songs ('I Don't Wanna Go Down To The Basement'), break-up songs ('I Don't Wanna Walk Around With You'), drug songs ('Now I Wanna Sniff Some Glue'), party songs ('Let's Dance'), unrequited love songs ('I Wanna Be Your Boyfriend'), war imagery songs ('Havana Affair') – the whole gamut of teen confusion. It was America . . . New York City . . . Queens . . . Forest Hills, in a microcosm. Life reduced to its essentials, shorn of the bullshit thrown at adolescents by know-it-all adults. *Ramones* was brutal, funny, hard, unrelenting and, most of all, human.

(Author's own essay on the debut Ramones album)

DANNY FIELDS WAS a charismatic figure on the NYC scene in 1974, a Harvard Law School dropout associated with Andy Warhol's art crowd – "forever the coolest guy in the room," as *Please Kill Me* put it – who co-edited *16 Magazine* and had a gossip column in *Soho Weekly News*. While doing publicity for Elektra in the Sixties, he'd worked with The Doors, and signed The Stooges, whom he later managed, and MC5 [the radical Sixties politically charged Detroit garage band credited with being a major influence on punk]. He got fired for defending the MC5's right to say 'fuck' in their artwork. He then moved to Atlantic where he was also fired – this time, he claimed, for openly detesting Seventies prog rock dinosaurs Emerson, Lake & Palmer.

It was February 1975 before Tommy Ramone – under considerable pressure from Johnny to deliver some "names" into the Ramones' inner circle of admirers – managed to talk Fields, and *Creem* writer Lisa Robinson, into coming along to a show. Few people took the Ramones seriously. Gigs would end abruptly in a melee of confusion and shouting as someone lost their place in a song, or Joey forgot the words. The bickering had started.

Lisa edited *Hit Parader* alongside her husband Richard (who later produced New York Dolls singer David Johansen's solo albums). She was also the American editor for *NME* and ran *Rock Scene*, a picture-led teen magazine of influence. Clearly, rock critics were thin on the ground back then.

"In the music industry, we read *Rock Scene* religiously because there were always photos of parties that we had been to," explains Ida Langsam, Ramones PR between '87 and '96. "*Rock Scene* was like the Bible to people outside New York."

"Tommy Ramone was relentless – and that was before I knew him as a drummer," Danny Fields wrote in the foreword to the Ramones anthology, *Hey Ho! Let's Go!* "He promoted his band with a fervour that was astonishing. I was a great fan of a certain other group playing frequently at CBGBs, a group the Ramones hated for reasons aesthetic, personal and professional. As I would soon learn, the Ramones hated just about every other band in the world, especially ones that were getting written about in early '75 while they were being ignored – by the press, the music industry, the promoters . . . everyone but Hilly Kristal, who gave them a place to play, because who else would want them?"

"We felt he would like what we were doing," explains Tommy. "He was enthusiastic. We kind of idolised him because of his connection with all these famous people. It took a while for him to agree to become our manager – I think it was Lou Reed who finally convinced him. It was like a burden lifted from me."

Legend has it that a coin was flipped between the two writers, and that either the loser or winner had to go and check out the Ramones. Whatever the result, Lisa was the one to see them, and came back raving.

"True," Danny asserts in an email. "But I'm not sure if a coin was literally flipped."

"You have *got* to see this band," Lisa told Danny the following day. So he went down to the Bowery the next time Ramones played.

"I was sitting in front," Fields told David Fricke, "overwhelmed by watching Joey sing 'I Don't Wanna Go Down To The Basement' – 'I don't wanna go down to the basement/There's something down there.' It was a great lyric – and you believed him. The song was about primal fear, with an incredible beat, rush and power. I thought, 'This band is great, and that guy is great.' "

After the set, Fields introduced himself to the band

"I want to manage you," he said. "You've changed my life."

"Well," said Johnny, "that's very nice. But we really need a new set of drums. Can you buy us a new set of drums?"

A few weeks later, Fields took Sire records boss Seymour Stein's wife Linda along to see the band at a 23rd Street gay bar called Mother's.

"The first show we went to was hysterical," remembers Sire PR Janis Schacht. "They played for 15 minutes and then stopped because Johnny's guitar broke. [Photographer] Leee Childers was there, and Lou Reed. It was impossible to tell how many songs they played. I thought they were perfectly constructed – I'd been a contributing editor at *Circus* for seven years, so I noticed things like that. Joey was like a snake, wrapped around the microphone. He barely moved at all."

"I thought they were amazing," Linda says. "You'd hear them once and the second time you'd be singing along. I loved the energy, brevity and simplicity. I don't mean simple in a silly way. I loved the fact that there were four of them, the fact they were a band. I loved that they didn't have any sort of costumes, props, make-up and other nonsense.

"Tommy was highly intelligent and extremely literate, with a wonderful voice, and he did most of the business talking. Dee Dee was hysterical, ridiculous, charming and divine and a royal pain in the neck. He liked to be the centre of attention. Sid Vicious was such a groupie for Dee Dee, oh my God . . . Dee Dee didn't need heroin: he had his own natural energy and lack of it. Dee Dee was like a clown: adorable and testy. John was the most serious, the most obviously driven, full of Ramone energy and attitude. He could be frightening if he yelled at you. He's one of the great yellers of life, but he's nobody's fool. He doesn't sound as academic as Tommy, but I'll put my money on Johnny. He is extremely smart, honest, hardworking, and deep down . . . very deep, really deep," she laughs, "there's a sweet guy."

"Most of the run-ins I had were with Dee Dee," reflects Gary Valentine. "We didn't actually get into a fist-fight, but we did have to be pulled apart, when Clem [Burke, Blondie drummer] and I were playing pool in CBs. He'd obviously had a couple of drinks and started knocking balls around on the table, feeling pleased with himself. This goes on for a while when he says, 'I bet you think I'm acting like an asshole.' So I go, 'No Dee Dee. I don't think you're acting at all.' He got very angry. There was always something hovering, an underlying current of violence."

"I was going out with the drummer with Mink DeVille," recalls Gloria Nicholl, later to work with Janis Schacht at Sire. "Then I started seeing Stiv Bators [Dead Boys singer]. We'd sometimes go to CBGBs during the day to pick up money because Hilly managed his band, and Dee Dee would say in a loud voice: 'Stiv, is she still afraid of it? Does she still think that if she looks at it she'll get pregnant?' It was so embarrassing."

"He had a chip on his shoulder," ex-Blondie bassist Valentine says. "We were talking about playing bass one day at Arturo's when he said, 'I'm not a real musician like you are' because I'd used two fingers while he used one. The remark surprised me because I felt there was no rivalry between us."

In 1980, *Esquire* asked Danny Fields what made Dee Dee so distinctive.

"His IQ . . . his abiding sense of decency, justice, honour, integrity, morality . . . He'll also sleep with anything, which makes him very hot."

WALKING AROUND THE Lower East Side in 1975, you might have come across a flyer for a Ramones show, photocopied and assembled by Arturo or Tommy. A typical one stated in large type, *"Appearing at Performance Studios 23 East 20th Street, Friday April 11 9 P.M. Also C.B.G.B's 315 Bowery + Bleeker Monday + Tuesday April 14 + 15 11 P.M."*

A description of the group followed: *"The Ramones are not an oldies group, they are not a glitter group, they don't play boogie music and they don't play the blues. The Ramones are an original Rock and Roll group of 1975, and their songs are brief, to the point and every one a potential hit single. Contact Tome [*sic*] Erdelyi, Loudmouth Productions."* At the bottom were lyrics to six songs, including 'I Don't Care' and 'I Don't Want To Go Down To The Basement'.

On June 23, Danny and Linda arranged a private audition for Seymour Stein in a loft on Broadway and 20th. Stein offered them a singles deal on the spot for 'You're Gonna Kill That Girl'. The band declined, holding out for an albums deal.

"I had heard so many negative things about the Ramones and so many positive things," Stein told *Mojo* journalist Michael Hill in 2000, "that I didn't know what to expect. I certainly expected to see something visually exciting – and it was. I loved their songs. I can sing their songs. I don't know how many artists you can say that about, artists of the mid-Seventies onwards. They wrote great fucking songs. It was easy to see their influences were The Beach Boys and, to a certain extent, Abba. I loved them at first sight. Nobody wanted to go down the Bowery. Nobody. It was a great stroke of luck for me."

The following two days, the Ramones auditioned for Steve Paul's Blue Sky label and Arista.

"I remember a Miamis show where afterwards Dee Dee was going on about the Ramones being signed for a singles deal," laughs Valentine. "Everyone was sitting round the table, smoking a joint, asking questions – you know, 'What's it like? Are you still going to play CBGBs?' And he said, 'Well, y'know, probably, but not that often. We want to play the bigger places too.' He leaned back, with his pudding basin haircut and ripped jeans, satisfied with his assessment. I was keeping pretty quiet. I was the new boy in town. Then he added, 'We'll come see you guys, though. We don't want to lose touch.' I couldn't resist it. 'Wow, Dee Dee,' I said. 'It must be lonely at the top.' Everyone sniggered. I don't think he liked that."

On July 11, da bruddas played their first and only out-of-town show of the year – an ill-judged support to Johnny Winter at the Palace Theater in Waterbury, Connecticut in front of 2,000 kids (arranged by Steve Paul). First song, there was a smattering of applause. After that, the crowd turned ugly.

"It was a very nasty town," Dee Dee wrote in *Spin* over a decade later. "Before we went on, this cop who had heard us warming up said, 'I really feel sorry for you guys.' I've never got so many bottles or firecrackers or people giving me the finger. After that, we didn't want to play anymore, but we were too involved to turn back."

SEYMOUR STEIN WAS a music fan with an impeccable ear. From Brooklyn, with a Jewish upbringing, he started as a record collector, buying publishing and putting out Fleetwood Mac's early albums, and created Sire Records as a fan. Staff meetings with Seymour were memorable: one day he sang 20 years of Oscar winning hits, another time he called the Memphis operator and sang Chuck Berry's 'Memphis' on the line with her.

By 1978, he had an incredible roster including the Ramones, Talking Heads, [excitable Scots bubblegum rockers] the Rezillos, the irrepressible Undertones, Stiv Bators' scuzzy Dead Boys and Richard Hell [post-Television, and with his Voidoids, the band that created the tag 'Blank Generation'].

"The fact that [present-day Scots cutie pop stars] Belle And Sebastian write poetic songs about him is amazing," mulls Hill, "because you wouldn't look at Seymour and think of poetry. There's something about Seymour, though . . . he has this child-like enthusiasm that he shared with Joey. Seymour is a great collector of antiques, and is relentless in his pursuit of these objects to fill his many homes. His acquiring of bands and this stuff went hand-in-hand – with each new thing he saw, he got as excited as if it was the first thing he had ever laid his eyes upon. Maybe he's jaded in other ways, but not about music.

"His love of the Ramones is unconditional," Hill continues. "It's like a parent to a child. Here's the great apotheosis of the three-chord – or the two-chord in their case – rock song, or pop song: the distillation of everything he had believed in, in that moment. Seymour was truly a visionary."

BY COMMON ASSENT in America (if not in England) punk rock started over the weekend of July 16–18, 1975, when CBGBs put on a three-night Festival Of Unrecorded Talent featuring bands like Talking Heads, Blondie, the Ramones, Tuff Darts, The Fast, Television and the Heartbreakers (with Richard Hell and Johnny Thunders). The weekend was written up extensively both at home and in the British music press. *Rolling Stone* ran a full-page report, and the Ramones merited three quarters of the article.

As ungainly as Joey looked, he was certainly photogenic, wrapped around the microphone stand like a brittle moth, flanked by Dee Dee and Johnny on either side, legs unfeasibly far astride like a retarded Status Quo, guitars slung lower than anyone had seen before. This look, that rapidly became synonymous with Ramones (and was later mimicked by bassists everywhere – from Sid Vicious to New Order's Peter Hook) came about by necessity. It's easier to play down strokes the lower you hold your guitar. The haircuts, incidentally, were either arguably influenced by Dave Hill from Slade, or The Monkees. But whatever the origins of the Ramones' style, there was certainly something in the air that month.

"Before that weekend," Johnny explained to *Entertainment Weekly*, "we just thought we were fooling people. Me and Dee Dee would make jokes about it. We started to take it serious then."

"This was Woodstock on the Lower East Side," Valentine recalls. "It was the beginning, the semi-official, semi-conscious start of the scene recognising itself. It wasn't called punk right then, but shortly would be. There were different coteries of people on the scene: in standard leather jackets and jeans, and long hair. It was like charity shop chic, stuff you'd get out of rubbish bins or thrift stores. The bondage chic came later when the scene started becoming more defined."

Various characters stood out: a half-Chinese girl named Anya Philips who later starred in a *Punk* "graphic novel" called *The Legend Of Nick Detroit* with Debbie Harry and Richard Hell, and went on to manage No Wave artist James Chance [with his Contortions, a brittle explosion of funk and hard-edged attitude]. Anya had the Dragon Lady dominatrix look with her black leather, long fingernails and a cigarette holder. The club was popular with the late glitter, sleazy, Club 82 scene. Then there was the skinny tie mob, copying a look first made fashionable by Patti Smith, and picked up on by the boys in Blondie, and the Ramones crowd with their ripped jeans and plimsolls. Leather jackets were still associated with Lou Reed and the gay bondage scene, the heavy rough trade taking place on West Village.

"The big thing was black jeans and you couldn't get them anywhere," sighs Roberta Bayley, "and then Fiorucci started making them." Drainpipe presumably? "Yeah, and they were like $60 which was really expensive. And they'd have the contrasting gold thread so you'd have to go and dye them so it wouldn't show. Then Trash on Broadway started making black jeans for $20. Blondie used to be into that look: they'd find their shirts on 14th Street. Debbie was so into the vintage look. There was no dominant look until the hardcore era when people started being all spiky and pierced and tattooed. I was gone by then. I didn't like that look."

The *Soho Weekly News* called the Ramones the greatest singles band since The Velvet Underground, perhaps because of the Danny Fields connection – an odd statement, as the Velvets weren't exactly known for being a singles band. Fields recalls that early on, the Ramones would come to blows after their sets. "Johnny would be strangling Dee Dee, and there'd be press or fans waiting to see them," he says. "I'd tell folks they were just towelling off, give them a couple of minutes, and by the time people saw them, they'd be sipping a beer."

On September 19, the Ramones recorded a two-song demo 'Judy Is A

Punk' and 'I Wanna Be Your Boyfriend' in Westchester, with ex-New York Dolls manager Marty Thau. "They came out OK," Tommy says, "but we spent more time recording those two songs than on the real album."

"I FIRST HEARD ABOUT the Ramones in 1975 from Johnny Thunders," writes Thau, "who told me a new scene was developing at a little Village bar called Mother's and a hot new band called the Ramones were causing all the excitement. 'You should check them out,' he said, ''cause they're gonna stir some waves.' So I did, and thought, 'Here's a band I'd like to produce.' They had the music, the attitude, the look, and the street smarts to spearhead what was to be known as punk rock . . . and they did.

"I wasn't recognised as a producer yet, but having spent so much time in recording studios I figured I was up to the task. I was still managing the high maintenance New York Dolls, who were in the early stages of their implosion, but I knew it was just a matter of time before they'd break up. I couldn't picture myself managing anymore. I wanted to produce records.

"The Ramones were searching for a manager and were considering me. I made it clear I wasn't interested in managing anyone, but would like an opportunity to produce some demos with them to see how they'd fare in the studio. 'Let's do it,' they said. A week later we were off to 914 Studios in Blauvelt, New York, a funky little 16-track place north of the city where Bruce Springsteen and Janis Ian had recorded some of their earlier works.

"I discovered the Ramones knew exactly what they wanted: a duplication of their live sound with no added frills, overdubs, or gimmicks. I wondered if it was because they couldn't play more complex parts but eventually realised they believed less is more and one must keep it honest, keep it pure and never lose sight of the beat. High energy 'beat minimalism' was their governing philosophy and their reaction to the excessive production values that had crept into rock'n'roll in the late Sixties. They were striving for good old teen sounds you could dance to, sing along with, and feel way down in your gut, songs with lyrics about sex and love and drugs and r'n'r (Seventies style) that American teens would relate to. No 20-minute extended guitar solos or pretentious drum flourishes would ever be heard when the Ramones took the stage.

"The sessions began. Tommy was somewhat familiar with the recording process and helped direct his band mates through the recordings. Johnny and Dee Dee were tight-lipped; Joey was the butt of the others' constant teasing. A quiet and somewhat nervous type, Joey said little, delivered a near-perfect performance each take, and then quietly retreated into a corner, as we listened back to the tape. We completed the recordings in less than four hours – they were never mixed.

"A few days later the rough cassette was sent to Craig Leon, a young A&R man at Sire Records, who played them for his boss Seymour Stein. Craig was a close friend – we'd hang out together at CBGBs almost every night and see every new band appearing there. We knew we were witnessing rock history in the making as we revelled in the performances of future stars like Patti Smith, Suicide, the Heartbreakers, Richard Hell & The Voidoids, The Cramps, Talking Heads and Blondie . . . the future stars of the new punk rock era. Weeks later, Sire signed the Ramones. My demos weren't the only reason they were signed, but they did play a role and proved without doubt that the Ramones could make credible records. The doors to Seventies punk were kicked wide open.

"Craig was assigned the task of producing and did an excellent job, which resulted in their classic self-titled first LP. I was naturally disappointed that I didn't get the production assignment but was glad the Ramones were in Craig's hands."

(Marty Thau on http://tres_producers.blogspot.com: reprinted with permission)

IN JANUARY 1976, after months of negotiation, the Ramones signed a recording contract with Sire Records. Thau's demos, and the fact that Danny Fields – a respected industry figure – was co-managing them were enough to finally convince Stein that he should sign the band. Also, Sire was having real trouble with its distribution at the time and desperately needed some cheap new acts to help bolster its roster.

And the Ramones were certainly cheap.

"I was an A&R scout for Sire," says Craig Leon, the man many people credit with discovering both the Ramones and Talking Heads. Florida-born Leon had previously worked with the Climax Blues Band in Miami before coming across to NYC in the Seventies. In '75, Sire was a tiny label that was mostly importing European progressive acts. "We had an A&R staff of two," he recalls, "and a promotions staff of one. Seymour Stein would take trips over to England and go through the garbage cans and put out the stuff American labels wouldn't release. Then we started getting into the New York scene. I was actually after Patti Smith but we didn't have enough money to get her, but as a result of that I came across many of the CBGBs bands.

"I saw the Ramones with Talking Heads in 1975, and loved them. So I went back and did my little A&R report. Talking Heads seemed a little raw, but I definitely thought I could produce the Ramones. I was more into what they didn't do. Rock was becoming decadent - not in personal morals, the music was decaying. People would listen to long instrumental, pseudo-classical solos. The Ramones came on, and hit you over the head with what rock'n'roll was all about. Other bands had done that, like The Stooges and MC5, but the Ramones had a much more commercial pop aspect. Also, they had that very bizarre New York art viewpoint.

"Richie Gottehrer (who co-founded Sire with Stein in 1966) was my boss, so we kicked it around, debated whether they could actually make a record. Trouble was, the demo that Tommy had done wasn't particularly great and, to make it worse, Marty's demo wasn't so good. Seymour and Richie were interested from the very beginning. What clinched it was Danny's and Linda's involvement. Also, the deal was very, very cheap. I had advance discussions with Tommy, and we gave them enough money to buy a PA, and record the album."

YOU MUST HAVE seen Joey and Dee Dee write songs. Can you describe what it was like?

"I couldn't believe it. Joey would write songs with his one string on the guitar. I thought it was really funny and I tried to convince him to . . . you know, why don't we go get strings? He was like, 'No, it's OK. It works OK.' Joey always tried to keep things light and real, without much depth or . . . Joey's like a pop writer. He would write about what was apparently on the surface of things but looking at them in a way that most people would ignore and think of as superfluous. But once the song was written, it would tell you something about life that you had previously overlooked or ignored. Dee Dee was a lot different from that, a lot darker, always. Joey would write any time, any time of the day, any mood. Dee Dee wouldn't."

(Author's interview with Arturo Vega, 2002)

5

Meet The Ramones

ON FEBRUARY 2, 1976, the Ramones went into Plaza Sound, a radio broadcast studio on the eighth floor of Radio City Music Hall that featured a Wurlitzer pipe organ, the rehearsal room for [famed female dance troupe] The Rockettes, and an authentic art-deco décor straight from a Thirties musical with synchronised water routines. On February 19, they finished. It cost them $6,200 to record the 14 songs that comprised their debut album – or $6,400, depending on which account you believe, the odd $200 hardly making a difference in an era when major albums could cost $500,000. It took two days to lay the basic tracks down (live), and another two for Joey's vocals. The mixing itself lasted 10 hours, enough time to record an alternative mix that sometimes pops up accidentally on CD reissues.

Ramones clocked in at 28 minutes, 53 seconds. Craig Leon and Tommy [Ramone] Erdelyi produced.

"I used to deliver film to Radio City when I was a messenger," Arturo Vega says, "so I knew my way around the secret passageways and stairwells – I liked to walk along the ramp above the stage. I'd slip into the Rockettes' dressing room and steal their costumes, like the gold lamé pants and satin cloaks. It was great. I thought the band would be in there for ages, but after three days they'd finished."

"I can remember going to the studio and [the Ramones] had got there three hours earlier," Seymour Stein recounted on *Lifestyles Of The Ramones*. "I said, 'How's everything going?' and Johnny says to me, 'Things aren't going so great, we only got seven tracks down.' If everyone was like them, record companies would have no worries."

It wasn't that the band was cutting corners, not really: it took so little time because Tommy knew what he wanted. Most of the ideas had been worked out via the original demo: all that remained was to add a few extra sounds to the original blueprint – a genuine chainsaw at the start of 'Chainsaw', 12-string guitars and a glockenspiel to Tommy's teary-eyed love song 'I Wanna Be Your Boyfriend', the pipe organ, supplied by Leon, on a frenetic version of Chris Montez's 'Let's Dance' – and experiment with the stereo sound.

"It's like early Beatles or Cream records, where the guitar is in one channel, bass is in the other, drums in the middle," explains Tommy. (The alternative mix is more conventional.) "But it wasn't like James Joyce modelling *Ulysses* on *The Odyssey*. *Meet The Beatles* was an influence, not a model.

"I had trouble communicating with the engineer," he continues. "They'd never seen anything like us, and didn't have much respect for us, either. I wasn't very pleased with the vibe. Everything was rushed because it was low budget, and I had a bad cold. It was hard for me because I was playing the drums and I couldn't go back and forth to the control room because it took a minute to get there, and we had a limited budget."

In between takes, the band would order up cheeseburgers and French fries from the local luncheonette, or maybe a chicken Parmesan hero. There wasn't a lift in the building, so the band had to carry the Marshall amps up eight flights of stairs.

"The studio was massive, halfway in size between the two at Abbey Road," Leon recalls. "They don't make them that size anymore. Johnny's amp was in the Rockettes room, and we set up a metronome with a flashing light in Tommy's booth in the centre because we couldn't get a click track to go that fast. It was like, 'What's the tempo of this one – 208', as fast as it would go. 'What's the tempo of this – 208.' 'Let's do a ballad – 176!' Tommy wanted the swirling hi-hat sound that went through everything The Beatles recorded."

According to Craig, Hawkwind [a Seventies acid rock band, featuring a pre-Motorhead Lemmy] were a big influence on the Ramones guitar sound – "That relentless drone, like a loud version of the Velvets."

"If you could pin *Ramones* down to two records," he suggests, "it would be [Hawkwind's] 'Silver Machine', and 'A Hard Day's Night' [the Ramones were rumoured to soundcheck with The Beatles' song early on], with a little Phil Spector and Beach Boys and Herman's Hermits thrown in. There was no conscious MC5 or The Stooges, the Ramones sounded close enough to them as it was. Anyway, who would want to reference those records – they're rotten sounding."

"I think Joey wrote like me," recounted Dee Dee in *Poison Heart*. "I don't think he knew anything really about guitar chords, or the verse, chorus and intro. Somehow he just banged out these songs on two strings of a Yamaha acoustic guitar and then Johnny Ramone would struggle his best to interpret it. Johnny would show me the bass parts to my own songs because I had no idea how they went. Tommy Ramone wrote 'I Wanna Be Your Boyfriend' and we could have made a million dollars on it, because the Bay City Rollers wanted to do it. But that's another story."

According to a *Trouser Press* interview in 1982, the band actually rehearsed Buddy Holly's 'I'm Gonna Love You Too', Tommy Roe's 'Sheila' and Roy Orbison's 'Crying' early on – the latter was even considered for inclusion in the live set as a slow song because, "We didn't see how we could play so fast for 35 minutes" (Johnny).

There were no outside players. There wasn't time. Instead, the engineer Rob Freeman and Leon sang backing vocals for 'I Wanna Be Your Boyfriend': "We tried it with Doug [Dee Dee]," laughs Leon, "and he'd get spit all over the microphone, he was so aggressive. After a lot of torture – it was supposed to be sweet – we did it." The band would come in after 7pm, so they'd get the cheaper rate, and work through till five in the morning. "Rehearsal and discussion took quite long, but actual recording was about a week. It didn't feel rushed."

"Craig would bring the tracks back to the office and play them so loud the windows would shake," recalls publicist Janis Schacht. And it wasn't like the band weren't aware of the album's potential.

"We used block chording as a melodic device," Tommy told *Rolling Stone*'s Timothy White in 1979, "and the harmonics resulting from the distortion of the amplifiers created countermelodies. We used the wall of sound as a melodic rather than a riff form: it was like a song within a song – created by a block of chords droning.

"I'll tell you what else was distinctive," he went on, "the hypnotic effect of strict repetition, the effect of lyrics that repeat, and vocals that dart at you, and the percussive effect of driving the music like a sonic machine. It's very sensual. You can put headphones on and just swim with it. It's not background music."

"Wait a minute," White countered. "Johnny told me the first LP sounded so primitive because that was the best you guys could play at the time."

"Yes," Tommy conceded, "but there was *always* intelligence behind it. If every untrained musician doing the best he can decides to make a record, he's not going to get a Ramones LP out of it."

Ramones was released on April 23 to partial critical acclaim but disappointing sales (it reached Number 111 on the US charts). "The first album only sold 7,000 copies," recalls Schacht, "even though I had a two-level horizontal file cabinet: one for the Ramones' press, and one for all the other Sire acts."

A preview party was held at the label's West 74th St building that, *Melody Maker* journalist Chris Charlesworth recalls, didn't last long because "the album was over pretty quickly".

"If it had been Atlantic launching the new Led Zeppelin album," Charlesworth reflects wistfully, "it would've been all up-market with huge speakers and a wide variety of food . . . lobster, heaven knows what. This was fun, but scruffy. We were served this dreadful, sweet red wine, the worst I've ever tasted: bottles of it were pressed on us as we left. Two bottles of it stayed in my kitchen undrunk for months afterwards, real last resort stuff.

"I had yet to be attuned to this cosmic change in styles," the writer explains, "so I thought it was a big joke. No one could believe these 45-second songs. It was so brief. I went to see them a few weeks later at The Bottom Line with Dr. Feelgood and came away thoroughly bemused."

TOMMY TOLD ME that the Ramones actually slowed the songs down on their first album because they feared no one would understand them otherwise.

"It's amazing to think what their songs would've sounded like even faster. Because in 1976 they seemed impossibly fast – like, 'How could anybody play like that?' The thing is if you listen to the songs, they do have verse chorus verse."

Yeah.

"They actually are songs – but, in 1976, songs that were two minutes and 10 seconds long were considered too short. Yet, in 1966, a song that was two minutes and 10 seconds long was considered average. American Top 40 radio, if you went over the three minutes mark, nobody wanted to know you. There's that possibly apocryphal story about Phil Spector putting the wrong timing on 'You've Lost That Loving Feeling' by The Righteous Brothers because it was too long and nobody would play it. It may be a different record or a different song, but the point is the same – what wasn't a song in '76 was all you needed in '66. And when you talked to Joey about the music that meant the most to him, he'd talk about The Kinks and The Beatles and The Ronettes, Phil Spector, Shangri-Las – all from '64, '65, '66. That was everything Joey did, to get everything into two minutes and 10 seconds. Why wouldn't you do it that way?"*

Yeah.

"What do you need 19 minutes to sing about oceans and dragons for? Cut it out

* Fact – not apocrypha. The record's playing time on the original Philles single is listed at 3 minutes 5 seconds. It really is much longer – all of 40 seconds longer. Spector had insisted that timing be put on the label on purpose, fearing that radio programmers wouldn't play a record that was 3.45 long, no matter how good it was.

– it's wholly unnecessary. And, in that sense, he was of exactly a like mind with Johnny."

(Author's interview with David Fricke, *Rolling Stone*, 2002)

MICHAEL HILL WAS another journalist who saw the band at The Bottom Line that May of '76.

"It was as if the whole Class Of '75 was in that room – Debbie Harry and members of Blondie; Tom Verlaine, and perhaps Richard Lloyd [both from Television]; of course Seymour was there, and maybe Andy Warhol," he recalls. "I remember walking in and seeing everyone I idolised semi-solemnly sitting there at those tables. It seemed so incongruous because the Ramones were so loud and assaultive, and so anti-everything a record company would showcase at the Bottom Line. It was a wonderful introduction in a way, because it showed up the whole dichotomy of where the music business and music itself was at, and where the Ramones were at, which was such a different place. When you saw it in its milieu, it all made sense.

"I'd seen Patti Smith very early on, when she had just a trio – that was incredible, but it was also part of a bohemian legacy, the Beat Poets. Television had their roots in rock music and jazz, the Talking Heads too. But seeing the Ramones was a complete shock.

"That first record," Hill adds, "separated the men from the boys. You could really clear a room."

It still can.

Kenneth Tucker was reasonably spot-on when he reviewed the show in *Soho Weekly News*: "The Ramones' bullets of two-minute rock provide just the right sort of ugly jolt the Underground has always wanted to inflict on a mass audience," he wrote, before comparing da bruddas to a "wonderfully perverse junk food – Liquorice Pop Tarts, say", and calling Danny Fields the Gertrude Stein of the New York Underground. Although Tucker accused the Ramones of perpetuating urban sexism through their "moronically elementary lyrics", at least he acknowledged the "knowing parody" of songs like 'Judy Is A Punk' (the term "punk" was clearly charged with more meaning back then). Also, he appreciated their "vulnerable" romantic side, and the music's instant energy rush.

Reactions to the album were likewise varied.

Future Ramones producer Daniel Rey was a 15-year-old living in Red Bank, NJ, into The Stooges and The Dictators: "On Friday we would get together and party and listen to all the records my friend had five-fingered from the record store he worked at," Rey recalls. "One weekend, he came home with the Ramones album, and when we first heard it we couldn't stop laughing – it was so fast, and there were no guitar solos. It sorta sounded like the New York Dolls because it was so heavy. We were staring at the cover: who are these guys? Come the following week, it was all we could listen to. I don't think I've listened to Uriah Heep since."

"Of course it all sounds the same," wrote Dave Marsh in *NY Post*. "It's supposed to."

"My favourite review," laughs Schacht, "was the one from California that described *Ramones* as the sound of 10,000 toilets flushing."

WNEW-FM DJ Vin Scelsa assured his place in both Ramones and punk lore through his initial reaction: "I was one of those old hippie DJs," he told *Lifestyles Of The Ramones*, "pretty staid, pretty conservative, but known for playing the fringe bands. I was hot to hear the Ramones. So I got the record, played 'Blitzkrieg Bop' . . . it immediately segued into the next song . . . into the third song . . . halfway through that, I took the record off and hurled it across the room." Scelsa later recanted his sins.

Seymour Stein loved it, but was less than happy with Dee Dee's use of Nazi imagery and the German references in songs like 'Today Your Love, Tomorrow The World'.

"You can't throw away 20 years of Jewish upbringing in Brooklyn, nor would I want to," he explained. "But I soon got over it."

Tommy, too, was unsure about the effect such taboo subjects would have on the band's career: "I was very disturbed by it," he says, "but I wasn't going to censor Dee Dee's songs. I'm sure it must have hurt us tremendously."

"IT'S VERY SIMPLE to me," explains Arturo Vega. "It's an exploration of the dark side. I believe that true good doesn't exist until you face evil and conquer it, and the best way to conquer evil is to make love to it. And the best way to make love to something is by turning it into art. But, of course, people are so afraid."

I thought it was because Dee Dee liked to watch old war movies.

"You know," says Vega. "Publishers can use swastikas on book covers, but not on records. That's an established rule. The swastika is a symbol, like the eagle. I was wearing fluorescent swastika armbands in 1973. I told Tommy I was going to use a photograph of an eagle and a swastika for the Ramones: he had all sorts of reservations about that."

What did he say?

" 'Oh, I wish you wouldn't.' "

But Joey's Jewish! How can anyone take that stuff seriously, a Jewish boy singing, "I'm a Nazi schatzi/Y'know I fight for the fatherland" [on 'Today Your Love . . .']?

"Exactly."

"Punk was the last great reaction to the Second World War," explains Blondie biographer Victor Bockris. "After the war, you had the Beat generation, the abstract expressionists, Francis Bacon, and those great Fifties artists. Then it was the Sixties, the rock'n'roll generation. I was born in 1952. My generation, the punk rockers, grew up totally affected by the war. All our comic books, our games, our films were about it. The reason the punks wore Nazi uniforms and flirted with fascist iconography was for the same reason the Stones had. It was like, 'Stop fucking telling me about the war.' And having grown up in Germany, Dee Dee had a slightly more European sensibility than any of the other genius New York artists, Patti Smith included. That's why he used those images."

"There were so many offensive things in our songs that people would've been in an uproar about," Johnny remarked deadpan. "If we'd actually been selling records."

OTHER SONGS DIDN'T have such troublesome connotations.

The album's opener – and first single – 'Blitzkrieg Bop' (written by Tommy, with contributions from Dee Dee) was a straightforward glitter stomp, the baying bubblegum teenage lust of the Bay City Rollers' 'Saturday Night' reduced down to a few simple, aggressive words and harmonies. Of course, with a title like that it was never going to receive much radio airplay: unfortunate, as it remains one of the catchiest of all the punk-era songs.

"Dee Dee was a huge Rollers fan," explains Rey. "I know he would have liked them to cover 'Boyfriend' – back then, they were one of his favourite groups. He liked their songs' pop and power, and he also felt a camaraderie. He felt the Ramones were the American urban version of the Rollers."

Tommy's original line of "They're shouting in the back now" on 'Blitzkrieg Bop' got changed to "Shoot 'em in the back now" – a non sequitur, but far meaner. Dee Dee also changed the title from 'Animal Hop' to its more war-like counterpart.

"I wanted a rallying song," Tommy explains. "I was trying to think of a good rally when I remembered The Rolling Stones' version of [Rufus Thomas'] 'Walking The Dog'. Where Mick Jagger sings the line, 'Hi Ho's nipped her toes'. We used to joke about that. Johnny would say, 'He's going, "Hey ho, hey ho, hey ho, hey ho",' and he'd say it real effeminate."

Like *Snow White And The Seven Dwarfs*?

"Something like that," the drummer laughs. "So I went with that. I thought it would be funny."

'Boyfriend' was written in direct response to all the 'I Don't Wanna' songs the Ramones started with – 'I Don't Wanna Go Down To The Basement', 'I Don't Wanna Walk Around With You'. "The only positive song we had was 'Now I Wanna Sniff Some Glue'," Tommy explains. (All three were written by Dee Dee, with an assist from Johnny on 'Basement'.) "We were all very frustrated. We escaped from our anger with humour. Dee Dee would write with an almost Dada sensibility."

"Tommy 'The Pervert' Ramone wrote this one," Dee Dee told *Spin*. "There always seemed to be some 13-year-old girl around, and he'd go, 'Wow, Dee Dee, that girl likes you!' And I would think, 'What the hell is he thinking about?' When you're 22, you don't want to go out with a 13-year-old – you want something in a mini-skirt. The monster girls – they followed us everywhere!"

Then there were all the songs inspired by the Ramones' love for late night TV: 'Havana Affair' (like a Cuban spy film), 'Basement' (directly inspired by Seventies slasher movies) and 'Chain Saw', a straightforward tribute to *The Texas Chainsaw Massacre*, that wickedly rhymes "massacre" with "me". And let's not forget the street-fighting snarl of 'Glue' and 'Loudmouth', either.

The Joey-penned songs were more upbeat: 'Beat On The Brat' was drawn from the singer's experiences growing up in Queens, and the chord change is lifted directly from Sixties pop hits like 'Yummy, Yummy, Yummy'. "I was living in Forest Hills, walking around the neighbourhood," he explained to Donna Gaines, "annoyed by all these rich ladies with their bratty kids."

'Judy Is A Punk' – perhaps the first known use of the word "punk" in a song – was another similarly warped tale of interpersonal relationships, written about two crazed Ramones fans, local juvenile delinquents. With its finger-clicks and knowing repetition, 'Judy' is deconstructionist post-modernism in its purest, most unconscious form. "Second verse, same as the first," the singer yells, in an inspired moment of knowing self-deprecation.*

It was all any of their fans needed to know.

* The line was actually copped from Herman's Hermits 1965 US No.1 'I'm Henry The VIII, I Am'.

ROBERTA BAYLEY'S PHOTOGRAPH of the four members slouched against a brick wall, hands in pockets, Tommy stretching his belly and Joey (as ever) hunched over so the two musicians strangely look almost similar in height, sneakers and leather jackets and straight-leg ripped jeans to the fore, shot in black and white, has long passed into rock iconography. It's almost impossible to judge the expressions of the musicians, hidden behind shades and bowl haircuts: surly, menacing, street-wise tough. It has since picked up any number of awards.

Of course, it wasn't planned.

"People don't like having their photograph taken," Roberta explains. "I think that's why people liked me as a photographer because I work really quickly. For that album cover, we maybe shot two rolls of film. It was only the 28th reel of film through my camera. I'd only been taking pictures for a few weeks."

It was taken just across the road from CBGBs, right off 1st Street. John Holmstrom recalls that first off Roberta tried to shoot them in Arturo's loft and it didn't work too well. So they took them to a playground round the corner. "They did not like having their picture taken," Holmstrom laughs. "They were not cooperative."

Roberta's shoot was never intended to be the cover: they were for Holmstrom's *Punk* magazine. Sire had hired a professional photographer to take the pictures, and he blew their entire budget of $2,000. "You know when you take a picture from below and go up the nostril?" asks Roberta. "That's what these were like: really unattractive, and the band felt so. So they were desperate for pictures. They looked at the ones I'd taken for *Punk*, and offered me $125 for that shot and another for publicity purposes. That was the deal."

Punk magazine is credited with helping ferment and crystallise the nascent NYC punk scene. It was started by cartoonist Holmstrom with money from Ged Dunn Jr, and "resident punk" Legs McNeil in tow, after the trio heard the first Dictators album in the summer of '75. *Punk* began defining the music they liked through use of one simple device – if they liked it, it was "punk".

"The Ramones did *not* call themselves punk rock," Holmstrom told *NY Press* writer George Tabb. "Nobody else in New York City was calling themselves punk. We were total outsiders to the scene, and forced the word on them. A lot of people kind of resented that."

Punk carried interviews with the Ramones, Iggy Pop, Sid Vicious, Blondie – it even put Lou Reed on its first cover. What was coolest about it though were Holmstrom's cartoons – inspired by great US illustrators like *Mad*'s Harvey Kurtzman and *Fantastic Four*'s Jack Kirby – and its great sense of visuals. There was a Patti Smith graffiti contest, where readers were invited to scribble all over a press photograph of her, and send the results in. There was a Top 100 of . . . well, everything . . . later to be copied incessantly. Joey Ramone suggested the magazine should run a "Punk Of The Month".

"Joey loved the magazine," Holmstrom told me. "Even if he hadn't been in it, he would have liked to have written for it. He drew a picture of Danny Fields for us for the Iggy Pop interview – and we credited it to Raven. It must have been an old glam name of his."

A main feature was the photo-led stories that featured local rock stars enacting a story told through cartoon-strip dialogue. The famous Bayley shot of Joey Ramone and Debbie Harry in bed together came from the feature-length *Mutant Monster Beach Party*, also starring David Johansen, John Cale and Andy Warhol. (The strip helped inspire the only Ramones movie, 1979's *Rock'N'Roll High School*.) Another featured legendary rock critic Lester Bangs and Handsome Dick Manitoba.

"Legs wrote *Beach Party* with Joey in mind," says Holmstrom. "We had trouble getting that made because he was sick so often. He'd be in hospital, but whenever he was around he was the most cooperative guy. He took a trip to Coney Island for just one photo."

Despite the popularity of the sleeve (the belt buckle on the back was supplied by Arturo), it was Bayley's final session with the Ramones. More established photographer Moshe Brakha was chosen to shoot the second album cover.

"I saw an article in *Vanity Fair* recently," Bayley comments, "where Beck picked out the *Ramones* sleeve as one of his favourite album sleeves of all time. He said, 'I like the Ramones because their record covers all look alike.' Well, that's because everyone tried to do my photograph again. First, Sire waste their budget on some shots they never used, and then they throw away $3,000 on a terrible follow-up. Isn't the music industry wonderful?"

6

Today, Your Love . . .

WHEN DID YOU first encounter the Ramones?

"When I was sleeping on Brian James' floor in Kilburn, and we were having our first rehearsals. He'd play The Stooges, MC5, New York Dolls and Ramones non-stop – to get the Marc Bolan and Gary Glitter out of my brain, I think. Brian had this vision: he was looking across the Atlantic at what was going on there. We couldn't work out what the Ramones were singing about. We'd play this game, 'What are they singing?' We thought 'Listen To My Heart' was 'next stop – trip to Mars'."

Is it fair to say that the first Ramones album completely changed punk in the UK?

"It kick-started it, yeah – although it depends on what you mean by 'punk', because some people look back to the Chocolate Watch Band and the Electric Prunes, stuff like that. But in London, yes. When they played that gig at Dingwalls with [Ramones label-mates, Sixties-influenced, jangling San Francisco rockers] The Flamin' Groovies, everyone in the audience pretty much went out and formed a band. Their huge wall of noise, it was sensational. Instantly, it changed everything in my mind about what could be done with the band. I remember thinking, 'Oh crikey, must get one of them guitars' . . ."

What, the Mosrite – the old surfing guitar?

"That's right. But I thought it must be some kind of new-fangled blitzkrieg guitar."

Did you get one?

"Yeah, but unfortunately the baggage handlers at Lufthansa smashed the bloody neck off it. I think they had a weakness in that department. I never used one on Damned records because I was the bass player. By the time I graduated to the guitar, I was on Gibsons."

Why do you think the Ramones were such a big influence on punk?

"It was a fresh, wild, powerful sound, and it was easy. You could plonk their record on, grab hold of a bass or a guitar or whatever, and jam along. That's how I used to practise – and Sid Vicious as well. I remember being in [Sue] Catwoman's

flat on Ealing Broadway, and Sid would be sitting in the corner, jamming along to the Ramones' album."

Sid took Dee Dee as his role model, didn't he? Not necessarily the best of examples to follow . . .

"That's the thing. The British may have taken some influence on the musical side, but not the drugs. I couldn't work that out. Mostly, we weren't interested in smack and that. Anyone can write a rock song, but the genius of the Ramones was that they had these brilliant tunes coming out their ear holes. So they can't have been so dumb, can they?"

Not really. They had a massive pop sensibility.

"Totally. I don't know what the British punk scene would've been like if the Ramones hadn't come over in '76. Or whether it would have happened. They pulled it all together. At the time, it was Eddie & The Hot Rods, The Stranglers . . ."

Dr. Feelgood.

"Yeah. The Ramones added biker jackets to the scene as well. Music in the mid-Seventies was dire, all those songs about pixies and castles, appalling. There was Little Jimmy Osmond, David Cassidy, Barry Blue. And then the Ramones came along, and all of a sudden music was fun again.

"I loved the way they mixed the first album, with the guitars right up in your face. The drums are there, driving it along, but they're not overbearing. Nowadays, sound engineers are so proud of their immense drum sound on stage, they make it unbearable. I always suggest to my sound person that if they've never mixed a punk band before, they listen to the Ramones' first album. We took their influence when we recorded Damned Damned Damned *– we deliberately under-produced it to keep it energetic and not over-glossy. I hate to slag off the Pistols again, but theirs was too over-produced."*

(Author's interview with Captain Sensible, The Damned guitarist, 2002)

IT WAS THE industry showcase at The Bottom Line with Dr. Feelgood in May that helped spark everything off: here was another band, playing a much more recognisable hard-edged bluesy rock – but with bags of attitude. And yet Dr. Feelgood had managed to reach Number One on the UK album charts with their *Stupidity* live album – a far cry from America where 'Blitzkrieg Bop' was up against Wings, Paul Simon, Steve Miller and far more heinous musical crimes.

Suddenly, the Ramones were alert to the possibilities abroad.

First, however, they needed to play outside lower Manhattan – an achievement Danny Fields still ranks among his finest – especially as no club in their targeted area of Boston would book them.

"We found a semi-abandoned bar in a downscale Cambridge neighbourhood and charged $2, splitting the admission with the bar owner," Fields wrote in the introduction to the Ramones *Anthology*. "I collected the money at the door. It was also the occasion of our first radio interview, with Oedipus, in a basement at MIT."

"It was on the ocean, a sleazy beer-stinking big ballroom called Frolics," Dee Dee recounted in *Please Kill Me*. "I couldn't cop dope that morning and I was getting sick. It was winter and it was cold, and after the show we went back to some fleabag motel."

Once there, the bassist – starting to go through withdrawal – put a blanket over the sink in his motel room, ran the tap and sat underneath the sink, pretending he was under a waterfall, anything to distract from the pain. The band was there for three days, and each night it got colder.

"We were interviewed the next morning by a kid from *The Harvard Crimson* at the Treadway Motor Lodge," Fields told Michael Hill in 2000. "I said, 'Did you see the show?' and the guy said, 'Yeah,' but they were afraid to come up front because they thought we might vomit on them. They must have read that the Sex Pistols vomit on their fans, or that it was some kind of theatre of confrontation, but it was so not that."

Andy Paley, later to play with the Ramones with his brother in The Paley Brothers on the soundtrack to *Rock'N'Roll High School* also saw the NYC band play that same late February night:

"I went along with Jonathan Richman,"* Paley enthuses. "It was great. Joey and Jonathan had a mutual respect and admiration for bubblegum pop records, and shared a similar sense of humour. There weren't many people like that around back then, so when you met someone as into Tommy James & The Shondells as you were, you spoke to them." Paley and Joey also bonded through a mutual love of Abba and The Beach Boys. "I couldn't stand the endless guitar solos these sensitive, self-indulgent acts would play. The Ramones played short, compact songs that made a point quickly, and they didn't take it too seriously either. They weren't part of any scene, but out on their own."

Someone else who loved the Ramones was LA scenester and DJ, Rodney Bingenheimer – a man who certainly knew his pop music, having grown up

* Incredible, poetic, minimalist Seventies rocker whom Paley was producing at the time – Richman's 'Roadrunner' has been covered by everyone from the Pistols to The Pastels, and his role as narrator in *There's Something About Mary* is a real treasure: he was rumoured to be the first person to dance to the Ramones: certainly, the brevity and directness of his Modern Lovers, which included a pre-Talking Heads Jerry Harrison, and the way they hated hippies – see laconic anthem 'I'm Straight' – were a big influence on the early Ramones.

around Phil Spector's studio. While Rodney was still a kid, he met Mick Jagger and Brian Wilson, acted as gopher to Sonny Bono, and was present for the recording of Ike & Tina Turner's peerless 'River Deep Mountain High'.* In 1976, he launched his *Rodney On The ROQ* New Wave and Sixties show on KROQ-FM. The Ramones were his first guests.

"I knew everyone would be into them," he says. "I got a test pressing of their album from Danny Fields at a Bay City Rollers interview at Century Plaza Hotel, and I told him I'd love to have them on. I liked them because they were fast and punk rock, but not angry punk – more like pop punk. 'Sheena Is A Punk Rocker' could have been 'Help Me Rhonda' [Beach Boys]. Johnny did all the talking, and we got a phone call from The Runaways [Joan Jett's first band, an excellent all-girl hard rock outfit put together by impresario Kim Fowley] who were out on the road, saying 'We love you guys.' "

In San Francisco, future Sire Records General Manager Howie Klein began setting up one of America's first punk rock radio shows, having seen the Ramones in August. "The Ramones were like the Johnny Appleseeds of the whole New Wave movement," he told *Lifestyles Of The Ramones*. "Wherever they'd go, a local New Wave scene would start. They'd come to town, leave, and two weeks later there were 10 bands that had started."

On the whole, though, radio ignored the Ramones and anything connected with "punk", fearing for their livelihoods.

"The Ramones didn't stand a chance," Paley explains. "It wasn't so much their image as their sound – as much as I thought they were fun, the radio people didn't. Radio hasn't been very good in America for a long, long time. Originally, in the Fifties and early Sixties, you'd have great regional DJs in different towns, but it got worse and worse, and then the hippies came along and FM radio took over, and it got turned into a weird corporate thing. Like when you hear Jonathan sing 'I got the AM radio on' [from 'Roadrunner'], AM was so much better than FM. The stations weren't into classic pop – and the Ramones wanted to make fun music, in the tradition of 1910 Fruitgum Company, Every Mother's Son, and the girl groups."

You could argue that the Ramones finally went off the boil when they lost sight of that pop heritage – sometime following the release of 1984's fine *Too Tough To Die*, when someone (Johnny probably) decided that he'd had enough with chasing the hit and experimenting with the sound, and it was time to concentrate on the aggression, and the live shows.

* A song covered and stripped right back to callous-ripping raw guitars by the Ramones' Australian counterparts The Saints in 1977, incidentally.

There was an excellent single in 1985, the anti-Reagan 'Bonzo Goes To Bitburg' – hated by Johnny, a staunch Republican and card-carrying member of the NRA – and it was downhill after that. Still, that's 10 years of unadulterated genius – and even so, every album right up to the Ramones' final shows in 1996 had one or two moments of guaranteed brilliance. But I'm getting way ahead of myself.

"ENGLAND WAS AMAZING," says Tommy. "In New York they hardly knew we existed, and in England we were treated like stars. We sold out Dingwalls and the Roundhouse, it was very exciting – meeting the up-and-coming English punk bands that came to our soundcheck at Dingwalls, members of the Pistols, The Clash, The Damned, Chrissie Hynde of The Pretenders . . . It happened so quickly it was a blur."

"In those days," Fields writes to me, "Europe was famously hipper than America. The English were always trend-crazy and lived in a country compact enough to have a trend sweep the whole culture overnight."

"It was such a low budget," Dee Dee told *Mojo*. "I was like a kid then, and I thought I'd be staying in, like, a Hilton Hotel and not a bed-sit in Shepherd's Bush and getting sandwiches instead of dinner."

"Oh, it was so hot," Linda Stein recalls. "And it was really cool because for some reason all the Warhol crowd was in London that week and everyone came. There was absolutely no air-conditioning any place and there was record-breaking heat. Ice! That was the problem. There was no ice! There were all these warm drinks, nowhere to cool off. That was the cry: 'No ice!' "

The Ramones made their London debut on July 4, the same day as America's bicentenary, on a day of stifling heat. Six weeks before, they'd been playing in front of 50 people at CBGBs. At the Roundhouse, 2,000 excited British fans turned up – spurred on by reports of the Ramones in the press.

"One guy at the Roundhouse kept yelling, 'Don't play music,' " Tommy recalled. "You couldn't tell if he was for us or against us."

"Jeez," *NME*'s Charles Shaar Murray wrote in November '75, "I'd give a week's pay just to see them explode over an unprepared audience at, say, Dingwalls. They're simultaneously so funny, such a cartoon vision of rock'n'roll, and so genuinely tight and powerful that they're bound to enchant anyone who fell in love with rock'n'roll for the right reasons."

Nick Kent, reviewing *Ramones* on import the following May for the same paper, suggested that the Ramones, even more than Kiss, were the real children of The Archies, before adding that, "*Ramones* is an object lesson in how to successfully record hard rock. If you pride yourself on being a sensitive human being," he pointed out, "this record will gag on you like a Gatorade and vermouth fireball.

"The Ramones don't say much," the critic concluded – after a smart nod to both Iggy and Jonathan Richmond [*sic*]. "They're pretty vacant. But they rock out with a vengeance."

Next Big Thing fanzine editor Lindsay Hutton was at the London show, having travelled down from Scotland: "I'd bought the first album when we were down a few weeks earlier at a Kiss concert, because I was obsessed with New York punk rock. As soon as I saw a picture of Joey, I knew that there was no way these guys couldn't be good – the same held true for The Cramps [often overlooked peers of the Ramones, who revelled in a dark, primordial garage sound, with no bass and B-movie imagery]. I had terrible hay fever until I got into the dankness of the Roundhouse – The Flamin' Groovies were great, The Stranglers were lamentable, and the Ramones absolutely blew us away. We met them at the side of the stage: they were thrilled that people from Scotland had come to see them, and gave us wee baseball bats. Dee Dee asked us where they could buy Bay City Rollers records, and we sent them off to [Camden record shop] Rock On in search of glam rock."

The "wee baseball bats" were miniatures of the Louisville Slugger, black, made to help promote the 'Blitzkrieg Bop' single. PR Janis Schacht wanted them to read "Beat On The Brat" but was advised they'd be considered weapons, so Sire settled for "Ramones: A Hit On Sire Records" in America, and "Blitzkrieg Bop" in the UK.

Afterwards, a rumour spread that the Ramones had pissed in the beer they'd given one of their guests, Johnny Rotten. Tommy denies it. "That's not true," he angrily says. "I think they did it once – though certainly not while I was around – and it got transposed onto that occasion. We were happy to see him. They admired us."

The Clash, too, were quick to pay their respects – Johnny remembers various members telling him they were still rehearsing because they weren't confident enough to start performing. "Are you kidding?" he told them. "We can't play. If you wait until you can play, you'll be too old to get up there."

Mickey Leigh remembers it slightly differently. "Tommy was popping Valium and his hands were shaking because he was so fucking nervous," he told *Please Kill Me* about the Ramones' first meeting with Joe Strummer's gang.

There was some animosity, however, as *Melody Maker* journalist, and early punk champion, Carol Clerk recalls: "Glen Matlock threw a glass at the Ramones," she says, "which later led to the Pistols being banned from many London venues, even though it was only plastic." Outside, JJ Burnel of The Stranglers, with various friends, was squaring up to his opposite number in The Clash, Paul Simonon – who had the support of Dee Dee, Phil Lynott [from Thin Lizzy], and Steve and Paul from the Pistols. "Joe Strummer and Hugh Cornwall were just standing there, going, 'Oh look. Here's my bass player fighting your bass player.' "

Gary Valentine claims that Johnny once chased the Sex Pistols manager, the self-serving Malcolm McLaren – who, even to this day, claims punk had more to do with middle-class London fashion houses than working class alienation – out of a Ramones dressing room at LA's Whisky a Go Go with his Mosrite. "McLaren was running around trying to get a record deal for the Pistols, but everyone remembered him from a few years before with the New York Dolls [where he latched onto Richard Hell's ripped T-shirts and claimed them for his own]. He said something to Johnny – and Johnny had a fiery temperament. He could take offence and react in a real expressive way at the drop of a hat. Maybe he just wanted to take the piss. So he showed him his guitar."

SOMEONE ELSE WHO was present in London was Sid Vicious, pre-Sex Pistols.

"Sid idolised Dee Dee," Arturo Vega says. "He started wearing that chain with the padlock because Dee Dee was wearing one in '76 when the Ramones first went there.* Sid was just an imitator. I like to call Joey the king of punk, but Dee Dee is the dark prince."

"Me and Sid used to hang out together, and it was Dee Dee Ramone that set the standard for me, and for Sid as well," Paul Simonon told journalist Scott Rowley about wearing his bass as-low-as-it-can-go. "And we both adopted accordingly. It is hard, but I've got really long arms. Did you not see them dragging along the floor? Maybe there's a half-measure where you can have it at your waist, but I preferred it like that: you had more room to throw it around . . ."

THE *NME* CRITIC was disparaging in his review the following week.

"I reckon [the Ramones] are closer to a comedy routine than a rock group," sneered Max Bell. "[Dee Dee] is possibly the most half-witted

* Dee Dee has claimed that he actually gave Sid that self-same padlock, originally a gift from Connie.

specimen I've ever seen hulk over the golden boards . . . singer Joey flapped around centre in a fair impersonation of Batroc. When he stood sideways, I couldn't see him at all . . . The [Ramones] appeal is purely negative, based in their not being able to play a shit or give a shit. The thinking process involved in evaluating their performance is non-existent. It's first step moronorock strung across a selection of imbecilic adolescent ditties whose sole variation lies in the shuffling of three chords into some semblance of order . . ."

God, there were some dumb journalists around.

Melody Maker's Allan Jones was hardly any kinder: "It has been suggested that the ominous panache of the fiercely retarded music perpetrated by the Ramones, with its moronic emphasis on a violently expressed nihilism, had captured effectively the mood of aggression and terminal discontent some have divined in the behaviour of contemporary adolescents . . . Rock may well be on a disaster course. But they will do nothing to avert disaster. And if we're going to go to the wall, let's at least go with some dignity, not to the strains of 'Judy Is A Punk'."

Maybe the press had simply been caught on the hop. American punk was actually quite dissimilar to its British relation. It was more of an "art" thing. The Sex Pistols actively courted irritation as a tool: the band were happy when shows got cancelled as a result of the latest foul-mouthed burst on TV because they knew it meant more publicity – and sales. 'God Save The Queen' was a sneering blast of disillusionment at the established order. The Clash were politically charged – or at least gave the illusion of it. The Damned were more obviously fun, but soon copped an attitude. Punk rapidly became a working-class phenomenon in the UK: in America, certainly in '76, it was mostly the preserve of a few arty New York types like Television and the Ramones.

Other bands existed in other cities – for example, Cleveland had the pre-Dead Boys and Pere Ubu amalgam, Rocket From The Tombs, and Electric Eels – but away from the media glare. And punk was a media-led movement.

The Ramones had no intention of spitting on anybody.

Punk spread like wildfire through Britain, and soon became synonymous with pop, eventually throwing up a startling array of disparate styles that didn't just derive from hard rock and bubblegum, but reggae (The Slits), funk (The Pop Group), Goth (Siouxsie & The Banshees). What other choice did British youth have? They knew they wouldn't earn more than their parents (a state of mind that didn't occur in America until the Nineties, and grunge, hence the smartly titled Sonic Youth documentary from 1991, *The Year Punk Broke*). It became vital for bands in Britain to be seen as independent – which meant sidestepping then-accepted routes of communication.

Several fanzines sprang up following the Roundhouse show, the most famous of which was *Sniffin' Glue* – its title clearly inspired by the Ramones song – put together on Xeroxed A4 sheets by South London bank clerk Mark Perry.

"I used to read *NME*," the writer explains, " and it carried all these exciting reports about Ramones and the bands coming out of CBGBs. Nick Kent's review of their first album sounded so exciting. So I went up to a West End import shop, and bought it. I couldn't believe how exciting it was, and how different. One time I was in Rock On, trying to find out if there were any magazines I could read about these bands in. There weren't, so the people behind the counter suggested flippantly that I should go and start my own. So I did. I got out the typewriter, did the old cut and paste, with the felt-tip marker. 'Now I Wanna Sniff Some Glue' is my favourite song off that album – and glue is also the most punk drug, the one you'd choose if you had no money, skint. It fitted in so well with what I thought the new music was about."

"Here's a chord," *Strangled* fanzine wrote [a line often wrongly attributed to Perry himself]. "Here's another. And here's another. Now go away and form a band." Mark Perry soon followed their advice, fronting the experimental ATV.

"They weren't noisy rockers like the Heartbreakers," Perry recalls. "They seemed shy. The Ramones were like kids. They had that innocence. It was one of their charms."

"There must have been about 20 fanzines or so," Linda Stein recalls. "Every kid had a fanzine. There had never been fanzines before. I decided to have a fanzine press conference in our apartment in Gloucester Place in London. There were so many people, so cute and proper. It was so great. The fanzines were mimeographed. Some of the editors were actually quite bright and academically astute."

The song didn't inspire only magazines, though. The August 19 edition of the Glasgow *Evening Times* bore the headline "Glue Sniff Death Shocker", above a story relating how James Dempsey, MP for Coatbridge, Lanarkshire was trying to get the first Ramones album banned after a spate of glue-sniffing related deaths – that actually had nothing to do with the music. As Danny Fields pointed out in the *NME*, "Why should the song be banned? War films aren't banned on the grounds that they advocate violence."

"Shit," Dee Dee remarked. "It's a good thing we split from those assholes 200 years ago. I hope they don't really think we sniff glue. I quit when I was eight."

What with the stupid Nazi allegations, the drug headlines, the speed of the songs and the perceived "cartoon" image of the Ramones, it seemed the British press had more than enough controversy to keep them happy.

"What stupid Nazi allegations?" Fields asks, via email. "Coming from the fashion-statement Maoism of that dress store owner and his stooges in the press, no doubt. [A reference to McLaren, one assumes.]

"Yeah," he adds sarcastically, "Seymour and Linda Stein and I would gladly further the careers of Nazis."

"MANY OF OUR lyrics are downright psychotic," explains Tommy. "That, in itself, will be something people find controversial. We weren't looking for controversy like the Sex Pistols. We had interesting songs. Malcolm McLaren was older than us, and a troublemaker. We were mature enough not to cause problems.

"We always felt humour was a vital element of good rock music. It may have been a cartoon in a sense that it was sometimes a caricature, or light-hearted – but if it was, it was a very complex and multi-dimensional one. People are offended by humour when combined with music – they think it trivialises or makes fun of it. But nobody loved rock more than we did."

"The reason we were called cartoon," Joey told me in '89, "was that we had distinct personalities. Most people are afraid to let their personalities be seen because they want to appear serious. They want to be looked up to, but they're not real – they only exist on poster boards. The Beatles had all different identities and personalities. Were they looked upon as a cartoon?"

They had their own cartoon series. The Ramones would've made a great cartoon show.

"In that respect, yes. I can see it. But no, we're not cartoon-ish. We're very authentic and genuine people. Most bands are just cardboard cut-out stand-ups."

(Various interviews with author)

IN AUGUST, THE RAMONES played 13 dates in California. The press was ready for them. "Can you imagine a mother's reaction after noticing a teenager's fascination with this tale of sibling rivalry?" the *LA Times* critic asked about 'Beat On The Brat', comparing the band to the fascistic futuristic gangs that roamed through *A Clockwork Orange*, before admitting that the Ramones were more a joke than a threat. *San Francisco Examiner* compared da bruddas to swine flu, but Art Fein, writing in *LA Free Press* about their Roxy show (once more with The Flamin' Groovies) stated, "I may not have seen the future of rock'n'roll but I have seen the Ramones and that may be even better."

"It was weird going back to America afterwards," says Tommy. "We thought that everything was set up and all we had to do was to make a new record, and release it. We kept doing that, album after album, and it wasn't happening. It was very frustrating. I didn't get it. I still don't."

The Ramones played a total of 73 shows in 1976, just warming up. Back in New York and CBGBs, for the weekend of September 10, Ed Stasium – shortly to produce *Leave Home*, the Ramones' second album – finally caught up with the band.

"It was like standing in the middle of a railway track and having a locomotive come straight at you," he recalls. "The crowd was pogoing, jumping up and down, the stage was only two foot high, it was just packed. If I hadn't been with the band I would never have got in. It was sweaty, stinky rock'n'roll to the max and it was great. I couldn't understand where everybody had come from. It was a whole new world. The entire crowd was dressed in T-shirts and jeans."

Arturo Vega recalls going to CBGBs with Joey Ramone, and playing pinball with him till four or five in the morning. ["Who needs to sleep?" sang wistful English punk poet Patrik Fitzgerald. "I play pinball till three in the night. Ain't got a job. Ain't got a home. But I like my lifestyle."] And when they closed down, the pair would stay there and talk to the bartender Merv. "Joey loved drinking," Vega says. "He would drink a lot in the early days."

David Kessel, later to help Phil Spector record *End Of The Century* with the Ramones, also saw them for the first time that year. He was full of admiration: "It was totally audacious to have that sort of Buddy Holly simplicity to their music at a time when the record companies all wanted to sign the new Carly Simon or John Denver. It was adventurous, humorous and very intelligent, very New York. I've seen a lot of acts in their prime – Cream, Rolling Stones – but the Ramones totally commanded the audience, and were in control of rock'n'roll."

"We invented alternative touring in America," Dee Dee told Michael Hill for *Mojo*. "We were the most stubborn band there was. We would go everywhere in our van [with Monte Melnick as tour manager – he came onboard after the June 20 Ohio show after managing to collect the money for a show that had flopped]. We had the windows of the car broken sometimes by rednecks, even in Connecticut. But we kept touring. We'd drive back and forth, back and forth, across the country with the van, with about 14 people in it. We could always tell when a person was a musician by their pained, hunchback-type walk when they just got out of the van. It's a miracle we didn't get killed in an accident . . . We would drive at ridiculous speeds after the show to get home, we would drive all night, we would drive on LSD, in blizzards, in the snow . . . but we always got an audience."

WERE YOU WITH the Ramones on their first visit to the UK?

"Yeah."

How was that?

"It was great. It was dead in the States, and there was no audience. The people that would come to the first shows at CBGBs, the cool Soho crowd, were thinking, 'Oh, this is the next cool scene. Andy [Warhol]'s going to love these people.' It was more an intellectual or artistic approach than real rock'n'roll fans. New York had the bands and England had the fans – that was the biggest discovery and the biggest pleasure. To realise, 'This is the public the Ramones deserve.'

Do any incidents stand out in your mind?

"The day that all those punk bands came to pay tribute. I didn't know who they were and I kind of thought that they looked cool. Johnny Rotten was trying to get in through a side door. I didn't know who he was until later. I said, 'You want to come in – come in.' It took him . . . I made him repeat the sentence about three or four times because I couldn't understand a fucking word he was saying, but what he was asking me was, 'Will they be mad? If the Ramones see me sneaking into their show, will they beat me up?' That's what they thought the Ramones were like, a tough gang band."

They look like tough guys.

"That's what he said. Will they hit me? The most memorable thing, though, was the audience. They were jumping up and down. That was the biggest revelation."

Did people not dance at CBs before then?

"No, not at all, nothing."

I can't imagine people just standing and watching the Ramones. Was it because they played too fast or . . .?

"It was way too fast for anything. The crowds weren't that young. People saw them as some kind of minimalist artists."

Because Danny Fields was part of the Warhol crowd?

"Yeah, very much."

Maybe it's because New York is so cosmopolitan. It's only in the big cities that you get those art crowds.

"True. Also, the state of the economy in England was in such bad shape. The young people were desperate – they needed something to help them express their

frustration and rebellion. When the Pistols came up with 'No Future' it made total sense to them. That's what I thought was the big difference between the Pistols and the Ramones, because the American kids were still expecting to make more money than their parents. Americans always expect that . . . until very recently . . ."

Until the Nineties, which is when punk happened in America.

"In the beginning, punk in England was a social movement, and here it was entertainment. The kids wanted to have fun. Here, it takes a long time. It's so massive and the business side don't want things to change too rapidly – they have to milk it first before they will allow it to go into the next phase. The Ramones were successful in the UK because the audiences were there."

(Author's interview with Arturo Vega, 2002)

7

D-U-M-B/Everyone's Accusing Me

I WAS SPEAKING TO Andy Shernoff [Dictators, also bassist on Joey Ramone's solo album], and he pointed out that one of the reasons why Ramones didn't get the airplay they might have expected was because the imagery in some of the songs was quite . . .

"Bizarre?"

Yes. When I was in New York last December I bought the video compilation and it was like "oh . . . OK . . ." I was quite surprised.

"That's true . . . the feel to the songs, the lyrics, maybe wouldn't sit well on radio. Also, some of the better songs were the weirdest and the sickest. Joey would write certain songs for airplay – 'Sheena Is A Punk Rocker'. But a song like 'I Wanna Be Sedated', which would have been great on the radio, you couldn't get played because of its theme."

I know. It's sad. When I used to travel around America in the early Nineties, I'd sing that song whenever I got to an airport or something. Strap me down in a wheelchair now. Hurry, hurry, hurry before I go insane. That was how I felt. I can see how the radio stations wouldn't play that. But maybe they would now – maybe it just takes that long. You know, what's interesting is that it's the Golden Jubilee for the Queen in Britain right now and every single magazine, every single newspaper is using punk imagery. It's taken them 25 years to catch on.

"I was there for the Silver Jubilee."

Did the Ramones get caught up in it?

"Not really. It was just on the telly, the newspapers and stuff."

Do you think one of the reasons the Ramones never had a hit was because of the punk tag?

"Well, yeah, we had a lot of problems. A lot of people were afraid we were going to change the music industry and they would lose their jobs – there was a fear of that because we were so revolutionary. Another thing was that virtuosity was irrelevant to what we were doing – so that was a threat too, to musicians. A lot of people just didn't like us. It was like 'this is ugly' or 'this is violent' and then there was the punk imagery. The nature of the publicity the Sex Pistols got tainted the whole scene.

People were wary of us like we were going to throw up problems, which we never did because we were very professional. But people were worried and scared about it."

It's interesting, because The Clash managed to break free of that, didn't they?

"Yeah, well, they very shortly adopted ska and reggae and changed direction. They acquired an image of respectability early on, and that helped them a lot."

Critics could understand The Clash, though, because they weren't doing anything that wasn't . . . if you looked beyond the punk tag, they were The Rolling Stones updated. The music establishment could understand that. The Rolling Stones were revolutionary in their time but they'd become assimilated into the system. It's like if somebody came along . . . well, I was going to say if someone came along like the Ramones now, it wouldn't be a problem, they'd probably sell millions . . . but they already have, haven't they? Bands like Green Day and Rancid and Blink 182 . . .

"Yeah."

(Author's interview with Tommy Ramone, 2002)

BY THE END of 1976, the music industry was starting to catch up with punk – or New Wave, as savvy sorts like Seymour Stein started to call the music influenced by the Ramones and the Sex Pistols. *Billboard* ran a front-page story in November, detailing recent signings like Television and The Dictators (Elektra), Talking Heads (Sire), Blondie (Private Stock). Atlantic released *Live At CBGBs*, but – lacking names like the Ramones and Blondie – it failed to impress, with its second division acts like Lou Reed/Van Morrison-influenced Spanish singer Willie (Mink) DeVille and the lacklustre Tuff Darts.

"The three bands I worked most closely with were Suicide [a blunt, minimalist duo who matched the Velvets' ethos to rudimentary disco], Blondie and the Ramones," says producer Craig Leon. "They all shared a similar ethic: trying to get back to rock's roots with a peculiar New York twist. They'd go for different recording techniques, depending on their record collections – for Suicide it was James Brown, Elvis Presley and early rock'n'roll, Vince Taylor's 'Brand New Cadillac'. Blondie was girl groups, Shangri-Las, Caribbean music. The Ramones was classic British pop moulded with MC5, Stooges and The Velvet Underground. The Ramones sped the Velvets' relentless beat up."

In America, the Ramones released 'Boyfriend' as the follow-up single to 'Blitzkrieg Bop', backed with live versions of 'California Sun' and 'I Don't Wanna Walk Around With You', but there was a problem of how to market such an obvious tearjerker from four tough-looking guys from Queens.

"They chose a picture of us looking dreamy and not so threatening," laughs Tommy. "It didn't matter. I came up with the whole concept of the song on the way to the grocery store. I was trying to write a jangly, Beatles-esque song like 'Eight Days A Week'."

An interview that ran in *Creem*, late '76, gave an insight into the Ramones' living arrangements: "Walking down the street with Joey Ramone is like having a pet giraffe and taking it to Gem Spa with you to buy the latest copy of *Zoo World*," author Pam Brown wrote. She went on to detail how the singer slept in his leather jacket, kept a plastic bug zoo, and had hundreds of LPs lying around an old record player in an attic somewhere.

"He always smiles and never lies," she added, "but makes up great stories about people getting hit by buses, girls turning into vegetables and giant cockroaches breaking through walls . . . A 250-pound cherub named Jenny followed [the Ramones] all over California during their recent tour there. She says they changed her life. She sends one of them a letter every day."

In late October, the Ramones began recording their second album *Leave Home* in Sundragon Studios, a loft on the eighth floor of 21st Street and Fifth Avenue associated with radio jingles. Tommy describes it as "a nice room, cosy like a living room, with a handmade Roger Mayer console".

"It had one creaky elevator, the slowest elevator in the world," recalls producer Ed Stasium. "If you went up in it with the equipment, it would go at half-speed. You'd end up walking up the stairs most of the time." Stasium had been asked in to engineer the album by Tony Bongiovi – a veteran producer from Motown and the Record Plant, where he'd previously employed Tommy.

"I'd never heard Ramones before although I'd heard of them, via Lisa Robinson's *Rock Scene* magazine," Stasium says. "I'd been in the great white north [Canada] for over a year. I would listen to bands like Pink Floyd, Peter Frampton, Fleetwood Mac and The Eagles on Montreal's CHOM radio." Stasium recalls he was late for the sessions because his daughter was born two-and-a-half months early – so Bob Clearmountain recorded three or four tracks with the band on the first day.

"I got in, and I was like, 'What the heck is this?' " he continues. "After an hour, I got it. I thought it was great: it's what every kid wants to do – it wasn't about virtuosity but the feel, and the lyrics were so ridiculous! It gave me that good smack in the face everyone could use every 10 years." He pauses, and veers off at a tangent. "We desperately need one right now. I want to assassinate the person who invented the vocal tuner, and all these punk bands who try to sound like Blink 182 . . ."

"Joey brought Ed in – he had a hit record with 'Midnight Train To Georgia'," says Tommy. "He never heard a group like us. He was a little shocked."

Stasium sang backing vocals on a couple of songs. "The simplicity, the power and the comedy," he says, "that's why I latched onto them – and their personalities. They're very likeable people. The songs have extremely memorable melodies, too."

There were still no guitar solos, either.

Most of the songs were recorded live, in one or two takes – Joey in the booth, laying down the guide vocal with Dee Dee counting him in. "It was straight in, straight out, no messing: Shure FM-57 microphone on the Marshall amp, standard settings, probably a Neumann U-87 microphone a little further away, turn up the amp and . . . boom. It was very professional. No one wanted to waste time, or money. Joey was a workhorse. He knew exactly what he was going to do – his songs were embedded in his mind and soul. When Joey double-tracked his vocals, all the nuances were exactly the same."

There was an appreciable leap in sound quality between *Ramones* and *Leave Home* – much bigger than between the next few records.

"We had a better studio with better engineers," explains Tommy, who co-produced the record with Bongiovi, "and we also had more time."

I don't mean this as an insult, but the first album sounds almost like demos.

"Worse," disagrees Tommy, still the perfectionist, "the demos sounded better. I did the demos."

"That's the difference between making a record for $6,000 and spending a few dollars more," thinks *Rolling Stone* writer David Fricke. "But nobody was going to give the Ramones any money. They were used to that – they weren't exactly getting paid a fortune down at CBGBs. Hilly was not handing out free vouchers for champagne. It was like 'get on, do it, get off', and they treated the record the same way."

"*Leave Home* didn't have many overdubs," says Tommy. "We tried to keep them down until *Road To Ruin* where Ed Stasium and I played a lot of the guitar. The Ramones didn't like being in the studio: we wanted to get straight back on the road again. Johnny played acoustic on some of the songs. I tried to keep the drumming straightforward, simple and driving – like Stax Records, and Charlie Watts [Rolling Stones]."

LEAVE HOME WAS released on January 10, 1977.

The 14 songs clocked in at just under 31 minutes – at two minutes 12 seconds per song, that's just two seconds above the prescribed peak for Sixties pop perfection. More songs about retards, 'Nam casualties, glue and girls; it continued where the *Ramones* left off – literally. The first 30 or so Ramones songs were written before the band signed to Sire, and recorded in near chronological order.

"Danny invited us to listen to *Leave Home*," recalls cartoonist John Holmstrom. "He brought us a couple of beers. We sat down and it was kind of wild because, in his apartment, for the first time I saw the naked picture of Iggy. We didn't like to listen to music in that room. So he plays us the record. I think they were worried that it was too slick and far off from the Ramones sound – like you pointed out earlier about the difference between their studio and live sound on *It's Alive*. So we listen to the whole thing and we're going nuts, we love it. Danny says afterwards, 'What song do you think is the hit?' With him, that was always the big question – 'What's the hit?' So we tell him that 'Carbona Not Glue' is easily the best song and he says, 'I was afraid you'd say that. That's the song we can't release as a single.' That summed up the Ramones' double-edged sword for me. They couldn't be successful because they were the Ramones. They were always at their best when they were doing songs about sniffing glue and other stuff."

That song actually got left off the album in Britain.

"Do you know why?"

It was a brand name of a cleaning fluid.

"Yes. Carbona threatened to sue. It's weird because they actually did Carbona. Joey told me that they experimented with Carbona, and they sniffed glue. I always thought it was a joke before he said that."

And it's better than glue?

"Yeah, apparently Carbona is better than glue. The brain damage to the scene, though, is probably through glue-sniffing because that is deadly stuff."

Soon after *Leave Home* was released, Sire removed the song to avoid potential lawsuits – replacing it with 'Sheena Is A Punk Rocker' (US) and 'Babysitter' (UK). Five thousand copies of the album were pressed up in Britain, creating instant collector's items.

"I'm sorry," wrote Tony Morris, MD of Phonogram UK, in a personal letter to Seymour Stein, "but I have to say we cannot promote product which extols the virtue of 'dope'. Carbona is apparently available, and more dangerous than glue."

Stein responded by stating he felt censorship was a far greater evil than either Carbona or glue – "and something that in good conscience I cannot be party to."

"Something like 'Carbona Not Glue' has to be tongue-in-cheek," Tommy declares. "It's absurd, like saying you should try something *more* poisonous. But 'Sniff Some Glue' – I have a feeling Dee Dee was talking about his childhood, how he thought it was a release when he was a kid. I thought of it as parody. Maybe it wasn't."

"There weren't too many parents wanting their kids listening to 'Beat On The Brat' and 'Carbona Not Glue'," agrees Sire PR, Janis Schacht. "(The) Ramones lyrics were funny, though. Joey would be hysterical with laughter whenever he came up with a new lyric, like 'We're A Happy Family'. It would just tickle him. 'Sitting here in Queens/Eating refried beans.' How could they come up with something that silly? They would laugh and laugh. That sense of humour keeps the music alive today. Joey wrote a lot of the love songs as well, he had a good heart. Dee Dee wrote the more tormented numbers like 'Don't Come Close' – when you'd speak to him in the early days, he sounded like he was existing on one tiny corpuscle of blood. He never knew where he was or where he was supposed to be. There was an intelligent brain in there. He just wouldn't use it."

Other songs were equally as demented. 'Gimme Gimme Shock Treatment' was a group composition, written in Arturo's loft with all the fruit flies, that continued the Ramones' obsession with psychotherapy; 'You Should Never Have Opened That Door' was another late night horror movie re-enacted over three chords; 'Commando' with its riot of rules and instructions to Vietnam vets to "eat kosher salami", rapidly became a massive live favourite.

'Suzy Is A Headbanger' added to the lineage of weird characters that began with 'Judy Is A Punk' and continued with 'Sheena Is A Punk Rocker': simple, mindless, headbanging glory that'd do even the Ramones' metal peers Motorhead proud.

Damn. There's so much great stuff on *Leave Home* – Dee Dee's ode to Connie, 'Glad To See You Go' with its Eddie Cochran-style riff; the affectionate nod to Freddy Cannon and 'Palisades Park' on 'Oh Oh I Love Her So' with its opening couplet: "I met her at the Burger King/We fell in love by the soda machine"; the paean to departed youth, 'Babysitter'; the full-on romp through The Riviera's surf classic 'California Sun' . . .

Every one is a classic.

"We were already doing 'California Sun' in our set," Johnny told Fricke for the *Anthology* notes. "We were probably aware that The Dictators had it on their album [*Go Girl Crazy*], but we didn't care. We were also doing 'I Fought The Law' by Bobby Fuller but we had trouble with the stop [in the last verse], so we dropped it right away."

The first single from the album, 'Swallow My Pride', was written by Joey in direct response to the reaction the band got after returning home from the UK in '76: when the president of Sire's distributors ABC came down to see the band at CBGBs, he was reportedly wearing a powder-blue leisure suit. "That was about signing with Sire," Joey told Legs McNeil and John Holmstrom for *Rolling Stone* in 1986. "It was about how the first album didn't skyrocket. There were a lot of things that were fucked up in those days. Sire was then distributed by ABC. They really sucked. We'd fly to some city where we were going to play and there'd be no one there to meet us at the airport. So you swallow your pride."

Money was a problem, too: the little the Ramones made was being ploughed straight back into the band. "I was only making $125 a week," Dee Dee complained later, "and I had a $100-a-day dope habit."

'Sheena Is A Punk Rocker' came out as a single before 'Swallow My Pride' in the UK – as the follow-up to 'I Remember You', another ballad that failed to hit. Perhaps the reversal of order happened because the British label thought the juxtaposition of the word "punk" in the title would have the exact opposite effect on radio programmers than in the US – they'd embrace it. The policy worked: 'Sheena' became the band's first genuine UK Top 40 hit in the summer of 1977 – hitting Number 22 on the back of an intensive publicity campaign that included free posters given away with the first 10,000 12-inch singles sold, and a free T-shirt offer.

'Sheena' is quintessential Ramones: like its follow-up single, the matchless 'Rockaway Beach', you can virtually taste the hot asphalt and splattering fire hydrants of NYC's over-heated summer sidewalks, ice creams on the Bowery outside CBGBs, within its bubblegum grooves and Beach Boys-style harmonies.* It foams over with an infectious, starry-eyed enthusiasm impossible to resist. The music has as much to do with the sneering, angry, safety-pinned side of punk as *South Pacific.* Unfortunate then, that it was released in America at the time the media was working itself into a froth of indignation over the Sex Pistols' (supposed) vomit-splattered exploits.

Of course it flopped in that most conservative of Western countries.

* This more punchy single mix differed to the album version eventually released on the Ramones' third album *Rocket To Russia.*

"The tragedy of the Ramones is if they'd just had one hit early on," thinks Roberta Bayley, "then it would have pulled the whole thing up. It was the same with Blondie – they had all those Top 10 hits in England at a time when no one would touch them in America. They didn't know 'Heart Of Glass' would be a hit. It was a fluke. No one had a clue. I'm sure they thought doing a disco remix was a terrible idea. Debbie was signing a lease on a $600 a month apartment. Not to denigrate Blondie's talent, but it was Debbie's beauty that caused the businessmen to stick with them. The Ramones were never going to inspire that loyalty in anyone – that bunch of reprobates, that bunch of freaks!? Who's going to back that? But think about it: why were the Bay City Rollers huge and not the Ramones? It makes no sense."

"I played 'Sheena' for Seymour Stein," recalls Joey in the booklet to *Hey Ho Let's Go!* "He flipped out and said, 'We gotta record that song now.' It was like back in the Fifties; you'd rush into the studio because you thought you had a hit, then put it right out. To me, 'Sheena' was the first surf/punk rock/teenage rebellion song. I combined Sheena, the Queen of the Jungle, with the primalness of punk rock. Then Sheena is brought into the modern day: 'But she just couldn't stay/She had to break away/Well, New York City really has it all.' It was funny because all the girls in New York seemed to change their name to Sheena after that. Everybody was a Sheena."

'I Remember You' is a haunting, hurting torch song, among the sweetest ever written. With just a couple of lines – "I remember lying awake at night/And thinking just of you/But things don't last forever/And somehow baby/They never really do" – the Ramones capture more emotion than a thousand flowery poets and chest-beating stadium rockers like U2 will manage in a thousand lifetimes. 'What's Your Game' sees Joey's voice going into Ronnie Spector trembling overload for almost the first time: sweet backing "oohs" and an acoustic guitar help tell the story of one more outsider, one more girl shunned by the pack.

'You're Gonna Kill That Girl' is just as memorable: a three-minute vignette of violence and betrayal that could've been taken straight from The Shangri-Las and *West Side Story*'s *oeuvre* of doomed teen love – and proved that the Ramones had ample grasp of dynamics. Sections of the press took offence at this one too: mistaking the song's dark humour for misogyny – good job that Dee Dee never completed the infamous 'Cripple' . . .

Then there was 'Pinhead' . . .

One day in 1976, after an outdoor show had been rained off in Ohio, the band went to an art-house cinema to see the movie *Freaks*, Todd Browning's 1932 Gothic horror masterpiece. At the film's peak, there's a famous scene where the troupe of sideshow performers that have been scorned, swindled and shut out by the outside world finally take their vengeance, and start razzing the villain, chanting "Gooble gabba, gooble gabba – we accept you, one of us." Dee Dee streamlined the chant, and came up with the magnificent "D-U-M-B/Everyone's accusing me" slogan that climaxed every Ramones live show till the band's demise in 1996 – replete with roadie in pinhead mask waving a giant "Gabba Gabba Hey" sign aloft.

"We simplified 'Gooble gabba' to 'Gabba gabba'," explains Tommy, "and 'We accept you, one of us' – meaning that all the freaks were welcome to join the Ramones. It was our way of goofing on the media, for saying we were not too bright."

"We had fun with 'Pinhead'," Stasium told David Fricke. "They had this 'Gabba gabba hey!' chant, and I started messing with the vari-speed control on the tape machine, just as a joke. I'd speed it up and slow it down, and Dee Dee's going, 'This is cool!' It ended up being on the record. You can hear a little chipmunk voice going 'Gabba gabba'."

The song is essence of Ramones.

"*LEAVE HOME* IS pure rock'n'roll," wrote *NY Post*'s Dave Marsh, showing a fine understanding of basics. "This is a genuine item."

Charles Shaar Murray agreed in the *NME*, despite taking The Archies/ Saturday morning cartoon analogy a fraction too far: "It's magnificent and you should buy it right now," he wrote. "I mean *right now*, yout'. You ain't getting any younger and this album's getting older all the time."

"The Ramones are one of the most perfect groups ever conceived," wrote the *Sounds* journalist. "Thick? Never."

To help promote the album, Sire gave away a Ramones *Leave Home* silver letter opener, designed to look like a switchblade. "Joey didn't throw many of those from the stage," Schacht laughs. "Beyond the baseball bat and letter opener [and full-size cardboard cut-outs], we didn't do much physical promotion. I tried to get Joey to do a radio ad for *Leave Home*. We spent an entire afternoon with a little tape recorder in his house. It was hilarious. I wanted him to do it the way he spoke, so it had 40 y'know's in it. They hired a professional to do it in the end."

A proposed double headlining tour of the UK with the Sex Pistols fell through due to lack of time; and Joey also missed *Leave Home*'s listening party after being hospitalised for an ankle operation. The incident also caused a couple of seasonal dates – at CBGBs, and in LA – to be cancelled.

"I spent a lot of time in the hospital with Joey," recalls Schacht, "two

New Year's Eves in a row. He had a bone infection in his foot that kept recurring. They would have to scrape the bone and it would keep him in there. So we took out the Spector Colour sign in Times Square, and posted a message saying 'Get well, Joey Ramone'. Then that kettle exploded in his face the following November [about which, more later]. Somebody brought him a stuffed parrot, and it just sat there on a perch, perfect for him. I gave him an (artist-illustrator) Edward Gorey book to try and expand his horizons."

On January 28-30 in Boston, the Ramones returned to what they did best – playing live. These were followed by a handful of dates at CBGBs at the start of February with Suicide in support, including one night when they rushed back to the Bowery to play three sets after supporting Blue Oyster Cult at Nassau Coliseum in Long Island in front of a partisan crowd of 20,000 metal fans.

"I remember that Blue Oyster Cult gig," says Tommy, "but I didn't realise we raced back – but if we did, we did. That would have been no big deal to us. Our sets were short, and we were young and full of energy. I have no idea what the audience response was – whether they hated us, were mystified by us, liked us or ignored us, they were so far away. We didn't get booed off the stage anyway."

"That show was nothing next to the Black Sabbath ones in December '78," Arturo suggests. "Those were really bad. Yeah, they booed, and yeah in Long Island, they hated the band, but it was no big deal. The shows with Black Sabbath were more serious because they were billed as a battle of punk against heavy metal. The metal fans were by far the majority of the crowd, so they came ready to kill – and they tried, aiming at the band with cans full of beer. After six songs, the amps and stage were all covered with garbage. That was scary, but it got worse."

"It was when we started playing 'Surfin' Bird'," Joey recalled, "and everything in the world came on. It started raining carburettors and whisky bottles. The stage manager was about 65 and he told us he hadn't seen anything like it since the Stones first played America."

"Someone threw an ice pick and it landed right next to John's foot," the lighting man continues. "That was in San Bernardino, CA – next, we did Long Beach where Johnny was hit by a can of beer, and the band walked off stage. They came back, but you know . . ."

"I went to at least 50 Ramones shows," says John Holmstrom. "Besides seeing them at CBGBs, I would travel with them. I went to the University of Connecticut to see them once. I went to New Jersey. I saw them opening for Blue Oyster Cult, a very traumatic experience for them – the stage on its own was bigger than CBGBs. Joey was in the middle, with Dee Dee and Johnny about half a mile away from him. They tried to compensate for it by jumping higher and spinning around faster. They were booed mercilessly."

Other established acts supported in 1977 included The Kinks, Peter Frampton and Toto. ("The Kinks had us so crowded down stage," Joey recalled, "that I couldn't even stand up straight. They told us that they were fucked over in the past and so now they're gonna fuck everybody else over.") It wasn't until they started headlining that the Ramones were able to play on suitable bills – for example, the shows in LA at the Whiskey in February with Blondie, where Phil Spector came down to see the band for the first time. [About which, more later.]

One of the kids who saw them that year was music critic David Fricke: "I'm originally from Philadelphia, so the first time I saw the Ramones was at the University of Pennsylvania, April '77. It was in a tiny, seated venue with rows of school desks and wood chairs – like going to an eighteenth-century schoolhouse. My friend and I sat in the front row, right in front of Johnny's amp. It was so fucking loud. It was deafening. And you'd look over, and there was Joey towering over you. It looked like he went on forever into the sky. The spread-legged stance, Dee Dee yelling 'one-two-three-four' . . . it was so intense. It had to have come from New York – it was very much a gang thing, but a New York gang like *West Side Story*. They clearly weren't from LA.

"It was obvious they weren't from Manhattan either," Fricke clarifies, "but Queens – their compatriots at CBs, like Television and Patti Smith, Blondie had more of an art vision. All those bands had grounding in poetry, in pop culture, in modern art. The Ramones had that through Joey's mother – but Dee Dee was from Germany, an army brat. He'd gone through drug situations. And Johnny was very conservative, very much a tough guy. So it was Queens, not Manhattan."

The Ramones played almost 150 shows in 1977: famous rock stars would stop by CBGBs to see what the fuss was about.

"I remember Lou Reed told Johnny he didn't play the right sort of guitar," Joey laughed. "I don't think that went over too well with John. He'd bought the Mosrite because it was all he could afford, and because it was unique, a trademark. So John thought Lou Reed was a bit of a jerk."

Iggy Pop was also aware of da bruddas' reputation. At Fields' behest, he visited the Ramones in their loft. "They were good guys. They told me they liked my stuff, and I felt good about that. Their first album was a terrific record, but I looked at the way every guy was named Ramone and it reminded me that's what Danny Fields tried to do with us. Danny made me 'Iggy Stooge' on the first album without asking. They called it product identification. Yeah, like America's gonna run out and say, 'Oh, that's Iggy Stooge, yeah, we'll buy him right away.' I was somewhere between furious and suicidal over that. So when I saw *Ramones*, I thought Danny had finally got his Muppet band."

"I first saw the Ramones on March 15, 1977, in Denver," recalls NYC producer Don Fleming [Alice Cooper, Teenage Fanclub]. The Ramones were opening that night for Nite City, a (by all accounts) awful band led by [ex-Doors] Ray Manzarek that included a pre-Blondie Nigel Harrison on bass and a Desmond Childs wannabe named Noah James. The country rock audience wore flowers in their Joni Mitchell-style curly hair, nice sweaters and corduroy jackets. "Al Jourgenson [singer with punk electro outfit Ministry] and Jello Biafra [outspoken front-man for highly politicised Eighties CA punk band, Dead Kennedys] were at the same show. It was fucking amazing – the raw energy, the no-bullshit speed. I went backstage and Joey was complaining the only song he'd heard the entire tour was (Al Stewart's) 'Year Of The Cat'. He told me about this Australian band he said sounded like them, The Saints – so I picked up their first album and it was great."

"When Johnny hit the first chord, the 10 of us in the front row who knew who the Ramones were knew this was going to be much more extreme than the record gave us any right to expect," reminisces Biafra. "For the next 20-40 minutes, the Ramones mowed down everybody in the room. It totally blew me away, in part because I kept turning around and seeing the looks of shock and horror on people's faces, them going, 'No, no! Make them stop!' and I'm going, 'Yes, yes! More, more!' "

"Johnny lost a couple of picks during the show," Fleming remembers, "and I grabbed one of them. A couple of weeks later, The Runaways came through town and I ended up giving the pick to Joan [Jett]. Then the next time there was a show in Atlanta – February 25, 1978 – with the two bands on the same bill, I snuck in with Tom Smith and we hid in the rafters to watch the soundcheck. The band came off stage at the same time as we ventured out to buy some popcorn, and we said, 'Great soundcheck. Do you want some popcorn?' Joey went, 'That's my favourite food,' grabbed the whole bag and started chowing down on it.' He was real nice."

BETWEEN APRIL 23 AND June 6, the Ramones embarked upon an extensive tour of Europe, with labelmates Talking Heads – right at the height of punk in the UK.

"(The) Ramones had this whole vibe of leather, loudness, and *extreme* girls, in high heels and usually some kind of bondage dress, with bleached blonde hair done up really big," Heads drummer Chris Frantz told Jim Bessman for *Ramones: An American Band*. "Johnny's girlfriend wore a black rubber dress with armpit hair sewn into it."

April 26 saw the band travel for 18 hours to Marseilles for a concert, only for it to be cancelled when it was realised there wasn't enough power for the amps: in Paris – where Frantz joined Dee Dee in searching for pot – the Ramones found temporary nirvana: there was a McDonald's restaurant, a rarity back then. Shows in Holland, Sweden and Finland followed.

"We never ran into trouble while we were touring," states Arturo, "just a couple of [speeding] tickets. The first time we went over to Finland, it was Cold War territory – the Russians were all over the place. They brought dogs to the show, looking for drugs or weapons or I don't know what. The authorities followed the band everywhere. But nothing happened."

The first UK date took place in Liverpool, May 19. "We had millions of fans and people following the band," exclaims Linda Stein who has described the 1977 European tour as being like *This Is . . . Spinal Tap*, with arguments over who would sit where in the van. "We had a mini-mania. You could spot our audience from the street. They didn't have safety pins in their ears, they didn't have spiked hair, they didn't have the military look – they looked like kids in their denim and long hair, and maybe a motorcycle jacket if they could afford one. It was certainly not the heavy metal glam rock look. In England, it was crazy because of the Sex Pistols. Your tabloids looked down upon us. If Carnaby Street was in New York it never would have happened. We never had anybody in costume on Kings Road the way you did.

"And the audiences as you went north," she continues. "Oh my God! We played Leeds; we were all freaking out that night. We played Slough College, and we gave that pyjama band, The Boomtown Rats,* a big start that night."

"I love this," starts Arturo. "Uh, The Boomtown Rats were opening for us, I think in Manchester, in some school, and Dee Dee must have been doing drugs that day – or maybe he did them right before they went on stage. So Dee Dee's playing and he's getting sick. So he goes to the side

* Seventies pop band fronted by Bob Geldof: known for exploiting American school shootings for Number One hits, and for keyboard-player Johnny Fingers' fondness for wearing pyjama shirts on stage.

of the stage and vomits. And he never stops playing . . .!

"Oh, I thought that was great," Vega laughs.

In Friars, Aylesbury – where the band encored with at least nine songs – Johnny got a large globule of phlegm spat at him, as gobbing was the brief (media-fed) craze.

"I want that person thrown out," he snapped to a roadie.

"Nasty habit," he told *Zigzag* afterwards. "I don't know who started that, but you play better if they don't do it." The writer, Kris Needs, went on to detail how the previous time he saw the Ramones – at the Roundhouse – Johnny had blood pouring from his fingers, he'd been playing so hard.

"My fingers are so hardened so much now that I can't even cut them," the guitarist admitted. "That night there was blood all over my T-shirt, people thought I had blood capsules in my fingers."

The tour was a chance to renew old acquaintances. On a rare day off, the Ramones went down to Brighton on the South Coast to see The Clash play: "That was a great show," Dee Dee told fanzine writer Mark Bannister. "The Buzzcocks [classic Manchester punk-pop group known for their bittersweet, abrasive singles] were on that show. I was begging Seymour Stein to sign them up."

Mark asked Dee Dee whether The Jam also played.

"NO!" the bassist replied vehemently. "Someone else was on . . . The Slits. I don't know but . . . she was there! On the balcony and yelling in my ears [Dee Dee impersonates Nancy Spungen, Sid Vicious' legendary, doomed girlfriend] 'Oh Sid, Sid!' and I couldn't believe she had a British accent. [Dee Dee knew Nancy from way back, when she was a New York Dolls groupie.] I wanted to throw her off the balcony. But he needed her, I guess . . ."

The Ramones didn't enjoy the cuisine in Britain: "They hated the fucking Indian food," Stein sighs. "People don't understand. Italian food was exotic for these boys. We didn't have McDonald's on every corner from Hamburg to Glasgow, there were no hamburgers in England, and fish and chips did not fly – 'I just want a fucking hamburger'. England was the whole world to the Ramones."

The manager was impressed by Johnny's professionalism. "Anybody five minutes late would be fined $25 by John," Linda explained – a rule that (mostly) kept Dee Dee's drug-taking in check, certainly when it came to getting on stage.

"Johnny was businesslike," explains Janis Schacht, "very serious. He was always the same whenever I was around: 'How much money are we going to make? How far do we have to travel? What are we selling? What do we have to do to make things sell?' He was like that from the start. I never looked at him as a creative force, but he was the one who policed them as far as the drinking on the road goes, he ran it like a little army. They got fined for everything – turning up late, drinking, irresponsibility of any kind. John really saw it as a business. I don't know where the fines would go. But it would come out of their salaries."

The Ramones may have argued over the years, but they never let it get in the way of their main job – putting on a great live show. Biographer Victor Bockris thinks their turbulent relationships probably contributed to the consistency of their live performances.

"(The) Ramones just enjoyed playing," he states. "When you travel with people and start hating them [as would happen to 'da bruddas' within a couple of years], it's difficult to deal with, but the exhilaration of the music overrode that. They had that wonderful sense of being on a mission that also gave their music a quasi-military quality and vital group mentality. Rock'n'roll bonds people together like sex: lovers can hate each other but still have great sex.

"I missed the ferocious argument period in '74," he continues, "that faded out by the time they started recording. But they definitely believed they played better if they went on stage pissed off – so they tried to make themselves pissed off before they went on."

Victor pauses, and continues with a story to illustrate his point.

"I remember one time when they were all travelling to a show in their van having a very nice, almost intellectual, conversation. We left them alone together in the dressing room for a few minutes, and the next time I saw Joey he was going 'Fucking YEAH man, fucking YEAH man' to himself – obviously pissed off. They stormed on stage, and gave a great show. Keith Richards said the same thing in 1979 – that as much as the Stones played their instruments, they played each other, and to get turned on in the studio or on stage, they had to get pissed off. It's a part of rock'n'roll. It's a part of everything – the legal profession, the army – people use antagonism to make things happen."

ON THEIR RETURN to the States the Ramones played in Madison, Wisconsin – and were promptly fined. They were supposed to receive $450, but their 30-minute set wasn't perceived as being long enough. It was around this time the quintessential Ramones on-the-road story took place. The band was in Texas, when they stopped to pick up some candy and supplies.

"When you're about 15, 16, that's when you start to learn how to live and stay alive," said Joey. "You learn the ways of the street or else you get fucked. What they teach you in school doesn't prepare you for life. Textbooks don't compare to living in the real world. Rock'n'roll teaches you how to live." Dee Dee, Tommy, Johnny and Joey. (*Bob Gruen/Star File*)

The Tangerine Puppets, circa 1966, with Tommy Erdelyi (far left) on guitar and John Cummings (in shades) on bass. (*Bob Rowland/Richard Adler/Jari-Pekka Laitio*)

The original Ramones on stage at CBGBs, 1976. "There were maybe 20 people in the audience," said Andy Shernoff. "The Ramones did 15 songs in 15 minutes, and it was great. They cut all the fat out. It was surf music, it was pop, it was hard rock – with a big beat." (*Ebet Roberts/Redferns*)

“Did the Ramones piss in other people’s drinks?” asks Gary Valentine. “It was impossible to tell at CBGBs. All the beer there tasted like piss.” Outside on the Bowery, Arturo Vega and friend (top right), Dee Dee and Joey (bottom right), and Ramones manager Danny Fields (bottom left). *(Godlis)*

On the subway: "Man, they were so New York… there was also something irreducibly American about them. They could have not existed in any other country, or in any other city, or been born in any other borough than Queens." – David Fricke. (*Bob Gruen/Star File*)

"Four brothers – I believed at first they were brothers. They all had leather jackets, they all looked the same and they sang songs like 'We're A Happy Family'... I liked the whole ripped jeans thing and sneakers... They were like the New York Beatles." – George Tabb. (*Michael Ochs Archives/Redferns*)

"One, chew, free, faw…" Joey (top left), Johnny (top right), Dee Dee (bottom right) and Tommy (bottom left). *(LFI/Bob Gruen/Star File/LFI/Godlis)*

New York, September 1976. "When we played live, we just played the (songs) faster because we felt them faster. We had to consciously slow them down in the studio. We were hoping for radio airplay." – Tommy Ramone. (*Bob Gruen/Star File*)

R-A-M-O-N-E-S - da bruddahs to da letter. (*Michael Ochs Archives/Redferns*)

May, 1977 – The Ramones pose on the site of the original Cavern Club in Mathew Street, Liverpool. "Without The Beatles there could never have been a Ramones, but as far as I'm concerned the Ramones are far, far superior to The Beatles." – Fanzine editor Lindsay Hutton. (*Ian Dickson/Redferns*)

"We all piled out," Monte relates with a grin, "and the look on the locals' faces told me they had no idea what was coming. So this person pulls me aside and asks me if I was the driver for these people from the Institution. I wanted to humour him, so I said, 'Yes, but don't worry, they're just out for the day.'

"Then there was the time in Bremerton, Washington, we played a half-hour set in a lumberjack bar," the tour manager adds. "They got a little testy because they were used to bar bands playing for an hour-and-a-half, so the Ramones played the entire set again. They *really* didn't know any other songs. The lumberjacks didn't care as long as we kept playing."

On August 6, one of the infamous Tony Parsons *NME* interviews appeared – the articles that helped reinforce both the British music press' (mostly unjustified, because the critics ain't got the guts) "We build 'em up to knock 'em down" reputation, and the Ramones stereotype as D-U-M-B.

Ironically, the band member that Parsons had on the end of the line that day in Queens was Tommy Erdelyi – the most articulate and musical Ramone. Parsons, a stooge in the McLaren/Bernie Rhodes Sex Pistols/ Clash camp, obviously had a Bad Interview Day and contented himself with making fun of Tommy's accent and tongue-in-cheek replies.

The uniform of leather jacket, T-shirt, cheesy sneakers and ancient Levis with knee ventilation, the journalist sneered. Are they the only clothes the brothers have got?

"Yeah, dat's all the clothes we've had for tree years now," Tommy replied [his speech is as the *NME* printed it].

"How long?" Parsons asked pedantically, unable to understand how other races could have different accents to his own.

"TREE YEARS!" Tommy repeated impatiently.

"Ain't it getting a little samey?" the critic jeered.

Tommy was having none of his sarcasm: "Well, it kinda smells, especially in the hot weather," he laughed, making fun of the D-U-M-B question. "But we jest hang it out the window fer a while an' den it ain't so bad."

Fair's fair. The feature was a genuine laugh riot. The trouble was, it was laughing *at* them, not *with* them.

The Ramones didn't forgive the British music press for a long time after that.

A week later, on August 16, managers Fields and Stein held a meeting with Premier Talent – the booking agency behind The Who and Led Zeppelin – frustrated at the way the Ramones still couldn't get on decent bills. Knowing that punk's reputation may have put the agency off, Fields took the precaution of videoing a show at Chicago's Uptown Theater – and bringing along his own TV and tape deck to Premier's office. (Entertainment companies generally didn't have video equipment in those days.) Tim McGrath – who was to become the Ramones' agent for the next 14 years – was initially suspicious of the band's "anti-establishment stance" and Joey's unique look. McGrath far preferred such (frankly crap) groups as The Doobie Brothers, Journey, and Supertramp.

It was McGrath who was responsible for matching the Ramones to The Kinks, the infamous Black Sabbath shows, and Eddie Money. You'd have thought someone would've said something.

AUGUST 16, 1977 was also the day that Elvis Presley died.

Joey Ramone and some friends were hanging around the Lower East Side, distraught. Nobody could think of a fitting homage for The King. "Then somebody got the idea we should buy some fresh brains," said Joey's friend, Deer Frances, who was there that day, speaking at a tribute to Joey in 2001.

"We went to CBGBs and we put the brains all over the place!" she recalled. "People played anyway."

8

Teenage Lobotomy

HOW DID YOU get involved with doing the sleeves for Rocket To Russia *and* Road To Ruin*?*

"It was Johnny. At first, he wanted us to do the inside cover to Rocket To Russia. *We were originally going to do it like a* Punk *magazine spread – photographs, cartoons, lots of different stuff. Joey wanted to do a shoot for 'Teenage Lobotomy' with a cow's brain. So Roberta took the photo at the Ramones' loft and after that we went to CBGBs and put the brains all over the place. We put them in the pinball machine, on the bar, on the stage, waiting for people to find the brains. It was a lot of fun, but Johnny didn't like the mixed media. The Ramones liked the picture of Bugs Bunny [used to illustrate the lyrics to 'Rockaway Beach'] – so I did all the cartoons on the inner sleeve. That was a lot of work for a couple of days."*

I'd imagine.

"Then Johnny asked me to do the back cover as well. He described what he wanted: the pinhead and the missile, you know, the little African guy in Africa. I talked with Johnny an awful lot back then. He was always fun to talk to. He was a good ideas guy. For Road To Ruin, *this fan had sent him a drawing of the band with a lobster claw coming out of the speaker and a snake.* They wanted it redrawn more professionally without the snake. They wanted to know who could draw it. I said Wally Wood [famed comic book artist, renowned for his work on Fifties* Mad *magazine – the comic that shaped a generation's humour] would be perfect, but he was ill and suggested that we use one of his assistants, Paul Kirchner, who did* Dope Rider.*"*

I don't know if I know that.

"It was a very good comic strip about a skeleton, from High Times, *like a spaghetti western. Paul drew similar to Wally, but was flightier in style. So he took the drawing and reinterpreted it in three dimensions. They didn't like it. He did 30 sketches and put them up on a wall in a room and Johnny asked me to pick one out.*

* Gus MacDonald gave the illustration to Arturo Vega outside a venue in Glasgow during the Scottish "punk rock weekend" of May 1977. Gus' original featured Tommy on drums.

They were awful. He said, 'John, what are we going to do? The cover's due in three days.' I was trying to bring out the next issue of Punk*, so I said, 'OK, pay me a lot of money and I'll do it.' "*

And did they?

"I got $1,000 – pretty cheap, I think."

Did you get any merchandising rights?

"No. I should have held out. I don't make any money from the T-shirts or anything. Sometimes I think I should sue but . . . a word is a bond."

When you were doing the cartoons for Rocket To Russia*, what thought process was going through your mind?*

" 'How fast can I get this done?' With 'Ramona', I did a picture of a little punk rock girl, what could be more quick?"

Were you consciously trying to make them funny?

"They were funny lyrics so I tried to do something fun interpreting them. I didn't have time to think about it, you know? Every record, it seems like they had to do it all last minute so there wasn't much time to be clever."

(Author's interview with John Holmstrom,
Punk editor and sleeve illustrator)

THE RAMONES STARTED recording their third album, *Rocket To Russia* on August 21, 1977 at Media Sound in midtown NYC – an old Episcopalian church funded by the people who'd put up the money for Woodstock. Engineer Ed Stasium had recorded there in March 1970, with his former hit band Brandywine: "It had a Neve 8078 recording desk, a wide selection of old microphones and great acoustics." Media Sound had one of the biggest drum sounds around, not that you can tell from *Russia* because Tommy – co-producing with Tony Bongiovi once more – kept the drums down in the mix.

Popular Ramones legend has it there was a female engineer named Ramona present – true, but she had nothing to do with the song of the same name: "Johnny had her kicked off the session, no women were allowed to be around," Stasium explains. "The song would have been written well before they met her."

Bongiovi – who'd just mixed the 'Star Wars Theme' disco hit – was in the process of building the Power Station. The Ramones were the first group to be mixed there. "The third floor was bare except for the control room," Stasium recalls. "We had no outboard gear, no effects, no digital reverb, nothing. The reverb you can hear is actually from the stairwell on the East Side of the building where we set up a couple of speakers."

There wasn't much hanging around at the studio in between takes –

time was too tight at $150 per studio hour. Johnny would lay his guitar part down, and leave straight away afterwards; Joey, who was becoming more perfectionist about his vocals with each record, stuck around longer; Tommy, of course, had to be around.

The album cost between $25,000 and $30,000 to make – small by major label budgets, but a fair leap from *Ramones*.

"It doesn't matter if you spend $100,000 or $30,000," the guitarist explained. "It's best to do it quickly. If the engineer said a take was good, we'd go on to the next one. You don't wanna sit there and bullshit: it's your money they're spending."

Johnny played all the guitars, except for the extra part on 'Sheena Is A Punk Rocker', for which Stasium took down his old Stratocaster for The Beach Boys feel. Stasium also sang background vocals on a few songs, the sweet "oohs" – and again missed out on both percentage points and a production credit because, "I was naïve. It happened later on *It's Alive*, *Road To Ruin* and the rest of them. When Tony asked me to come in on these albums, I thought I was producing them – then they'd come out and have a different name on them. 'Ah,' I was told. 'Next time you'll get production credits.' "

"Tony Bongiovi didn't do anything on this album," Johnny claimed in a 1982 *Trouser Press* feature. "He wasn't even there!"

For sustenance, the band devoured cheeseburgers, French fries, milkshakes, grilled cheese . . . "Probably hamburgers," thinks Stasium. "That's all we ever ate."

"We were on a roll, in high gear, touring and everything," Tommy told David Fricke. "We thought we were gonna make it, that we were on the launching pad. Even if it was a little difficult to write the songs because we had to write 'em in hotel rooms, once we got into the studio, we felt we were in control – that we were in our prime."

A major theme on *Rocket To Russia* [originally called *Ramones Get Well*] is mental illness – 'Cretin Hop', the peerless 'Teenage Lobotomy', 'I Wanna Be Well', 'Why Is It Always This Way?', 'We're A Happy Family' – the band influenced by their late night diet of schlock horror TV and warped comic books, drug abuse [Dee Dee], and Joey's spell inside a mental institution. But it was so comical, so human. Nowhere did you feel the Ramones were patronising their dysfunctional subjects and cretin dancers: the grinning manic faces of Holmstrom's cartoons – owing more than a nod to comic book god Harvey Kurtzman, creator of *Mad* magazine – that accompanied the lyrics made everything look such FUN, like [Bugs Bunny/Daffy Duck artist] Tex Avery given a shaved haircut and a

Grade A Lobotomy. Hilarious. The songs on *Rocket To Russia* were perhaps the funnest – and funniest – in rock music since the Bonzo Dog Doo Dah Band, and The Beatles recording, 'You Know My Name (Look Up The Number)' in the Sixties.

"I don't know where the mental illness thing came from," says Tommy. "I think we were all trying to get as mentally unsound as possible. The guys were major fans of B-movies – and maybe they were major fans of institutions. I'm not sure."

"Joey and Dee Dee didn't think of themselves as freaks," suggests Arturo, "but they were aware people considered them *outsiders*. And it's something that is now related directly to mental patients as in outsider art. I think they thought it was funny that there were people like that, and that people like that were OK in this world. That was the message – it's OK. Everything's going to be all right."

If there has to be one, *Rocket To Russia* is the Greatest (Studio) Album The Ramones Made, Official. It certainly contains some of their finest songs.

"If there is a greatest Ramones song that I recorded, it has to be 'Teenage Lobotomy'," Ed Stasium told Fricke for the *Anthology*. "It's a mini-Ramones symphony. It has every element of what's great about them, in one song: the big drum intro and the 'Lobotomy' chant; the little background-harmony oooohs; the subject matter." Stasium also pointed to the bewildering array of time and key changes in Johnny's finely crafted chord progressions, perfectly attuned to Dee Dee and Tommy's rigid tempo. Johnny wrote some of the sections, Tommy wrote others. "Not a lot of bands had modulations in their songs," the engineer explained. "The Ramones always had modulations. They were always changing the key."

'Lobotomy' is a solid-set Ramones classic – it rhymes "cerebellum" with "tell 'em", for Christ's sake – the equal of both 'Sheena' and the call-to-arms chanting on 'Cretin Hop'.

"1-2-3-4," Joey sings with obvious relish on 'Cretin Hop', "cretins wanna hop some more." Tommy's hi-hats go into overload, as Johnny and Dee Dee lay down the rock solid rhythm base. "That came from when we were staying in St Paul, Minnesota," Joey explained. "We went some place to eat and there were these cretins all over the place. And there was a Cretin Avenue, where we drove into the city."

'Rockaway Beach' is even better, if anything – insanely catchy, with harmonies and a false ending on the chorus that would have done Brian Wilson proud. Two minutes, six seconds of absolute pop nirvana. It was a natural subject for a band so in love with Sixties Americana and the surf guitars of The Ventures – a paean to a sandbar at the southern end of Queens, written by Dee Dee (on tour in England in the van).

"Dee Dee used to take the bus down there – he was more of a beach goer than the rest of us," Tommy Erdelyi told Ira Robbins. "I was there maybe three times in my life. It was a long schlepp from Forest Hills [Queens]." Joey agreed. "Dee Dee spent a lot more time there than I did," he says. "It was more of a hangout for him and Johnny."

Of course, 'Rockaway Beach' was released as a single in November '77 – perfect seasonal timing for its "chewing out a rhythm on my bubblegum" summer splendour. Not.

"It was out of our control," says Joey. "A lot of things were ridiculous when it came to our releases." The single reached the heady heights of Number 66 on the *Billboard* chart, and earned the dubious soubriquet of being the Ramones' biggest hit in America.

"Have you ever been to Rockaway Beach?" *Punk* magazine's former resident punk [and co-author of *Please Kill Me*] Legs McNeil asks in the sleeve-notes to the 2001 CD reissue of *Rocket To Russia*. "The place is a sewer. Crowds of vicious girls in bikinis and high heels, drinking tallboys of beer out of little brown paper bags, waiting to get into the next fight. Everyone [is] stoned on Quaaludes and Tuinals . . . to romanticise such a toilet was akin to writing a ballad about finding true love at Spahn Ranch."

But that was the genius of the Ramones: they could find beauty in the unlikeliest of spots.

AN EARLY REPORT on *Rocket To Russia* in *NME*, dated October 15 (a month before the album appeared) stated that 'Here Today Gone Tomorrow' represented a break with the first two albums: "It is a slow love ballad sung with a certain degree of tenderness." Even more startling (apparently) was the inclusion of a guitar solo – the Ramones' first – not exactly lengthy, granted, a fair statement in brevity, but shocking because, as *Village Voice* critic Tom Carson wrote, "for the first time in 15 years, you weren't expecting one".

Ironic then, that this song was one of the earliest Joey ever wrote, penned before the Ramones existed. "It was about someone having to pay the price," explained the singer somewhat literally. "Know what I mean?"

Other highlights include a couple of fast-paced love songs, 'Locket Love' and 'Ramona' – the latter illustrated with a Holmstrom drawing of a sweet punkette in regulation leather jacket and ripped jeans standing by a bleak tenement wall.

Elsewhere, 'I Don't Care' strips back the negative minimalism of the early 'I Don't Wanna' songs to their logical conclusion – 'I don't care," Joey lamented with a scarifying intensity over and over again, "about that girl." "I don't care," he repeated again, countless times, "about this world." That was it. "Why get bogged down in specifics?" McNeil asks rhetorically. "Just chuck the whole lot."

Two stand-outs are the covers: a full-on version of 'Do You Wanna Dance?" – a hit previously for Bobby Freeman, The Beach Boys and Bette Midler, but never with such unbridled joy – that got issued as a single in early '78 in both America and Britain with rare tracks on the B-side (US: 'Babysitter'; UK: 'It's A Long Way Back To Germany', a magnificent paced-out drawl of loneliness). Then there's the show-stopping take on the 1964 Trashmen hit 'Surfin' Bird' with its "poppa-ooh-mow-mow" and insane guttural laughter in the break – picked after the Ramones caught The Cramps playing an equally raucous version.

"We had to do 'Surfin' Bird' over a couple of times," Stasium told David Fricke. "I don't think Joey was singing along [on the basic track], and it's hard to follow without a singer. It's basically one chord. And for the hole in the middle – Joey's vocal noises – we just stopped and guessed how long his part would be."

"When we were playing 'Surfin' Bird' in California '77," Joey recalled, "some kid tied a rope around the legs of a dead seagull and started swinging it around like a lasso. He was swinging it round and round, and let go, and it wrapped itself around Dee Dee's throat."

'We're A Happy Family' is the song that sums up the Ramones' deranged worldview best – a hilarious tale of everyday folk in Queens, dealing dope and gay dads. It's like the Ramones theme, a history lesson for the fans that wondered where da bruddas' pantheon of freaks came from. Of course, everyone is off their head – the classic dysfunctional American family as depicted in films like *American Beauty* and 2001's *Royal Tenenbaums* (which also featured 'Judy Is A Punk') – why wouldn't they be?

"The mental illness on the album was probably there because of the mental illness in the band," Stasium says, before hastily adding, "I'm joking. Nothing was seriously wrong with the Ramones, except Joey's obsessive/compulsive disorder. Every time Joey left a room, he had to put his foot back in for a second, no matter where the room was. It became a problem particularly when Monte was trying to get him out of the dressing room, or onto a plane, as sweet as he was.

"It's like a funny horror movie," the engineer patiently explains. "They weren't seriously thinking about a teenage lobotomy. It's a joke."

"I grew up in New Jersey in a suburban neighbourhood," says Carla Olla [guitarist with Deborah Harry, and Dee Dee Ramone in the Nineties], "so *Rocket To Russia* was like finding a piece of gold at the age of 14. I played it over and over. I was like a kid in a candy store. It was funny, first of all. There weren't many bands that didn't take themselves incredibly seriously. I went to see them play live as often as I could – skip school, run away and be deaf for three days. I was a big Johnny fan, I liked how low he wore his guitar, I liked the fact he drank Yoo Hoo. He intimidated me. He still does. He's the hard-nosed one, the one yelling at the crew telling them they got paid too much."

Rolling Stone's Steve Pond called *Rocket To Russia* one of the essential records of the Seventies. Robert Christgau gave it an "A" in *Village Voice* (rock'n'roll, of course, being another subject to be marked coldly like mathematics or biology). In the *NME*, Nick Kent wasn't so enthusiastic: "This album is little more than the sum of the aforementioned parts," he wrote, "[or] maybe the fact the latest Ramones chapter has appeared at almost the same time as the Pistols' LP has brought on my jaded reaction; perhaps actual passion, neurosis and frustration are the real meat of rock'n'roll."

What, like the Ramones expressed in every one of their early songs – but with liberal doses of humour? Fellow UK critic Karl Tsigdinos was closer to the truth when he stated, "The only thing that matters when spinning a Ramones record *is the record itself* . . . understatement is nearly always best." Kent's reaction, however, was a fair indication of the divide that started to come down between the Ramones and their British cousins – not "serious" enough for the politicised music press, and not "arty" enough to be lumped in with their former CBGBs peers like Talking Heads, the Ramones were becoming outcasts in the scene they'd helped inspire. No one likes to be seen enjoying cartoons, even though everyone does. (It wasn't until the advent of *The Simpsons* two decades later that the much under-appreciated art form received mainstream respectability in America.)

The Ramones situation wasn't helped by a couple of incidents that occurred towards the end of the year, either.

'WHY IS IT ALWAYS THIS WAY?' asked the final song on *Rocket To Russia.*

Sire signed a distribution deal with Warner Bros., giving the label the full backing of a major for the first time. In August, the Ramones played a couple of dates in the Northwest with Tom Petty And The Heartbreakers;

in October they undertook a mini-tour with Iggy Pop. But just as the Ramones were getting ready for the big time, the Sex Pistols released *Never Mind The Bollocks* and became the stereotype of punk for all time: safety-pins, shock tactics, drug overdoses, spitting, bad language, bondage trousers, ponce managers flouncing around claiming they invented the wheel, the works. Any chance the Ramones had of getting airplay disappeared in a welter of outrage.

"I walked into Media Sound on the first day," Stasium told *Mojo* journalist Michael Hill, "and Johnny had the Pistols' 'God Save The Queen' record and he said, 'These guys ripped us off and I want to sound better than this'. And we put it on and said, 'No problem . . .' "

"Warners were all geared up to break the Ramones," explains Seymour Stein, "and when that didn't happen, unfortunately they got tarnished with an image of being a cult band. Just one big hit, and they could have sold a million albums. That's all it would have taken."

Then, on November 19, Joey was involved with a major accident before going on stage at the Capitol Theater in Passaic, New Jersey that involved the singer going to hospital with second- and third-degree burns – *after* the show took place.

"Joey did these breathing exercises," explains Linda Stein. "He suffered from asthma. He had to take care of his throat. All I remember is that he got severely burned by the vaporiser, and we took him afterwards to the hospital where he stayed for a week, in agony. The water from the vaporiser must have spilled on him. He was really a mess. I don't know how come he did the show."

"Joey came out in this white cream like Bob Dylan on the *Rolling Thunder* revue," recalls Stasium.

Janis Schacht remembers the night differently: "It was something his voice teacher had told him to do, breathe steam to clear the sinuses – you're meant to do it over an open pot, not a teapot. Someone had put plastic over its nozzle and it exploded in his face."

Joey was rushed to hospital where they put cream over his face.

"Unfortunately," Schacht continues, "that's the worse thing you can do to a burn, it should be ice. So he went back and did the entire show without missing a beat – the salve melting on his face, like a clown, white white white. I'm standing next to Linda Stein who has no idea how badly burnt he is. I wanted to kill her – why was he on stage? Instead of taking him to hospital afterwards, they took him home. He couldn't speak the next day. It was a terribly serious thing.

"He ended up in New York Hospital Burn Center for three weeks –

not one," she corrects. "His entire throat filled with blisters. I gave him a Snoopy *Little Paint By Numbers* kit to keep him happy. On the British tour the next month, you could still see the burns on his chest. He never liked talking about that."

The remainder of the US tour had to be cancelled. During the band's first full gig after the accident, in Carlisle, England, Joey leaned too near the microphone, leaving a piece of blistered skin six inches long hanging from it.

Joey put the trauma to good use, however, when he wrote 'I Wanna Be Sedated' backstage at Canterbury, England in December [this is the reported town: it's more likely to be at Cambridge]. "He called me up while he was in hospital and had me write down the lines, 'I wanna be sedated/And Matt tried to have me cremated' [Matt was the roadie who set up the exploding teapot]," Schacht laughs. "That was usual for Joey. He would often call me up and play stuff to me on his two-string guitar, stuff that tickled him."*

"I was there when Joey wrote 'Sedated'," says Stein. "He was just sitting writing, all curled in like Joey used to curl in, on paper ripped out of a notebook."

Also, around October, the band had their truck and all their equipment stolen, including Johnny's cherished blue Mosrite. It was never recovered.

"We lost almost $30,000 worth of equipment," Dee Dee told *Zigzag*'s Colin Keinch. The band went on to reveal they were on a salary of $100 a week – "that's about £55," Johnny translated. "Touring costs us $750 a day, and sometimes we only get paid as little as $250. In San Francisco [where 'Rockaway Beach' was Number One on the radio station charts], we'll probably play at Winterland to 4,000 people for just $750." Someone was getting ripped off.

Johnny told the writer that he'd found the Sex Pistols show at Brunel University two weeks before "terrible . . . terrible . . . they were just boring. I couldn't believe they could be that poor."

The feeling was reciprocated: The Pistols' singer also claimed he found Ramones boring. "Listen, mate," Rotten told a *Circus* journalist, alert to the necessity of not losing his sarcastic cool. "I used to work in a shoe

* Joey played a short-necked, two-string – sometimes four – Yamaha that he stole from a guy who'd come over to Arturo's loft. He was aiming to buy it, but then the guy ripped Arturo off for $500 and Joey got so annoyed he decided that "the only way I was gonna give it back to him was over his head." Joey wasn't the most accomplished guitarist: "Some of [the strings] age, y'know," he told Lester Bangs. "Sometime you have to, like, yank 'em off with pliers." He'd also played "mop" and "pool cue".

factory, and you heard the same fuggin' noise all day long. I don't need it."

On Xmas Day, the Ramones saw The Kinks' Yuletide concert at the Rainbow Theatre in London.

On the day following the *Zigzag* interview, the Ramones also played at the Rainbow – New Year's Eve, 1977. Writer Victor Bockris, who spent the evening with the group, picks up the tale.

"They were very innocent, fresh and sexy," he recalls. "It was very pleasing to see, because people who've been on the road so long normally get toasted. Dee Dee was the most attractive because he was such an animalistic natural person. He had a strong sexual vibe in his joy of being alive."

Support that night came from Scotland's Rezillos, and Billy Idol's rather risible part-time punks, Generation X: "They had a little buzz about them at the time," explains Linda Stein, "so we thought we could charge more. We had balloons come down from the ceiling during 'Pinhead' – it was a really big production for us. I was standing on the side of the stage with Danny Fields when Billy Idol spilled a bottle of champagne over my head thinking it was punk. I was livid. I took him by the collar, up against the wall and said, 'You're a fucking idiot.' "

"I walked in the dressing room after they came off stage," continues Bockris, "and Sid Vicious was sitting on a stool with Nancy kneeling in front of him, her head buried in his crotch. He looked very beautiful, vibrant and alive. Johnny Rotten was also there, surrounded by his entourage, maintaining his stony silence."

Afterwards, the band clambered into three enormous limos with the journalist and management, and went to Elton John's restaurant: "They were pissed off with Seymour because they didn't think there were enough posters around," Bockris recalls. "I thought it was pathetic – here were the Ramones, having just played a great gig, and there was no party laid on for them, no reception. Instead, they got shunted off to a chic restaurant, sitting in an empty room waited on by men in kilts. Only Dee Dee had a girl with him."

Linda Stein disagrees: "We had so many parties for them in different places – at Morten's in Covent Garden, the John Reid restaurant. Sir Elton came to one of their shows. I have a photo of him backstage dressed all in black with a policeman's hat. I was wearing clothes from Seditionaries with the trousers held together. He thought it was a hoot."

"You have to know when to quit," Elton told Johnny Ramone. "I feel exhausted and I'm 30. I don't want to finish up an old rock'n'roller."

Dee Dee's girl was possibly Vera Colvin – who the bassist married in early September 1978. (A 1976 edition of *NME* stated that Johnny was living with his wife Rosanna in Queens, but the Ramones jealously guarded their private lives. The band was a team, a gang, and that's all anyone needed to know.) A 1980 report in *Melody Maker* stated that Dee Dee first met Vera at Max's Kansas City, and didn't call her again until the girl he was living with kicked him out. Tommy remembers the wedding: "It was very nice, a regular church service and there was a banquet affair afterwards. The priest gave a speech about the sanctity of marriage. It was fairly big . . . the bride must have had a big family. It may have been on Long Island."

Dee Dee got Vera's name tattooed on his arm, and the couple stayed together until 1989, a month before the bassist quit the Ramones. Johnny – in a distant echo of early Beatles' shenanigans – feared for the group's image and refused to publicise the marriage.

"I was glad when Dee Dee married Vera," says Arturo. "She would help keep him under control. Plus, I liked her, and I believe love is a great medicine for many illnesses."

Danny Fields and Linda Stein felt Dee Dee should've had a string of affairs with stars like Farrah Fawcett, "so when I found out [he] was getting married," Linda told *Please Kill Me*, "I couldn't believe it. But he chose to be completely domesticated and settle down in Whitestone, Queens – with his cutlery and his porcelain and his dinette set . . .

"The great thing about Dee Dee," she explained, "is that he slept with everybody . . . and he made you feel good. He was a professional hooker! Dee Dee and I had an affair – and I'm the mother of two!"

HAVE YOU EVER felt bitter about the Ramones' lack of recognition?

"Well, I feel real good about what we've become. We've always done it our way, never compromised. We've always maintained high ideals and integrity. We revolutionised rock'n'roll music and brought a whole new attitude and excitement to music and turned the world around, and influenced about every band that's come after us from '75. Our album in 1976 really was shaking things up. We were a catalyst and didn't get quite the recognition that we deserved, but I'm comfortable too. I wouldn't put us on his level, but I always liked the way David Bowie maintained what he wanted to do without being a big glitzy star. A lot of artists become these major stars but there's no credibility to them even though they're very credible. We never played at that magnitude, but then indirectly we have. Everyone holds us in high regard. You walk down the street and kids come up to you and say, 'You guys are the best. You inspired us to start a band.' It feels good, to retain your initial beliefs and to practise them. A lot of bands lose sight of what they're doing."

What were your initial aims?

"To be one of the most exciting bands around . . . It was a very genuine thing. Rock'n'roll in the late Fifties and throughout the Sixties, through its infancy to the experimental period, was exciting and fresh, and it was fun, a buzz. In the Seventies, it became like big business, very formulated and watered down, polished over. That's what we were reacting against when we were starting out. In '76 it was the height of disco in America with Donna Summer and corporate rock like Boston and Journey and Foreigner, and the Southern thing – The Eagles, Linda Ronstadt. Also, you had bands like Styx and Pink Floyd that weren't playing exciting music, that weren't playing for the audience. They were playing with a little bit of arrogance. What we did was reassemble music, pick it apart and strip it down and reassemble it. It was almost like a clog in the coil that you have to flush down the drain. Let the fresh air in. Let it breathe. That's what we did. Also, people were taking themselves a little too seriously. We put the fun back into it. That's how it was meant to be – fun and exciting and with guts. That's what we accomplished.

"From then to now, things look a lot more promising. Everything is more uptempo and exciting."

It probably depends where you look.

"1976 and 1977 in America and England reminded me a lot of '64 and '65, the British Invasion. There were a lot of artists being innovative and imaginative. You had the Pistols, The Clash and The Damned and The Saints from Australia, but you also had The Pretenders. It was real strong. Now it's getting back to how it was when it fucked up – the metal bands, the corporate fluff, the totally superficial music. It's bullshit. There's a minority of things that are really good and tasteful and imaginative and innovative."

Does that make it important for the Ramones to still be around?

"Yeah. We're probably more important than ever. We don't kiss ass. That's why we don't have Number One triple platinum albums. We've never bowed or compromised to get ahead. That's not important to us. We have substance. We know what's good and we know what we like and we give a shit."

(Author's interview with Joey Ramone, 1989)

THE BRITISH TOUR was recorded and later released in April 1979 as the 28-song, double album set *It's Alive*. (At 17.821428p per track – as the British advertising campaign had it – the album must have cost £4.99, then.) Most of the songs were taken from the Rainbow show, where 10 rows of seats were ripped out and thrown on stage. Astonishingly, the album didn't come out in America until the Nineties – despite being one of the greatest live albums ever, to rank alongside James Brown's first two

Live At The Apollo volumes, Motorhead's *No Sleep Till Hammersmith* and The Who's *Live At Leeds* – God knows what Sire were thinking.

It's Alive captured the band at their very peak: songs present include . . . everything really. Hit segues seamlessly into hit. It's the perfect Ramones album.

"You know what listening to the Ramones is like?" asked Charles Shaar Murray* in the *NME*. "It's like eating cherries or peanuts or Smarties: you can never have just one.

"A Ramones live double album!" he enthused. "28 tracks of non-stop fun! Why isn't the radio like this? Why should you have to buy Ramones records just to be able to hear perfect pop songs streamlined to the nth degree fired at you at perfect rock velocity with machine-gun precision? Why didn't the Ramones exist before Jerry [sic] Hyman, Derek [sic] Colvin, Tommy Erdelyi and John Cummings invented them?"

Murray went on to (correctly) point out that *It's Alive* sounds less like a standard double live album than an effortless panorama of Top Five hit singles – "the finest lesson imaginable in the art of pop single construction from a group who've yet to have a proper hit." The review ended by pointing out that "to Ramone" is a verb, and that "this album Ramones more than any other record ever made".**

"We recorded *It's Alive* on the Island Studios mobile," recalls Stasium, who finally got a co-producer's credit (with Tommy). He laughs. "I remember there was a lot of Swedish porno magazines on the bus. Other than that, it was very calm. The album is a terrific representation of the band in 1977 – the Ramones always played faster in a live situation than on record. That came from Johnny's philosophy of 'Get in, get out, see how many songs you can fit into 30 minutes.' Occasionally, Joey would have to stop singing because he ran out of breath or skip words because they were going so fast."

Talking to gay activist singer Tom Robinson, Dee Dee revealed he achieved his high energy level while recording the bass overdubs by drinking "lots and lots of black coffee".

WHY WERE THE SONGS so much slower on the early studio albums than on It's Alive*?*

* The journalist was a long-time Ramones fan who once had the cheek to ask Art Garfunkel at a Savoy Hotel, London, press conference whether he thought his music might benefit from a Ramones influence. Everyone laughed, embarrassed. Art was lost for words.

** Incidentally. Look for the vinyl not the CD when searching out a copy: the sound is far superior.

"Because we didn't want to totally distance people. When we played live, we just played them faster because we felt them faster. We had to consciously slow them down in the studio. We were hoping for radio airplay."

Why England?

"Because at the time, we didn't get to play many big theatres and it was one of the biggest shows we'd ever played. It was in London, so it was easy to get the facilities."

Did you see that advert at the time: two albums, 28 songs, 54.36 minutes . . . was speed that important?

"It was important to Johnny – he thought of it as his virtuosity, that he could play faster than other people. Also, he just liked it fast. I liked things fast, but solid – if they're played too fast they come apart at the seams, so my job was to make sure that didn't happen. It must have been rough on Joey. He didn't complain, but it must have been rough. You have to understand how unique it was back then, to play fast. It was way before the hardcore bands and speed metal bands started. We were the only ones doing that."

(Author's interview with Tommy Ramone, 2002)

9

Touring, Part 1

". . . YOU'RE TALKING ABOUT 23 years. What tour? We did everything. You'll have to be specific."

OK – when they were touring the UK, what was that like, the first couple of tours?

"The early tours in Europe were very hard because we're talking about the Seventies and coming from the United States, we were used to conveniences – TV all night, 24 hour shops. But in Europe back then, there was no TV all night, there was no late night shopping, that all happened later on. Showers were something that I missed a lot, that's something else the Europeans don't like to have – they have a hose or something if you're lucky. It's all baths. No mixer taps, which is another concept I don't understand, why you would turn on this and turn on this and mix it in the bowl. I want to turn on the tap and have the water already mixed. Stuff like that mattered to us, being Americans going to Europe back in the Seventies. It was pretty difficult for us."

I know that the UK has a bad reputation with touring bands.

"Yeah, and the food also. Food in England is . . . that's why they developed a taste for Indian food because that's the best meal you can get in any city."

Reports of early Ramones tours say they'd go to bed early. Is that true?

"Well, they weren't a party band. They couldn't stay up too late – and that's why they lasted so long. I mean, this group lasted over twenty something years. That's amazing – managers don't even last that long. So they really couldn't. I mean, on the road, you get up early, you travel, long distance usually, you do a soundcheck, go back to the hotel, get ready, get to the place, play, eat, then you're exhausted."

And there's usually nowhere to go afterwards, anyway.

"Exactly – and if there was, well, they weren't a party band anyway. They had their little things, but basically they kept it pretty tight."

For sure, because bands that party non-stop are going to last two years max. Were you there when the Ramones exerted such an influence on the UK punk scene?

"I was there for the second tour. I only missed about three shows with the Ramones. In '76, they did two shows in England, but they couldn't afford to bring many people with them so they brought Mickey [Leigh, Joey's brother] along. They came back a second time to England . . . The Clash, Johnny Rotten, Sid Vicious – yeah, I was there for that."

I also read a report that said the '77 European tour was like *Spinal Tap* – the argument over whose girlfriend was sitting where in the van. Is that true?

"Not really, no. It wasn't that bad. There were times when someone wouldn't talk to the other people but basically when the girlfriends were on the road, they kept them calmer than when they weren't."

Did the Ramones get on early on when they were touring?

"Well – they grew up together in the early days. Yeah, basically they were all friends and got along. They all did what they had to do. Johnny is a heavy-duty Yankees and baseball fan – into stats. He collected photographs of players, cards and memorabilia . . . Whenever there was a game, he'd sit up front and listen to the game."

Did he ever actually play baseball?

"I don't know."

George Tabb said he saw them play touch football a couple of times.

"They'd throw around a football once in a while. I never saw them do anything heavily athletic, any of them really."

So they got along fine, then . . .

"There were different phases. There were times when we could get a big bus with separate compartments, which was better, and then there were times when we had to get vans and everybody was squished in and people weren't talking to people. That was hard."

Yeah.

"But they were never impolite."

The way it's been described to me is like a dysfunctional family who still loved each other.

"Yeah, exactly."

Which . . .

"You know, hate and love."

Which makes sense – if you're going to be around somebody for 23 years, you're going to have your ups and downs.

"Yeah. You have to know how to be diplomatic about it, know when to say and when not to say something and just keep to yourself. It would just be verbal stuff. They never had a fight."

No – I can't imagine that.

"I mean, they got on my nerves and I told them to fuck off too. I'll tell you my favourite joke. 'What's the difference between a toilet bowl and a tour manager? A toilet bowl has to deal with one asshole at a time.' "

It's a good joke.

"It's an old joke."

(Author's interview with Monte Melnick, tour manager)

10

Flatbush City Limits

EARLY ON, THE RAMONES were Tommy's band. There's little sense denying it. Look at the album sleeves – there's the drummer, standing front centre, glowering. It was his impetus and leadership. He made sense of the others' talents. He was older. He was more experienced, in the studio and on stage. Sure, Joey and Dee Dee wrote most of the songs and supplied the creativity. Sure, Johnny was the taskmaster, the General. Sure, Johnny and Joey later developed a Jagger/Richards hate-hate relationship that helped to fuel the 2,000 plus live shows, and ensured the band would not break up, not for a phenomenally long time – they had too much to prove to each other. Sure, Dee Dee served as an intermediary between the warring front men, and Marky was a great solid rock drummer, and CJ later provided a fan's enthusiasm that enabled the Ramones to keep going way past anyone's expectations when he joined on bass in the Nineties.

And, of course, the Ramones could never have continued without the faith, determination and graft of unsung heroes like Arturo and Monte and the rest of the road crew – and musicians like Daniel Rey, Ed Stasium and Andy Shernoff.

But it was Tommy who started it all, and created an ideal strong enough that it lasted for 23 years straight – even though he was missing at the helm for 18 of those years.

Look at the evidence.

The first three Ramones albums (when Tommy was in the band) are certified classics, no argument. No one denies that. Fourth album, 1978's *Road To Ruin* – Tommy leaves the band, fed up with the grind of touring, but sticks around to flesh out his production vision with Stasium – bona fide classic, very little argument, even with the acoustic guitars. Few would be foolish enough to deny that.

Then what happens?

The Ramones are a gang. That's what Tommy taught them, and what they believe in so fervently they can't lose the mentality even when it's to their detriment. So they close up shop, and decide they can't have anything to do with deserters, it would be a sign of weakness: after *Road To Ruin*, that's it for Tommy's involvement – aside from a brief return on 1984's comeback album *Too Tough To Die*, the last great record the Ramones made.

In the same way *Ramones* defined the mindset of early Ramones – pop-punk bubblegum, with deranged lyrics and a healthy sense of humour – *Too Tough To Die* set out the stall for the remainder of da bruddas' career: hardcore punk, mostly minus the bubblegum, with deranged lyrics and not so much humour because life was becoming more serious, this was a job.

Shunting Tommy aside may not have been deliberate – legendary Sixties Wall Of Sound producer Phil Spector came on the scene, and a pop fan like Joey wasn't going to pass up on the opportunity to work with one of his idols. But again, look at the evidence. First, there came that spate of albums where the Ramones were going full out in the search for that elusive hit: *End Of The Century*, *Pleasant Dreams* and *Subterranean Jungle*. Fans argue about these. I'd claim the first two as genuine classics, and possibly the last despite the dodgy drum sound (sorry Marky) – the songs are fantastic. As Scots fan Lindsay Hutton says, " 'The KKK Took My Baby Away' . . . fucking Jesus Christ, that's about as great as it gets." But, post-Tommy, the cracks were beginning to appear.

First, the band started claiming individual songwriting credits. Dee Dee and Joey wanted some credit and acclaim as writers. The publishing money was still being split equally, however. Then, Joey and Johnny had a major falling out. By March 1980, Joey and Johnny had stopped speaking entirely (much more on which later). The Ramone Myth was grating on its participants. The band failed to renew Danny and Linda's managerial contracts. Yet they never stopped touring.

In 1978, 154 shows.

In 1979, 158 shows.

In 1980, 155 shows.

And so on . . . right up till 1996 and the final tour.

It hardly mattered that after *Too Tough To Die*, the studio albums became patchy, still with flashes of brilliance but, in the main, stale rehashes of former glories. The Ramones had long stopped believing the studio was a true representation – on stage was where they belonged, where they could communicate directly with their fans, bypassing the machinations of a record industry that had never supported them, playing countries like Argentina and Brazil and Spain and Japan and Finland where they were held as Rock Gods. The Ramones were a gang, and damn stubborn with it.

"People said they wouldn't last one album," explains Janis Schacht, "so they showed them. They kept going out of sheer spite – maybe they were too stupid to lie down, but they didn't need to as long as people kept coming to see them. The nice part was, their audience kept regenerating themselves."

Dee Dee explained it in his book: "We just needed something to do."

The Ramones were making money, and enjoyed being on stage – so why quit? Although driving five or more hours a day, weeks on end, in a van with someone you never speak to, might seem like a good enough reason to some. But then, loads of people are in jobs they hate, and stay in them for long past 20 years.

"The Ramones didn't have artistic pretensions," suggests Roberta Bayley. "It was better than working a coal mine. Also, the dysfunction of being miserable – if you're Johnny Ramone and you're saying 'turn off the radio, I wanna listen to the baseball' and torturing other people, you might enjoy that. You and I might not understand it, but some people get off on making others miserable."

"What else could they do?" asks NYC writer Rachel Felder. "If you'd been touring consistently since your mid-twenties, quitting might not seem like an obvious option."

IN JANUARY 1978, the Ramones undertook a three-month tour of the States, with The Runaways in support.*

Critics were still undecided as to the Ramones' worth. At the sell-out New York Palladium show, *New York Times* critic Robert Palmer (unrelated to the ersatz soul singer) suggested that "[Ramones] are the kind of joke one tires of very rapidly". In Madison, Wisconsin the club was picketed by the musical pressure group Committee Against Racism for the Ramones' "fascist ideology" – even confirmed fan, *NME*'s Charles Shaar Murray was uneasy with that joke, saying that 'Today Your Love . . .' was the only place where da bruddas' black humour overbalanced into genuine bad taste, "seriously out of order, mate, even from someone

* Runaways singer Joan Jett became the living embodiment of rock'n'roll during the Eighties with her monster solo hit, 'I Love Rock'N'Roll' – "so put another dime in the jukebox, baby". Ironic that it took a woman to define rock, such a fiercely patriarchal tradition. Jett went on to inspire a whole generation of Riot Grrrls in the Nineties, including Ramones fans Sleater-Kinney.

pretending to be a pinhead". (Odd that if the same joke had been made in a comic book, or film – see Chaplin's *Great Dictator* – it would have been hailed as amusing satire.)

Rocket To Russia failed to deliver (commercially): it was supposed to be the album that pushed the Ramones into the big-time. It didn't. The sense of feeling, of release that the band experienced while recording it, turned to frustration. Clouds started to gather. This was good news for the Ramones, artistically: they worked better when there was something to push against – but bad news for the individuals involved.

Their cartoon image was affecting the band, too.

"Once in Chicago, they threw bananas at us," Joey told Lester Bangs. "We picked 'em up and carried 'em home, so we had enough bananas to eat that day."

Cynth Sley, of early Eighties punk/funk dub group the Bush Tetras, saw the Ramones in Cleveland, January 16: "My roommate Barb and I had been playing the Ramones non-stop. She was going out with [film director] Jim Jarmusch long distance so we got all the cool NYC stuff when he came out to visit us. We were the only ones at the show not wearing flannel – and the only girls. I think the Cleveland crowd thought it was going to be a guy bar band. They were in shock and we were in heaven."

The pressures of touring were getting to Tommy. He'd never wanted to play drums in the first place. He only started because he was fed up with trying to explain his musical vision to self-serving fools. "It was hard on me," he says, "to be cooped up in a van and dressing rooms and hotel rooms. I felt I could be more productive behind the scenes. Also, I used to smoke at the time – and it used to annoy other people."

"Even though we were going well in Europe and England," Dee Dee recounted in *Poison Heart*, "life on the road with the Ramones was not an easy way to live. Johnny used to yell at everybody when he came off stage. When we returned to the States, we would go back to playing places at the same level as CBGBs. You couldn't win. Sometimes it seemed like people just came to the show to hate us and to look for a fight."

"Tommy didn't really leave," says Ed Stasium. "He was still involved in songwriting. He never considered himself a drummer. I do, his style is so influential to so many, but he wanted to get behind the console and produce."

The final show Tommy played with the Ramones took place on May 4 at CBGBs – a benefit for Dead Boys drummer Johnny Blitz who'd been stabbed in a street fight. Michael Sticca, roadie for the Dead Boys and

Blondie, got incarcerated in Rikers Island through the same incident.*

By that point, the Ramones – after considering various musicians including Sex Pistol Paul Cook, Blondie's Clem Burke and ex-Heartbreaker Jerry Nolan – had already lined up his replacement: Marc Bell, of Richard Hell's avant-soul Voidoids.

"Marky is the character that goes out in the backyard, plays, gets itself all muddy and dirty, comes into the living room and shakes itself out and gets everybody in the family and the furniture filthy," laughs Arturo Vega. "You wanna kill him but you don't – he's your pet, that's what pets do . . ."

MARKY RAMONE WAS born Marc Bell on July 15, 1956 in Brooklyn, New York – and grew up in Flatbush.

"Flatbush was a tough gang-related neighbourhood," the drummer says. "The greasers were still around when I was nine – figuring out if they were hippies or what. If you grew your hair a little long you were called a faggot or a queer, and I'd say, 'Go fuck yourself,' so I'd get into a lot of fights. You wear leather jacket, jeans, dungarees, that's all. What are you going to wear – glam pants and high heels? You'd get your ass kicked."

Marc is the son of a pro-union longshoreman (now a lawyer, having graduated from Brooklyn Law School), while his mother ran the Brooklyn College music library. As a youngster, he went on the 1963 UN civil rights march on Washington DC, and participated in several more with his liberal parents.

"There was always music around. When I was eight, my mother told me to come in and watch The Beatles on *Ed Sullivan* – that's what started me off wanting to play drums, Ringo. He kept the beat and had a good sound – that's the whole idea, keep it tight and put your drum fills where they belong. I loved Mitch Mitchell [Jimi Hendrix's drummer], too, and Buddy Rich. I can hold my sticks both ways, military and regular style."

Marc was young enough to be part of the Sixties generation, but he wasn't a hippie child – he liked The Beatles, Dave Clark Five, The Searchers, The Rolling Stones, The Kinks, The Who, Cream, and Led Zeppelin's first album.

It was at Erasmus High School that Marc recorded two albums with the

* The NYC scene's fondness for shock tactics nearly resulted in Blitz dying in hospital, according to *Please Kill Me*: "The doctors started working on Johnny immediately," Sticca recounted in the book. "But when the surgeon saw Johnny's swastika, he just stopped working on him. The surgeon was Jewish. A black doctor came over, and said, 'We can't stop doing this, man.' The black doctor saved Johnny's life."

teenage prog metal trio Dust. The two other members were Richie Wise, who produced the first two Kiss albums, and Kenny Aronsen, later to play with Joan Jett and Billy Idol.

"I was 16-years-old, dressed in leather jacket, jeans and bangs," Marky says. "You can see it on our sleeves. To this day, people ask if that's where the Ramones got their image. Johnny told me he came to see us in the Village, but I didn't know him then. You do wonder – those albums came out five years before *Ramones* did."

Dust broke up in 1972, and Marc started hanging around Nobody's on Bleeker St, a haunt of the New York Dolls. After the Dolls' original drummer Billy Murcia died of a drugs overdose, Marky tried out for the job – only to be beaten to it by Jerry Nolan. "I played 'Pills', 'Personality Crisis', and 'Trash'," he recalls. "I started doing all these crazy drum rolls and the idea was simply to keep the beat. That's why Jerry got it. He was five years older than me, but he was more in sync.

"What did I like about the New York Dolls?" He laughs. "I liked the fact we partied a lot. They had charisma and a style that was very New York. [Johnny] Thunders was a very cool guitar player, born July 15 like me, but four years earlier. They'd go down to Chinatown to get the stuff they liked – the connection. Jerry and Johnny would want me to walk with them. I would, but then I'd stop off at a bar and have a few drinks – I didn't want to get too involved. Dee Dee got into a situation with Richard Hell on the Lower East Side once, like a knife fight but they managed to escape it. I never did heroin, but it was a big thing back then."

The scene moved to Max's Kansas City – where artists like the Dolls, Teenage Lust, Kiss and the Harlots Of 42nd Street would get drunk in the back room. It was at Max's where Marc – with fake ID because he was so young – met transsexual Georgia rocker Wayne County with his baby doll negligee. He later joined his group, the Backstreet Boys.

"The best thing that happened when I was playing with Wayne County was when he kicked Dick Manitoba's ass in CBGBs," says Marky. Wayne/Jayne later attained further infamy with her self-explanatory titled single 'If You Don't Want To Fuck Me Baby, Fuck Off'. "Dick was gay-bashing him. So Wayne showed him who the real man was and sent him to the hospital."

"I met Joey in 1975 at CBGBs," the drummer reveals. "He was very emotional, very quiet – you could tell he was abused in his early life. I don't want to get into family matters, but I'm sure that happened at school – he used music as a way out. We would goof around together. Politically, he was a liberal. He couldn't stand Republicans. He was the opposite of

John, basically – maybe that's why we created all the great songs. We had those differences."

In the spring of '76, Richard Hell asked Marc if he wanted to join the Voidoids, best known for their epoch-defining 'Blank Generation' single (and Sire album): "I had no idea the song had something special, but it was embraced in NYC and London and LA – in fact, it was embraced more in New York than any Ramones song. I loved the words and I loved the moody chord changes. Richard started punk, with his ripped clothes and safety pins, not out of fashion but because he had no money. It would be a straight choice between cigarettes, food and clothes – among other things.

"We toured Europe with The Clash for six weeks in September 1977, and had a lot of fun with Joe and Mick and Topper, but Richard didn't like getting spat on. I didn't mind. I love England, that's where all my idols come from. The beer was great. The Indian restaurants were great. But when we got back home, Richard said he didn't want to tour any more."

One night in CBGBs, in December 1977, Dee Dee mentioned to Marc that Tommy was leaving the Ramones: so, if he ever wanted to join . . . "Dee Dee was a great drinking buddy," Marky reminisces. "I would never cop with him, but I'd smoke pot with him. He was like a bomb waiting to go off."

Marky was asked officially by Johnny to join the Ramones in March 1978, at Max's Kansas City. Also present were Johnny Thunders and girlfriend, and Marky's wife. The audition was held the next day in a studio on West 27th Street: the drummer played 'Sheena', 'Rockaway Beach' and 'I Don't Care'. Once in, Marky had three weeks to learn the set: 31 old numbers, and nine new songs. His first show was in Kansas City on June 29. A couple of nights later, the Ramones were chased by a gang of crowbar-wielding Grateful Dead fans, angry that da bruddas hadn't played for three hours. Tommy presented Marky with his white Rogers kit (as favoured by Dave Clark of the Dave Clark Five), which he used with Slingerland and Ludwig and Rogers snare drums. He later replaced that set with a Tama (as seen in the film *Rock'N'Roll High School*) and, after that, a Pearl.

"I'm playing so quick with the Ramones, I don't have time to whirl a stick," he exclaimed, describing his new style. "It wasn't hard to learn because I sat there with a drum kit, headphones and the tape on 10 hours each day. Tommy would sit behind me until I got it right, so I learnt the eighth-notes real quick – that's something a lot of punk drummers try to do, but can't. Heavy metal drummers usually play with their arms and shoulders. I play with my wrists and fingers."

ON MAY 31, the Ramones went back into Media Sound to start recording their fourth album – the first to go all out for the elusive American hit single. But how could it succeed where such radio-friendly songs as 'Sheena' and 'Rockaway Beach' and 'Blitzkrieg Bop' had failed? That was the big question.

"Tommy and the boys decided they needed to make a record that had commercial appeal," says Ed Stasium. Either that, or pressure was being exerted from above: it was time the Ramones started repaying Sire's faith in them with sales. "We came to a decision that Tommy and I would try different bass and guitar parts – keep what the Ramones were, but appeal to a broader audience."

"It was difficult to know how to market the Ramones," admits their Sire PR Janis Schacht, who left the company in January 1979. "When we had The Paley Brothers,* we were able to create a teen market for them, the same way you'd do in the early Sixties, by putting them in teen magazines, and on the Shaun Cassidy show at Madison Square Garden. We couldn't do that with the Ramones. Even early on, though, we knew they'd appeal more to some markets – 50 per cent of our mail came from Japan, this one girl would send the most amazing cartoons . . .

"But the Ramones were so critic-orientated," she sighs. "It's hard when a band is on the road and there are no records in the stores, as was the case when ABC distributed Sire."

The 12 songs on *Road To Ruin* took over three months to produce, and was the first Ramones album to break the half-hour barrier – by 61 seconds.

"We had a bigger budget, we knew what we were doing, and we had a new drummer with a different style," explains Tommy Erdelyi. "Marky was a professional drummer. He has a powerful dynamic sound. We were able to make real good use of that. I was free to shape the sounds, and be in control."

"We made a conscious effort to get songs over the two-minute mark," explained Johnny. "It was very hard to continue writing 14 songs an album. Everybody else has eight."

* The Paley Brothers were pop contemporaries of Ramones from Boston, who'd earlier in the year recorded a cover of Richie Valens' 'C'Mon Let's Go' with them at The Beach Boys' Brother Studio in Santa Monica when Joey was sick in hospital with asthma. Andy and Jonathan sang lead vocals. "I was very impressed at the complete utter preparedness and swiftness of the Ramones," says producer David Kessel. "They were 100 per cent professional. It was like the troops hitting the beach." 'C'Mon Let's Go' was the last Ramones record Tommy played drums on, and ended up being played on *Rock'N'Roll High School* as the credits rolled at the film's end.

There was a diner down the stairs where the Ramones would order takeaways: burgers, fries, Hero subs, Chinese . . .

"I put on a lot of weight eating that garbage," Erdelyi complains. "You sit behind a console for 12-14 hours a day. It's not healthy. I would go out and watch some cable TV, but mostly I worked." The basic tracks took two days to record with two or three takes: no guide vocals. That wasn't a problem because, as Tommy explains, "We rehearsed like that because Joey wanted to save his voice. We spent a little more time recording the vocals – with each album, that time increased. My guess would be three to four days."

There had been acoustic guitars on *Rocket To Russia* – 'Locket Love', 'I Can't Give You Anything', 'Why Is It Always This Way?'; Johnny at one point instructing Stasium to make him sound more like Steve Miller – but on *Road To Ruin*, their use became blatant, especially on the heart-rending take on The Searchers' 'Needles And Pins', 'Questioningly', and the first single off the album, Dee Dee's disturbing love song, 'Don't Come Close'.

'Don't Come Close' was disliked by many Ramones fans, including Johnny himself: "Johnny hated that song," laughs Stasium. Their annoyance is easy to understand: Jesus, a country and western song sung by that gawky kid with the queer voice from Queens, appearing on an album by the notorious American punks . . . how ya goin' to sell that one? As Legs McNeil points out in the reissue's booklet, "It echoed the desperation of the situation. If you have any doubt how panicked the record companies were by punk, remember that Seymour Stein would place advertisements in trade magazines demanding, 'Don't Call It Punk, Call It New Wave'."

Yet it's a great track, as fine (and also hated) as the soulful 'Questioningly' (a song that doesn't sound out of place on a mix tape next to The Bee Gees' 'Massachusetts'). 'Questioningly' was one of the earliest songs Dee Dee ever wrote (on a folk guitar). The imagery of loneliness in Manhattan, with its whisky-soaked TV movies and choked-down memories of former lovers, is so evocative: "In the morning/I'm at work on time/My boss tells me/That I'm doing fine".

'Needles And Pins', meanwhile, is pure heartache. A cover of the Sonny Bono/Jack Nitzsche tune, it beautifully suited the overall downbeat mood of the album – even though the song was first cut for *Rocket To Russia*.

"I helped Joey with the lyrics to 'Needles And Pins'," reveals Schacht. "We were sitting by the pool at the Hotel Tropicana in LA. It was three in the morning, and Joey was desperately inebriated and worried that he'd be found out – the Ramones were fined if they were caught drunk on the road. It was sort of a theme, researching songs in hotels. I can remember throwing batteries into the pool as Joey studied the words to 'Surfin' Bird'. It's not exactly a difficult song to learn."

The fact that 'Don't Come Close' was followed up as a US single by 'Needles And Pins' can only have helped to alienate sections of the Ramones' fan base. People were worried they'd "do a Status Quo", and turn their back on the hard rock that had become synonymous with their sound, favouring stadium-filling soft rock ballads instead.

This is probably where the great split came in – some Ramones fans appreciated the versatility of Joey's voice, and figured the Ramones' forte lay in releasing great pop-punk singles in the tradition of Spector and The Beach Boys, and the Sixties groups. Then there were those who, like Johnny, felt the Ramones had a unique sound – and should stick with it.

In the UK, the follow-up single was far more recognisably Ramones. With its surf harmonies and fast guitars, 'She's The One' was a minor hit. It sounds effortless, the sort of song everybody imagines bands can toss off in a couple of minutes and few rarely do. Of its time, it's an equal to the pop thrills with which both The Undertones and Buzzcocks (two bands inspired by the Ramones) were constantly hitting the British charts, and shouldn't be undervalued.

The album's opener, 'I Just Want To Have Something To Do', meanwhile, begins with an evocative image of "Hanging out on Second Avenue/Eating chicken vindaloo" and ably captures the age-old frustration of being a youth with pent-up energy and nowhere to take it: shards of guitar and feedback ricochet past your ear as the song builds up inexorably. The band's frustration at their situation was beginning to show – and this feeling continues in Dee Dee's paean to his fucked-up childhood, 'I Wanted Everything'. The title is in the past tense: the Ramones seem aware that certain of life's illusions have already passed them by. The sad tale of betrayal, 'I Don't Want You', has a similar edge.

Next to these three songs, the cartoon lines in 'I'm Against It' about hating Jesus freaks and circus geeks, Burger King and anything – sound plain retarded. That's stupid as in stupid stupid, not clever stupid. The Ramones were fast outstripping their early roots; and the honesty of songs like 'Questioningly' and 'I Don't Want You' rang even truer when put next to throwaway – if slightly worrying – odes to insanity like 'Go Mental' and 'Bad Brain' (both fine songs to jump up and down to, however).

" 'Go Mental'," wrote Lester Bangs in *NME*, "celebrates escape from pervasive misery through psychotic regression and murder resulting in a rubbery barbiturate catatonia staring at a goldfish bowl." He was probably on drugs.

'It's A Long Way Back' closes out the record in disturbing fashion – a song about Germany, written by Dee Dee, the pull of his soul's distance from his homeland all the more redolent because he, more than most, was aware of what The Shangri-Las meant when they sang 'I Can Never Go Home Anymore'.

"Me and Tommy played on all those songs, absolutely all of them," Stasium states firmly. "There was no reason we should have been credited – us studio rats don't care about that. Johnny would come in every day to hear what we did. He'd say, 'Eddy, you and Tommy finish that stuff up, put some good guitars on, and I'll come and listen to it when you're finished.'

"Johnny is a specialist guitar player," the producer continues. "Nobody in the world can do what he does – but the Ramones wanted to augment what was there, and he didn't feel he wanted to do, or was capable of doing, these things. For example, the way 'I Wanna Be Sedated' was double-tracked with my Stratocaster."

'Sedated' is a solid-state Ramones classic – memorable, funny, with all the elements that go to make up the Ramones archetype: the eighth notes on the cymbal, the chugging guitars, the background harmonies and the lyrics.

"My 10-year-old nephew knows that song," laughs Stasium.

Aside from the "exploding kettle" incident, another inspiration for 'Sedated' came from being cooped up in a tiny tour van for hours on end: "It came out of something Dee Dee said," Joey told me, "about feeling like he was in a space capsule. That, and the way England was all closed down over Christmas when we were there."

"We spent a little time making 'Sedated' more produced," Tommy says. "We were trying to get a single. Which was bittersweet, because we knew it wasn't going to get played with the word 'sedated' in it."

Is it true that you and Ed played the extra guitar parts on *Road To Ruin*?

"Yes," the musician sighs, "but I don't know if John wants that in print. He's sensitive about that. It doesn't really matter, anyway. They're Ramones songs because they're written by the Ramones, done by the Ramones – but they're an extension because they don't have the Ramones sound. It's still the Ramones, though."

"People liked *Road To Ruin*," Stasium insists in the *Anthology* booklet. "I was talking to Slash of Guns N' Roses once, and he was like, 'Dude, that's the best record ever. I learned how to play guitar by listening to *Road To Ruin*."

THERE WERE A COUPLE of songs recorded during the *Road To Ruin* sessions that weren't released at the time – 'I Walk Out', and 'Slug', a Fifties/Sixties-style pop anthem with a memorable "S-L-U-G" hook. 'Slug' got left off the album because, as Johnny explained to *Zigzag*, "we're trying to get away from that oldies sound". Significantly, Joey's forte was the "oldies" sound.

The song initially appeared as a computer programme in *K-Power*, a children's magazine edited by John Holmstrom that appeared when home computers first hit the market.

"It was aimed at kids," recalls Holmstrom. "We had a lot of teenage hackers in the office, hanging out, reviewing computer games, causing problems. They wanted to do a music issue – so Chris [Frantz] and Tina [Weymouth, both from Talking Heads] reviewed a lot of stuff, and Joey allowed us to use 'Slug'. There wasn't much computer software around back then, so the magazine would print the code. The Atari version of 'Slug' was the best because the program made a little dancing worm that would crawl across the screen to the music. I made my one and only appearance on MTV to talk about it."

"[My brother] Dan and I added piano on 'Slug'," recalls David Kessel, shortly to work on the *End Of The Century* sessions. "You can hear some extra percussion, and both of us sang on the background vocals. Joey really liked the song, but the rest of the guys seemed unsure."

THE PRESS DIDN'T know what to make of *Road To Ruin* when it appeared. Some took the presence of songs like 'Questioningly' and 'Don't Come Close' as an indication that punk was, indeed, dead.*

Others were more positive. *NME* made 'She's The One' Single Of The Week, while managing to avoid describing it; *Village Voice*'s Tom Carson suggested that "what was once a one-joke dead-end is now an endless vista"; Kurt Loder, in *Circus*, called the album a "graceful and good-natured holding action".

"The guitar breaks bring tears to my eyes," wrote another *Village Voice* critic (without sarcasm – he was being favourable).

* The cry "punk is dead" went up almost as soon as the movement began, and fresh claims occurred every week until around about the start of 1979 when, with Sid Vicious physically dead and the Pistols split up, The Clash making dub-based records and the Ramones releasing country-tinged singles, it was deemed official. This, of course, meant it was merely starting. As Holmstrom pointed out in an interview with George Tabb, "When *Punk* went out of business in 1979, we'd never had better sales, but all those idiot trendies kept insisting that it was over with, and the next thing you know, everybody was playing disco music."

In *Trouser Press*, however, Scott Isler really went to town: "By rejecting the role of new wave idiots savant, they've become (just) another loud rock band," he wrote, after laying into the "amoral morality tales" of songs like 'I Wanted Everything' and "flatly normal romanticism" of 'Don't Come Close'. "We expect triteness from the Ramones, but not mundanity."

His last line cut to the chase: "What the Ramones need is time to figure out who they want to be now that they don't want to be the Ramones."

"It's our *Berlin*," Joey told Lester Bangs – referring to Lou Reed's equally downbeat and mistrusted (and now generally accepted to be classic) album.

Bangs wanted to know if the group had been feeling frustrated at the lack of mass acceptance. "Well, it's been steady but slow," Johnny demurred. "But when you see groups just pop up doin' what everybody else had been doin' and become big all of a sudden, when we feel that we're one of the few groups doing something original . . ."

He let the sentence trail off.

"I don't feel desperate, not yet," the guitarist added, "although I don't feel like waiting another two years to get big."

"I guess everyone is on the verge of a breakdown," he said elsewhere. "You're on a thin line, and sometimes you start falling over. We're hanging on."

"*Road To Ruin* is probably my favourite Ramones album," says George Tabb, "just because it's got all that power, plus you hear acoustic guitars in there. It's beautiful. It's complete balls-to-the-wall rock'n'roll. All the Ramones albums were great, but *Road To Ruin* especially has a brightness that I've studied for years and tried to copy. I asked John about this – 'How did you get it to sound so . . .?' – and he says just one word. 'Tommy'."

THE SUPPORT FOR the August 21 Ramones show in New Haven were a bunch of teenagers from New Jersey called Shrapnel. Shrapnel were a glam pop-metal band whose gimmick was to dress up in army gear, and bring out a cardboard tank at the set's climax. They were managed by *Punk*'s resident punk Legs McNeil, and notably featured Dave Wyndorf (vocals - later to form the blistering Monster Magnet, a heavy NYC grunge act) and future Ramones songwriting partner Daniel Rey (guitar).

"Legs wasn't that great a manager," laughs Daniel, "but he was great to hang out with. He did teach us some vital stuff, though – like how to get in free to clubs and get free beer, and how to throw parties."

The Ramones were in reasonably buoyant mood through 1978, downbeat albums notwithstanding – at least in public: "It's building," Johnny told *Zigzag*'s Kris Needs. "Finally we can work the whole country.

Before, we couldn't get jobs [gigs – that was Johnny's term for them] in the South."

"We saw swamps," said Dee Dee, excited, "and we went into this shack to eat, an old shack – Southern fried chicken!"

In September and October, the band returned to tour Europe and the UK. It was on September 7, the day of the Stockholm show, that the Ramones discovered one of their biggest heroes, Keith Moon, had died.

"When I found out Keith Moon died, it really killed me because I loved him," recalls Marky. "I loved his maniac crazy drumming, I loved him as a nut job, but a funny nut job – too bad that he drank too much and died. But he made me smile, and wonder what in the hell he was doing – that's what I wanted to get over, the energy and the response from the people back to me. Of course, from the other Ramones too – it's not my band, it's the Ramones."

By this time, the Ramones were consummate professionals. No drink or drugs before shows (road crew included), no unclothed groupies in the luggage racks – as Kris Needs and Colin Keinch wrote in another *Zigzag* article, "This band prefers to watch TV rather than chuck it out of the hotel room window." In Hammersmith, both Dee Dee and Johnny had their other halves present (Vera and Roxy, respectively). The *Zigzag* writers commented on the rather haphazard way the UK dates had been booked: "Whoever planned this tour must have got a map of Britain and thrown darts in it blindfold," they sarcastically wrote. "We're surprised Penzance wasn't slotted in after Glasgow."

Johnny and Dee Dee were reported as retiring early (probably because their partners were present), but Marky and Joey were willing to sit up late and drink in hotel bars, rearrange the plastic letters on hotel notice-boards (Joey) and stagger round, trousers accidentally opened (Marky). "There are no outward signs of internal strife," the pair stated. "They rely on each other to get through the pressures. Close, real close."

In Dublin and Belfast, *Sounds* journalist Dave McCullough failed to be impressed by the "mock threats" of the live show, writing, "Cosiness is creeping into their music like a fat rouged peroxide Middle-West stage mother at last pushing her beautiful offspring into dire B-movies," despite admitting that the kids went "bonkers". He did, however, praise Joey's voice during the Dublin soundcheck, after hearing his rendition of 'Needles And Pins' – "I'll bet he's never used [that voice] on stage, bending and curving notes in fully fledged crooner fashion." McCullough took the slower songs on *Road To Ruin* as a sign the band was feeling disillusioned and that jadedness was creeping in . . .

"You think so?" asked Dee Dee, astonished. "We're in show business. The lyrics just reflect what's going on with us. Maybe you're right . . ."

Johnny insisted to McCullough that it was easy to get into the American Top 10, and when the writer pointed out that the Ramones hadn't exactly made any sizeable dents yet, Johnny replied "Aw, it's the radio programming. We're as big as most bands over there." What? McCullough replied, astonished. Like Boston, Styx, Foreigner?

If the Ramones stood any chance of US airplay, it evaporated after October 13, the day Nancy Spungen died at the Chelsea Hotel – with her boyfriend Sid Vicious, ex-bassist of the Sex Pistols, accused of murdering her. Sid was incarcerated in Rikers Island, where $50,000 bail was posted for him. Shortly afterwards, Sid was sent back to jail after he attacked Patti Smith's brother, Todd, with a broken Heineken bottle in Hurrah's nightclub. These tragic events followed a disastrous tour of the States in January where Sid's band had imploded, and left a trail of bitterness and recriminations that lasts even to the present day. If the American media thought punk was disgusting before, then it was beyond the pale now. A couple of catchy, country-tinged Ramones singles weren't going to alter that fact.

"We've had a lot of job rejections," Johnny told *Rolling Stone* journalist Timothy White in an article that appeared in February 1979, the same month Sid Vicious was found dead in a Greenwich Village apartment, from an apparent heroin overdose. "We had a lot of radio stations taking us off and rejecting us. We had a job offer at Notre Dame with Foreigner, and Notre Dame turned us down. We got pulled off stations after the *Weekend* show with the Sex Pistols. It had nothing to do with us. We don't look or act like them. We weren't out to ruin the music business. There's room for everybody."

Everybody, except for the Ramones, it seemed.

WHO WAS THE pinhead? Would it be one regular person?

"It was the drum roadie. I was the first pinhead. The mask was made for the movie. We were in San Francisco [December 28, 1978, with The Tubes] doing this outdoor show at the Civic Centre in the middle of the day. I had nothing to do – there were no lights – so I decided to put on the mask and kick and wave at the crowds.

"The pinhead in the movie was a friend called David Moon, who ended up doing the merchandising. Later on we would have guest stars, like during the last tour, at Lollapalooza, Lars from Rancid."

(Author's interview with Arturo Vega, lighting manager)

11

Touring, Part 2

"LIKE THE SONG says, 'Touring touring was never boring'. Uh, it was great. It was their bread and butter. It's what made them survive. The fact their live shows were so successful, and the audiences were so exciting, was very important."

What was it was like to travel with them in the bus?

"They didn't travel in a bus. They travelled in a van. Monte would drive."

Did he always drive?

"Yes. If it were going to be an extremely long drive, Johnny would drive as well. He was the only one that drove as well. Otherwise, he'd sit in the passenger seat next to the driver – but the first row would be his whenever he wanted to lie down. And then the next row was, I think it was Dee Dee, then it was Joey, and then Marky. I used to travel with them a lot. Very often, I would sit down with Joey, or Johnny wouldn't lie down in his rows and somebody else would sit there, and I would take a row. And uh, they had a ritual, about going to a 7–11 after every show."

Really?

"Even if it was just going back to the hotel, they would stop at a 7–11. To get cookies, milk, something for the hotel room. And it was cordial; it was always nice, you know. I enjoyed it."

What kind of diners would you eat at?

"It depends on what part of the country you are in. A big favourite toward the end was Cracker Barrel in the south. If not that, it would be McDonald's or Burger King. Sometimes, there'd be little shops or convenience stores that had some specialty. We also liked the big truck stops in Texas where they had video games and a big store – that was like being in an amusement park, especially at the beginning that was a thrill."

Did any of them have special dietary requirements – like in the Nineties, when Joey was eating more healthily?

"That was only at the very end. For a while, he would have a big steak before the show – before he stopped eating meat completely. They always had pizza before the show. They would have hamburgers. They would have fish. There was no big predilection for anything, except the tacos. When we'd stop in LA on the way back from Hawaii or Japan, and we had a couple of hours to kill, everybody would want to go to a taco place."

What, Taco Bell?

"No, real tacos, little ones. So we would only do it when we were in California or New Mexico, Arizona. Not Taco Bell. That was not a favourite at all."

Were there any kind of rituals that the band would do before they got on stage?

"Joey had his throat-warming exercises. He did that all the time – the warming-up, the steaming, the drinking of the tea."

What, herbal tea?

"Yeah, with honey and lemon, that kind of thing. The only ritual was the pizza, right before the show, and then we'd warm up in the dressing room. Johnny with a guitar, and Marky with a little set of padded drums . . ."

How many songs would they do?

"A good amount – four or six."

Would it always be the same songs?

"No. It would be whatever facilitated things for them to start playing. Uh, but pizza was the only ritual before show time – just plain cheese, the round ones, nothing extra. They'd always ask for it on the rider, and be very upset if it wasn't there."

(Author's interview with Arturo Vega, lighting manager)

12

Mutant Monster Movie Mayhem

ON AUGUST 11–13, 1978, over the course of three nights at Hurrah's, NYC, the Ramones auditioned for film director Allan Arkush.

Arkush was a protégé of the King of the B-movies, Roger Corman – the man who'd brought motorbikes, young nurses and women in chains to the drive-in, the man responsible for *Death Race 2000*, *Little Shop Of Horrors* and *Psych-Out*, the definitive 1968 Hollywood flower-power exploitation flick, complete with The Seeds, Strawberry Alarm Clock and Dean Stockwell in headband. Producer Corman had shot over 200 films, and had as fine a grasp on disposable pop culture as any. Johnny Ramone was a fan. "I like his movies," the guitarist said. "They got a lot of violence and action."

Growing up in Fort Lee, New Jersey, Arkush daydreamed in class – about having go-kart races in the hallways, blowing up the school and having The Yardbirds come over and play. Fleshing out his dreams, he and future *Gremlins* director Joe Dante came up with a treatment for a movie called *Heavy Metal Kids* [after the Todd Rundgren song] for possible production by Corman's New World Pictures. Corman wasn't too impressed – it was 1978, disco was happening, and he much preferred the idea of nude cheerleaders bouncing around a gym to the strains of Donna Summer.

Arkush was undeterred. The filmmaker wasn't much of a punk fan, but he had seen the [ironically enough] Roger Corman-inspired *Mutant Monster Beach Party* photo-spread in *Punk* magazine, starring Joey Ramone and Debbie Harry. Still working on his rock film treatment – now re-titled *Rock'N'Roll High School* and pitched somewhere between the classic Fifties Jayne Mansfield rock'n'roll film *The Girl Can't Help It*, Jerry Lee Lewis' *High School Confidential* and *Freaks* – he flew to New York to see the Ramones.

"Auditioned?" exclaims Marky, incredulous at the idea. "No, he knew us. Well, first he wanted Cheap Trick and they said no. [The Who-influenced power pop band were probably too expensive for a film eventually made for $300,000 in three weeks flat.] Then we said 'yes' and he wanted us immediately. Our image was more suitable for the high school thing."

"I knew [Cheap Trick's] *Live At Budokan* would be a big record," Arkush stated, "but Roger didn't get it. Then I had to tell him that the Ramones weren't a disco band, and that it had to work out of frustration and anger – not people with money. It was about how rock music functions in every teenager's fantasy life."

"Allan Arkush told me that Corman wanted to know who the Ramones were, and why should they be in the movie," Holmstrom recalls. "So Allan showed him a copy of *Beach Party* and that was the end of the discussion."

On November 26, the Ramones cut two songs in a single day with Ed Stasium for inclusion in the movie – the first, the title track, written by Joey as an affectionate parody of Sixties beach-flicks and still one of the catchiest Ramones songs around. The second was the tearjerker 'I Want You Around', perfect for a film supposed to encapsulate teen angst. Legendary Sixties girl group producer Phil Spector later remixed both tracks.

Filming began in December, at a deserted Los Angeles Catholic school in Watts: "The high school depicted was patterned after my own real life high school," Arkush told *NME* in 1979, "which in turn was probably patterned after the Gulag Archipelago: no jeans, no sandals, no rock'n'roll music, no long hair and absolutely no dissent."

Rock'N'Roll High School was faithful to the oldest portrayal of rock in film, as a tool of teen liberation. "When you get out of here," declares heroine, cheerleader-type Riff Randle, played by PJ Soles (*Carrie*, *Halloween*) with perky alacrity, "nobody's even gonna remember you went to high school, much less whether or not you skipped a few classes."

The movie was low rent social satire: from the Ramones-hating authoritarian principal of Vince Lombardi High School, Miss Togar [played by former Warhol Factory actress Mary Woronov], who discovers that mice explode when exposed to rock music above a certain volume, to the finale where the entire school blows up. "It was so real," shudders Marky. "I felt the heat, plus we were all wearing our jackets – and it was 80 degrees anyway." All this, because Ramones Number One fan Randle is banned from seeing her favourite band.

Joey explained the plot to *NME*'s Philippe Garnier on set: "There's this bunch of kids in their high school, they're all fans of the Ramones and they use the Ramones to sorta . . . rebel against the authorities. But like, there's a lot of gags, y'know, like in front of the ticket-line there's gonna be this Indian, and someone asks him what the hell he's doing here, and the Injun says, 'I'm a scalper' . . . y'know, kinda dumb, but it's funny . . ."

Basically, the film is diverting fluff, indistinguishable from a thousand others, except for one crucial difference. It features the Ramones.

And there are some great Ramones moments . . .

The scene where the band engage in their pre-show ritual of eating pizza, and Dee Dee utters the immortal line, "Hey pizza!" ("The whole movie was like a goof," sighs Linda Stein, "and they hated making it. Dee Dee had one line to say, and he couldn't get that right. They must have retook that scene 30 or 40 times, but it was beyond him.")

The scene where Joey serenades Riff in her dreams, to the strains of 'I Want You Around'. (Riff pulls back the shower curtain to discover Dee Dee playing bass – the bassist was known for taking four showers a day.)

The scene where Joey tears into a leg of chicken and throws it away while singing "Eating chicken vindaloo" from 'I Just Want To Have Something To Do'.

The scene where Principal Togar asks, "Do your parents know you're Ramones?"

The scene where the hip science teacher (Paul Bartel) remarks, "People say that your music is loud and destructive and lethal to mice, but I think you're the Beethovens of our time."

The scene where the Ramones draw up outside The Roxy in a pink Cadillac driven by DJ and friend Rodney Bingenheimer, and walk down the street, playing their instruments. You can see real tour manager Monte Melnick in the shot, walking behind the band, talking to the fake manager. ("Johnny hated that scene," Linda remarks. "He couldn't understand the concept of lip-syncing. Something like that wouldn't even be discussed. They were extremely pure.")

"We filmed some scenes in the Whiskey, upstairs in the dressing room," says Rodney. "There's a poster of Cherie Currie on the wall that I donated. [Seminal LA punk band] The Germs were there."

"Every time we went down to the school," Marky recalls, "there would be fans giving me and Dee Dee pot, throwing bottles of beer over the fence. We'd be out till five in the morning, and have to get up at eight. Most of that movie, me and Dee Dee were high on Quaaludes and hung over from the night before."

Dee Dee got arrested while staying at the Tropicana, but *en route* to the jail he slipped into a coma, and was rushed to hospital to have his stomach pumped. "We were flat broke at the time," he commented. "I only had enough money to buy two damn Tuinals and a beer every day."

Although it was fun, and a blast, and a great opportunity for the fans to see Ramones in concert – albeit with the sound out of sync with the visuals, and the annoying spectacle of Riff Randle and her friends bouncing up and down in between numbers, looking about as far away from the Ramones uniform of sneakers and ripped jeans as it was possible to get with their blow-dried LA hair – the film did da bruddas a great disservice. Corman's films appealed to the lowest, trashiest denominator – and the script called for a band that was D-U-M-B. Ramones played the part to perfection, tearing into pizza, grunting in monosyllables and looking all surly and mean. It helped reinforce the stereotype.

Not that those in the band saw it that way.

"Johnny was not smiling," recalls Linda, "but he was smart enough to know what a great opportunity the whole thing was – and it was. We'd sit around this extremely elegant coffee shop called Duke's, downstairs at the Tropicana [where Andy Warhol shot *Heat*]. We thought we were going to be huge."

"I went to see *Rock'N'Roll High School* with Joey seven or eight times," says Janis Schacht. "When you look at him in 'I Want You Around', it was so him. The rest of them were doing what they were told, but he took that moment and gave a true picture of himself. Sweet, sexy . . . I thought he was ugly when we first met – I called him Godzilla – but within a year he was the sexiest man around."

Corman wasn't happy with the resulting film – he thought it cost too much, and didn't understand why the Ramones featured so prominently. *Rock'N'Roll High School* was released in April '79 in the US and failed to make an impact, probably because it was awful – patchy distribution not helping. The acting is wooden, the cast lame, the dialogue forgettable. Chicago took to it, though: after a favourable review from local critics, and an inspired billing that saw the film paired with *Grease* and *Dawn Of The Dead*. The film came out in the UK, January 1980, to tie in with the release of *End Of The Century*.

The soundtrack record was also lacklustre: the aforementioned Ramones tracks and Paley Brothers collaboration, plus a fine medley of Ramones songs live (including 'She's The One'), filled out with the usual generic numbers that had little to do with the film – Brownsville Station's 'Smoking In The Boys Room', Alice Cooper's 'School's Out' (again!), Chuck Berry, Eno . . . The one song of note is an appalling rendition of the title track by PJ Soles, so bad it's brilliant. The cover was a *Mad*-style cartoon drawn by WM Stout – when every Ramones fan knew Holmstrom was the only man alive for the job.

Paul Rambali was spot on in his *NME* review: "If *Rock'N'Roll High*

School was the cinematic equivalent of the Ramones, it would be a smart film disguised as a dumb film and dedicated to the three 'r's. That's right: fun, noise and delinquency. As it is, it's a silly film that tries to be a dumb film. It plays like a feature-length episode of *The Monkees* starring the Ramones."

The video to the single of 'Rock'N'Roll High School', released in 1979, showing the Ramones goofing around in a classroom, was one of the first to be played on the fledgling MTV, when the station started in 1982. Not that it helped sales.

"Do you realise how boring it is to make a movie?" asks Monte. "It's really boring. You sit around for hours while they do the scene. Then you sit around for another couple of hours while they set up the next scene. And it's extreme boredom between. It was kinda interesting watching the whole thing, though."

HOW WAS JOEY to live with?

"Great. You know what? In all the years I knew Joey, we never had one disagreement, not one. Both Johnny and Joey's mother said the same thing to me, you know? 'Boy, you knew another Joey than the rest of us.' They thought I idolised him too much – but I never had a problem with him at all. Joey loved being with people that he appreciated or that he felt appreciated him. I'm not saying he was perfect – far from it – and I saw him being mean to other people. It just never happened with me."

Yeah, I understand. What would you do when you were hanging out?

"We used to watch a lot of TV."

What kind of TV did he prefer?

"Well, for instance when we were in California, when we were making Rock'N'Roll High School, *and he wrote 'Hanging out in 100B, watching* Get Smart *on TV' ['Danny Says']. 100B was our room. Sometimes Joey and I used to share rooms, sometimes Joey, Dee Dee and I, depends what kind of a day we were having. We'd watch comedies."*

What is Get Smart*?*

*"*Get Smart *is that show with the crazy detective (Don Adams as Maxwell Smart) who has a telephone in his shoe – that movie [*Inspector Gadget*] is based on . . ."*

Oh yeah, I know what it is. Did you watch cartoons?

"Yes we did. We didn't have a favourite. We liked them all. It was all fun."

What other stuff would you do apart from watching TV?

"We'd go out and play games – pinball, he liked that a lot."

(Author's interview with Arturo Vega)

AN ARTICLE THAT appeared in *Rolling Stone* in February 1979 gave a fair indication that cracks in the band, brought on by four (five) unsuccessful albums and three years of constant touring, were beginning to show.

"I'm sick of not selling records," Joey muttered as journalist Timothy White watched him peer into the mirror in a cramped dressing room at Philadelphia's Walnut Street Theater. "I want to draw more people to the shows, make something happen. If the new album isn't a hit, I'm gonna kill myself."

Fresh from their European tour of October '78, the Ramones were on the road in the States again to promote *Road To Ruin*. Despite worldwide sales of 250,000, it had failed to reach the US Top 50.

"Anything new is discouraged," Joey told *The Face* bitterly in 1980. The fact that the Ramones were hardly new at this point had clearly escaped the singer. "It's like a big brainwashing process, heavy metal crap and Olivia Newton John. Anything with no feeling involved. If it's spineless it gets played."

White reported that, post-Tommy, Johnny appeared to have taken on the role of group leader – leading the band through an impromptu pre-concert discussion on timing and pacing, stopping off briefly to berate Danny Fields for not ensuring there were posters of the band outside the theatre, and to enquire after record sales in secondary markets.

"Watch the beginning of 'Cretin Hop' tonight," he scolded Marky. "You came in wrong again last night. You're just not hearing it."

"OK," Marky said meekly. "Tell it all to me again."

"No, we'll *play* it once quickly," Johnny ruled as he plugged his white Mosrite guitar into a small practice amp.

Later, White saw Joey whisper urgently to Linda Stein, who immediately instructed everyone to leave the dressing room: "Excuse me everybody!" she boomed. "Please clear the room! Joey wishes to be alone to wash his face!"

The Ramones toured North America constantly, slogging it out: "Getting in the van with them in '79," says Janis Schacht, "must have been the same as travelling with The Troggs. There was a real Ronnie versus Reg thing happening with Joey and Johnny [Schacht is referring to a famous Troggs session tape wherein every petty disagreement between the English band was exposed]. I stopped going to see them after 1980. Once they started setting off the explosions and jumping off the amps I lost interest. The feeling had gone. They reached a point where Joey would sing two words a line, otherwise he couldn't keep up."

The Ramones played their last show at CBGBs on April 10 – a benefit for the NYC Police Department, to go towards buying bullet-proof vests.

Another time, John Holmstrom opened for the Ramones with his own unique Cartoon Concert. "It was like a Ramones cartoon rock video," the illustrator reveals. "I would show slides of cartoons, and do the voices of the characters. I cut it down to 15 minutes. I didn't want to bore anybody. I would do 'I Wanna Be Sedated' and have pictures of people going nuts. It was very traumatic for me."

Joey started to namecheck newer bands in interviews – not London Ramones-influenced bands like Erazorhead [precursors of the Eighties psychobilly scene] or punk deadbeats Manic Esso's Lurkers [who made the Ramones sound intellectual with songs like 'Just 13' and 'Suzie Is A Floozie' – oddly, they now have a distinct retro charm]. The bands Joey mentioned contained friends, relatives – Shrapnel, managed by Legs McNeil, and The Rattlers [his brother Mickey's band: Joey sang background vocals on one of their records].

While Joey liked his music and his alcohol, Johnny liked being the boss and Dee Dee liked his drugs, it was the newest member who would frequently get into scrapes – both on the road, and off. It wasn't always his fault, though.

"Sting [The Police's sanctimonious, smug singer] came up to me once," the drummer recalls, "and he was like, 'Where do you get those leather jackets from? Woolworths?'

"That's like a Walmarts in America," he explains. "He was goofing on me because he knew it would affect me. So I looked at him, and said, 'What's the matter, didn't you get your fish and chips today?' He looked stunned, so I said, 'Thank God for Bob Marley because without Marley you wouldn't exist.' He was shocked I came back so fast. We had to get used to a lot of ribbing because we were doing something unique that people didn't understand, the only way they could cope was to put us down."

13

Touring, Part 3

"JOHNNY WAS THE ONE that looked into the business side of things."

OK – so Johnny would organise the riders?

"Johnny wouldn't want the promoters to spend money on anything superfluous."

I can see that.

"Promoters were afraid of John because they knew that he wouldn't let them get away with anything as far as the band being cheated out of something. John would demand to see numbers on everything. But at the same time he wouldn't want them to spend money unnecessarily."

He kept a record of everything, didn't he?

"Everything. He had a little black book where he would write everything about people and how much they had been paid. So the rider didn't have anything unnecessary, anything that wasn't going to be consumed that night."

Were there a standard number of encores each night?

"Yes – two encores, two songs on each encore."

OK.

"That was the standard procedure. Rarely they would go beyond that – they would sometimes, but very rarely."

What about the sets? Presumably it would be the same set on each tour?

"The set didn't change very much at all. There were probably a couple of songs that were performed on every single one of the 2,263 shows."

They would have done something like 'Pinhead' . . .

"You know – 'Blitzkrieg Bop', 'Pinhead', 'Today Your Love . . .' was always there. Whenever a new album came out, they would play three, four at the most. It was mostly three songs from the new album, and that was it. They knew. There was a reason why their live shows were so successful – because people got what they wanted."

Yeah, I can totally see Johnny being really practical about it and saying, "Look – people aren't coming along to hear the new album."

"It worked with some bands, but not the Ramones. The set didn't change very much."

(Author's interview with Arturo Vega, lighting manager)

14

C'mon, Let's Rock'n'Roll With The Ramones . . .

For some fans – and Joey, almost certainly – the Ramones' fifth album, the Phil Spector-produced *End Of The Century,* was the zenith of their career. The Wall Of Noise meets The Wall Of Sound.

To others – Johnny, definitely – it was the beginning of . . . if not the end, then a series of bleak years where the group wandered directionless through half-hearted album after half-hearted album, until managing to regroup at the end of the Eighties and recapture an audience that stayed faithful for as long as the Ramones could race through the songs on stage. Of course, the fact that the Ramones had turned into a franchise by that point, a tribute band that happened to feature a couple of the original members and little of the original vitality, seems to have escaped virtually everyone in this school of thought. There again, there were certain factions that viewed Joey's astonishing and unique voice as disposable – no more vital to the Ramones than a good live drum sound.

But whatever camp you fell into, the pairing of the Ramones and Spector seemed to make sense – on paper.

The Ramones' roots lay in the baroque pop of the Spector-produced Sixties girl groups like The Ronettes and The Crystals – albeit with a minimalist interpretation that stripped away the lush harmonies and 20-piece orchestras, the introductions and codas. Just because Johnny played LOUD with relentless down-strokes that initially cut his fingers to ribbons didn't mean the Ramones' spiritual brethren were MC5 or The Stooges, or any of the angry late Seventies British punk bands. Their music was pop – Beach Boys, Beatles, Herman's Hermits . . . Indeed, it was such classic pop that their record company couldn't understand why the Ramones weren't one of the biggest bands in the world.

The fault must lie, they reasoned, with the production, and the image – so Tommy Erdelyi, the man more responsible than any for the Ramones' vision was out, right after he'd helped create four of the Definitive Albums

Of Rock Music. Period. It was time to pull in the "name" producers – and to lose the leather jackets, while they were at it. And where better to start than legendary recluse and control freak Phil Spector – the man behind 'He's A Rebel', 'Be My Baby', *A Christmas Gift For You*, 'You've Lost That Loving Feeling', 'Unchained Melody', 'River Deep, Mountain High', and later The Beatles' *Let It Be*, plus solo albums from John Lennon and George Harrison . . . the list goes on. Phil was already a hero and inspiration – and a confirmed fan of the Ramones.

The trouble was Spector had some . . . er . . . *individual* ways of recording.

"HEY MAN!" PLEADS a panic-stricken Dee Dee Ramone. "If ya hit me, I ain't gonna hit ya back! I've got too much respect for ya . . .! Anyway, I don't know how many armed bodyguards ya got hidden in the kitchen who'll come burstin' through the door with their guns blazin' if I do!"

Nevertheless, Dee Dee stands his ground. Arms pressed rigidly against the sides of his body, fists clenched, eyes half-closed, bracing himself for a KO punch that is never actually launched.

"Just leave me alone, will ya!!" he hollers defiantly at Phil Spector – who, after handing me his automatic pistol for safe-keeping, is executing a fast Ali Shuffle inches in front of his distraught house guest.

Joey, Johnny and Tommy silently anticipate his next move. If there's got to be a rumble, they're ready – if somewhat reluctant.

"I came over here this evening at your invitation," pleads Dee Dee, who's no longer talking to Spector but screaming at him at the top of his powerful lungs, "to admire your house, listen to your music and party, not to fight with ya, so just cut it out, before someone gets hurt!!"

I don't think Dee Dee's referring to himself.

(Roy Carr, *NME*, May 21, 1977)

"I'M UP AT PHIL'S house one night, with the Ramones and Rodney [Bingenheimer]," Carr starts. The critic was in LA to write a screenplay for the Phil Spector story, starring Al Pacino (it was later shelved). The night in question happened in February '77, after one of several shows where the Ramones and Blondie played the Whiskey A Go Go as alternate headliners.*

* "Blondie were great that night," Dee Dee wrote in *Poison Heart*. "Deborah Harry was smashing, and wearing [a really] short mini-skirt. All the boys were crowding the front, trying to get a look up her skirt at her white bikini briefs."

"Phil was under the illusion that the Ramones were Joey and his backing band," Carr explains.* "He was very interested in Joey's voice – it reminded him of Dion [di Mucci, responsible for classic early Sixties doo-wop hits, and later worked with Spector in the Seventies]. He offers to sign the Ramones to his label. He tells me I can manage them, and he'll be the producer. The Ramones don't know what to make of it, especially when he asks them how many records they've sold.

"So he disappears into one of his many rooms, and comes out with a computer printout with their sales figures on," continues the journalist. "He tells them that *Ramones Leave Home* sold less than *Ramones* and offers them $50,000 each. Cash. He's like, what d'ya want – cars, girls? He offers to call Marty [Machat, famous show-business lawyer who worked with Sinatra], who's staying at the Beverly Hills Hotel, even though it's one in the morning – 'He'll bring the cash with him.' So, whether he can do it legally or not, he's offering to sign the Ramones for $200,000 cash – you could see them wondering, what should they do? They had problems handling $50 each."

The Ramones turned Spector down – but it didn't stop him from phoning them up after each album, and suggesting they should record the next one together. "Do you want to make a good album, or a great one?" he'd ask Joey, a big Spector fan. (As David Fricke points out in the *Anthology* notes, the fact that Phil only rated *Rocket To Russia* as "good" should've been enough to tip someone off something was awry.)

"The thing is, he may well have been able to sign them," Carr suggests. "Sire was part of Warner Bros., as was Phil's label, so it would've been a straight switch. They weren't doing much, and – as he told them – if they didn't watch out, their career was over."

Spector's legendary bodyguards Dan and David Kessel were also big Ramones fans. They were playing Ramones songs in a frat party band before California had even seen the real thing. In '78, the brothers produced a cover of The Beach Boys' 'Surfin' Safari' for Bingenheimer with the Ramones as his backing band, under the alias Rodney & The

The bassist went backstage to pass on his regards, only to find his way blocked by a man dressed in a batwing cloak, devilish black beard and moustache, and dark aviator shades: "The crown prince of darkness, Mr Phil Spector himself." Dee Dee claims Spector took an instant dislike to him – a claim that probably says more about his paranoia than the producer's, because Phil invited the Ramones back to his Spanish-style villa in Beverly Hills regardless.

* The producer also thought that Debbie Harry could be the Eighties Ronnie Spector.

Brunettes.* After they finished, David Kessel phoned Spector to play him the songs, and he told them to pick up some pizza and bring the band over: "We stopped at Piece O'Pizza on Santa Monica Boulevard," he recalls, "and got two extra large pizzas, with pepperoni, mushrooms, onions and green bell pepper.

"That's not from my notes," he laughs, "that's how I always order pizza. We also threw garlic on them. So off we went to Phil's. There were a lot of laughs, a few guns, plenty of pizza, and a lot of talk about real rock'n'roll. A few weeks later, Dan and I were invited to Phil's house to join in a meeting with Seymour Stein. The result was *End Of The Century* on which both my brother and I played guitar and lots of handclap percussion."

RECORDING ON *END Of The Century* began at Gold Star Studios in Los Angeles, on May 1, 1979 – the Ramones immediately freaked out by the presence of large oxygen tanks (designed by Brian Wilson) and an underground swimming pool that doubled as an echo chamber. This place had history – as well as Spector's own mighty productions, Eddie Cochran, The Beach Boys, Sonny & Cher, Buffalo Springfield, and Iron Butterfly (among others) had recorded there. It was intimidating.

"I recall a lengthy chat with Joey Ramone by the Gold Star Coca-Cola machine – which only stocked Tab – in the hallway late one evening," recounts *Melody Maker* stringer Harvey Kubernik in the unabridged sleeve notes to the *End Of The Century* reissue. "Joey was so stunned when I told him The Who mixed 'I Can See For Miles' at this studio, he took off his glasses and shook his head in amazement."

In the main control room, where the volume could go as loud as 130 decibels, Spector had an entire series of hand gestures worked out for communicating with his engineer Larry Levine – who suffered a heart attack during the sessions. It was certainly too loud for normal speech.

"Phil was insane," recalls Ed Stasium, nominally musical director, invited along in a Henry Kissinger "mediator" role. "The volume was incredible. He would make the band do take after take after take. I have it written down. He listened to 'This Ain't Havana' over 300 times. No one knew why. He'd do a lot of jumping up and down and swearing and sign language to Larry. If he wanted a snare drum, he'd imitate the snare drum. If he wanted more reverb, he'd slap his tongue with his hand.

* It matched an earlier track the DJ cut with Blondie under the name the Little GTOs. Both songs later surfaced on 1984's *Rodney Bingenheimer Presents 'All Year Party' Vol I.* 'Slug' was recorded at the same session.

"Phil wouldn't tell us where we were recording," Stasium admits. "We came out for pre-production on April 19 and Phil had three studios on hold. He told the band to go to Gold Star, and Monte to go to Rumbo [the Captain & Tennille-owned studio where the first Guns N' Roses record was made]. Phil wanted to make the biggest record ever – not *my* biggest record ever, or the Ramones' biggest record ever, or Phil's . . . but THE biggest record ever. He would point at his eye with his finger, this will be Number One, the biggest thing you've ever worked on, be prepared."

The producer drove the group to distraction – popular legend has it he made Johnny play the opening chord to 'Rock'N'Roll High School' for eight hours straight. The guitarist walked out, and Spector ordered him back. "What you going to do?" Johnny asked. "Shoot me?" He wasn't idly joking: Phil had already pulled a gun on Dee Dee after the pair had got into a boys' own "my gun is bigger than yours" type argument. Johnny went as far as to book a flight to New York, and it took a series of frantic phone calls between Stasium, Spector and Stein before he returned. It was a hard time for Johnny. Not only did the way Spector work run contrary to his whole ethos, his dad died during the recordings.

"It wasn't eight hours, but it was an enduring length of time," Stasium corrects. "I played some of the guitars myself. Phil was doing something in the control room, to this day no one knows what, he was searching the cosmos for a sound and with that antiquated equipment he couldn't find it. At the end of the day Johnny was, 'I'm outta here.' The rest of the boys were up in arms."

"I wouldn't say Johnny was at his happiest," sighs Kessel. "It wasn't their usual rhythm. Johnny was like, 'Hey man, can we get fucking rocking?' and Phil's like, 'Wait, I'm not ready to deal with you.' I wouldn't call them arguments. I'd call them different points of view expressed with passion.

"Johnny is a powerful, innovative guitar player, a hundred per cent Buddy Holly with a Mosrite and a Marshall amp," the bodyguard continues. "He must have lifted weights because all those down-strokes are a physical gymnastic by themselves."

Kessel has a slightly different take on the gun story, too: "Dee Dee would have been the first to admit he was a little rambunctious," he says. "And that's to put it mildly. He was uptight, arrogant and a mean bass player – basically a good guy, using the music as an expression of his aggression. Phil was from New York himself. He just wanted to clarify the relationship a little. Yes, the gun stories are true. It's not offensive. It's merely factual reporting."*

"Yeah, one time he was a little under the influence, and started waving the guns around," says Marky. "The place was a nuthouse. I walked into his kitchen, and there was a killer Saint Bernard in there, tied up. The gate around the mansion was electrified, all these dead moths. He had bodyguards who were black belts in karate. Maybe he was paranoid about certain deals in the past. Maybe it was his drinking. When you drank like we did, there was always some reason . . ."

Before the Ramones' job, Spector was mugged in the parking lot of a Sunset Strip Italian restaurant. Dee Dee admitted some of the tension was created from his side: "The Ramones were a pain in the ass," he told Kubernik.

"I had a great time with Spector," Marky admits. "I don't know about the others. He had a picture of his kids on his piano, and we would go out to The Roxy with his bodyguards and party and drink all night. And, of course, he would have his guns on him. They didn't have metal detectors then."

On nights off, all the Ramones except Joey would go and see *Alien*: "The boys saw it every evening and day they had off!" Spector wrote to Kubernik. "Joey asked me to come down to the Whiskey when they were filming the video, but I declined. He wanted me to do a 'Hitchcock' type thing."

Spector loved Joey for his New York sound, his lyrical interpretation and his attitude. Kessel too: "He obviously wasn't an opera singer," he explains, "but he used what he had brilliantly, and Phil taught him a lot about voice control."

During mixes, the band would eat herring, tongue and corned-beef sandwiches from Canter's deli. Joey was in Seventh Heaven, working with a certifiable legend: "Joey loved every minute," smiles Stasium. "He didn't want to leave. He loved Phil. Phil loved Joey. Joey had a little bit of Ronnie in his voice. They were buds."

But Spector still managed to freak out one of his biggest fans.

"One time, Joey was sitting at the piano next to Phil learning an arrangement, with the words written out for him by Phil on a piece of paper," recalls friend Joan Tarshis. "When he was ready to leave he folded up the paper, and put it in his pocket. Suddenly, he knew he'd done something

* As a little coda to that, Kubernik recalls an evening when the Kessel brothers wore matching shoulder holsters with .38 pistols while strumming acoustic guitars in the studio. "OK, gun section," barked Phil. "Play!"

really wrong. He knew if he left with that piece of paper, he was not going to leave – if you know what I mean. So he had to figure out how to put it back without Spector knowing that he knew that he was putting it back."

"[Someone] would bring Phil these tiny little Dixie cups of Manischevitz wine," Joey recounted in *Rolling Stone* in 1987, "and before long Phil would be drunk out of his mind. He'd be stompin' on the floor, cursin'. 'Piss, shit, fuck! Piss, shit, fuck! Fuck this shit', and that would be the end of the session."

"The thing was, Phil had never worked with a band before, his artists were more of his own conception," Joey told Jaan Uhelszki, with the benefit of hindsight. "Phil liked to dominate and manipulate, so it was a little strange. But I felt like I was performing for the master. He's a passionate, high-drama person. I still admire him – but during his episodes nobody was enjoying any of it. We were all pissed off with his drinking, his antics, high drama, and the insanity."

Seymour Stein – who'd just sold Sire to Warner Bros. for a large sum of money and a seat on the board of directors – was forced to sue Spector to get the Ramones' master tapes back for release.

Johnny hated that album, didn't he?

"Yeah," says Monte.

"THE RAMONES WERE very much utilising the pop structure, but it wasn't just a matter of speeding it up. Even some of Joey's vocal techniques mirrored that girl group style. My father was very touched by Joey, flattered but respectful. He realised the honoured position Joey has in punk, and music in general. Many people see the Ramones as a punk rock entity, but my father has a way of seeing them as transcending those shackles . . ."

People around the Ramones feel if they hadn't been called punk rock, they would have been more successful.

"It is like that with every genre – genres are very restricting."

Did your dad tell you stories of the Ramones at all?

"Every time I've enquired, he's treated it as a somewhat blurry area in his past like, 'Oh you know, it was crazy. Joey was crazy. They were all nuts. It was great.' He feels accomplishment in everything he's done and he's never worked with something he isn't extremely passionate about – but I don't know if he feels that's one of his most accomplished works. His memories are much more candid of, say, John, or any of The Beatles' experiences. With the Ramones, it embodied the spirit of punk rock itself, this chaotic discontent."

Why did he want to work with them?

"He was looking for that passion that the other people he worked with had about

music and he wasn't finding at the time. He's extremely liberal and disdainful of popular conventions, and he saw the Ramones as a total move against everything, which he wanted to be a part of – not to conduct or control, but just to be immersed in it. It was his way of symbolically being a part of what punk stood for."

So he was into the whole idea of punk?

"Yeah, very much so. He really saw them as sincere – they weren't about image. Joey wore the same thing every day. He was a lot like my dad in that way of submerging within his own presence."

The recording of that album is kind of legendary, the stories around it . . .

"Stories of what?"

Well, like how your dad kept them locked up.

"Whatever. My dad has intimidating ways of going about hard work, but I can't think of one artist who will say that that kind of imprisoning atmosphere was not eventually the most productive way of going about things. I don't know everything about the stories. If they're true, they produced something good. And they're good anecdotes."

Totally. There was a documentary on your dad, where the Ramones were being interviewed. It was very funny because it was mostly Johnny speaking . . .

"That's the wrong one to pick. He's a Republican for Christ's sake – he thanked George W Bush in his induction speech [for the Rock'N'Roll Hall Of Fame, in 2002] or something equally repulsive – put that in your book."

Whatever. I could see that Johnny's way of working would be at odds with your dad's way of working. Johnny's idea was you get in, you get out, you put everything down in two days and then you leave. The story runs that the Ramones would always have about $100,000 to record each album, but they would only spend $60,000 and split the rest up between them. 'Why spend more? We're not going to sell more.' And then you hear stories about Phil Spector working and reworking the opening chord to 'Rock'N'Roll High School', right – how much money that must have cost? It must have driven Johnny crazy.

"I hear such mixed things about that album. Some people tell me it was the worst Ramones album."

That album's fucking great, I love that album.

"Aesthetically, and in all other ways, it's superb."

That version of 'Baby, I Love You' is as good as the [Ronettes] original and that's saying a lot. The first three songs . . . I can still to this day remember where I heard them. I'd spend all my money on records, so I never had enough left over for a proper record player. It was my first year of college, and I had a portable Dansette mono record player but the speaker didn't work. So I was hunched over the record, trying to listen to the needle on the grooves. My brother and I discussed End Of The Century *before it came out. I took the hardcore line, taking issue with the fact it had strings on it. He was like, 'So what? If it's good, it's good.' That's the last time I tried to be cool about something.*

(Author's interview with Nicole Spector, 19-year-old daughter of Phil)

"THE PHIL SPECTOR album is one of the greatest albums ever made," exclaims George Tabb. "I know that John didn't like it, but all the fans loved it – the Ramones can think whatever they want. Yes, it was a Joey solo album – but you got to hear him sing 'Baby, I Love You', and yes, the guitars were in the background, but there was a nice wall of strings. When you hear 'Danny Says' with the guitar picking out the intro, and this wall building up behind it, it's beautiful. I can understand why Johnny hated it."

Of course he hated it. It's disrespectful. Phil Spector was recording with the Ramones, so he should have used the Ramones. It ripped up the blueprint and stomped all over the pieces. He should've done a solo album – and called it that. But that too would've veered radically away from the Ramones' gang mentality. (When Dee Dee decided he needed to make a solo album at the end of the Eighties, he left.)

But Dee Dee appreciated *End Of The Century* before he died, though: "Now I realise more and more," the bassist told Kubernik in spring 2002, "Joey's voice had a real deep, deep part of the Ramones' sound – and that started with *End Of The Century*. Phil Spector and Joey were a great combination. Phil brought out the romanticism in Joey. I never thought that would have been an appeal of the Ramones. But he met girls everywhere in the Ramones' songs: The Cat Club, The Burger King, 7–11, every time he turned around, he spotted someone else. He was a romantic guy . . ."

Wait a minute! It took 28 years after the Ramones formed for Dee Dee to realise that Joey's voice was a vital component of the Ramones' sound . . .! Jesus. Talk about not recognising your own strengths: that cavalier attitude may explain why on the final few albums, the band didn't even keep their one remaining recognisable trait – Joey's voice – and got Dee Dee's replacement, Ramones *fan*, CJ to sing many of the tracks.

Whatever. Dee Dee is right to pick out Joey and Phil's shared romanticism: the theme of true love was one the singer returned to time and time again, despite the fact he never married. *End Of The Century* features plenty of such moments: the darkly devotional 'I'm Affected', underscored by an inspired echo on the voice and menacing backing track; the Ronettes cover version; and one of the album's absolute knock-outs, the mini-teen symphony 'Danny Says'.

"The title was inspired by Lou Reed songs like 'Candy Says' and 'Caroline Says'," Joey told David Fricke. The title was also a tribute to Danny

Fields who, in his former days as part of the Warhol entourage, worked with Reed. "We were in LA at the Tropicana, I'd met someone kind of special, and when we woke up, we really did watch *Get Smart* on TV."

That someone special was almost certainly girlfriend Linda, shortly to be the cause of a major rift in the band – one that Johnny and Joey never recovered from. The song itself is magnificent, evocative, lines like "Soundcheck's at 5.02/Record stores and interviews/Oh, but I can't wait to be with you tomorrow" perfectly encapsulating the loneliness and distress caused by extended periods spent travelling on the road, rootless, just dreaming of security – any security. Musically, it's 'In My Room' meets . . . *Ramones*, Joey sounding almost naïve in his child-like intonations.

'All The Way' also references touring: but this time it's the power of the live experience that comes blasting through the distorted guitars and super-charged drum sound – Monte gets a mention, albeit disparagingly. Like 'High Risk Insurance' and Dee Dee's 'This Ain't Havana' and the rather disposable 'Let's Go' with its mercenary-praising lyrics (co-written by Johnny and Dee Dee), the song is a straightforward Ramones rocker – sounds great and everything, but you know both Stasium and Erdelyi would've recorded this side of the Ramones better.*

"Johnny was the new Link Wray," Dan Kessel told Harvey Kubernik. "We were proud to be Ray-Men. David and I would thrash on our acoustic guitars all night long until our hands were bloody and raw. We'd mainly play rhythm, staying out of Johnny's way."

For 'The Return Of Jackie And Judy' – a self-referencing Ramones song in the style of 'Sheena' and 'Judy Is A Punk', and a worrying sign that the band was starting to run short of ideas – Spector utilised an ensemble of hand-clappers, including Bingenheimer, Kubernik, Jeff Morrison, Maria Montoya and Phast Phreddie.

As Marky indicated later, "It was corny."**

"It wasn't my best album," Dee Dee told Kubernik. "I was writing and writing, and I realised I was in danger of being a rock star and becoming frigid. After *End Of The Century*, I had to go back to the craft of songwriting.

* After Joey told Lester Bangs the story of how the band had had bananas thrown at them, the critic remarked, "Someday they'll probably write a song about it, and no doubt it'll be a great one." 'Havana' indeed mentions bananas in the chorus-line.

** The track was also released in 1980 by RSO, as the B-side to 'I Wanna Be Sedated', a tie-in with *Times Square*, an unremarkable teen-orientated movie that incorporated the *Road To Ruin* stand out on its soundtrack. Around the same time, Sire put out the 'Meltdown With The Ramones EP' in the UK, for no discernible reason. It featured 'Boyfriend', 'Here Today', 'Something To Do' and 'Questioningly'.

But then, we weren't doing it as a band anymore. We lost each other on the road."

The album reaches its unassailable peak when Spector tackles the pop stuff – 'Rock'N'Roll High School' revamped, and beefed up considerably. Then there are the Sixties organs and saxophones and what sounds like an entire orchestra of drums on the opening cut, 'Do You Remember Rock'N'Roll Radio?' with Sean Donahue supplying the memorable DJ talk-over intro: "C'mon, let's rock'n'roll with the Ramones."

Joey's voice has rarely sounded more vital: the Wall Of Sound blares out passion and colour – appropriately enough for a song that namechecks the great bands and DJs of the past, and harks back with a tangible yearning for the simpler days of the past. If one song sums up the entire Ramones' belief in Sixties pop and themselves, this is it. What a way to start the new decade!

" 'Do You Remember Rock'N'Roll Radio?' might be seen as a Joey song, but it applied to all the band," Dee Dee says. "When I was in Germany, they had a hard time getting music out, Radio Free Europe or Luxembourg. I used to listen late at night and it came on from the channel. I'd hide under the covers with a tiny transistor radio."

It made for a great single.

THE ALBUM'S OTHER single 'Baby, I Love You' is something else again.

For a start, Spector was jealously protective of all his previous work, especially any involving his former wife Ronnie's old band – the couple were involved in a protracted lawsuit over ownership of material for years. Seymour Stein convinced him to change his mind.* Then, there was the fact that none of the Ramones – aside from Joey, obviously – are on the recorded version.

"It's true," admits David Kessel. "There's Barry Goldberg on keyboards, and the legendary and lovely Mr. Jim Keltner on drums. I remember him turning around to me, saying, 'Huh, my kids are not going to believe I'm on a Ramones record – Beatles, Bob Dylan, whatever, dad!' Sure it excites controversy because of the strings and the beat, but it went Top 10 in England. What's the problem with folks? Chill out. Did anyone get pissed when The Beatles changed styles and grew? Don't pick on those records, they're good records."

"I realised that it was a mistake," Johnny said afterwards, "and it was the worst thing we've ever done in our career."

He's wrong. The production on 'Baby, I Love You' is incredible – the

* Spector originally wanted the band to cover Bob B. Soxx's 'Not Too Young To Get Married'.

soaring strings, the double-tracked vocal harmonies, the thunderous wall of drums, the almost disco rhythm – pure heartbreak and denial and wonder, all wrapped up in 3.49 minutes of pop perfection. One of the greatest singles ever – that's *ever*, not just the Ramones. It remains the Ramones' best-selling UK single.

The sight of the Ramones performing on *Top Of The Pops* the following spring was quite something: union regulations meant that the BBC orchestra had to perform (or mime) the string parts, and the camera kept cutting between Joey all hunched over the mic like a grotesque stick insect, and band looking all moody (surly, actually) and the musicians in black tie and tails. Years later, to add injury to Johnny's insult, the track was used in a baby commercial for nappies, and also as an ad for the Yellow Pages.

Marky recalls a similar television experience for different reasons: "When we did 'Rock'N'Roll Radio' on *The Old Grey Whistle Test*, Roger Daltrey had the balls to come up to me and say, 'You guys are never going to amount to anything in your leather jackets.' So I started goofing on him. I was like, 'Roger, go drink your fucking tea.' He was 5′ 6″ and I was 5′11″ and I wanted to give him a little smack round the head. I was mad but I kept it cool. When The Who was starting out, he was Mr. Mod and I'm sure no one ever said anything to him."

"We got a lot of new attention because of the chart success of that single ('Baby, I Love You'), especially in Europe," Dee Dee told Harvey Kubernik in 2002. "In Holland and Spain we got a lot of TV shows. It got to be scary. We'd get to the Apollo Theatre in Glasgow, Scotland, and we'd been playing it for years, all of a sudden all these very young girls were at the gig – not for the Ramones, but for 'Baby, I Love You'."

'Chinese Rock' also attracted controversy, for different reasons. Dee Dee claims he wrote the song when he was staying at Chris Stein's apartment [which he incorrectly recalled as Deborah Harry's] with Tommy – but gave it to Johnny Thunders' Heartbreakers to record* after Johnny refused to let the Ramones play a song that mentioned hard drugs, specifically heroin. (Glue was OK.) Then the Heartbreakers turned round and said it was theirs. Who knows the real truth? As far as energy levels go, the original version wipes the floor with Spector's recording.

"Richard Hell just wrote the riff in the middle," Dee Dee told Charles Shaar Murray, "and the others had nothing to do with it. We don't glorify shooting dope. The Heartbreakers were proud of being junkies, but when

* Recorded in 1977 The Heartbreakers' anthem 'Chinese Rock' was released as a single, and appeared on their *LAMF* ('Like A Motherfucker') album.

we do it it's just a straightforward account of what an addict's life is like. Shooting dope is a lifetime thing, but you can't sniff glue for more than a few months – because your hair falls out and you can't do nothing, and then you die. 'Now I Wanna Sniff Some Glue' was an obvious joke."

"It's like an Andy Warhol thing," explains Roberta Bayley. "Andy would say 'what should I paint?' and someone would say 'paint what you like' and so he would paint blood. Write about what you know. The Ramones were writing about suburban . . . even though Queens isn't the suburbs . . . experiences like sniffing glue. So you try to figure out what else to write about . . . copping heroin, that's Dee Dee. It's not something the Ramones did. It didn't fit into their image, so they gave it away."

They did it in the end.

"They were running out of material. They had to do something."

WHAT DO YOU like about the Ramones?

"I tend to enjoy art for many different reasons, but aesthetically and musically I love the Ramones in that essential way you can't describe. But I also have some sociological reasons for liking them because they did an amazing job of expressing not necessarily angst – though it was angst-ridden – but discontent with the government, social conventions, and artistic standards. They broke through a major threshold that was pretty stalwart, whether or not people recognised that. So it's as much political as it is simple essence."

Right. The Ramones weren't really punk rock, as such. Punk rock means something different. The Ramones are art punk – like Talking Heads, Arto Lindsay, Sonic Youth. It's not an accident, the way they sounded. They clearly had an idea of what they wanted to do. They're like a minimalist painter. It's not like somebody just goes, 'I'm going to put a line on a sheet of paper' – they have an idea of why they want to put that line on the sheet of paper.

"Yeah, but they still have the line on the paper. That's why it was so relatable to a wide audience rather than a mere intellectual."

When did you first hear them?

"I don't know, when I was maybe 13."

Were you scared?

"No, I was enthralled. I didn't gain much of a musical appreciation for anything until I was 14, 15. I kind of drifted away from the Ramones and then I got reunited with them when I started college a few years ago. They're an omnipresent force to me. I almost feel contradictory forming opinions about them. You either like the Ramones, or you don't – and when you do, you like them with every vessel. Why do you like the Ramones?"

I can sing along with them. Because the only singer I ever wanted to sound like was Joey Ramone, not that I can. I lived in Seattle for nine months, for my leaving party we had a karaoke machine. I got up onstage with a local punk band and we did a set of entirely Ramones covers, thus fulfilling a lifelong dream.

"The Ramones fill that hole that pop is supposed to, but has failed to do recently – which is to make life simple without making it simplistic."

(Author's interview with Nicole Spector)

AFTER NEARLY SIX months spent mixing the album (Stasium reckons Spector did three complete remixes), *End Of The Century* appeared in January 1980. It was reported as having been recorded in five different locations, and cost over $200,000 to make – a minor fortune to a band struggling to make ends meet.

"Actually," Stasium says, "everyone goes on about what a gruelling three or four months in the studio that album was, but we spent two weeks tracking the instruments, not including overdubs and vocals." A fact borne out by the Ramones tour schedule – 100 shows between June 8 and the end of 1979. And, although the sleeve listed five different studios, that was down to Spector's paranoia – the band only visited one studio.

The press loved it. "Old 'fans' who resent Spector's meddling or the Ramones' own mainstreaming," wrote Scott Isler in *Trouser Press*, "are depriving themselves of a joyously subversive experience. Sometimes a little camouflage doesn't hurt." In *NME*, Max Bell wrote, "This is the best thing they've ever done, first two albums included" (but remember, this was from the man who slagged off their debut UK show).

People magazine suggested that the "Ramones sound bigger, fuller and more polished then ever. Spector hasn't mixed away the underlying rawness and driving delivery that made the group the first New Wavers to attract national attention. The Ramones seem sure to crack the Top 40 this time." *Rolling Stone*'s Kurt Loder wrote that it was "the most commercially credible album the Ramones have ever made, as well as being one of Spector's finest efforts for years". And it made *Time*'s Best Records of 1980.

On one level, *End Of The Century* proved Sire right – Spector's presence helped it sell more than any other Ramones record to date, this side of the *Anthology*. It reached Number 44 on the US charts, but it left the entire band feeling resentful and confused.

According to *Poison Heart*, Dee Dee didn't even remember being around: "To this day," he wrote, "I have no idea how they made *End Of The Century*, or who played bass on it."

"He played bass, definitely," states Marky. "I was there with him. And I have a good memory."

THE CONTROVERSY DIDN'T stop with the recording.

For the first time since the group's inception, the Ramones weren't wearing their leather jackets on the sleeve: instead there's a soft focus *Hit Parader*-style shot of the musicians trying to look dreamy (and miserably failing: the way Johnny looks would give any pubescent girl the screaming heebie-jeebies), dressed in colour-coded T-shirts. It was photographer Mick Rock's suggestion to leave the jackets off – and Dee Dee and Joey voted against Johnny 2–1 on the final sleeve. Marky, not being an original member, didn't have a vote. The decision caused a massive ruction between the band members: Johnny felt betrayed at what he saw as Joey's increasing sloppiness and lack of commitment to the group. (Joey, by this point, was drinking heavily and it was starting to affect his songwriting skill. Plus, he was frail and prone to accidents. Johnny saw this as a weakness.) The fact that 'Baby, I Love You' was recorded after the remainder of the Ramones left the studio didn't help.

But, as Johnny indicated later, the rift in the band started when Tommy left: "Tommy was our main spokesman," he explained. "Joey had the least to say. Dee Dee and Joey would go along with me if I went along with Tommy. Once Tommy left, it became a power struggle." Johnny suggested that the reasons he and Joey never got along were personal, but "75 per cent artistic differences".

"They were trying to blame the jackets for our lack of success," Johnny commented bitterly. "So we put the leather jacket photo on the inside sleeve. I thought it was selling out.

"We all knew [Phil] wasn't the right person to produce us," he continued. "That's why we avoided him on *Rocket To Russia* and *Road To Ruin*. We agreed to do it because we thought his name would help us out. That was enough of a compromise without having to go and take pictures without our jackets. And, because of that, me and Dee Dee had a falling out."

YOU MET Phil Spector in '77, didn't you?

"Yeah."

How was that?

"It was a very complex event."

(Author's interview with Tommy Ramone)

15

Favourite Ramones Song

" 'I Wanna Be Sedated' " – Andy Paley

"The one that goes 'duh duh duh duh duh duh duh . . . Hey ho/Let's go' . . . 'Blitzkrieg Bop', first song on the first album – what a way to start a career" – Captain Sensible

" 'We're A Happy Family' – anything that makes me laugh is good" – Carla Olla

"Oh gosh, probably the intro to the first record, 'Blitzkrieg Bop', 'Sheena', 'Rockaway Beach', 'Boyfriend'. I liked them doing surf stuff and California stuff" – Craig Leon

" 'Loudmouth', that's a defining Ramones sound and song and message . . . 'Sheena Is A Punk Rocker' and 'Cretin Hop' " – David Kessel

" 'It's A Long Way Back To Germany', 'Sitting In My Room', 'Wart Hog', 'Outsider', anything at all off the first three albums" – CJ Ramone

" 'Commando'. I'm into Vietnam songs right now" – Don Fleming

"Changes every day, for today it's 'I Don't Care'. I also love Dee Dee's 'Born To Die In Berlin' and 'Commando' and 'Today Your Love'. I used to have perfect recall – thank you Carbona, thank you glue!" – Donna Gaines

" 'Sheena', you can play it on acoustic guitar" – Gary Valentine

" 'Howling At The Moon' – great guitar riff and lyrics. Also 'We Want The Airwaves', 'Someone Put Something In My Drink' " – George DuBose

" 'Something To Do' – it reflected my life at exactly that moment. I lived on 4th and 2nd, and would go and eat Chicken Vindaloo. I too had that annoying East Village teenage ennui, just hanging out all the time, what's to do for fun?" – George Seminara

" 'Somebody Put Something In My Drink', 'Beat On The Brat', how can you listen to that without dancing? 'Rock'N'Roll Radio' . . . all the quote unquote singles were great" – Ida Langsam

" 'Sheena Is A Punk Rocker' – I'm surprised you can't hear me when I'm in my car, cranking it up, windows down, singing along at the top of my voice" – Janis Schacht

" 'We're A Happy Family' " – Joan Tarshis

" 'Danny Says', is one. That's always been a favourite. 'I Wanna Be Sedated', too. Is that three? 'Sheena' " – Joey Ramone

" 'Carbona Not Glue', 'I Can't Give You Anything', 'Bad Brain', '53rd And 3rd' 'Loudmouth'. Everyone remembers 'Blitzkrieg Bop' and 'Sheena', but those are a little too cute" – Kim Thayil

" 'Danny Says'. I can just pick that out, watching *Get Smart* on TV. I think of it as a Christmas record – 'There ain't no Christmas, if there ain't no snow'. 'I Wanna Be Sedated' " – Lindsay Hutton

"Tommy – 'Sheena'. Myself – 'Sedated'. Dee Dee – 'Today Your Love', 'Havana Affair', 'Pet Sematary', '53rd And 3rd'. Joey's stuff is great, too – 'I Just Want To Have Something To Do', 'Rock'N'Roll Radio', 'Sheena'. I could go on and on" – Marky Ramone

" 'Freak Of Nature' – I like that one. I don't know why, just the ta-ta-ta-ta. 'Wart Hog' " – Monte Melnick

" 'Danny Says'. The Ramones wrote the best lyrics in the world" – Nicole Spector

" 'Sheena', 'Beat On The Brat'. I love their covers – 'California Sun', 'Needles And Pins' . . . 'Somebody Put Something In My Drink'. 'Rock' N'Roll High School' " – Rodney Bingenheimer

Favourite Ramones Song

" 'Suzy', 'Carbona Not Glue', 'Glad To See You Go', 'Pinhead' . . . 'Gimme Gimme Shock Treatment' " – Tommy Ramone

"It always used to be 'She's The One' " – Mark Bannister

16

'She Went Away For The Holidays . . .'

THE RAMONES MAY have been feeling increasingly fractured, but they still toured relentlessly. The schedule for 1980 included a two-month trip to Europe, five nights in Chicago in May, a week long visit to Japan in July followed by a fortnight in Australia and New Zealand, and another six weeks in Europe towards the year's end bolstered by the success of 'Baby, I Love You'.

The Ramones were in the odd position of being a successful touring band without a hit record – at least at home. Bewildered by the success of contemporary New Wave acts like The Police, Cars and Blondie, and cut asunder by their choice of producers from the nascent hardcore punk scene starting to take hold in places like LA (X, The Germs and Black Flag), Minneapolis (Minutemen), Arizona (Meat Puppets) and Washington DC (Ian MacKaye in his pre-Fugazi band, Minor Threat), the Ramones needed a change of pace, and fast. So they lashed out – getting rid of the elements that helped make them so great: Tommy, the leather jackets and the minimalist artistic vision.

Nothing was working. Danny Fields and Linda Stein's five-year contract was due for renewal, and the Ramones had the option to renegotiate or seek fresh management – they decided on the latter. There was a new name on the credits to *End Of The Century*: Gary Kurfirst Management. "We never had any warning," sighs Linda. "We were fired through the lawyers."

"I can't say I blame them," reflected Fields philosophically. "Five years and still not sold any records, but they'd played all over the world and were famous."

Kurfirst was another Forest Hills graduate. He was tough where Fields was artistic. The new manager had got his start during the Sixties, promoting acts like The Ronettes, The Shangri-Las and Leslie West – all big Ramones influences. He staged the 1968 New York Rock Festival in Flushing Meadow Park, starring Hendrix, The Who, The Doors and a plethora of other stars. Moving into management, Kurfirst picked up Free and Peter Tosh, and, during the CBGBs era, The B-52's and Talking Heads.

"He was a very enterprising young man in his early thirties," says Gloria Nicholl who left Sire to join Kurfirst in 1980. "He's very hard-headed. He's always looked the same, although I'm sure he wasn't bald when he was a teenager – but that's how I remember him."

It was via the Heads Kurfirst first encountered the Ramones, in November 1977.

"[Talking Heads] were in Boston," Kurfirst told *Village Voice*'s Bill Werde, "and we were in a nasty fight with the headlining band [the Ramones] – they didn't want to let us use their stage lights. Finally David [Byrne, singer] walks up and says, 'Screw it!' They played the whole show with the house lights on."*

Trouser Press wanted to know what Kurfirst could do that Fields couldn't: "He has the right temperament," Johnny explained. "He's aggressive and answers to things."

"The old fight, fight, fight," Joey butted in.

Not that his presence necessarily helped sort out the situation. Buoyed by the partial success of *End Of The Century*, Warner Bros wanted to keep the Ramones radio-friendly, and were looking for more outside producers to soften their sound. Much to Johnny's continued chagrin.

"The Ramones do certain things better than anyone else," he said. "Any speed metal band that starts tomorrow, we can top them. The combination of punk and pop we play we do better than anybody."

Speed metal? Someone was starting to believe in his own myth a little too much: contrary to popular legend, the Ramones never played 25 songs in 20 minutes, or whatever the ridiculous claims were made for their set's brevity early on. They actually sped up as they grew older: four songs gave way to a few more in 25 minutes, gave way to 33 in 75 minutes, the pace growing faster and faster. The Ramones were never, ever, a speed metal band.

Leave that to the young bloods.

IN FEBRUARY, THE RAMONES experienced a nasty moment when a stage collapsed underneath them in a football stadium in Milan, Italy. Also on

* "My first impression of the Ramones," remarked Byrne, "was that this was real art rock. The concept was so strong and so focused it became invisible. People almost didn't notice that it was tongue-in-cheek."

the bill were street-level British punk band UK Subs. The Red Brigade provided security.

"In countries like Spain and Italy, they don't like to pay for anything," laughs Arturo Vega. "There were about 40,000 people inside and 20,000 outside, trying to crash the gates. I had to sneak in through a bathroom window. Inside, it was total chaos, when all of a sudden I saw everything shaking and moving on stage, and the band walking off. It was really bad. It was a simple set-up – front and back truss, but the front went out into the audience. Fortunately, the cables held it and it didn't come down in a wham, but slowly. Then the ambulances came . . .

"In those days," Vega continues, "if you played a town that was controlled by the Communists, then the people on the Right would try to cause trouble at the show to make them look bad. And vice versa. It made for very interesting situations. At another Milan show, they were throwing rocks this big. When one cracked the cymbal, the band just walked off. It was scary."

This was the year I first saw the Ramones – February 9, Rainbow Theatre, London – with fading power-pop combo The Boys in support. Outside, we fearfully discussed what we'd do if the NF skinheads (then a nasty presence in British punk, with their right-wing leanings and shaved heads) started throwing kids off the balcony, like it was rumoured. We needn't have worried. The show was turbulent, mesmerising, relentless – from the opening salvo of 'Blitzkrieg Bop', 'Rockaway Beach' and 'Rock'N'Roll High School', to the time-honoured "Gabba Gabba Hey" sign being waved aloft by the pinhead in front of the crush of heaving bodies, to the chants of "Hey ho, let's go" echoing down the platforms on Finsbury Park tube long afterwards.

I caught them twice more that month, each time even better.

"I saw them at the Bataclan in Paris," recalls journalist Roy Carr. "After the show, with the crowd still yelling for more, Joey asks for a bottle of iced coke. He doesn't drink it. He just pours it over himself. When we went out to eat afterwards, they had the exact same clothes on."

New York PR Lisa Gottheil also saw that tour: "There was a weird guy in my math class called Eric – cute but odd," she says. "He asked me to go to the Ramones with him, on the college campus. I'd just heard of them – my mom bought my little brother a Ramones record to drum along to, on the recommendation of the record store clerk. Up until then I'd been listening to a weird array of music – Frank Zappa, Pink Floyd, Journey. Eek! I loved this record but knew nothing about punk. So I said yes to Eric. My first date ever. He was 15. I was 14. What to wear?

"I really wasn't sure," she continues. "I wore army pants and a white T-shirt and, as a belt, a bandana. Oh good lord. He, of course, was a punk rock dude, pogoing the entire time. I sat there, loving the show but too self-conscious to dance. I was a total geek. But that night I met three guys I would hang out with for the remainder of Junior High and High School."

In September, the Ramones headlined a New Pop Festival in Rotterdam, above UB40, The Undertones and ska acolytes Bad Manners. "(The) Ramones [are] a joke that we can all join in with. Which explains why I love them live," journalist Andy Gill wrote, "but wouldn't dream of buying their records."

The road crew's T-shirts read "Ramones Non-Stop World Tour" – because, as Gill pointed out, if the band ever stopped gigging, they'd be finished. Indeed, when the Ramones cancelled some dates in August after an open-air show in Central Park, it was deemed newsworthy enough for a lead item in *NME*.

"I feel bad that we never went to Russia," Arturo says. "They did get offers, but Johnny wasn't about to put up with the Commies."

Another significant tour was the Ramones' first visit to Spain – among the first rock bands to play there following Franco's death a few years earlier. The Spaniards were in full-on party mode. They'd been waiting for 36 years. The occasion was a joint headliner with Mike Oldfield on September 26, 1980 on the steps of the old imperial palace in Barcelona in front of 200,000 people.

(Mike Oldfield *and* the Ramones? Wow!)

"All the big important guys from the Communist Party were sitting in the front row," recalls Vega. "They freaked out when they saw our *Rocket To Russia* backdrop* because they thought it was their time to assert their authority – close American bases in Spain, stop NATO from deploying new weapons. Fortunately the chaos among the crowd was so big, everything started collapsing. So they lost interest in the backdrop . . ."

Seven days later, they played a bullring in Madrid.

THE RAMONES WERE starting to get the third degree in the UK music press, as journalists realised there was more to da bruddas than met the eye – especially in the wake of an album that exploded the myth of the Ramones sound. First up for scrutiny was the band's rather twisted sense of humour.

* It was more likely to have been the Ramones Presidential Seal as seen on the back cover to *Leave Home*.

"Taste is a thin line," Johnny conceded in *Trouser Press*. "We sing a song about glue: that's within taste. You sing a song about pinheads because there are no pinheads. But to sing about retards would be in bad taste. Cretins?"

The guitarist looked puzzled.

"Cretins are fun," offered Joey.

The band enjoyed teasing critics. In a *Sounds* interview, the Ramones tried to convince the journalist that her hamburger was made from roundworms – "You have to be rational about it," suggested Dee Dee. Later, they showed a worrying naivety when confronted with Northern England's multi-culturalism: "One place was absolutely full of *Indians*," exclaimed Johnny. "And we keep seeing these Chinese Mexicans or somethin'. Do you think they're Cambodians?"

Record Mirror's Ronnie Gurr reported on Dee Dee's antics with something approaching awe: "Oi'd really like to get a pichur of me givin' lallipawps to littul kids," he had him as saying. "Oi troid last night. Oi awfered this kid some candy but he wouldn't take it, caws he taut it had LSD on it or sumfin', hur hur . . .

"Aww hey, you goys, can we go and get our pichur taken in a pet shawp?" the bassist pleaded. "We can get pichurs of us strokin' baby bunnies, or sumfin'."

Witnessing the Ramones backstage, Gurr pointed out it was unlikely either Dee Dee or Johnny played the more intricate parts on *End Of The Century* – "It's clear that both guitarists have difficulty even tuning their instruments," he wrote, perhaps with some prejudice. A known Stranglers fan, Gurr went on to commit such crimes against music as signing The Stereophonics and Kula Shaker. "Dee Dee has three identical souped-up white Fender Precision Basses with red scratch plates that his guitar roadie tunes up," he wrote. "He is handed one, and belts hell out of it until it goes out of tune. Then he simply straps on another and ditto. Johnny does likewise with his black and white Mosrites and Hoey six stringers."

Charles Shaar Murray didn't make the same mistake of underestimating Johnny in *NME*: "Johnny is the Ramones' most remarkable instrumentalist," he wrote. "He drives his guitar like a racing driver going round hairpin bends, maintaining the constant deadpan roar so earnestly mimicked by every '77 garage band. If the Ramones had never existed there would be no band for whom Johnny could possibly play guitar. If Johnny had never existed, the Ramones would never have the right guitar player."

Gurr reported that Dee Dee was the only married Ramone – Johnny and Marky had regular girlfriends (Roxy and Cynthia, respectively), while Joey had just got engaged to a Linda. This was at the end of January 1980.

Murray also mentioned Linda: "She is small, blonde and fizzy," he wrote, "hyperactive, grinning. She fusses over her lanky, ungainly boyfriend, indulges him, nurses him [and] showers him constantly with affectionate abuse."

A while afterwards, Linda left Joey for Johnny.

"JOHNNY COVETED LINDA," says video director George Seminara. "So, I guess, he made her an offer she couldn't refuse, and eventually she married him. One of the great stories about their relationship is that he wanted her to get a boob job . . . [George is illustrating a point here, not being literal] . . . but he didn't want to pay for the entire job – so he paid for the left breast and she paid for the right breast. Or vice versa. She's very nice, attractive, maybe mid-forties, works in a posh Beverly Hills saloon as a colourist – and has one hell of a rack. Johnny seemed to like her to have it on display one way or another. They're still married."

"Joey always talked about Linda," explains Jaan Uhelszki. "I think he was hung up on her until the end. He started dating this Japanese woman Lisa, I think primarily because she had the same birthday – July 24 – as Linda. He never forgave Johnny. Joey always said he'd never do a reunion tour because Johnny wanted to. He'd often talk about how Johnny was really Mickey [Leigh]'s friend. They were never warm, fuzzy companions."

"Johnny was a criminal when he was young," sighs Gloria Nicholl. "He used to throw stuff off the roofs in Queens at old ladies and stuff. He never got caught – someone else always did. He was horrible. He still is.

"He's a bread-head, a shit-head and he stole Joey's girlfriend," she continues. "I knew her, because I hung out with her cousin Janis who had a column in *New York Rocker*. They were loud, fun, typically New York girls. Janis reminded me of Ruby Wax. Johnny had a girlfriend named Roxy and when he wanted to be with Linda, he would tell Roxy he was visiting his uncle in Philadelphia. Johnny was unkind to everyone in the band. He wasn't nice when he was young and isn't nice now."

"Johnny Ramone?" asks Marky. "He's a nice guy, opinionated, conservative Republican, into sports, very All-American. He started a guitar style that a lot of people tried to imitate and really couldn't. He was business-minded, and cared about the quality of the group. Yes, he shouted at people. That girlfriend story is true, yeah – but, you know, may the best man win, all's fair in love and war. No one fucked each other in the ass, or stabbed anyone in the back. You had to be blind or stupid not to see what was happening. I saw it going on, but I didn't want to get in the way of love or jealousies – it happened to me too when I was 22. What you gonna do? There are many more fish in the sea."

Unfortunately for Marky and the Ramones, the singer didn't view the situation in the same light. Johnny was already at odds with Dee Dee over the leather jackets on the sleeve of *End Of The Century*, and becoming increasingly irritated with Marky and Joey's heavy drinking which he saw as being detrimental to the band. Now Joey was refusing to even speak to the guitarist.*

"Johnny crossed the line with me concerning my girlfriend that he happened to like a little too much at the time, creating total conflict with me in our close-knit situation called (the) Ramones," Joey told Uhelszki for *Mojo* in 1999. "He destroyed the relationship and the band right there, early among other things. Twenty-two years of constant touring with people you don't really care for was enough – I am much happier now. My reasons are personal, [relating to] things that suck, that people don't do to each other, especially inside a band. [Some] things are off-limits. If you want the band to blossom, get to its fullest, you don't cross that line. And I never felt any love for John anyways. There were people who I felt closer to in the band, like Dee Dee."

SO WHAT DID Joey and Johnny fall out about?

"Linda."

Tell me about Linda.

"OK. Linda was basically . . . we all hung out at CBGBs. Linda was a very short, skinny, blonde-haired girl. She started going out with Joey and then she started cheating on Joey with Johnny. This broke Joey's heart and this was the big rift between them."

When was that?

"I understand around the time Pleasant Dreams *came out. Joey had pictures of her. The* Punk *magazine that never came out had a cover story on* Rock'N'Roll High School *and Joey took a lot of Polaroids for it, including ones of Linda. Then somebody told me that 'The KKK Took My Baby Away' was written about Johnny. I was baffled that Joey stayed with the Ramones because he could have had a successful solo career – but after Sid killed Nancy and punk rock fell apart, it felt*

* Stories like this are not uncommon among rock groups: Roger Waters Vs Dave Gilmour (Pink Floyd), David Lee Roth Vs Eddie Van Halen, various band members sleeping with other band members – see Fleetwood Mac, Hole – particularly when the groups contain both male and female musicians.

like 1975 again. Joey was like, 'We're the only rock'n'roll band out there. Everybody else has quit but we're never going to quit. We're always going to be the Ramones.' "

Also, what do you do after you've been a rock'n'roll star?

"Joey always had projects. He didn't have a problem with that. It's funny – Johnny talked about retiring even in the mid-Seventies. He always talked about how he was going to open up a bar some day."

(Author's interview with John Holmstrom)

17

We Want The Airwaves

RECORDING ON THE Ramones' most under-appreciated and difficult album *Pleasant Dreams*, started on March 30, 1981. The record company and management were still pressing celebrity producers on the Ramones, despite a series of demos recorded with Tommy and Ed Stasium towards the end of 1980 that kicked ass, old time style.

Dee Dee's behaviour was becoming increasingly erratic, fuelled by the drug addiction. Joey and Marky were lushes – in fact, Marky's drinking problem caused him to miss a show on October 10, 1981. "I was drinking in a hotel with Roger Maris, a New York Yankee [baseball player]," Marky recalls, "and he was dying of cancer and I got trashed. The next day I was supposed to play a show in Virginia Beach. But I was in Ohio and had to get there on my own. I said, 'Fuck I wasn't [allowed] to drink.' I knew I had a problem. They knew I had a problem." Add to this the ongoing estrangement that Johnny had with both Dee Dee (musically) and Joey (personally), and, in 10cc's Graham Gouldman, a producer that none of the band particularly cared for, and . . .

"The turmoil," remarked Johnny dryly, "was starting."

Johnny, having expected to retire by the time *End Of The Century* appeared, was now on the verge of quitting – but he couldn't. The job wasn't completed.

"Tommy produced the demo, and it was like the fifth great Ramones album," says John Holmstrom, "but they gave it to Graham Gouldman and he ruined it."

Joey, his heart broken, began to turn his attention to politics. Always more at home with his own, and Marky's, bohemian left-leaning upbringing than Johnny or Dee Dee's militaristic beliefs, he started writing lyrics that reflected his new found sense of injustice. 'The KKK Took My Baby Away' was the signal – whereas before the Ramones considered it amusing to be second or third generation immigrants pretending to be Nazis, now it was clear where their singer's allegiances lay.

Joey wanted to use Steve Lillywhite, impressed by his work on Johnny Thunders' 1978 solo album *So Alone*, but the future U2 producer wasn't established enough for Sire, and Seymour Stein preferred Gouldman because of his proven track record – he'd written Sixties hits for The Yardbirds ('For Your Love', 'Heart Full Of Soul'), The Hollies ('Bus Stop') and Herman's Hermits ('No Milk Today'). Also, 10cc were in limbo: Gouldman's songwriting partner Eric Stewart had recently been in a car crash.

"We weren't really communicating," Johnny told *Rolling Stone*'s Colin Devenish. "[Gouldman] was a lightweight pop guy. I knew I was in trouble on the first day when he said, 'Your amp is buzzing too much. Can you turn down your volume?' He wasn't right for the Ramones, that's all. We had no choice. Once you don't have the commercial success it's hard to maintain as much control over things as you'd like."

"John didn't like him," says Monte Melnick, a big Gouldman fan. "I did. He was a real professional, you know?"

"Johnny," remarked Dee Dee caustically in *Poison Heart*, "would be pleased if it were Christmas and there was a Christmas tree with nothing but presents for himself under it."

"IN THE EARLY days, we'd be on the road almost 365 days a year. It probably got us really tight, but at the same time it caused a lot of friction and tension. There were a lot of bad feelings round the Pleasant Dreams *period. It was a real rocky time. It probably would have split up most bands. Me and John had almost no communication whatsoever. You can't run an organisation or a band or a government like that. Things had to change. Maybe they were a little too militaristic. Maybe the egos were running a little too wild. In that period, I got disgusted with the majority of the songwriting. For me, songwriting came natural. In the early days, it said the Ramones wrote everything. It wasn't. It was me. It was Dee Dee. Some songs were written in collaboration.*

"When things broke down, I felt like – fuck. Maybe there was a bit of spite or envy or revenge at that point. There was a breakdown in the machinery of the band. Things were rolling, but not the way they should have been. It wasn't a total breakdown. I don't regret that Spector thing. I'm happy that we did it. But Pleasant Dreams *and* Subterranean Jungle . . . Pleasant Dreams *was a strong album but Graham Gouldman wasn't right for the job. We wanted to produce it ourselves.*

"We got pushed into using Gouldman. He'd written great songs for The Yardbirds, but he didn't understand us. He lacked aggression and depth. Some of the songs came out OK, like 'We Want The Airwaves', but for the most part it wasn't us."

I like that album. I think people underestimate it.

"I don't know," Joey sighed. "Maybe I'm just seeing it from the inside. There's a lot of strong stuff on it. Then we signed a new contract with Sire, and stated that the future as far as artistic freedom went was our way or no way. Too Tough To Die *was the first album released like that, and it was right on. During the* Pleasant Dreams *period we lost a lot of our fans. They didn't know where we were going."*

(Author's interview with Joey Ramone, 1989)

PLEASANT DREAMS IS not the half-hearted affair Ramones lore makes out.

Its sleeve, however, is the absolute nadir of Ramones' artwork – a lazy, barely formulated portrayal of . . . It's hard to say precisely what. A black silhouette of a man stands hunched under a two-tone (green and yellow!) spotlight, for no discernible reason – although the style could be loosely termed New Wave. Perhaps. (Research shows it's based on a still from the 1953 movie *The House Of Wax*, but the criticism remains.) No wonder the Ramones look disconsolate, framed by shadows, and with the leather jackets back, in a small photo on the reverse – this was a plain and obvious insult to a rock band with the most perfect image in the history of rock'n'roll.

"Tell me about it," sighs Holmstrom. "I'd been involved in three of the first four record covers. The photo shoot for the first, the cartoons for the third and the front cover for the fourth. I knew what the Ramones wanted – Arturo and I shared that. They could have come to me for *Pleasant Dreams* . . . I don't know what they were thinking. It's one of the ugliest record covers of all time."

The basic tracks were recorded at Media Sound, while Joey did a lot of vocals in England, with background support coming from Sparks' vocalist Russell Mael (on Joey's Fifties-style plea for domestic harmony, the Four Seasons-esque 'Don't Go'). As a signifier of how fractured the group were, Dee Dee wasn't even aware Mael was on the album until Joey mentioned it in a later interview. As a bassist himself, Gouldman taught the Ramones to think of the bass as a melodic instrument, and introduced Dee Dee to the concept of minor chords – the Ramones hadn't previously had the ability to utilise anything but the most obvious keys. For the first time on a Ramones album, songs were credited to individual writers – Joey wrote seven, and Dee Dee five. It was another crack in the gang façade.

"Joey wanted it, I guess," commented Johnny. "I thought we always did things as a unit, a group."

Gouldman over-layered the aggression with sweet harmony. Perhaps the "bop-wop-shoo-wop" vocal breaks weren't too surprising: Joey recorded with doo wop group The Mystics around the time of *Pleasant Dreams*.

"He had a great voice for that," says Holmstrom. "Joey actually has a horrible voice for some of the songs where the Ramones tried to be punk rock – that's what's so weird about that band. But that's also what makes them stand out because there are so many punk rock bands that have a growling singer. It gets so boring."

The album's only US single – outrageously – 'We Want The Airwaves' was a slightly caustic blast from Joey at the policy of radio DJs to play only the blandest of singles. "Where's your guts," he asked, "and will to survive/And don't you wanna keep rock'n'roll music alive?" Noticeably, there was a direct quotation from The Doors within the lyrics – the only time that happened, apart from the famous Herman's Hermits lift in 'Judy Is A Punk'. The Ramones were bitterly aware that their love for Sixties pop music and rock'n'roll was increasingly turning them into in an anomaly in an era when 12-inch disco remixes and synthesisers ruled – the irony that the sound of their protest was cleaned up wasn't lost on Johnny, either.

'The KKK Took My Baby Away', with its hammering drum intro stolen from Cheap Trick's sensational 1977 pop hit 'He's A Whore', and backing vocals courtesy of Gouldman, is classic Ramones – a chorus that's both ridiculous and redolent, guitars that threaten to tear your head apart, and sweet Beach Boys-style backing harmonies, topped off by a raucous "Hey! Ho!" chant. The second British single from the album, 'She's A Sensation' and 'Let's Go', are both its equal: effortless, Joey's voice deep and in full control, the chorus and instruments complimenting each other with élan.

" 'KKK' could be about the Linda situation," suggests George Seminara. "Johnny does have some pretty stringent right-wing leanings. One time the Ramones were in Germany, he wanted to buy a Hitler autograph and people flipped out because it's against the law there. He was just applying logic: where would be a better place to find one? Johnny would probably have become Warren Buffet, or one of those big CEO types, if he hadn't heeded the clarion call of rock'n'roll. He's quite the expert on movie posters, baseball cards and autographs in general. Johnny's an interesting fellow – at times, he seems educated, sophisticated, but he's also taciturn, and it's hard to stay on his side, because he demands a certain amount of subservience."

Joey denied any hidden agendas, though: "I must have written 'KKK' about seven years ago," he told *Trouser Press*. "The bridge is recent, within a year's time."

You can lose your heart within the singer's torched '7-11'. Joey details in time-honoured girl group fashion the beauty of young love that takes place among the most mundane, humdrum of surroundings – convenience stores, Space Invaders machines, record swaps – before the entire story goes horribly wrong, again in classic girl group fashion. The oncoming car goes out of control – "It crushed my baby and it crushed my soul". If ever a man was born out of his era, it was Joey Ramone. This man was female teen angst personified.

"I always wanted to write something about a 7-11," Joey explained. "We don't fly, we drive on tour – and, after 15 hours, the 7-11 is a welcome sight, like our second home. It's taken the place of candy stores."

"I love *Pleasant Dreams*," Marky says, with the benefit of hindsight. "I love the production. It was the Ramones during their punk pop era, and I like pop rock a lot – catchy tunes, things with a lot of minor chords. And that album had it. *End Of The Century* should have sounded like that. There are demos around. I have them all, without the background horns, and the 30 people in the studio, and the percussion, but it is what it is . . . It's Phil and you can't get enough of him."

"There were albums where I became totally disinterested," Johnny admitted, "and didn't write anything, like *Pleasant Dreams*. The Ramones were losing the respect we'd earned throughout the years."

"We were really striving for quality with the songs," Dee Dee told *Trouser Press*. "It was like a neurosis: quality, quality, we want quality. We made three different sets of demos, five or six songs each at least."

In his 'It's Not My Place (In The 9 To 5 World)', Joey namechecks various pop culture icons – rock critic Lester Bangs, Phil Spector, Clint Eastwood, 10cc, Allan Arkush, Stephen King . . . There's even a tribute to The Who's 'Whiskey Man' thrown in. *Village Voice*, meanwhile, praised the singer's 10-note leap in the song's chorus.

"There was a normality about Joey's voice that was really inspiring," comments David Fricke. "Like Bob Dylan or Neil Young, he never got compared to other singers, but had an unconventional voice. He sang directly from his emotional centre without any of the prettiness we usually associate with melody. Those early records have really strong melodies – but then he'd sing them in a way that sounded like any guy you knew, but not like any guy you knew."

Dee Dee's songs, too, are simply fine – even if Gouldman's production style doesn't sit quite as well on his harder-edged numbers. 'Sitting In My

Room' is teenage ennui in the style of 'I Just Want To Have Something To Do', only this time its hero can't even be bothered to leave the comfort of his boudoir to venture outside. 'Come On Now' is another sparkling rush of blood to the head from the "comic book boy", a pop song to rank alongside any from The Dave Clark Five or 1910 Fruitgum Company.

'You Sound Like You're Sick' returns to the bassist's traditional institutionalised theme. 'You Didn't Mean Anything To Me' reflects the despondency and self-doubt Dee Dee was feeling in both his own life and the Ramones – with lines like "Every dinner was crummy/Even the ones for free" – a theme that Joey also picked upon, rather more obviously in 'This Business Is Killing Me'.

"Skies were cloudy everyday," Dee Dee wrote. "Nothing wanted to grow. We had our last chance. I think I told you so."

Indeed.

"THEY HAD PROBLEMS with the whole punk thing. The whole punk thing was not kind to the Ramones."

Surely, it was obvious to anyone the Ramones were trying their hardest in the early Eighties to move away from punk, put it behind them? And then when the hits didn't come, they went back and embraced it wholesale, which personally I found really annoying.

"I'm glad you know that because it was very strange the way they were acting round then – remember, they didn't call themselves punk rock, we did. I called them, Alice Cooper and The Dictators, punk rockers. They never used the word themselves."

Yeah, but with Too Tough To Die, *Ramones hit the pause button and went back and deliberately embraced punk. That was the album when they turned their backs on what they'd been doing – it's great and everything, but afterwards . . .? After* Pleasant Dreams *it seems they lost interest in writing pop songs.*

"I think it was Tommy's mistake, actually, on Road To Ruin. *He should never have suggested doing a country song."*

I always thought Joey had a great voice for singing country.

"Yeah, he did, didn't he?"

(Author's interview with John Holmstrom)

THE PRESS REACTION in September was muted.

One British music paper gave the album four stars (out of five), suggesting that, "Gouldman has succeeded where Spector failed, coercing the brothers into the Eighties on a wave of sympathetic, harmonic skill. This is a powerful Ramones album. This is a melodic Ramones album. This is a Ramones album *with songs*." The writer also pointed out the irony of choosing the heaviest track, 'Airwaves' to lead the assault on the singles chart with so many other pop gems bubbling under.

US magazine patronisingly called the songs "message-free ditties" and said the Ramones were one of a kind – "that's why [they] don't fit into Top 40 rock". "What's in their future?" the paper asked. "Oh, we'll keep touring, keep recording, do more and better," says Johnny. "Nothing much."

Robert Palmer in the *New York Times* wrote that *Pleasant Dreams* "sounds like a New York version of The Beach Boys – the tempos are considerably faster, but so is life in the big city." *Village Voice* threw in a Buddy Holly comparison, as favoured by David Kessel. But *Musician* accused Gouldman of diluting da bruddas sound, and forcing them to adopt other musical styles.

"For me, it was the perfect combination," says Janis Schacht, who also worked with 10cc as a PR. "If they'd let Graham change the lyrics a bit, the album would have had major hits. 'The KKK Took My Baby Away' had the best melody ever, but difficult lyrics – with a few minor changes, it would have been Number One, no problem."

"Their subject matter stopped them being more popular, without a doubt," agrees George Seminara, "the whole concept, the way they looked . . . The mechanism that the Ramones hated from the beginning kept them down. When the Ramones played Forest Hills Tennis Court, Seymour brought along his new signing and said she was going to be the biggest thing in the world, and Joey was like, 'Yeah she's cute, but I can't see it.' It was Madonna. She was willing to do what it took. The Ramones weren't."

Yet still the band continued to tour – 96 dates in 1981, down on previous years, but more than most. Mark Bannister saw them that year: "Back in those days, their intro tape was military drums," he wrote, "but Ennio Morricone was the intro ['The Good, The Bad And The Ugly'] when they came back to play at the Hammersmith Palais. They became my undisputed favourite band. *Pleasant Dreams* was out, and I loved it. It's a great album – a bit poppy, maybe, but what the hell's wrong with that?

"The Ramones always did have a strong pop sensibility," he continued. "That's what made them the greatest. They understood rock'n'roll. Trouble was, the industry and the majority of the public wasn't interested. But it made you feel special to love a band that wasn't having hits left, right and centre. They were outsiders.

"We hung around the Palais in the afternoon. In front of us in the queue were some French punks sniffing glue out of a plastic bag. It really stunk. Afterwards, we froze our arses off walking around Victoria Station half the night waiting for the milk train back to Canterbury, but it was worth it."

The fans may have been enjoying themselves, but it wasn't so great being a Ramone: "Dee Dee punched Joey once in a restaurant, because Joey said something about his wife or something," Marky told *Spin*. "He had his glasses on, so I thought that was wrong. We were like brothers – brothers fight, brothers argue. I always felt I was in the middle of the bickering. Every time I'd talk to Joey, Johnny would get upset; if I talked to John, Joey'd get upset. Then there was Dee Dee with his schizophrenic personality. He was on a lot of pills. He'd jump out of the tour van and want to fight everybody. Johnny would tell him to come back in, or he'd kick his ass. Dee Dee was afraid of him, so he'd run back in."

"I was extremely hated," Dee Dee complained. "Nobody in my life cared about me. To be in the Ramones, you kind of had to be miserable. 'Suffering at its best,' is what Johnny used to say."

The musicians certainly needed to retain their warped sense of humour to stay . . . well, not exactly sane . . .

"I liked to throw fish heads off of hotel balconies into the pools when people were out there swimming," laughs Marky. "Big fish heads. I'd see one fall into the pool and people would jump right out because it was full of blood and crap. I'd have it wrapped up and throw it off the balcony, because the pool was usually out the back, you know?"

Yeah, right.

"What else did we do?" he wonders aloud. "In Japan, me and Dee Dee would drink a lot of sake and walk around Tokyo asking everyone where Godzilla was. The police had to escort us back to the hotel, and we would crawl from the elevator to our rooms."

What kind of jokes would you tell?

"Jokes?"

Yeah – bands always have their own personal humour.

"We never had jokes. We just thought certain things in life were funny, you know? The Ramones weren't a joking band. We never really let anybody backstage. We just played the show to the best of our abilities, and then went back to the hotels, and partied with the people we wanted to party with. It would always end up with me and Dee Dee in the same room till the wee hours of the morning."

AS A FURTHER SIGN of discord, Joey recorded a duet with Holly Beth Vincent, the feisty singer of New Wave pop act Holly & The Italians – a fairly straight cover of Sonny and Cher's fluffy togetherness ode 'I Got You Babe'. The single was made in England, over Christmas 1981, at Manor Studios – engineer Steve Brown went on to record Wham! Joey was wearing a flowery shirt on the sleeve: enough of a symbolic gesture to send shockwaves through Ramones fans everywhere.

Where had the leather jackets gone? Was Joey about to go solo?

"It was a dream come true for me," Holly said. "I'd started out listening to a Ramones test pressing from a girlfriend of mine from high school who was working for ABC Records. A couple of years later I'm singing with Joey."

The single flopped, despite a series of music press adverts that showed the two singers pictured in a heart bubble together – thus scotching any further rumours. Holly & The Italians later toured with the Ramones in the US.

In an *NME* questionnaire in November '81, Joey revealed his current favourite records included 999's *Obsessed*, the Swinging Madisons, U2's 'I Will Follow', Squeeze, Iggy, all three Buzzcocks albums, Phil Spector's *Greatest Hits* and The Rattlers (his brother's band). Tellingly, among his dislikes, he wrote "all this technical synthesiser bullshit (not to say it's all bad) – have people forgotten about guts and soul?

"Condemnation of guitars calling them obsolete," he added, "the ones responsible for rock's sterility."

Another Ramones collaboration, 'Chop Suey' – this time with Kate Pierson and Cindy Wilson of the Kurfirst-managed B-52's, and Debbie Harry on backing vocals – appeared on the soundtrack to *Get Crazy*, Arkush's 1983 follow-up to *Rock'N'Roll High School*. The track was as undistinguished as the film – the first time in their career that the Ramones had released a bona fide stinker.

Not bad after six albums.

. . . SO JOHNNY IS listening to his baseball in the dressing room. What would the other Ramones be doing?

"Heh – alright. Joey was quiet. Joey was very, very shy. When we used to go to parties, Joey would be standing alone and you'd think, 'We should go talk to him – he looks so lonely over there.' Because he was such an icon, a lot of people had trouble approaching him, they were afraid. Once you engaged him in conversation, he was brilliant, totally nice . . . totally sweet. Dee Dee and Marky were like the 7th graders of the band."

Were they the bad boys?

"Yeah, but like the bad boys from 7th grade – not high school. These guys – chicken farts – ha ha – maybe 3rd grade. Dee Dee would go 'chicken farts' and Marky would go 'chicken farts', 'chicken farts', 'elephant farts'. 'Ha ha ha, elephant farts.' Seriously. This could go on for hours between these two. Then they'd go 'chicken beak boy' – they had all these weird names they made up. When Monte talks about driving a Special Ed bus, he's referring to them. They would act like total retards. But it was cute. They were having a good time."

That's interesting because I've spoken to Marky a lot over the phone and he's really articulate. It's not like he's stupid or anything.

"Right, no. Marky's . . . I think his mom's a left-wing librarian – he's a smart guy. But on the Ramones level, the music was . . . everything was Dada. It was very simple, very Dadaistic, like 'duh, chicken farts . . . huh huh.' Dee Dee was the idiot savant of the band, he would instigate most of this, and Marky would play along. This went on for a long time, like years."

Did they get up to pranks?

"Yeah – the thing about the Ramones was – and everybody will tell you – they liked to piss in the beer. Anybody tell you about this?"

Tommy denies that it ever happened.

"Well, maybe with him it didn't, but it certainly happened with me."

Really?

"Yeah, so – OK, I only worked for them for a few days. I couldn't drive the truck right, it was a terrifying job – it wasn't the one I signed up for. I was going to be Johnny's guitar tech but I didn't need to move eight Marshall cabinets a night, you know? Screw that. So Johnny's like, 'Hey, have a beer, have a beer.' 'Alright . . . it tastes terrible!' And everyone in the road crew is laughing, and I'm like, 'Why are you guys laughing?' They go, 'Everyone pissed in your beer. Ha ha – they got you.' I was like 'You guys suck!' Whatever . . . they got me.

"My job was to tune the guitar between songs, make sure Johnny had towels and fill his water bottles . . . So it's my last show and I piss in his water bottle. The T-shirt guy saw me do it. I got my dick out and I pissed in his water. Johnny comes offstage, grabs the bottle, goes back for the encore, and it's like . . . 'Argh!' He looks at me and I just smiled. You know, they drove me home that night anyway.

"Each guy had his own row of seats in the van. John was always up front going, 'Monte blah blah blah,' and the others would be listening to Hair *or some other Sixties soundtrack. So Johnny would say something like, 'Will you tell Joey to shut up and play some different music?' and put on a baseball game – so Joey would go 'Monte, tell John that I want to listen to the soundtrack from* Hair.*' Then Monte would say 'Johnny, Joey wants to listen to the soundtrack from* Hair.*' Johnny would go, 'Tell that asshole I have to hear the game.' Monte would say,*

'Asshole, Johnny says you're an asshole and he wants to hear the game.' These guys were right next to each other, but that was how the conversation split. Dee Dee would be lying down on his seats, and Marky would be trying to ignore all the crap. It was so cute.

"Then Monte was like, 'OK – who wants to go to the bathroom? You want to go to the bathroom, raise your hand.' So two guys would raise their hands. Then Monte would go, 'Dee Dee, do you have to go?' 'No.' 'Are you sure because we're not going to stop until we get back to the city.' 'I don't have to go.' 'Are you sure?' 'OK, I do.'

"One of my favourite memories in the whole world is – I walked into this men's room, in a McDonalds outside of Newhaven or somewhere, and me, Joey, Johnny, Marky and Dee Dee all walked into the bathroom together, with our leather jackets, we all walked up to the urinal and pissed at the same time. I was like, 'Wow, I wish I had a fucking camera – this is my dream come true. I'm standing here with my dick out, pissing with the Ramones.' Of course, Joey and Johnny wouldn't stand next to each other at a urinal, you know? They had Dee Dee and Marky in between them."

(Author's interview with George Tabb, part-time Ramones roadie)

18

Touring, Part 4

. . . EARLY EIGHTIES, WHEN Marky was in the band, what would it have been like in a typical Ramones dressing room?

"John didn't like to have a lot of people around. He kept it very quiet. No parties, women or booze – it was very businesslike. They had their warm-up before the show and couldn't see anybody anyway."

Yeah. Would they do their own . . . when bands get to a certain stage, they get their roadies to do the soundchecks.

"That's basic organisation. Sometimes we'd have to drive hundreds of miles, so they couldn't get to do a soundcheck. But mostly they did their own soundchecks. They liked to do soundchecks, it was very important to them."

Yeah.

"But if they couldn't make it, the road crew would test everything – it was simple, bang a guitar, bang a bass, sing into the mic."

Over the years, how did the crowd change? Was there a noticeable shift?

"It got bigger. In the beginning it was mostly younger kids but, as the years went by, it was both young and old."

In late Eighties footage of the Ramones playing, there's some crowd surfing.

"Yeah, first it started off with pogoing, then a little bit of jumping into crowds, then all of a sudden they were on top of crowds, then the moshpits. The spitting was horrible – that was disgusting. I'm glad that stopped. The crowds got crazier and crazier. Some of these clubs we'd play would be in small cities and they'd go, 'Whoa! What's going on? Stop the show,' and we'd have to say, 'Don't worry – that's just the way these kids like it.' Myself – I can't understand why any kid would want to go and slam his head into somebody else, spit on somebody, have somebody spit at them. I can understand the pogoing, the jumping up and down, getting excited. But the moshpits and the slam dancing got totally out of control and jumping on people with your combat boots . . . oh god. A little crowd floating, surfing – fine – but jumping down on people from a six foot high stage? People get hurt. What's it going to evolve into next? Have they got weapons? Are they going to start beating each other up?"

I know – it's a real jock thing.

"You don't see many women in there, that's for sure."

(Author's interview with Monte Melnick, tour manager)

19

Pranks And Muggings [Aren't] Fun . . .

WHAT WAS YOUR favourite tipple?

"It depended on the time of day. In the morning, it would be champagne. In the afternoon it would be Martinis and at night, it wouldn't matter any more because I'd be so wasted that it was probably straight up vodka, 100 per cent proof. I didn't give a shit about the mixing."

Was there a moment when you realised the drinking was getting out of control?

"There were a few. I'm driving along Flatbush Avenue [Brooklyn] in my 1960 Cadillac in the 90 degrees heat, and I stop off in a bar to have four double Martinis. I get back in and start driving, when all of a sudden I black out. The weight of my leg goes onto the gas pedal and I go right through a furniture store window. It was three in the afternoon, people were shopping and there were kids on a bus stop waiting to go home from school. My windows are electrical so you can't open them from the outside, and the cops have their guns drawn and are saying to me, 'You're going to get out or we're going to get you out.' They take me to the jail for 'Driving While Under The Influence'. I could have killed 10 kids at the bus stop. I could have killed people in the showroom of the furniture store . . . and I was in jail for a night and I didn't like it. I didn't learn my lesson, though.

"Another time, I was driving along with two roadies – one in the front and one in the back – and I drank a bottle of red wine. I own a few cars. This was a '68 Coupe de Ville Cadillac. I felt something hot. I thought the roadie had dropped a cigarette. But the seating got fucked up because the wiring was brittle. I dropped out of the car, put it in park and the whole car went up in flames. If I had of stayed in the car a few minutes longer, we would have all been on fire. The cops came, the firemen came – off I went, 'Driving While Under The Influence' again. I didn't even have a licence. I didn't have nothing, you know? I was dodging it. The same judge, the same bullshit, the same accidents.

"Next thing I knew, I said, 'I'm going to stop on my own.' It's the third day I stopped drinking. I felt really shitty, you know? I go to my parents' house, I look in the back yard – I see a shape forming and it's a big fucking dinosaur looking right at me. I turned away, rubbed my eyes – which you do as a reaction – I looked back

and it was closer. It's the DTs. So I run out of the house, go back to my apartment, which was around the corner, and I hid under the covers. All night long, that's all I saw – bugs, insects, snakes – flying crazy animals. I had a dog – I didn't take him out and he shit all over the floor. I remember stepping in shit. Then I was sweating under the covers, screaming but hoping nobody would hear me.

"The next day I put myself into a rehab centre. That's where you hear the screams, the yelling, the moans and everything. They take away your shoelaces and you start to see things. They come up out of nowhere. You sit in a chair, just about living, just about existing. You can't wait to get out, but you know if you get out you're going to come straight back . . .

"They wanted me to go to AA meetings. That's where you mingle with people who have the same problems. But in the beginning, I didn't want everyone knowing my fucking secrets."

Yeah, I understand.

"I didn't know who these people were. 'Hi – I'm Marc, I think I'm an alcoholic.' And then one guy goes, 'Well, why are you here?' I go, 'Why am I here? Not because I want to get sober – I'm here because I don't want to hurt other people and everybody keeps telling me to go. I don't want the DTs any more.' He goes, 'You're an alcoholic.' So I go, 'OK – I'm an alcoholic. I'm Marc and I'm an alcoholic.' So I started getting looser.

"After four weeks, I came out. I was good for about seven weeks then I had a slip, I went on a binge. This is where I had the fight with Johnny Thunders at the Mudd Club. We were all in the bathroom. Johnny wanted to shoot up, and I wanted to take a leak – because I was drinking, obviously. He punched me. I punched him. Clem held me back. Another guy held John back. I could have smeared him . . . Then I realised: 'I'm fighting with my friends now?' So I had to go through a real bare bone rehab – like an army barracks place. No nonsense, no bullshit, right? You wake up and you go to your six o'clock meeting in the morning even before breakfast. You come back – you do chores, whatever they tell you. When I got out of there, I started making meetings where I live, I absorbed everything and that's what stopped me from doing it any more. That's the whole deal."

Yeah – presumably you miss it, though?

"I don't regret it. I had a lot of fun. I enjoy drinking. I just don't enjoy getting out of control."

It's hard. If you're in a rock band, you sit around for hours – before the show, after . . . you need something to help you come down from the high of performing.

"Alcoholism affects anyone in any business – it doesn't have to be the rock business. There are people in the entertainment business who know how to handle their liquor. They find things to do when there's nothing else to do. They entertain themselves, they go out and see the city or town, and then they come back and play.

Me, I sat there with my booze and my bottle. But it's in Wall Street, it's in construction businesses, it's in politics. It affects the individual differently. If you're an alcoholic, you have a disease. Instead of going out in a cab, looking at the sights, looking at record stores, I would have the bartender come, and say, 'I want some Jack Daniel's now. Leave me the bottle, give me a shot glass, and that's it.' I would hide my breath – I would get something like Ambesol or some heavy shit to hide it. I could perform. I was able to play. Some people can't. I was able to keep the beat, no problem. But what I wasn't able to do was control my temper."

So when you stopped using the alcohol, what did you do instead?

"I started building cars, collecting sci-fi posters, toys, practising more on the drums – anything to keep my mind off the booze. After a while the urges go away."

(Author's interview with Marky Ramone)

IN OCTOBER 1982, the Ramones started recording their seventh studio album, *Subterranean Jungle* at Kingdom Sound in Syosset, Long Island.

Both Johnny and Joey talked about quitting, but neither would. Sire were still determined to bring in outside producers – and, at the Ramones' suggestion, asked Kenny Laguna, manager and producer of Joan Jett (now post-Runaways, and cutting some fine classic rock), if he could take control. Laguna was more of an arranger, so he suggested using his co-producer Ritchie Cordell – responsible for some of the Ramones' favourite Sixties pop by Tommy James & The Shondells and 1910 Fruitgum Company ('Indian Giver').

Cordell suggested Glen Kolotkin as co-producer – Kolotkin had produced The Chambers Brothers' 1968 counter-cultural hit 'Time Has Come Today', and also recorded with Jonathan Richman. With Stasium momentarily out of the picture, Johnny brought in Heartbreakers' guitarist Walter Lure to supplement his playing.

"Ed Stasium and Daniel [Rey] and Walter always played along with Johnny, either to accentuate certain things or to bring out certain chord harmonics," Marky explains. "John never played lead guitar. Walter was a friend; Daniel was a friend; and if the producer could play guitar, he'd play. That was it."

Dee Dee, meanwhile, was still having trouble mastering the basics: "I go by the dots and frets, so [Johnny] has to tell me where to play," he revealed. "I don't know the names of the strings even."

In a *Rolling Stone* article of the time, Cordell recalled that the Ramones were unhappy with the previous two albums, and attacked him as soon as he walked into the studio. "I was so upset after 15 minutes that I tried to leave and walked into a closet. They didn't trust me for over a week but then they were very open to suggestions."

Subterranean Jungle is a frustrating album. In places, it's horrendously over-produced – Spector had his Wall Of Sound, Gouldman had his Sixties pop harmonies vision, but Cordell seemed to be aiming for a hard rock sound that may have sat well with Joan Jett, but not with a band whose aggressive drive was the last thing they needed tampering with. Also, it's disorientating that the record starts with two cover versions – reasonable run-throughs of the Music Explosion's 'Little Bit O' Soul' and The Boyfriends' 'I Need Your Love', but with little power and a vocal style that sounded suspiciously like shouting, not the familiar heartfelt embrace. Two covers? At the start? The Ramones didn't even bother with one on *Pleasant Dreams*.

The fact that Joey's songs were credited to "Joe" Ramone was an indication of the general attitude: a few years back, someone would've picked up on such a howler. Now, no one seemed to care. Warner Bros. didn't even bother releasing a single from the record in America.

Perhaps Joey's voice was weakening after so many years on the road: Dee Dee sang an entire verse of his own disturbed 'Outsider', and for the entirety of his (frankly more ridiculous than frightening) 'Time Bomb'. To hear the bassist sing was weird: this wasn't the Ramones we knew and loved, but a strange alien beast that for the first time in their career seemed to be directly responding to peer pressure – but peers 10 years the Ramones' juniors, the hardcore kids.

'Psycho Therapy', an old-school Ramones song co-written by Johnny and Dee Dee, was the beginning of a long period of studio mediocrity – unfortunately, Johnny loved it: "I wanted to do a hardcore song to show the hardcore people that we can play as fast or faster than they can," he told *Rolling Stone*. "*Nobody* plays faster than us."*

Speed was John's craft, his trade. It was the one thing that he felt he could do better than anyone. No wonder he felt threatened by the new

* The video of 'Psycho Therapy', directed by Frank De Lea, was the first promo to cause a major censorship controversy on the nascent MTV channel. The film told the story of a wayward youth thrown into an asylum, and forced to undergo a brutal lobotomy. Just as he goes under, he starts hallucinating the doctors' heads as decaying skulls: and as they make the incision, a monster bursts forth, grotesque and leering like a twisted version of *Alien*. MTV classified the film as "offensive", and refused to show it: though whether it was because of the skulls, the cute monster or the insensitive depiction of mental hospitals it wasn't clear. Despite several frantic amendments, the Ramones album that it was hired to promote had slipped from the charts before the TV channel started to sporadically screen it.

breed of hardcore bands – like Suicidal Tendencies, Minutemen and Circle Jerks – who placed a premium on aggression and velocity. Yet these bands and Johnny himself missed a vital truth about the Ramones: this wasn't *only* what they did. In both Dee Dee and Joey they had two extraordinary pop songwriters.

"I was walking home from my psychiatrist's office one day," Dee Dee told *Melody Maker*, "and remembered 'psycho therapy' was one of the terms he used. I walked to rehearsal 'cos it was so nice that day, and just started singing the phrase. It was weird, 'cos I wasn't getting along with Johnny then, and decided I wanted to be friends with him again. So I said, 'Will you write a song with me?' and we got down together and wrote it, made it real Ramones-like."

'My-My Kind Of A Girl', just one of three Joey songs on the album, was another classic girl group style gem, with uncredited backing vocals supplied by Sixties British pop singer Petula Clark ('Downtown'). "When I saw you on 8th Street," Joey croons. "You could make my life complete, baby." The singer is so clearly in love with the idea of love itself, it makes the heart melt.

"The thing Joey wanted more than anything in life was to have Ramones songs used in movies and commercials," explains Janis Schacht. "That's why he kept throwing in references to places like Burger King. He so wanted 'My-My Kind Of A Girl' to be used in a Burger King commercial."

There are some other great songs present – Joey's return to the Thorazine-fuelled riotous imagery of 'We're A Happy Family' in the album's closer, 'Everytime I Eat Vegetables I Always Think Of You' (a song in a title, almost – in the old days, it would have been); Dee Dee's unashamedly beautiful ode to a (partly) innocent youth that he never experienced 'In The Park'; and his full-on rock anthem 'Somebody Like Me' with its no-nonsense lines, "I'm just a guy who likes to rock and roll/I'm just a guy who likes to get drunk/I'm just a guy who likes to dress punk/Get my kicks an' live up my life".

Oddly, the third and final cover is excellent: a blistering version of 'Time Has Come Today' (later released as a single in the UK) with a virtuoso vocal lead from Joey, and solid guitars, only marginally marred by the production: "I did some demos for *Subterranean Jungle*," says Ed Stasium. "Those are good songs. On the final version of 'Time Has Come Today', though, the recording technique did some wacky out-of-phase thing on Johnny's guitar so if you listen to it in mono, the guitar disappears from the mix. No guitars on a Ramones song: pretty embarrassing."

Joey, unsurprisingly, was indifferent towards hardcore: "I just hear it as sounding all the same," he told *Rolling Stone* in '87. "I don't hear anything that's earth-shattering or that knocks me out."

"I don't understand how anyone in a punk band could be a liberal," Johnny complained a few years earlier. "Punks should have no politics or be right wing: otherwise, they're just hippies dressed as punks."

"I'm proud of John's politics," Dee Dee said. "He's a good American. When the cops used to harass us all the time, he thought they were just being good cops. He just doesn't like to see Americans get shit on."

The power struggle within and around the band continued right up till the final shows, and beyond. Indeed, post-Joey (and now Dee Dee) the bickering has become stronger. One suspects that in the early Eighties, Joey had the upper hand – his search for pop perfection echoing the record company's needs. But then the drinking got out of hand, and the hit failed to materialise. So Johnny decided it was time he took artistic control.

Marky never had a say, and Dee Dee was in another world entirely.

No wonder the entire Ramones camp embraced Nirvana (and to a lesser degree grunge) so wholeheartedly when they appeared – here, at last, was another band able seamlessly to match a hardcore sensibility to a pure pop heart.

THE SLEEVE TO *Subterranean Jungle* – although not a patch on Roberta Bayley and John Holmstrom's earlier offerings – at least showed the band wearing their leather jackets again, standing on the Sixth Avenue local to Coney Island. The positioning of the musicians is odd. Joey is sitting down at the back, Dee Dee wears a white T-shirt that is too bright to be real, you could miss Marky looking through the side window – and the graffiti on the train's outside has clearly been added after the shoot. The entire picture reeks of inauthenticity: an air brushed, MTV-friendly vision of punk that had little to do with the Ramones' original image.

"I was hired by the art director Tony Wright to photograph the Ramones," says George DuBose. The pair had met via The B-52's: DuBose shot their debut album sleeve. "The Ramones had a concept to be photographed in a subway car and they wanted me to go to the train yards at the end of the line.

"I photographed different set-ups, and then Johnny asked me to tell Marky to go look out of the window, because they were kicking him out of the group but he didn't know it yet. When Tony put the cover together, the car was pretty clean – most of the graffiti was added on afterwards. We found out later the Ramones weren't happy with it, because it looked too fake."

The Ramones played only around 70 shows in 1982, reflecting their inner disharmony. They included notable dates with Cyndi Lauper's surprisingly fine New Wave band Blue Angel in May, in Jersey City with Robert Gordon (same month), a free show in Virginia Beach (April) to make up for the one Marky was too drunk to play at – plus a couple of big concerts in September and November.

The first was at the US festival in San Bernardino, California, where the Ramones played the punk rock segment in front of 300,000 people – other bands included The Police, Talking Heads and The B-52's. Ramones went on second after Oingo Boingo, in blazing sunlight – their 'The Good, The Bad And The Ugly' opening music being particularly effective among the dusty surroundings.

The other was a show in Bangor, Maine with Cheap Trick, promoted by Stephen King – afterwards, the band went back to the best-selling horror writer's house, thus beginning a friendship that would culminate in one of the Ramones' closest brushes with the American charts (Dee Dee's title track for the 1989 movie *Pet Sematary*).

The Ramones didn't venture out of America the whole year – rather an odd decision on the management's part, as their hardcore support was undoubtedly in the UK, continental Europe, Japan, Australia . . . anywhere that wasn't the States, in fact. But that's Americans for you – seriously xenophobic when left to their own devices.

"A cop pulled us over the other night after a show in New Jersey," Dee Dee told *Rolling Stone*. "Really patted us down, searched us twice. He seemed very upset when he had to let us go."

"He put a flashlight down my pants," said Johnny. "It isn't fair. We did a benefit at CBGBs for their bullet-proof vest fund."

"Customs officers have the same attitude," added Joey.

"Where was that country they held us up for so long?" asked Johnny. "France . . . and Hawaii. They don't like Americans there."

The band's final date of the year was on November 27, 1982, in Islip, Long Island. It was also Marky's last show with the band until his return in 1987.

"I'd bought a bottle of vodka to the studio," says Marky, "and I was nipping on it with Walter (Lure]. I hid it in the garbage. Dee Dee found it and ratted on me. He was no angel himself. He was doing cocaine and pot and all that stuff. I would never have done that to him. I forgot about it because obviously we're still friends. The only song I'm not on is 'Time Has Come Today'. I'm glad because I don't like that album. In fact, that's the album I hate the most – I hated the production, I hated the producer, he's the only one who wouldn't let me get my own drum sound. He wanted to use this modern shitty drum sound that sounded like a drum machine and, you know, I didn't care at that point because I was drinking. After that I got a call. 'We don't want you in the band anymore.' "

Johnny Thunders' drummer Billy Rogers replaced Marky on the final track. He didn't work out as a full-time Ramone, so after a series of auditions, the band chose Richie Reinhardt – formerly of NYC band Velveteen.

Richie joined in time to feature in the two videos shot to help promote the album: 'Psycho Therapy' and 'Time Has Come Today', the latter set in a church, a spoof on a Gospel Revivalist Meeting featuring many of the Ramones' friends.

Although roundly reviled by many fans, and suffering from lacklustre production, *Subterranean Jungle* isn't nearly so bad at all. "It's to do with the age you first heard the Ramones," thinks Slim Moon, boss of Kill Rock Stars, the Olympia Riot Grrrl label that later released a duet between Ronnie Spector and Joey Ramone. "It's my favourite album. 'Psycho Therapy' is great. I remember the clerk who sold it to me was just appalled. 'This isn't a real Ramones record.' I like the classic first two records, too. I'm not a purist about it."

NO ONE'S REALLY described Richie Ramone to me.

"I never met him."

You never met him?

"No."

Oh. Did he exist?

"Yes, he existed."

Was he made up?

"No. He was a friend."

(Author's interview with Arturo Vega)

RICHIE REINHARDT PLAYED 400 shows with da bruddas (with Arturo Vega working the lights) after he joined in 1983, appeared on several videos, wrote a handful of songs – including 1986's excellent 'Somebody Put Something In My Drink' UK single – yet no one I spoke to who was around the Ramones during this period will talk about him. It's like he disappeared off the face of the earth (he hasn't – he was last sighted at Joey's funeral in 2001). The Ramones Myth may have become tarnished over the years – first we discover they're not brothers, next we discover they lied about their ages, that Johnny doesn't play all the guitars in the studio, that they're not a Happy Family, that their clothes are not everyday wear, but a uniform. It was still potent enough, however, to cover its tracks in one last – seemingly pointless – gesture.

Hours spent trawling the 'net under the names Richie Ramone, Reinhardt and Beau (the name he went under when he drummed with Velveteen) turn up little biographical information. Velveteen released one album, the six-track dance-rock offering *After Hours* in 1983. Richie was also reported to have drummed with Annie Golden's New Wave Brooklyn outfit, The Shirts. In the official Ramones biography, Jim Bessman's *An American Band*, the drummer has one line devoted to his arrival. It's like he never existed. Did someone dream those 400 gigs, all the interviews he sat in on, the New York Dolls-style guitars on 'Somebody Put Something In My Drink'? (Joey shouts rather than sings his way through the latter – ironically, his own drinking had affected his vocal chords by that point.)

So this is what we know – Richard Reinhardt was born on August 11, 1957.

He officially became Richie Ramone at a show in Utica, New York on February 13, 1983, signed autographs as Richie Beau during that year's American *Subterranean Jungle* tour (when the band noticeably avoided Europe again, as they also did in 1984), played with the band until 1987 when he abruptly walked out over a dispute in pay and . . . disappeared.

"I just can't remember that much about him. It was like . . . you always knew Marc Bell would come back," says Gloria Nicholl. "He was nice, but Johnny treated him as a sideman and paid him sideman wages. He was never really a Ramone. He paid him like 150 bucks a week or something insulting. But that's Johnny for you. He used to take pleasure in being vile – some of it's put on, and some isn't."

ON AUGUST 15, a New York tabloid headline boasted, "Battered Punk Star Fights For His Life". Johnny had got into a serious brawl with Seth Macklin from punk band Sub-Zero Construction in front of his apartment at four in the morning – the report had him offering assistance to a drunken girl. Accounts vary.

"The Ramones had been playing Glenmore [Queens] that night," recalls Holmstrom. "We got out in front of Paul's Lounge, and I was talking to Johnny for about 10 minutes. I guess I was the last person to see him before it happened. I didn't hear anything or I would have run back. The next day I pick up the paper and find out he got his head kicked in. He came close to getting killed."

"Johnny was going out with this girl who was a drunk," explains Marky. "I know, because I was seeing her before him. One evening he catches her with this other guy in front of his house and starts swinging his bag at him. Next thing he knows, he gets kicked in the head, gets a concussion and ended up on the intensive care list at hospital. The other guy knew karate, and Johnny didn't. He fell down and the guy started stomping on his head so he had to get an operation on his skull. [He had a fractured skull.] Six or seven weeks later – he started playing again. That's amazing."

"I never saw what happened or what led up to it," Johnny remarked at the time. "The kid got arrested and went to jail."

When the guitarist returned from hospital, he'd had his head shaved, and needed to wear a baseball cap for a few months. "It was hardly covered in the British press," says fan Mark Bannister, "but it made front page news in New York. I made a 'Get Well Soon' card and carried it around for days, getting everyone I knew to sign it, and sent it off to the address on the back of the album. I was thrilled when I got a letter back from Johnny."

"WE HAD SO much fun playing pinball. We would hang out at CBGBs for the pinball more than the music. Then Joey moved to 9th Street in this big apartment building between Second and Third. That was kind of weird because Johnny was up the block on 10th Street between Third and Fourth. We used to hang out at this place called Paul's Lounge [in the front of Joey's building] – they had great pinball machines. That became like our second home. They had the Kiss pinball machine."

When I started coming to New York, I used to go to Max Fish just to play the pinball. They always had the newest ones there.

"We'd always try to get four people on the machines. I think that's why I hung out with Joey a lot because he liked to play. Dee Dee would hang out at CBGBs, but he wasn't there every night like Joey would be. With Joey, it was like his home away from home. It was right across the street and Paul's Lounge was in between. They all knew him. He'd walk into Paul's Lounge and they'd be like, 'Hey, Joey!' He practically owned the place."

Who was better at pinball, you or Joey?

"When we started, I was because I'd been playing more. Joey and I were pretty even. I was never that good at pinball – a real wizard would kick my ass. I never learned how to tilt it. It's like anything – the more you play, the better you get. We were playing a lot in those days."

Did you drink spirits or just beer?

"Only beer. I remember Joey getting pretty drunk one night, hitting a few beer bottles and smashing them against the bar. He got away with it. Anybody else would be . . . Merv was the big bartender. He always took care of Joey and would encourage him, like, 'It's time to go home now Joey.' He didn't do any real damage. I never saw Joey get violent or anything. Dee Dee could get violent."

Yeah, I can't imagine Joey getting violent.

(Author's interview with John Holmstrom)

20

Touring, Part 5

. . . "JOEY TRIED ALL kinds of things. We toured so often, it was really tough on him."

Yeah. What things did he try?

"Drinking teas. He would do vocal exercises all the time. Monte and I were always looking out for him, making sure that he would have a scarf around his neck when he came out, things like that."

Yeah – you can't mess with The Voice. I can remember seeing the Ramones perform on *The Old Grey Whistle Test* around the time of *Too Tough To Die* and Joey had lost his voice. He was singing really low down.

"It would happen. What was amazing was that he would get better in the middle of a tour."

Really?

"His vocal chords would get stronger and he would overcome. At the beginning it'd be tough but then he'd reach a point where instead of getting really, really bad, he would get better. It happened most of the time, if not all the time, because we never had to cancel a show because he couldn't sing – not once."

That's incredible.

"That's how he was. He would overcome about any situation. The Ramones were a highly disciplined working machine and the promoters loved them for it. The Ramones were never late for anything; they never cancelled for any reason. The promoter felt very safe booking a Ramones show."

And they knew it would always be the same show . . .

"Yeah. That was Johnny – he may not have been creative, but he kept things together. He looked after the band and the band's interests. He protected the band from unscrupulous promoters and record companies."

The Ramones were massive in South America, weren't they?

"Very much. It took about 10 years to develop, but once it took off, it got bigger and bigger. They were bigger than The Rolling Stones. They toured the same year (1995), and the Ramones sold more tickets."

Yeah, Monte was saying the reason for that was because the promoters in those countries would also run the radio shows – they made sure people heard the Ramones.

"The Argentinian promoters had the TV and radio stations, but you can only promote a band so much. The insanity they provoked in people could not be implanted."

(Author's interview with Arturo Vega, lighting manager)

21

The Song Ramones The Same

BETWEEN 19/11/81 and 24/2/85, the Ramones didn't play outside the States – apart from a handful of dates in Canada. That's a long time to be banging your head against a brick wall: considering the exalted status the Ramones had attained in Europe, Japan and the Spanish-speaking countries, it seemed an absurd decision not to have them travel abroad.

Right enough, the band were barely speaking to each other, the drinking was out of control, a new drummer had joined, Joey was in and out of hospital because of his body's frailty, Johnny had nearly died, punk was out of fashion, Dee Dee was taking far too many drugs . . . but this was the Ramones! An entire generation of bands had sprung up influenced by their no frills approach – indeed, by this point, it was becoming easier to find a musician not in love with the first three Ramones albums than one who was. NOFX, Bad Brains, Hüsker Dü, Suicidal Tendencies, Newtown Neurotics, Sniper, Billy Bragg, The Go-Go's, Sonic Youth, Shop Assistants, Membranes, R.E.M., Fear, The Vandals, UK Subs, Marine Girls, U2, Velvet Monkeys, The Germs, Black Flag, Dead Kennedys, Orange Juice, Half-Japanese . . . you could hear elements of da bruddas in all their sounds. And the list went on and on. Their leather jackets were models of cool: the ripped jeans and street-tough stance had been adopted countless times over as badges of credibility. Wear a Ramones T-shirt, and you were in – it didn't matter what you looked like, or what music you really dug. Lack of mainstream success only increased the Ramones' currency.

A glance at the Ramones tour itinerary shortly after Richie joined reads like an American travelling salesperson's dream . . .

Utica, Philadelphia, Poughkeepsie, Wellesley MA, Boston, Middlebury VT, Southampton LI, Danbury CT, Burlington VT, Philadelphia, Philadelphia, Brooklyn, Brooklyn, Washington DC, Washington DC . . .

. . . New Haven . . .

. . . Hartford . . .

. . . Boston, Amherst, Atlanta, New Orleans, Beaumont TX, Dallas, Houston, Austin, San Antonio, La Cruces NM, Phoenix, LA Palladium with The Dickies (an LA punk band who specialised in racing through songs at cartoon-fast tempo), San Diego with Tom Petty, Stray Cats and Bow Wow Wow (Malcolm McLaren's post-Pistols, rather fun, teen scam), Pasadena, Goleta CA, Santa Cruz, Palo Alto, San Francisco, Sacramento . . .

And all this between February and April . . .

"Their show was like a machine," explains Daniel Rey. "Nothing was left to chance. It was great opening for them in Shrapnel because after we did it a few times we became part of the family. We'd get the 'Hey Ho Let's Go' chant throughout our set. We must've opened for them a 100 times.

"They'd meet in front of Joey's house," he continues, "waiting for Joey to come down. They'd always tell Joey they were leaving at five when they'd have to leave at 5.30 because then Joey'd come down at 5.30. It was like a comedy troupe the way they carried on. Part of being in a band is that routine and the little gags you make that are only funny to you. They were very funny and wry, like mischievous kids on a school trip. Monte, the tour manager, would be like the substitute teacher who had to put up with them."

The Ramones' lean period may have been between '83 and '87, but they still played between 80 and a hundred shows across North America in each of those years.

Perhaps the band stopped going abroad because someone – the management, the musicians themselves – felt the early Eighties craze for synthetic pop, and the New Romantics, was at odds with their music. Joey indicated as much in an interview conducted with *NME* in early 1985: "The last time we were in England it was the boom of the synthesiser music and it seemed that's what everybody wanted to hear," he stated. "Maybe they thought we were passé or something."

In the same article, Dee Dee whined that "this is the first time anyone's paid any attention to us in a lot of years", and when the writer pointed out it was the first time they'd been abroad in years, the bassist retorted that the management had told the band that the promoters didn't want them. It was everybody else's fault, clearly.

"The first four years we went to the UK," Arturo Vega explains, "the audiences got wilder and wilder, and more energetic. But they also forgot about you faster. We became old hat very quickly in England. By then, it was like everybody [in the band] had given up, except they wanted to continue touring because that's how we made a living. It was a tough time."

"It was probably because Johnny was in one of his 'I hate English people' and 'I hate Europeans too' phases," thinks Gloria Nicholl, who opened a UK office for Kurfirst Management in 1983. "Johnny was such a xenophobe. He had to stay in a Holiday Inn and get CNN TV and would only go to McDonald's to eat. The other three loved every minute they were away."

After the relative failure of *Subterranean Jungle*, the band renegotiated their contract with Sire/Warner Bros. in America, but not from a position of strength. Seymour Stein still held the faith, but Sire was a part of Warners. The Ramones were offered a three-album and video package only, no singles. This didn't please Joey, a singles fanatic: "It's like somebody cuttin' your tongue out!" he complained. "Besides, you don't have a sales tool . . ."

"That period was difficult," explains Daniel Rey, "because the Ramones had been in a band, on a bus, non-stop for years. There was some animosity. Most bands would have broken up in that two year period between *Subterranean Jungle* and *Too Tough To Die*."

I guess that's why they came up with that title.

"Yeah, you're probably right," Rey laughs. " 'We are the Ramones, we do what we do and fuck you.' "

Yet still the shows kept coming . . .

1984: New Haven, Boston, Queens, Philadelphia, Roslyn . . . Portland ME, Providence, Waterbury CT, Brooklyn, Washington DC, Manchester NH, Albany, Hartford . . . Ithaca, Cortland with Cheap Trick and David Johansen, Garden City LI, New Haven, Mt Ivy NY, Richmond VA . . .

At a Palladium show in LA, the riot cops showed up, helicopters circling, after some of the 5,000 strong crowd started hurling bottles at security. "The cops were beating kids with sticks!" Joey reported, sickened. "It was fucked up."

"It's definitely been more violent," the singer stated elsewhere. "The guys out there in LA are *sick*, know what I mean? I've been doing a lot of smashing kids in the face with my mic stand, but they seem to like it – and I guess it gives me more to do."

THE RAMONES STARTED recording their "comeback" album *Too Tough To Die* in the summer of 1984, at Media Sound. Johnny was fed up with the pop experiment, and thought it was time to get back to the sound he felt the Ramones were associated with – punk, but not just punk. Hardcore. Loud thrashed guitars, guttural wrenched-out vocals, songs that had to be faster and faster . . . velocity over melody. Drums were upfront because that was the fashion in punk circles: any sign of emotion that wasn't negative and despairing was a sign of weakness, not punk.

How ironic that a movement that had its roots in breaking conventions rapidly became subsumed in a series of musical conventions even stricter.

If *End Of The Century* and *Pleasant Dreams* were Joey's albums, then this new one was definitely Johnny's. It was his vision, his sound, and he'd even started writing songs with Dee Dee again. Joey was singing in a deep, almost unrecognisable style, shouting half his lines. The effect was immediately harsher – perfectly complimenting the music. It was also disturbing.

The title was a direct reference to Johnny's near fatal fight, and also the Ramones' determination that all their efforts in staying on the road wouldn't go to waste.

"Every band that came out when we came out broke up," Joey told *Hard Times* in October 1984. Yet even at that point, Joey was talking of making a solo album – he was working on a heavy metal anthem called 'Rock'N'Roll Is The Answer' with Richie Stotts, ex-Plasmatics. "Also, the bands that came out when we came out [jumped] on the bandwagon because they weren't interested in their fans. They were interested in making money, like Blondie. Even though I like Blondie, but they went disco. And the Clash went dance-rock. Billy Idol is just nothing. It's like Hollywood punk, you know."

Dee Dee's songs were dark, unnerving in their despondency – the band, bitter at their lack of success, channelled their frustrations into the music. A couple of weak fillers aside, *Too Tough To Die* is a cracking album. It served as a necessary realignment for a band that had been floundering as to which musical direction they should take. For better or for worse, it was now decided.

The main reason *Too Tough To Die* sounds so great is its production.

The Ramones had returned to the combination behind the classic second, third and fourth albums – Tommy Erdelyi and Ed Stasium. It must've been a considerable climb down for someone, not that it was probably seen that way. Walter Lure again added extra guitar, along with – ironically, considering the band's supposed distaste for the instrument – some synthesisers supplied by Talking Heads' Jerry Harrison.

"They wanted to go back to the basic, classic Ramones sound," says Tommy, "so they gave me a call. It was a different atmosphere than before. Of course I would have preferred they all loved each other, but they felt what they were doing was important. And in order to survive, you have to make records. I tried to stay out of the personal politics."

"We mixed it at Sigma Sound," recalls Ed, "with the mysterious Richie on drums. He wasn't really a great drummer for the Ramones. He was more of a jazz musician. He could hold the beat, though."

In a 1985 *Sounds* interview, Richie indicated he didn't find it too hard fitting in: "I've always drummed in their style – steady and hard-hitting – but it was difficult working myself up to the speed. There are three speeds in the Ramones: fast, pretty fast and very fast."

"It's easy to forget about Richie," Stasium adds, "even though he was in the band for years, because he was so quiet. Maybe they asked us back in because it was the 10th anniversary . . . So we went back to the old studio."

Even so, management couldn't resist tampering with the formula: Dave Stewart of Eurythmics was brought in to produce the British single 'Howling At The Moon (Sha-La-La)', a pairing that surprisingly worked – it's a terrific pop song, written by Dee Dee about marijuana and survival, and dedicated to his wife Vera on the inner sleeve, keyboards (courtesy of Tom Petty musician, Benmont Tench) cascading across the song's intro, heralding as catchy a "sha-la-la" refrain as Joey has ever drawled. (Kurfirst also managed Stewart – thus are musical collaborations created.) Only trouble was, the song's totally unrepresentative of the rest of the album. Still, at least Stewart understood the concept of power, even if he did bail out of the recording halfway through.

"We finished that entire song first," recalls Stasium. "David wanted the drums to sound like a huge pile-driver – like one of those massive crane-type machines driving holes into the ground for the foundations of a skyscraper. He wanted to go out into the street and sample one, but we never got round to it."

If the Ramones had been trying to prove how "punk" they were to the new generation, that single must've thrown them off the scent entirely. Joey later furiously back-pedalled on his dislike of synths, justifying their inclusion by saying, "There are so many ways to use synths and orchestrations! Look at the way Zeppelin used 'em. That was no wimp-out."

Dee Dee was in fine form, having been revitalised by the hardcore scene – he was a fan of the actual music (more so than Johnny, who merely looked on it as a challenge to his job). The bassist wrote over two-thirds of the songs, and also sang two numbers – 'Wart Hog' (later to become a live staple) and the terrifying 'Endless Vacation' with its mocking chorus – in a voice that was far better suited to the Ramones' new "fuck sensitivity" sound. He sounded like he was gargling razorblades.

"I was amazed at how great Dee Dee was as a songwriter, and what a surprisingly good punk voice he had," recalled Marky. Indeed, the bassist's speed-rap on 'Endless Vacation' wouldn't have sounded out of place on English anarcho-punks Crass' trailblazing *Feeding Of The Five Thousand.*

"Dee Dee was a very unique character," said Johnny after his former band-member's death, "the most influential punk rock bassist. He set the standard that all punk rock bassists look to. He was a great lyricist. I'd write [the music to] something like, say, 'Wart Hog', and I'd give it to Dee Dee, and he'd just open up his book and start singing a page out of his book of lyrics. His songs were always my favourites. Anything I co-wrote, I co-wrote with Dee Dee."

Elsewhere, songs like the Joey Ramone/Daniel Rey collaboration 'Daytime Dilemma (Dangers Of Love)' and album opener 'Mama's Boy' were good solid rock – the former even giving a nod to old producer Phil Spector, courtesy of Richie's suspiciously Ronettes-style drum break in the middle. Shame the lyrics are so throwaway TV soap opera, and that the coda (a musical concept previously anathema to the Ramones) goes on far too long. 'Mama's Boy' (one of five songs co-written by Johnny) sets out the album's stall early on: "Couldn't shut up, you're an imbecile," Joey snarled. "You're an ugly dog." If the Ramones were going to take punk on, *they were going to take it on.* The inner sleeve was even set out like a Xeroxed fanzine, with the lyrics deliberately shoddily typed, in a fake approximation of the influential hardcore bible, *Maximum Rock'N'Roll.*

"It started out of necessity," says Rey about his input into the Ramones' music. The Shrapnel guitarist later became Dee Dee's songwriting partner. "The band needed songs. I had a little studio where we would make demos. Joey would write slower. Dee Dee was always reliable. He'd get a burst, and churn out four or five songs in an afternoon. Most of the time I wrote the music, and Dee Dee wrote the lyrics. It was easy because we had boundaries that we stayed within."

Joey was starting to lose his songwriting abilities: he never did manage to quite recapture the form that made early songs like 'Judy Is A Punk', 'Beat On The Brat' and 'Here Today . . .', so memorable. *Too Tough To Die* is a low point: three songs, and two are collaborations. 'No Go' is a fairly standard Fifties Gene Vincent-style rocker – like 'Do You Wanna Dance?', only more minimal. But the Dee Dee/Joey-penned 'Chasing

The Night' (with music from Busta Jones) was a classic – another hard-edged teen angst operetta, similar in feel to Tom Waits' 'Heart Of Saturday Night', that comes as welcome light relief at the end of side one. The drums pound way too fast as if the band are embarrassed to be playing along with Harrison's synthesisers, and Joey's voice is shot, but both add to the song's charm.

'I'm Not Afraid Of Life' contains some of the bleakest lines Dee Dee had ever written. "I'm not afraid of pain/But it hurts so bad," Joey sang in a near monotone, "Don't want to die at an early age." It was a chilling moment of self-realisation for the addict, one that he'd go through every so often. The song also touches on the threat of nuclear war. It's very claustrophobic, but the thought of Dee Dee maturing was almost more worrying than the song's sentiments.

"I saw a TV documentary about these people gettin' fired from their jobs just as they're gettin' ready to retire," he said, "and it struck me as real wrong. An' also, it kinda frightened me. When the time comes, I'm gonna get me a trailer right next to a deli and have myself a good time."

'Planet Earth 1988' continues the theme of pessimism and alarm – racial discrimination and the terrorist threat. It would've been far better suited to the bassist's voice than Joey's depressing monotone.

"I used to have no morals," Dee Dee told *Maximum Rock'N'Roll*, "then about four years ago I decided to quit taking heroin and started going to this programme, Odyssey House. This therapist, Harold, this black guy started teaching me about human feelings and that I was no different than anybody else even though I was a rock star. I even read the Bible to get some insight into the world and stop hating everything."

It rings a fraction false. The Ramones always shied away from preaching – Johnny felt it was the province of the hippies – yet here was Dee Dee discovering a social conscience that coincidentally echoed prevalent hard-core beliefs. Ridiculous lines like "I'm a Nazi schatzi/Yes I am" and pin-heads and cretins dancin' sat far better on the band then these newfound left-of-centre politics.

"Are you drawing on your stock of adolescent memories now you're in your thirties?" asked one *NME* critic.

Dee Dee: "No, we're writing as mature adults."

Joey (simultaneously): "No, I'm still a kid."

"America is pretty bleak, there's no hope really," Dee Dee explained later. "When we started out writing about politics, it was 'Hey, the Ramones are preaching left-wing propaganda.' But that's how we felt. We wanted to show we had feelings. We've gotten serious with this album."

Elsewhere, however (as early on as the album's press release), the bassist was trying to disassociate himself from his lyrics.

The other songs are fillers – the truly dire 'Danger Zone', where Dee Dee once again tries to get philosophical on our ass, and fails miserably; the brief Johnny Ramone instrumental 'Durango 95' that later became the live set opener (it's named after a restaurant opposite Paul's Bar which itself was named after a car in *A Clockwork Orange*); and Richie Ramone's contribution, the humdrum 'Human Kind'. Richie was a golfer: "Every time we pass a golf course, it's like, 'Oh, there's a nice one!'" Joey explained. "I played with him a couple of times, in South Carolina or somewhere, but he's real serious about it. Richie's makin' it *fun* to be in the Ramones again." Joey preferred go-karting.

In fairness, Dee Dee was originally meant to sing 'Danger Zone': "[The version with] Dee Dee singing is great – it's more punk," Johnny claimed. "The version that made it to the record, with Joey's vocals, is more polished."

It's during earnest, nonsense songs like these that one of the old Ramones' standbys – warped, sick humour – is most missed. Joey now wore grotesque leather trousers in photographs, in real rock star fashion. They – and the studded leather glove he also started wearing on stage – were at odds with the Ramones' street-level uniform. It's odd how this album was seen as a return to the old standards. It is, and it isn't. It omits vital components. Most of all, it missed the gang mentality that was so vital to the whole myth of the Ramones.

Too Tough To Die? Either that, or too darn stubborn.

"I BECAME FRIENDLY WITH Tommy because when I was at Warner Brothers, I was the A&R rep for The Replacements. Seymour was hot to sign them, and encouraged us to pursue Tommy as their record producer. At that point, I still thought of Tommy as another weirdo. He hadn't come on my radar as a fully thinking human being yet."

How was he as a producer? What was his modus operandi?

"This was a surprising thing, having only known him from his history, he was incredibly quiet and soft-spoken, to the point of being withdrawn. Tommy had an intellectual point of view that really differed from Joey's, which was much more innocent. Tommy would reference Warhol, and see the Ramones in this pantheon of pop art as well as . . . punk art. He never stopped thinking about what was going on at any moment."

He's older than Dee Dee and Joey and Marky, isn't he?

"Yes. Tommy has perspective. He knows that when the Ramones went over to

England, they changed the landscape of popular music. Whereas Joey was more like, 'Oh boy, I got to go to England! It was so exciting! Oh, and by the way this other thing happened!' He just had this childlike joy."

(Author's interview with Michael Hill)

THE COVER TO *Too Tough To Die* is probably the last great Ramones album sleeve.

The four members stand silhouetted in a blue light inside a tunnel, features barely discernible, waiting and primed for action. Behind them is one solitary blinding light, like a juggernaut's headlight. The lettering is big and solid and blocky – no-nonsense information. The back sleeve is a detail of a leather jacket.

"At this point in their career," recalls photographer George DuBose, "they could afford to have a cover that didn't show their faces. Which is what happened because my front strobes failed to fire. It was another one of my lucky accidents. Johnny wanted a picture that would evoke memories of the gang in *A Clockwork Orange*. They wanted to be photographed in a tunnel. In Central Park, Manhattan, there are a few tunnels, and I used the smallest one by the children's zoo.

"I got a case of beer and a couple of pizzas," he continues, "and it was shot at night. I hung up some clear plastic sheeting at one end, and had large strobe lights behind them shining into the tunnel, with blue gels. One time, the front light didn't flash and it gave this silhouette effect. The group ate all the pizza in the Winnebago, but they didn't want the beer. However, when I went to get one it had all gone. Dee Dee had snagged the whole case."

Too Tough To Die was released in America in October 1984. The reaction was part favourable and part sarcastic.

"Who'd have thunk it?" sneered *Village Voice*. "With Tommy producing again, these teen-identified professionals, mean age 33*, make what may be their greatest album, with the cleansing minimalism of their original conception evoked and honestly augmented. Dee Dee imitates Bugs Bunny on steroids on two well-placed hardcore parodies . . ."

Unfortunately, they weren't parodies.

"Their lyrics are vicious and very real," Dee Dee told *Maximum Rock'-N'Roll*, who also laid the same charge against them. "They're like anti-heroin songs and what you feel like. Like 'My skull lies bleaching in

* Correct, but the band constantly lied about their ages – Dee Dee claimed to be 28 in 1984, and 31 in 1985.

the dust' ['Endless Vacation'] . . . That was our attempt to play the new style. We did it to the strict rules of hardcore."

Rolling Stone were kinder, calling it "a significant step forward for this great American band", while *Creem* hailed them as the "most influential rock'n'roll band of the last 10 years". In *NME*, Mat Snow pointed out that "the topics to which they address themselves are largely free of such distracting frills as Mom and Luv. This year we're talking such Black Flag/Hüsker Dü subjects as nihilism, apocalypse and social ills." The songs on side two, meanwhile, "might have graced *Rocket To Russia* with some distinction. Need I say more?"

"It's full of Christmas cracker clichés and hilarious couplets such as 'Battleships crowd the sea/16-year-olds in the army'," another critic wrote. "But you can't fault the heart behind it."

Sounds, stalwart Ramones fans, reviewed the album twice – once on import, where Edwin Pouncy captured prevalent opinion by calling 'Wart Hog' a novelty song, and pointing out that "the Ramones' freak flag has been pulled down"; and again when the record was afforded an official UK release after the band signed with independent Beggar's Banquet at the start of '85. "When the going gets tough, the Ramones start punching. [This is] timeless, lovable and essential stuff," critic Dave Henderson wrote. "Kinda keeps you sane."

BUOYED BY THE reaction, the Ramones decided to cross the Atlantic again: in February '85 they played four dates in London, followed up a few months later by a proper European tour that included a massive outdoor festival in Milton Keynes, England on June 22, with R.E.M. and U2 (bands that had once feted the Ramones, but were now far larger than them). The same line-up – plus despised synthesiser band Depeche Mode – also played a festival in Werchter, Belgium on July 7.

"The Ramones had these wee short bursts of energy," explains Scots fanzine editor Lindsay Hutton. "Without The Beatles there could never have been a Ramones, but as far as I'm concerned, the Ramones are far, far superior to The Beatles. They touched a nerve. Joe was like our Elvis, his vocal style, his songs, everything . . . you felt he was talking directly to you. The Ramones and The Dictators are my favourite two bands of all time, no question about it.

"On the *Too Tough To Die* tour," he enthuses, "they played Glasgow Barrowlands [June 28] in front of 3,000 people. The place was as packed as I've ever seen it, and the sound was as loud as I've ever heard at any show. There was a point during 'I Wanna Be Sedated' where everything disintegrated into white noise, with Joe yelping over the top. It was like being in a church. Absolutely immense. I can always morph back to that, psychedelically, whenever I hear that song now."

"I thought the album was good," says Mark Bannister, "but there were a couple of songs I didn't care for, especially on side two, which seemed to fade away. Everyone was going mad about 'Wart Hog', but I'd been listening to hardcore bands like Bad Brains and The Cro-Mags, and, let's face it, they do that stuff much better. I went to two of the gigs during their run at the Lyceum [London], and I planned to stay at the back and watch for once, but as soon as I heard that crazy beat . . .!

"The sound was appalling," he laughs. "On the Wednesday night, they had a good shouting match onstage. For their second encore, they all started playing different songs but the mix was so bad most people didn't even notice."

That could well have been the same night, sweating profusely from dancing and not even caring that Joey could sing only half his lines, the band were playing at such a ridiculous speed, I shouted out, "Play us a solo," at Dee Dee during an equipment malfunction. The Ramones weren't exactly known for their spontaneity, but the bassist obliged. He did a "tooth solo" using his fingers inside his cheek, the way some people are able to. It certainly made this fan's night and that of quite a few people round me down the front: I wrote about it at length in my own fanzine later.

Dee Dee was going through his own particular hell around this time: in *Poison Heart* he recalled how the band would torment their long-suffering "road mother" Monte Melnick: "He was determined no one [would] ever pull the wool over his eyes," he wrote. "It was a drag. Marc Bell gave Monte the nickname 'Lambie', to drive Monte crazy on purpose. Marc would work himself up into a frenzy in the van, making lamb noises until Monte would flip. Then the Lamb would threaten to drive us off the road and he would step on the gas, shouting, 'We're all going to perish now, you fucking creeps. We're all going to get killed, Marc, because you wouldn't shut up. You're the Lamb, Marc! You!' "

So when Monte was asked to baby-sit the bassist and Joey on a promotional tour of England to help support 'Howling At The Moon', Dee Dee flipped out. "Why should I have to do interviews with the creepy English press?" he wondered. "The biggest assholes in the world." He got trashed on the flight, and was given the third degree at Customs. Then he amused himself by running up enormous bar tabs at the Kensington Hilton and insulting journalists at random. His PR for the expedition was Gloria Nicholl.

"He was totally messed up on that trip," Gloria recalls. "Dee Dee would teeter from one extreme to the next. When he married Vera he was trying to be a proper little suburban husband. Then he would take it all the other way – and any drug would do. I remember Johnny being rude and horrible to journalists later in the year – he insulted a German writer by talking about Hitler, puerile dumb stuff. Dee Dee was out of control. He'd drink and party and get totally wasted and totally screwed up and not come home, going mad, living life at 100 miles a second."

He told journalists he was learning the piano from an 80-year-old woman: "I've never known what fuckin' notes I've been playing on this [his bass] . . . I hate my parents for not giving me music lessons. They're real assholes. They'd have been real useful, me bein' a musician an' all."

"I'm inventing a new style that I call 'techno-punk'," he said elsewhere. "Where I play with a drum machine, an organ, a pump door flanger and stuff like that, doing hardcore Human League-type songs."

'Howling At The Moon' came out on 12-inch with a couple of previously unreleased tracks on the B-side: the first, 'Smash You', was written by Richie in what seemed to be almost a parody of a Ramones song with all the "don't go/don't go baby" and "hangin' out on 5th Avenue" lines – but a hidden gem nonetheless. The other track, a cover of The Rolling Stones' 'Street Fighting Man' is absolutely horrible – Joey's voice again all shot to hell, and the dark tune patently unsuited to the Ramones.

Dee Dee, at least, should've known better. As he told *NME* in 1985, when they asked him what first attracted him to Joey: "He was the first singer I'd seen who wasn't copying Mick Jagger." Exactly.

"I WAS IN A band in the Seventies called New Math. We went to college in Rochester, and when the Ramones played upstate, we opened the show for them. At the time we had this schtick going where we would ask the audience to throw money at us if they loved us or if they hated us, which worked out because you pretty much covered everybody that way. We did this with the Ramones, and we got showered with a lot of quarters and, as soon as we were done, we had to scurry off because it was a union hall. It was my first meeting with Monte – he was like, 'Get off the stage, get off the stage.' He and the crew picked up all the money and wanted to keep it. So we confronted him, like, 'Listen, you picked up the money. It's our money.' He was very gruff like, 'Get out of here, I got to get the band onstage.' But I would not let up on him so finally he took all the money out of his pockets and threw it at me.

"That was the first time I said hello to the band. Of course, they were gods to us then. Years later, in '84, I started working at Elektra. My friend Michael booked

the Ritz on 11th Street for years. We went there one night, and coming down the steps was Joey. And Michael said, 'Oh, Joe, I want you to meet Kevin. He's a big fan.' So Joe said hello, and asked if I wanted to go for a beer. We just hit it off. We must have talked for hours that night, exchanged phone numbers. Soon after, we were fast friends."

What did you share in common?

"Music. He loved a lot of Sixties English and American garage punk band stuff. He loved The Seeds, The Stooges, MC5, New York Dolls, Wizzard and Sparks . . . Joe clearly had a very eccentric experience as a kid. He was gawky, he liked different music, and he dressed the way his favourite rock stars dressed in the glam era. Can you imagine? Back then we loved to party, too. It's not hard to make fast friends when you're into alcohol and drugs. Also, Joey was really warm to people who loved his band. Right through to the end, he hoped they would be accepted in the mainstream, that something would get into a film."

Yeah.

"He always had time for fans. When we would leave his place to walk two blocks to get something to eat, it would take us an hour to get there because everybody would stop him on the street and he'd sign anything they had, pose for pictures."

(Author's interview with Kevin Patrick)

"MARKY AND ME were both friends for a while because we were both in recovery. That's when I stopped hanging out with Joey. I couldn't keep up with him, money wise. He would go someplace like the Ritz and afford to pay five bucks a beer. I couldn't. And I didn't want to sit there and have him pay for me all night. He started doing coke. I didn't want to do coke. It's unconscionable when people you're with suddenly start acting differently. The guy was very cool and . . ."

I can't imagine being with somebody who's doing coke when you're not.

"He really got into it."

(Author's interview with John Holmstrom)

TOO TOUGH TO DIE helped to restore the Ramones' artistic reputation, as did the second British single of 1985, the Jean Beauvoir-produced 'Bonzo Goes To Bitburg' – Joey's answer song to Ronald Reagan's controversial visit to a German cemetery containing SS graves. It quashed once and for all the ridiculous rumours that the joke quasi-Nazi imagery used in early Ramones songs was serious. To ram the point home, the sleeve featured a picture of Reagan.

Beauvoir was also a member of Little Steven & The Disciples Of Soul – Little Steven (Van Zandt), formerly Bruce Springsteen's guitarist, was so taken with the single that he asked Joey to join his former boss and Bob Dylan and Miles Davis, in the 50-strong Artists United Against Apartheid to record an album later that year. Joey sang a solo line on the 'Feed The World'-style protest single 'Sun City'.

Joey was moved to write 'Bonzo' (along with Dee Dee and Beauvoir) because he felt affronted as a New York Jew. "Bonzo goes to Bitburg then goes out for a cup of tea," sneered Joey. "As I watched it on TV somehow it really bothered me." The drum sound is all wrong – far too upfront and weak – but it hardly matters, the song is so (genuinely) angry and motivated: memorable and melodic, an unbeatable combination.

"What Reagan did was fucked up," the singer told *East Coast Rocker.* "Everybody told him not to go, all *his* people told him not to go, and he went anyway. How can you fuckin' forgive the Holocaust? How can you say, 'Oh well, it's OK now?' That's crazy."

"The Ramones were never political," Dee Dee explained, "but somehow we knew we'd got bunched into this right-wing kind of thing [probably because of earlier comments Johnny made about how every 'real' punk was right wing] and it was the first time we could make a statement to show we weren't prejudiced. We'd just had these skinheads at our gigs, punks walking round wearing swastikas."

Johnny, a staunch Republican, objected to the song – especially the depiction of Reagan as a chimp – and refused to play it live: "I thought Ronald Reagan was the best president of our lifetime," he stated. As a compromise, when the song appeared on 1986's *Animal Boy* album, it was re-titled 'My Brain Is Hanging Upside Down (Bonzo Goes To Bitburg)'.

The B-side contained 'Daytime Dilemma' and a Dee Dee/Mitch [Mickey] Leigh composition, 'Go Home Ann', fairly standard hard rock fare directed at an unwanted groupie with lines like "Never said I loved you/Never said I care", notable mainly for the presence of Motorhead's gravel-throated singer Lemmy on mixing duties.* The Ramones and Motorhead (a killer hard rock band in the tradition of early Black Sabbath)

* DuBose feels Mickey Leigh never got his just deserts: "Mickey is Joey's real brother, and he sang back-up on the song that was used on the Budweiser advert," he alleges. DuBose is referring to 'Blitzkrieg Bop' off the first album: Craig Leon (who produced the record) denies that Joey's brother was there, however. "There simply wasn't time for outside help," he explains. DuBose remains undeterred. "Someone once asked him whether he was making any money from the residuals," he continues, "and he said, 'What d'ya mean?' So Mickey went to Joey and asked him if he could have any money, and Joey went to Johnny and he said, 'Fuck no. Don't give him shit.' Mickey went to his father and asked him whether he thought it was right, and his father asked him if he had a contract. 'No? Then you shouldn't get paid.' "

were massive fans of each other: "There are only two bands in the whole world that are any good," Dee Dee told *Sounds* in 1995. "Us and Motorhead. They're a real important band playing genuine rough, raw music."

"I had to interview Lemmy one evening years ago," reports journalist Mark Spivey, "almost immediately after Motorhead had played at Rock City. It was less than 10 minutes after the show finished that Lemmy came in for the interview, sweat-soaked, and asked what I'd thought.

" 'Let's face it, you'll never be the greatest rock'n'roll band in the world, will you?' I replied.

"Lemmy wasn't best pleased. So I waited and said nothing more, hoping he'd ask what I meant before smacking me. I'd like to say something about rage being etched into his face, blood vessels bursting through pure anger, steam rising, and all that shit, but all I remember clearly is hoping I'd played this right or else I was fucked. I'm pretty sure his anger was tempered by curiosity and simple disbelief, but maybe that's because I know something must have stopped him losing it.

" 'What do you mean?' he asked.

" 'Well, the Ramones exist,' I said, still not sure how it would go down, 'so you can only ever hope to be the second best.'

" 'Fair enough,' said Lemmy, before adding, 'that's the only answer you could have possibly got away with . . .' "

22

Favourite Ramones Album

"*Ramones* – because that's the Ramones. People say it sounds too simple but that's what the Ramones sounded like" – John Holmstrom

"*Ramones* – the one that I worked on. They'd polished their style by *Rocket To Russia*, but the exuberance of *Ramones* is hard to top. *It's Alive* is great, too" – Craig Leon

"*Ramones*. I wasn't that aware of them after Tommy left. It was like when Brian Jones left The Rolling Stones, they were never the same after that" – Gary Valentine

"*Leave Home*, or *Ramones*" – Kim Thayil

"*Ramones* or *Rocket To Russia*. *Road To Ruin* was really good, too. Once Tommy was out of the picture there was a long period of mediocrity" – CJ Ramone

"*Ramones*, because it's the purest example of who they were. The first four are incredible. The mad grandeur of *End Of The Century* is really underrated, too" – David Fricke

"*Ramones* up to *End Of The Century* – I like them all equally" – George Seminara

"*Rocket To Russia* and *End Of The Century*. I'll go with *Ramones*, it gets me off the hook on both" – David Kessel

"*Rocket To Russia* – the first four were all solid to me" – Don Fleming

"*Rocket To Russia*, but I love them all. They've stayed with me all my life.

When did I love my parents the most?" – Donna Gaines

"*Rocket To Russia*. I feel this album has the most classic Ramones songs" – Johnny Ramone

"*Rocket To Russia*" – Brijitte West

"*Rocket To Russia* because that was my first" – Carla Olla

"*Rocket To Russia*" – Janis Schacht

"*Rocket To Russia*" – Rodney Bingenheimer

"*Rocket To Russia*. It appeared in the transitional period between the streetwise Ramones of *Ramones* to the slicker Ramones of *Road To Ruin*" – Ed Stasium

"*Rocket To Russia* – that was the Ramones at their peak, in songwriting, production and performance. My second favourite is a toss-up between *Ramones* and *Road To Ruin* for different reasons. The first album has great songs and it's almost like a lo-fi avant-garde record. *Road To Ruin* is a well-done, well-recorded album. Then *Leave Home*, something has to be at the end. But the Ramones never made a bad album" – Tommy Ramone

"*Road To Ruin* – it's got all that power, plus acoustic guitars. Then *Ramones* and *It's Alive*" – George Tabb

"*Road To Ruin*. One, I'm on it. Two, I love the production on it, and it's the first time lead guitar was present" – Marky Ramone

"*Subterranean Jungle* is really underrated, and, of course, 'The KKK Took My Baby Away' – fucking Jesus Christ, that's about as great as it ever gets" – Lindsay Hutton

"*Subterranean Jungle* – and the classic first two albums" – Slim Moon

"I don't have one. You got to realise, I listened to them for 22 years, 2263 shows. I don't sit at home and listen to Ramones albums, believe me" – Monte Melnick

23

My Brain Is Hanging Upside Down

THE RAMONES STARTED recording their ninth studio album *Animal Boy* in December 1985 – taking time off to play their semi-annual New Year's Eve show in NYC. In public, the mood was upbeat: the musicians enthused by the recent European tour. "Things are great when it's just the band," laughed Joey. "It's the girls who cause all the shit. Girls are troublemakers."

With typical Ramones logic, they dispensed with the services of Erdelyi and Stasium again, despite the fact that *Too Tough To Die* had been their most acclaimed album – by both critics and fans – for years, and brought in 'Bonzo Goes To Bitburg' producer Jean Beauvoir to oversee proceedings at Intergalactic Studios in New York. The group began to play to a slicker and more conventional formula. It was probably easier, and cheaper.

Joey, continuing his songwriting slump, only wrote two new songs for the record – 'Mental Hell' (a summation of his feelings towards the Ramones during the early Eighties) and the absolute rubbish 'Hair Of The Dog'. "What's so wrong with hair of the dog?" he sang. If Joey was writing about what he knew, then he needed to stop indulging as much, and rediscover his warped sense of humour. At least 'Mental Hell' has a great Buzzcocks-style middle section.

"It's not fair," Dee Dee complained to *NME* journalist Bill Black. "It's Johnny, man. Joey will present a great tune and Johnny won't do it because it's this or it's that. 'I'm not going to play minor chords. I'm not going to play lead. I'm not going to come to England.' For God's sake! That's why Joey's gotta do his solo album."

"It's not conflict," tempered Joey, ever the diplomat, "but I have ideas on the way I want to go. It's on the backburner. I'm still committed to this band."

"Me too," agreed his bassist. "I've got a solo album in the works, but I can't do it right now 'cos I've got to write for the Ramones." The band explained their reasons for dismissing Tommy as the producer with usual insouciance: "He cracked up, man!" Dee Dee claimed. "He did The Replacements album, then they put him away. But he does that every album. He holds it together long enough to record, then in the middle of mixing he starts talking to himself an' slapping himself."

"He likes to eat, y'know?" Joey said. "We would never get anything done 'cos he was always goin' somewhere to eat. It was a real reunion working with those guys an' a real exciting record to do, but . . .

"It's fun working with Jean, too," he added defensively.

THE MAIN PROBLEM with *Animal Boy* was that there was no longer one discernible Ramones sound: it sounds as disjointed as the band members probably felt. The guitar parts could've been played by anyone (and quite possibly were – Walter Lure again sat in), and Richie's drumming was slipping away from Tommy's original template. The Ramones were turning into a 9–5 job (night, not day).

Take 'She Belongs To Me', a sweet ballad co-written by Dee Dee and Beauvoir. It's a beautiful, lovelorn song, Joey does the "Ronnie" thing with his voice – absolutely ruined by synthesisers, where once Tommy would've put a sensitive acoustic guitar, or Phil Spector would've called in real strings. A few years before, Johnny would've complained vociferously at their inclusion: his silence points to the fact he didn't care as long as the job got done, the record was finished and the Ramones could get out on the road again.

Dee Dee's 'Crummy Stuff' is a straightforward fun punk-pop blast at the mediocrity of life, old style Ramones – again spoiled by the gimmicky, repetitive keyboards. 'Animal Boy' and 'Apeman Hop' are 'Cretin Hop' only not even a thousandth as good (cretins and retards are far more fun than beasts, sorry) – to use the George Tabb analogy again, this was stupid stupid, not clever stupid. As Mark Bannister pointed out to Dee Dee in 1994, it was like someone had said, "Let's write about cripples or something, because that's what used to work."

"I know," he replied. "That's all we would talk about, like, 'It's a good day if you see a midget.' But [that apeman] stuff was getting on my nerves. That was Johnny Ramone's idea . . ."

'Love Kills', written for inclusion in the (rather risible) Alex Cox movie, *Sid And Nancy* [it wasn't used], could've been drawn straight from *Too Tough To Die* but it's nowhere near as good. "Sid and Nancy were a mess/When you're hooked on heroin/Don't you know you'll never win/Drugs don't ever pay," Dee Dee sang, a fraction hypocritically. He sang to a style not his own, but like a sneerin', spittin' punk villain from an

Eighties TV sitcom. Something the Ramones never used to be.

The tracks Dee Dee co-wrote with Johnny just aren't very good. Toilet bowls and 10-inch erections sound out of place on a Ramones record. Again, it's stupid stupid, not clever stupid.

The far superior Sid tribute, 'I Don't Want To Live This Life (Anymore)' was relegated to the 12-inch B-side of the album's second UK single 'Crummy Stuff' – an amazing decision, as it's easily one of the Ramones' strongest songs of the time. Not a parody, not duplicitous, more a straightforward insight into Sid Vicious' mind, post-Nancy, from one of the few people qualified – but Dee Dee and Alex Cox had fallen out so he refused to hand the song over for use in the film. It was later accorded its rightful place on the Ramones' *Anthology* – where critic David Fricke referred to its "crushed-glass strumming and the [guitar's] judgemental howl.

"With a vivid, nasally hurt in Joey's voice," he wrote, " 'I Don't Wanna Live This Life' elevates the facts of Vicious and Spungen's sorry story to high pop drama: senseless death, the crushing burden of responsibility, consuming helplessness. The utter surrender Dee Dee etched into the song was convincing. It was, for him, also quite real."

Fricke, as ever, was spot on.

The three best songs, worryingly enough, had music written by non-original Ramones – Beauvoir and Richie. 'Bonzo Goes To Bitburg' – now re-titled 'My Brain Is Hanging Upside Down' at Johnny's insistence – won an award for best independent single at the New York Music Awards in 1985. But by the time it came to promote the album, the Libyan crisis had occurred, and Dee Dee was regretting the lyrics: "Poor Reagan, we should never have said anything bad about him. He's doin' so much *good* now. We should blow 'em all up. Kill 'em. Blow up England if we have to."

The Ramones, like all Yanks, were scared of being in England for fear of terrorist reprisals after America had once again created a crisis for everybody but themselves: Dee Dee continued to rant against anyone that showed the slightest inclination to be "anti-American" (as he called it) and whined about how the Ramones would get blown up when they played Berlin, because they were such visible "targets".

Then there was the excellent New Wave-esque single, 'Something To Believe In' (Beauvoir/Dee Dee again) – almost overshadowed by its equally fine video, filmed in a spoof of all the Live Aid charity singles then in fashion. Re-titled "Ramones Aid", and introduced by a suited spokesman explaining why we should contribute to the Ramones' cause – "Let's make this the most significant event of the Eighties" – it was reassuringly foolish, a welcome return to da bruddas' old sense of humour. There's a celebrity lookalike singalong; Monte Melnick handcuffed to a cop; gays holding hands in toilets, and any number of guests including Rodney Bingenheimer, Toni Basil, Holly Beth Vincent, The B-52's, Spinal Tap, Sparks, Afrika Bambaataa, X, Weird Al Yankovic, Penn & Teller, The Circle Jerks, Ted Nugent . . . all linking arms with one another in a parody of the nauseating sickly-sweet "Hands Across America" event.* So strong, it had the unfortunate side effect of making Dee Dee's heartfelt, lonely words seem almost a joke: but the song's still fine with its chiming keyboards.

Warners liked it so much, they released it as the Ramones' first American single in five years, backed with 'Animal Boy'.

Its double A-side in Britain, 'Somebody Put Something In My Drink', is also pure gold: black humour from the newest Ramones member, snarled and shouted in horrifying fashion – Joey's poor vocal chords! – with a killer hook.

"We wanted [Richie] to feel part of the band: we love the guy," Joey explained. "We never let the drummer write before, because John, Dee Dee and I felt like we were the band. Marc Bell would try to give us songs, but they weren't any good – he wouldn't even write them, his brother would. But Richie's a regular Phil Collins."

"Yeah," the drummer laughed. "I write on the piano."

"That was a personal experience," Richie said in *East Coast Rocker* about the single. "It was really bad, it was LSD. It was a practical joke but it could have turned to suicide. You put your Tanqueray and tonic down, and before you know it . . . I had to go to an institution for two weeks: they had to take me in a straitjacket. I wrote the song there."

You get the impression the drummer's tongue was firmly in his cheek when he gave this interview. In the same article, he talked of being tied to a tombstone in Woodlawn Cemetery out on Staten Island as part of the Ramones' initiation. "I still haven't recovered. I still go for treatment every 20 days. That's why we always insist on canned soda in our dressing room, and nothing open, ever."

That rule did actually exist – but it was more down to the Ramones touring entourage's predilection for "tampering" with drinks. Anything left open was seen as fair game for a few drops of piss.

* Sponsored by the *New York Times*, who attempted to have people hold hands across the entire USA for one day – Sunday, May 25, 1986.

ANIMAL BOY WAS released in May 1986, with a cover that showed the Ramones standing in front of a gorilla cage, with Richie clutching a chimp. "I wanted to use the Bronx Zoo for the shoot," recalls George DuBose, "but they said absolutely not. Plan B meant hiring Zippy the Chimp who starred in the Monkey Cam on *The David Letterman Show*. I built a monkey house out of wood and hung tiers from a chain. We had Legs McNeil and another roadie dress up in gorilla suits and hang out looking realistic in the background."

The album entered the UK charts at Number 31, probably because of determined marketing efforts on behalf of their British independent label. Most of the resulting British press centred on the by-now public differences between the Ramones – and the fact the band hadn't split up yet.

"We take rooms on different floors," said Richie half-joking.

"We can hate each other's guts but we go out there and play as a unit and it's fucking *great*," commented Joey. "For the past few tours we've had a bus, but on this tour we're economising and going out in a van. We toured England in a van and it was fun – sure we had fights, it was like psychodrama on wheels. But all that shit is just part of it."

"I think it would be a real shame," the singer told *East Coast Rocker*, "if we broke up and never had a major success. I'd like to see the Ramones remembered on a larger level."

In the *New York Times* Jon Pareles said that the Ramones "speak up for outcasts and disturbed individuals," making it rock album of the week, while *Village Voice*'s Robert Christgau – an old Ramones fan – wasn't so sure, saying it felt "ominously hit or miss", especially when contrasted with their back catalogue. The band was still upbeat, though.

"We don't want to become a parody of ourselves," Joey told *Sounds* journalist Jonh (*sic*) Wilde, "just to keep going because we *have* to. No way." He then appeared to contradict himself. "We don't need to break up, we could keep going forever."

The band was keen to correct a few misconceptions.

"When four people take credit for something one person wrote, it's almost like being robbed," Joey commented on the thorny issue of songwriting credits. "If you have anything to offer that's unique, it's your personality. In the early days we felt everything should be divided up four ways – and then three ways, after Tommy left – so once we made it, we all made it. In most bands, if you write a song, you get all the royalties for yourself. A big part of the reason we're still together is that everything is divided equally." Thus the generosity of Joey (and Johnny, the mainly non-creative partner) didn't extend to their drummers: a situation that would shortly create problems.

AFTER THE RAMONES finished recording, they played a handful of dates on the East Coast in April – rapidly followed by an extensive UK tour in May, including three dates in London. Richie, despite his blond hair, fitted in seamlessly. The rest of the year was spent touring the States, including a brace of shows with The Smithereens at the start of July, and an LA gig with major-league hardcore punks Social Distortion – plus another visit to Europe in time for the August festival season.

Of course, the year rounded out with a New Year's Eve show – this time in Roslyn, Long Island.

David Keegan was one fan that saw the Ramones that year. He was then playing guitar in his supercharged Ramones-meets-Velvet Underground-meets-Mary Chain female-fronted Scots pop band, Shop Assistants.

"Shop Assistants evolved into a group," explains David. "I liked Swell Maps, Raincoats when I first started it, and the Ramones were on the back burner – this was around the mid-Eighties when their records were OK. I built all these fuzz pedals and things that sounded like the Ramones, and became obsessed with the way their guitars sounded – three chords but there was so much happening in there, all these tunes and wonderful harmonies. So I started listening to them all the time again."

"I took David and Laura [Shoppies' drummer] and Rocky [from great unknown early Eighties Ramones-style Scots band The Dragsters] to meet Joey and they were thrilled," recalls Lindsay Hutton. The meeting happened on May 14, at Edinburgh's Playhouse.

"Joe was like a big daft laddie," Hutton says. "His enthusiasm was infectious."

"Someone must have given Joey a copy of 'Safety Net' [Shop Assistants' single] and he was like, 'Oh, I really like your record,'" recalls David. Keegan had recently started up the 53rd And 3rd label with Stephen from The Pastels – so they showed the singer a BMX Bandits record with the label logo, featuring his photo. "I was walking behind him going up the stairs and it took him ages, and I thought, 'Oh no, what's wrong with Joey?' It was really strange. Joey was fantastic, warm and friendly and really natural – I was really nervous meeting him, but it was fine. And Dee Dee was nice as well.

"The first Ramones record I can properly recall was 'Rockaway Beach'," David continues. "I was about 12, and liked Abba. I heard this and it was so tuneful and so right. I had this tiny little radio that'd only pick up Radio Luxembourg – we'd tape songs we liked, and they'd cut them off halfway through. The only punk band I liked was the Ramones, and also The Sex Pistols – but that was my friends' tastes, not mine."

Keegan was living in the tiny village of Newtonmore in the highlands of Scotland: he recalls no one needed to own records because everyone shared them. When he formed a band with his school friends, they covered Ramones songs and claimed them as their own, but the songs on *End Of The Century* were far too complicated to figure out.

"I really got into the Ramones around the time of *Road To Ruin*," David says. "Everyone at school loved them, someone had the album on yellow vinyl, someone had the singles, and then someone bought *It's Alive* when that appeared. *End Of The Century* was when everyone started having their own Ramones album."

ELSEWHERE, IT WAS (peculiar) business as usual, particularly when it came to booking dates . . .

"John Giddings at Solo pencilled in the only date I had available for a Ramones show," says Mark Spivey, former promoter at Nottingham Rock City, "but made it clear it was unlikely to happen as they were only going to play bigger venues. Sure enough, a couple of weeks later he rang to say they couldn't do that show, but could I make another date available? I rang round and failed, so I phoned John, making some facetious remark about disappointing my cat. I told him that my cat was called Ramona because, as a kitten, she'd ignored any music she heard, except *Rocket To Russia*, which caused her to walk over and rub against a speaker. Which was absolutely true. A few days later John rang again and told me he'd rearranged the entire tour to make the date work – adding, 'That's for your cat.'

"When the band arrived, Joey could barely walk. He asked if we could find a doctor to come to the venue and see him. It took some time, but I found one, and put Joey on the phone to talk to him, saying I'd get out of his way. He said it was OK, and said the same when the doctor arrived. I was, however, told I could never tell anyone what I was about to hear him say, as it would destroy his image. He then told the doctor that he'd been asleep the night before and had stretched out, getting his toe caught in a little tear in the sheet, and he felt stupid that it was hurting so much. It transpired that he'd dislocated his toe.

"There are also a couple of things I've heard which may not be true, but which would say a great deal about the Ramones as a band if they are," Spivey added. "Firstly, that each member had a roadie who could play/sing their respective parts. These roadies would often soundcheck for the band, playing entire Ramones songs. And secondly, that they used to rehearse for tours without using monitors, so that, no matter how bad the monitors in a venue might be, they were already used to playing in a situation that was even harder. I think that is an awesome approach."

"JOE HAD A REAL habit of being generous. He'd never be stingy and loved to throw a party, almost to the point of . . . 'You don't really know these people, Joe.' He loved finding gifts and schlepping them around the world for his friends.

"When he came back from Japan, he'd bring back little dogs or clocks that said 'Nihow'. He loved gadgets. We used to meet at the street level of his building, at Paul's Lounge, the neighbourhood bar. It was right on the corner of Third Avenue and 10th Street and even though it was in this real busy area, it was one of those places that you didn't notice unless you looked for it. It was just this very subdued, non-flash, Italian restaurant with a bar out front. That was our hangout – we would meet there and Joe would buy dinners for people, like every night.

"Sometimes the Ramones would be playing at The Ritz up the street, and endless streams of kids would walk by, little knowing that Joey Ramone was sitting right there. One afternoon we were sitting in the bar and Joe says, 'Look at that guy out there'. It was a bum going through the garbage pail on the street. Joe's looking out onto the street – and suddenly the look on his face was like, 'Oh my god,' and then you hear 'whoosh!' I turn around and he says, 'He just shot the garbage pail through the window.' Of course, this was a story that Joe must have told to 10,000 people over the next week."

When was this?

"This would have been '86 or '87. Paul's has been closed for years but it was half full of Ramones songs on the jukebox – Joe would bring people in and play Ramones songs. It seems we spent a lifetime hanging out in Paul's."

You were telling me about this surprise birthday party he threw for you.

"Right. We were in Paul's and he must have spent a fortune . . . I'd signed The Georgia Satellites in the Eighties and he flew them in from Atlanta to surprise me. He had Holly & The Italians come in from the West Coast. He worked out a set with Daniel Rey and Richie Stotts behind him. I knew nothing about the party. I felt awful, and wanted to go home and sleep. Poor Joe was coming up with reasons like, 'Let's go over to 8th Street and hang out,' and I was like, 'I'd rather sit here. I don't feel good.' He was like, 'Well maybe there's some new records in.' Finally he said, 'I heard that there's this new club over there and Alice Cooper is playing and it's unannounced'. I was like, 'Oh god, I fucking hate Alice Cooper.' So I just – because he's such a lovable person, it was easier to make Joe happy. We went over there and sure enough, it was the party.

"Many times he'd throw birthday parties for Arty, for Monte. He loved everybody to be happy and social and harmonious. He was very generous."

(Author's interview with Kevin Patrick)

A GREAT ARTICLE THAT appeared in *Rolling Stone* that year, written by former *Punk* stalwarts Legs McNeil and John Holmstrom, gave an insight into what it was like to be hanging out at Paul's . . .

Joey's long gangly body stands hunched over the jukebox. He's reading the selection like a Wall Street analyst studies the Dow Jones. "So what do you want to do tonight?" someone asks over the plates of half-eaten cheeseburgers, shrimp scampi, raw oysters, and crabmeat in avocado. "Pig Vomit's playing The Ritz," someone answers. "King Flux is playing the Cat Club." Both are within walking distance.

The conversation at the table turns to reminiscences of fucking to Ramones music as 'Danny Says' builds on the jukebox. Everybody offers a story and, finally, Joey is persuaded to tell one: "Yeah, I went home with this real nut once. She was nice, ya know, but she was still a nut, and she wanted to listen to us while we were in bed."

"What did she want you to play?" the whole table choruses.

Joey explodes into laughter just thinking about it: " 'I Wanna Be Sedated'."

That fairly innocuous, although personal, interview landed Holmstrom in hot water after it appeared. "I was desperate," the ex-*Punk* editor explains. "I needed money. And it was the first time anybody was going to talk about the problems within the band because . . . they were all good friends in the beginning. It was meant to be a fun article. We didn't want to make anybody think they were bad people. Just funny stuff – like how long Joey would take in the shower.

"If you hung out with Joey," he continues, "I guarantee you would spend two hours sitting in his apartment, waiting for him to dry his hair. He also had this obsessive-compulsive thing, every time he walked down the street. If he passed a kerb, he had to stop, walk back and touch the kerb with his foot. He had a lot of little oddities like that, which make a person more interesting except people don't like to see it written up in a magazine. They were telling us things like that – I think Joey said Dee Dee smelled bad or something.

"So we put it in the article and, right after it comes out, I go into Paul's Lounge and they're all sitting there with their girlfriends and I think, 'Fuck, they're here. I can't walk away, I'll just make the best of it.' I walk up to them. Stony cold. Dee Dee was like, 'I'm going to kick your ass.' You're going to kick my ass? What for? 'That fucking article you wrote.'

It was really ugly. I left before he could kick my ass, but I never saw the Ramones live after that.

"Legs was still friends with them. He said it was miserable being with them because all Johnny would say is, 'I'm getting too old for this.' They didn't enjoy the success they had. They were always bitter about the success they didn't have. They didn't have the hit record. They didn't get the respect for starting punk rock. They didn't get the respect they deserved for this, that and the other. They were so concerned with what was written about them and their image, unlike any band I've ever seen."

That surprises me. I wouldn't have thought they'd give a fuck.

"The thing is, they were all feeding us lots of stories because they all wanted to say bad things about each other in print. But once it came out, it was our fault."

Joey also interviewed actress Pia Zadora for *Spin* in August '86 – nice for him doubtless, but a little tame for everyone else. In typical musician fashion, he stayed away from asking a single penetrating question.

24

Gabba Gabba Rey

YOU WORKED WITH Joey closely. What inspired him to write songs?

"Usually it would be an event. It would stew around in his head and he'd turn it into a lyric. He'd never sit down and say, 'What am I going to write about?' Dee Dee would be more like, 'OK, we need some songs for the record' and get psyched up and write six songs. Two of them would be really bad, but three of them would be genius."

Did they throw much stuff out?

"Yeah, but we'd never record more than we were planning to use. We'd usually have about 20 songs to choose from. Everyone would make little demos and we'd vote on them. There were a lot of politics but mostly the best songs went out. We never recorded everything, because Johnny was like, 'No, you got 13 songs and that's it.' "

A few bands could learn from that.

"Yeah. Sometimes Johnny would say, 'The record's too soft, we need some heavy ones,' so Dee Dee would write some more. There was always this balance to a Ramones record. There would be one or two from Joey, Fifties ballad things, there would be Dee Dee's full-on hardcore rock songs."

Did you play guitar on any of the records?

"Sometimes, little bits, here and there. Again, that was just Johnny being practical. If I could do it in three minutes and it would take him 20, that would be wasting time. But he was always right there."

What food did they like to eat in the studio?

"By the Nineties, Joey was health-conscious so a lot of water and vegetarian stuff. Marc would eat anything that was put in front of him. Johnny didn't really eat in the studio. If it was time to eat, it was time to leave."

Can you describe Joey's apartment for me? When I saw it in '89, it looked like he'd just moved in. There were loads of boxes, and he opened one up and took out all these amazing Sixties psychedelic posters.

"Yeah, he got into that, which had a cool rock'n'roll logic to it. He was a bit of a

packrat. Stuff would accumulate and after a few months, I'd go in there and say, 'Come on Joey. Let's throw it out.'

"But back in the early days, when Joey was still partying a bit, I would go over to his house . . . He used to order coffee in the morning from the deli, two cups. He always felt guilty that it was too small an order so he ordered two bottles of Evian water. But he'd drink the coffee much faster than he'd drink the Evian water. So he'd have 10 bottles of Evian water, 10 deli bags and a lot of finished coffee cups. I'd go back two weeks later and there were like 200 white deli bags and 50 bottles of Evian water. We'd look at each other, surrounded by these bags and Evian bottles, and he'd ask with his wry sense of humour, 'Hey, you want a water?' He'd buy records, cool magazines and stuff when on tour. He'd come back from Japan with some cool Stooges box set or something. He was a rock'n'roll person."

He played me demos of all these bands, and was really excited about them. He was very supportive of young bands, wasn't he?

"Definitely. He liked that energy, that vitality. He was a full-time Ramone. As soon as he changed his name, he was Joey Ramone and not Jeff Hyman anymore."

Was that true of the others?

"I don't know. Dee Dee was always Dee Dee. When you become a celebrity like Dee Dee Ramone, people expect a certain style of behaviour from you and you fulfil that prophecy sometimes. But Johnny was always Johnny. He would only be a Ramone when it came in handy to get into somewhere, or something like that."

Can you describe the personalities of the Ramones?

"Sure. Dee Dee is oftentimes like a mischievous little kid, and sometimes erratic. He works on instinct, from the gut. I totally respect him. He's the best lyricist I've ever worked with. Johnny is very much a strategist and pragmatic about his approach to everything. He likes things simple and quick. Joey had the best rock'n'roll spirit of anyone I've ever known. Rock'n'roll saved his life and I think he knew he was saving other people. To the last moment, he believed in rock'n'roll, which is hard to do when you've been in the business for so long."

What kept them together so long?

"The Ramones were like a military battalion. They had this mission to get this stuff out there. After 10 years, when they realised they would never have a hit for whatever reasons, they fell into a routine where it was still a good living and they got a buzz out of playing."

(Author's interview with Daniel Rey, 2001)

IT WAS HARD to know who was the biggest fool in 1987.

The record industry, for never having given the Ramones a decent chance – yet it supported far less entertaining acts.

The Ramones, for continuing to make new albums and play shows – despite a media that was increasingly ignoring them.

Their fans, for continuing to support a band that didn't even believe in themselves any more and were content just to hack out a new record every couple of years as a half-hearted panacea.

Joey, for still believing that each new Ramones album was going to yield that elusive hit, and that he would finally be accorded his rightful place in the rock mainstream as an influential and talented musician.

Richie, for thinking that after four years and hundreds of shows, he might be put on parity with his band-members – naïve, perhaps, but understandable. Hadn't he written more songs than Johnny over the last few records?

Arturo and Monte and the other members of the Ramones' extended family, for carrying on with a cause that looked dead and buried – or maybe they were still having fun.

Something, surely, had to give.

Johnny had given up on the band, artistically: it was his trade, one that he did well and would see through till the end. Like many musicians, he had an almost morbid fear of having to return to the real world: he'd had enough of shitty jobs during the Seventies. If only he could see the band through for a few more years, he could finally retire . . . He knew the Ramones were not going to get a hit at this stage of their careers: they had two more albums to go with Sire and it was time to accept the facts and cut their losses. Doubtless, the Ramones would've produced themselves if they had the ability, but they didn't. So they did the next best thing, and got in a confirmed fan of the band – Shrapnel guitarist and Ramones collaborator Daniel Rey – for next to nothing.

"Johnny heard some four-track thing I did in my parents' basement for this punk band [The Dirge], and thought it sounded better than the Ramones' last record," recalls Rey. "Plus, I got along with all four of the Ramones, which was extremely unusual. Plus," he laughs, "they could get me very cheap because it was my first album. Hell. I would've done it for free."

Recording on *Halfway To Sanity* started in early 1987, again at Intergalactic Studios: saving money was high on the list of priorities: "It was a dingy place in midtown that somebody got a deal at. It's long gone now," Rey smiles. The band laid down the basic tracks in the afternoon, and Joey recorded his voice in the evening. It was quicker to learn the songs without any vocal, so they did – even though Joey wanted to work out how to phrase his singing.

"The other guys were very impatient," Rey admits. "They weren't really getting along at that point. Johnny and Joey had some problems."

Despite *Halfway To Sanity* being one of Rey's favourite Ramones albums, it's a low-point in da bruddas' career: not Rey's fault – he did the best he could with the material he was given, and at least he brought a consistency back to the sound – but Joey's songwriting had virtually dried up, and Dee Dee was churning out lyrics without any thought or insight. Plus, there was Johnny's new slick style of guitar-playing to contend with: the Ramones might've been trying to imitate hardcore punk but they were doing it without any of the passion or power of their late Seventies line-up.

"There was a real money crunch going on," says Ida Langsam. "Everybody was always worried about spending money with the Ramones – everything was always done cut-rate. It doesn't mean it wasn't done well. It was like, 'Where can we find to do it for less, who can we find to do it for less?' They were never afforded the respect a band of their calibre should have, and other bands much less worthy had much more respect afforded them. Everybody thought of them as the local band, everybody's friends – when are you going to break, when are you going to get big, when are you going to reach stardom?'

"There were problems between different people," Johnny explained. "The production, Richie. It was a real pain in the ass to be doing it. Nobody would listen to Daniel, they weren't letting Daniel do what he wanted and certain people were complaining. It became very difficult."

Joey did write one bona fide classic for *Halfway To Sanity*: 'Bye Bye Baby' (a song he later gave to Ronnie Spector when the pair recorded together in the late Nineties), a tear-jerking Fifties/early Sixties style girl group number with a beautiful chiming guitar sound that stands out like a sore thumb among the morass of songs about Weasel Faces and Worm Men – Joey *sings*, instead of shouting in what *Stereo Review* correctly described as "a creepy bullfrog baritone, like Mick Jagger doing his imitation of a sharecropper".

His 'A Real Cool Time' is also fine – a summer beach party/New York Cat Club tribute song – despite (or perhaps, *because* of) a melody line reminiscent of The Who's 'The Kids Are Alright'.* It became the first British

* Joey would DJ and present themed evenings at the Cat and the Ritz, starring friends like Handsome Dick Manitoba, Motorhead and Debbie Harry. A famous one took place on Friday, January 13, 1989, entitled *Holy Inquisition Circus Of The Perverse*. It featured 15 live bands, including Manitoba's Wild Kingdom, Cycle Sluts From Hell [a trash-glam female-fronted NYC band], Lords Of The Dead, plus mime artists, street art and ritual decapitations. Lemmy was cast

Spring 1978: Marky takes over from Tommy. "Marky is the character that goes out in the backyard, plays, gets itself all muddy and dirty… You wanna kill him but you don't – he's your pet, that's what pets do…" – Arturo Vega. (*LFI*)

Dee Dee marries Vera, September 1978. "Dee Dee would teeter from one extreme to the next," says Gloria Nichol. "When he married Vera he was trying to be a proper little suburban husband. Then he would take it all the other way – and any drug would do." *(Bob Gruen/Star File)*

April, 1979. "Image wise, it doesn't matter what you look like, as long as you're not a fucking asshole. If you have to act punk then you're not a punk. It's not an act. You either are or you're not." – Marky Ramone. *(Bob Gruen/Star File)*

"Joey… thought of it as his life's calling. There was nothing else he could do. Being this tall gawky guy who didn't look like every other Average Joe at school, he was forced to a certain marginal point of his adolescence where what he discovered about himself was that, if he was going to do anything, he was going to be a rock star." – David Fricke. *(Corbis)*

"We were like brothers – brothers fight, brothers argue." said Marky Ramone. "Every time I'd talk to Joey, Johnny would get upset; if I talked to John, Joey'd get upset. Then there was Dee Dee with his schizophrenic personality..." *(Godlis)*

A still from Roger Corman's *Rock'N'Roll High School*, the 1978 B-movie featuring the Ramones as themselves. (*Michael Ochs Archives/Redferns*)

Johnny on stage, with Arturo Vega's familiar Ramones insignia in the background. "[Johnny's] a nice guy, opinionated, conservative Republican, into sports, very All-American," described Marky. "He started a guitar style that a lot of people tried to imitate and really couldn't. He was business-minded, and cared about the quality of the group." (*Denis O'Regan/Corbis*)

Marky gets da beat. "I'm playing so quick with the Ramones, I don't have time to whirl a stick… Heavy metal drummers usually play with their arms and shoulders. I play with my wrists and fingers." *(Ebet Roberts/Redferns)*

Backstage fun with Joey. "He always had time for fans," said Kevin Patrick. "When we would leave his place to walk two blocks to get something to eat, it would take us an hour to get there because everybody would stop him on the street and he'd sign anything they had, pose for pictures." *(Jeff Albertson/Corbis)*

"You could spot our audience from the street. They didn't have safety pins in their ears, they didn't have spiked hair, they didn't have the military look – they looked like kids in their denim and long hair, and maybe a motorcycle jacket if they could afford one. It was certainly not the heavy metal glam rock look." – Linda Stein. The Ramones at work, as Johnny would have put it – just another of 2,163 jobs in 22 years. (*Denis O'Regan/Corbis*)

"The Ramones were like a family and you wanted to defend them to the death. That's why I think the Ramones got so big in the end: everyone was on their side, every outsider, every geek, every kid, every freak, every nerd, everybody was on the Ramones' side." – George Tabb, Ramones fan. *(Godlis)*

Dee Dee, Joey, Marky and Johnny. John Holmstrom: "They didn't enjoy the success they had. They were always bitter about the success they didn't have. They didn't have the hit record. They didn't get the respect for starting punk rock. They didn't get the respect they deserved for this, that and the other. They were so concerned with what was written about them and their image, unlike any band I've ever seen." (*Ebet Roberts/Redferns*)

single from the album, backed on the 12-inch with a faithful cover of the 1910 Fruitgum Co.'s 'Indian Giver' (Joey unfortunately sounding like English comedian Vic Reeves doing his "club singer" turn) and the synthetic, drum machine-sound on the throwaway 'Life Goes On' (the chorus clearly lifted from Slade's 'Cum On Feel The Noize').

Some of the other songs, particularly Dee Dee's dire "fun" numbers, 'Bop 'Til You Drop' and 'Go Lil' Camaro Go' (on which you can hear another Kurfirst client, Debbie Harry, faintly singing in the background) sound as if they've been tossed off in a couple of seconds – and probably were. Still, at least the bassist had enough wit to poke fun at his own situation: "You tried and tried/But you're a flop/You're 35/Still pushing a mop," Joey sang in his drink-ravaged voice on the former.

"John was fast in the studio," recalls George Tabb, who was also recording at Intergalactic during the *Halfway To Sanity* sessions, with his band False Prophets. "It was the funniest thing because John would be going, 'Enough, enough, it sounds fine. Don't waste any more of my money. You've got the sound right.' And Joey, the artist, would go, 'I gotta do my vocals, I gotta do my vocals,' and the drummer's going, 'But my drums!' Johnny was like, 'Fuck it. It's the Ramones. It is what it is and it comes out like that.'

"And he was right," George adds. "It was the Ramones. He was a good businessman about it. I heard a lot of people, other rock stars, don't like John – you know what? John was always nice to the boys, the teenager kids, the fans . . . he would always write letters back. The guy would send me a Christmas card every year, 'Best wishes, Johnny' – oh my god, Johnny Ramone has sent me a Christmas card!"

Two other songs stand out – both Daniel Rey/Dee Dee Ramone compositions. The first, 'I Wanna Live' is a feedback-drenched slice of hard rock that moves along at a fair lick. The lines "As I load my pistol/Fine German steel," were later echoed in an interview Dee Dee gave to Ken Hinchey and Mike Vought when the bassist started loading a live clip into his rifle for a photo session. Even at 2.39, the song is too long, though.

It was the album's second UK single – the video saw the band attempting to cash in on the hardcore craze, with grainy black and white footage of the Ramones on tour (based on Bon Jovi's *Wanted Dead Or Alive*): in

in the role of the Holy Inquisitor. "If Joey wasn't doing a Ramones thing," says Manitoba, "he was busy planning something. He was a great New York City party thrower. I grew up in the same scene as Debbie Harry and all that, but I would never call her up and say, 'Come to my party.' Joey could. Joey was the social glue."

their van, looking tired, on stage with skinheads dancing and Joey sporting a Corrosion Of Conformity T-shirt and that damn leather glove again. The kids are stage diving and moshing on each other's shoulders: two things the Ramones reviled in real life.

"They hated it and they tried to stop it as much as possible," affirms Arturo, "but it would happen. Kids are really resourceful. Once the law-suits started coming in, a lot of clubs tried to ban it, too. Sometimes the security made it difficult for them, you know. Once, we were in Tijuana – and, of course, in Tijuana, who cares! They were jumping from a balcony that was at least 20 feet high. Ha! Jumping into the crowd. It was too much. It was great."

Dee Dee looks scarily demented in the video – a little imp. Perhaps it's no surprise: in his book, he wrote that he showed up for the shoot in a maroon rap jumpsuit, gold chains and a kangol, nursing a horrendous hangover. The other musicians hit the roof.*

'Garden Of Serenity', meanwhile, is a reasonable attempt at hardcore thrash – certainly better than side two's dreadful, *stupid stupid*, 'I Lost My Mind' where Dee Dee starts imitating English punks like Johnny Rotten with his voice, clearly bored by the song's lack of *anything*, and the two Richie Ramone songs 'I Know Better Now' and 'I'm Not Jesus'. The last, a Black Flag soundalike, would've worked better with Dee Dee singing.

For the sleeve, George DuBose took the Ramones to Chinatown, where they set up in an old stairwell. "We got my cousin and his buddy to patrol the crowd," DuBose reveals – the pair are credited as the Husky Bros on the record. "We had red lights set up, a smoke machine, every-thing ready at 4.30 pm. After three reels, Johnny says, 'That's enough.' I tell him that Warner Bros. are paying me a shit load of money, but he's not having it. Monte goes, 'If that's all they want to do, that's all you get. You're covered. I'm your witness.' The whole shoot took 10 minutes. Then I had to go to a Jewish cemetery and shoot some green tombstones for the back cover. I also photographed Peking ducks hanging in the window of a restaurant, with glaze dripping off their tails, and we used them for the inner sleeve."

* Dee Dee then went on to recount a particularly demented tale involving firecrackers, peaches, alligators and a car that burst into flames before sinking slowly into a quicksand pit. He and his companions found themselves surrounded by alligators along a highway in Florida, and miles of swampland caught fire and burned completely. Eventually the sorry troupe made it to their Miami show in the back of a battered old pick-up truck, Zippy from Brooklyn still clutching the pinhead sign that he'd saved from the swamp.

SHORTLY AFTERWARDS, Dee Dee recorded his first solo record as Dee Dee King – a 12-inch rap 'Funky Man' (Rock Hotel). As a rapper, the former Douglas Colvin made a good security guard – he patently can't sing, and his flow is strictly no-go – but the single is surprisingly endearing. Like the artists Dee Dee cited as influences – Beastie Boys, Run DMC, Suicidal Tendencies (eh?) – it self-referenced, and swaggered with a ridiculous macho strut.

"That was very strange," says Daniel diplomatically. "Dee Dee went into the hospital for some mental maintenance. [The bassist claimed he was suffering from pneumonia.] His real name is Douglas, so the other patients started calling him Doug E. Fresh – and when he came out he was a rapper, and being a friend and writing partner I was supportive of his artistic venture."

The first person Dee Dee contacted when he left the hospital was Richie. He gave him a new name, Broadway, and also renamed his wife Baby Doll King. "I'd never really heard a rap record before," the bassist admitted. "I heard 'Rappin' Rodney' [a Rodney Dangerfield novelty record], 'White Lines' [Grandmaster Flash] and 'Genius Of Love' [Tom Tom Club, ex-Talking Heads]. Dee Dee King sounds a little like B.B. King, so I thought – what does he wear? A $700 sharkskin suit and silk: so I went out and bought 10 Adidas jumpsuits and matching sneakers, and I wrote 10 raps and decided I'm gonna make an album with Richie. I like Richie: he gets up early and he's a golfer."

The pair met Chubby Checker on a night out in Atlantic City, where Dee Dee got the idea to cover Chubby's 'The Twist' – later selling the idea to The Fat Boys, or so he claimed.

Later, Debbie Harry was rumoured to have recorded a couple of similar tracks with the bassist ['King Of Swing', and a version of Hendrix's 'Foxy Lady', with Harry rapping in French and Dee Dee in English] but they never appeared. Joey, however, did join the former Blondie singer on stage in December for an AIDS benefit, singing three Ramones songs – 'Go Lil' Camaro Go', 'Sedated' and 'Loudmouth'. A bootleg seven-inch of the event later showed up, credited to Joey & Friends: 'Live In NYC April 1st 1988' – showing his back-up included Andy Shernoff and Daniel Rey, with the unlikely presence of [Blondie songwriter/guitarist] Chris Stein on drums.

THE RAMONES TOURED the States solidly during '87, playing a handful of dates in South America in February – a continent where they would later become bigger than The Rolling Stones, at least in terms of ticket sales.

Then Richie left. His departure was unexpected – one can only imagine, if the band argued among themselves as often as was reported, that no one would've expected anyone to leave. However, Richie had had enough. Fed up with his wage – and the fact it was a wage – Richie walked out after an East Hampton gig on August 12, right before three shows in NYC (subsequently cancelled). As the band told it, the problem was that Richie went direct to the management with his grievances – that, and his partner had unduly influenced him. Richie had recently left his girlfriend for a new one, and got married – so the Ramones promptly blamed the situation on her. Women just aren't very rock'n'roll, at least in Johnny's world.

It's hard to know precisely what transpired, as Richie has been incommunicado since – he was last sighted working in a Florida hotel. And there was certainly no thought on the Ramones' side that Richie may have had a case to answer. A gang, remember? Time to close ranks again.

Blame the woman. It's far easier.

"I felt screwed," Joey said. "Me and Richie were friends. He was more than just the drummer. But he was out for himself. He said he would do the New York shows for $500 a night. I'm sure he felt he had us by the balls, as our album was coming out."

It occurs that if Richie went to the management, Joey only had the management's version of events: but whatever the reality, the whole incident left a bad taste in everyone's mouths, to the extent that most of the Ramones family won't speak about Richie to this day, despite everyone agreeing that – abrupt departure aside – he was a nice chap.

Perhaps a little sensitive managing might have been called for.

"He was my favourite," says DuBose. "He wrote some of the best songs, too. I thought it was a real shame when he quit. They should have kicked Johnny out instead. Richie was kicked out because he was making $250 a week as the drummer and wanted 25 per cent of the T-shirt proceeds, but the other three weren't happy at that, but he quit right before a gig and wasn't very professional. I remember thinking, why don't they fire Johnny because he's not even a good guitar player anyway – though he did play Mosrite guitars, as used by The Ventures and The B-52's. Johnny couldn't play his way out of a wet paper bag."

"They were a classic dysfunctional family," says Tabb, "but there was a real love there. When Richie left, John called me up and said, 'Hey, do you know any good drummers?' And I'm thinking, 'I could play drums,' but I suck. So I started asking around: 'Hey, do you want to play for the Ramones?' And these guys were all like, 'Well, how much do they pay? The Ramones are so yesterday. It's too simple for me. I'd get bored.'

Dumb-asses. Idiots. This was the biggest chance in the world! So they ended up having Clem Burke [Blondie], and then they got Marc back. I called Johnny and said, 'Who's the new drummer?' Johnny went, 'You'll see.' I was like, 'Holy crap – Marc!' "

Clem – by common assent one of the New Wave's finest drummers – lasted just two shows (August 28 in Providence, August 29 in Trenton). Johnny described his sojourn as a disaster. His drumming style wasn't right: it was too loose for the Ramones. "Double-time on the hi-hat was totally alien to him," Johnny explained. An uncredited review of Clem at the Trenton show at www.ramonesonline.com/clem.htm makes for interesting reading: not least because it gives an insight into the Ramones set.

(The following is edited.)

'Durango 95' (plays many of the fills wrong); 'Teenage Lobotomy'; 'Psycho Therapy'; 'Blitzkrieg Bop' (no major errors, but it is an easy song to play); 'Rock'N'Roll Radio' (Clem completely destroys the intro, forcing Johnny and Dee Dee to improvise); 'Freak Of Nature'; 'Gimme Gimme Shock Treatment' (unable to keep the tempo needed), 'Rock'N'-Roll High School' (misses fills between first and second verses); 'I Wanna Be Sedated'; 'The KKK Took My Baby Away'; 'Crummy Stuff' (at the end, Clem keeps drumming, and [finally] ends with a cheesy-sounding roll), 'Rockaway Beach' (not exactly like Tommy played it) . . . and so on, through 19 songs.

Now, that's fanatical.

"I was there at the photo session with Clem Burke. It was my first job with them," PR Ida Langsam says. "They were playing around with names. They said it couldn't be Joey, Johnny, Dee Dee and Clem Burke, and it couldn't be Clemmy Ramone, so they were going to call him Elvis Ramone.

"I'd been talking to Andrea Starr [the Ramones' personal manager at Kurfirst's Overland company] over a very long course of time to get their account," she continues. "I wasn't friends with them, but I knew them from being around the New York music industry. They seemed very removed. Other artists I've worked with eat, sleep and drink being in the music industry. The Ramones were the Ramones. These guys were always the way they were."

In his time away, Marky had been playing in Richie Stott's heavy metal band, King Flux and also his own M-80. Less than a week after being called upon, he was on stage as a Ramone once more, in Oyster Bay, LI on September 4.

"IT WAS THE same old thing," says Marky. "The new roadie introduced himself to me. I used the Ramones drums because I'd got rid of everything I had – all my drum kits, I didn't care. I sold them all. Then I got rid of that set, because I didn't like the wood finish, and colour. So Pearl Drums sponsored me for free – they sent me a black set when I joined, the colour I wanted, and a blue set for studio use. Then I ordered a custom-made silver sparkle set for the remaining years of the band. I toured with those for five years. Now that set is in the Hollywood Rock Hall Of Fame, next to Keith Moon's and Kiss's."

What was the big difference between the Ramones, first and second time around?

"It was the same. We'd warm up for about 10 minutes before we went on, go on, the count would start and that was it. The roadies would set the drums up real good – they dabbled in their pot and their drinking once in a while, but they always did their job well. First time round, it was the booze and the pot: Dee Dee and me staying out till six in the morning. I was a binge drinker. I drank when I drank and I drank. We always played good, though. It's still hard to believe."

"I once saw Marky drink 16 double martinis in Cleveland," confirms Monte. "The next morning during interviews, he threw up every 10 minutes. I have to give him credit for turning his life around. He used to have a tremendous drinking problem."

"When I came back I was sober," continues Marky. "I didn't want to be treated different, I didn't want them walking on eggshells. I just did what I had to do. They tried Clem Burke and he couldn't cut it. So they called me – I went to the studio and that was it. Nothing changed except me. Being straight is so much better: for 80 minutes you have to play 16th notes constantly on the hi-hat, and be ready for those '1-2-3-4's. You need to be aware of what's going on around you."

Did you find what you were getting out of it onstage was any different?

"No – I knew I had a job to do, to make people happy. All I ever wanted was to see smiles on the kids' faces."

So it was business as usual, except for George Tabb who'd just started his dream job – as a Ramones guitar tech, same night as Marky's first show back: "I knew the Ramones because of Johnny," he relates. "He was always nice to me when I was a kid hangin' around. Some of the other Ramones were very cranky to me on that tour, and I broke Johnny's guitar. I dropped his frickin' bridge down an air conditioning vent in New Jersey. I thought he was gonna kill me. All the roadies were like, 'Johnny's a terrible person – he'll scream at you.' Johnny came in, and put his head on my shoulder and said, 'Hey man, you fucked up, fix it up – no problem.'

"I'd see John glare at the other guys on stage when they made a mistake," Tabb continues. "That was a big thing with the Ramones. Johnny is a guy who likes his band really tight. But, again, that's what the Ramones are. It's this whole fascist imagery and the fascist music that works so well. He knew that everyone wants a Ramones show to be perfect, the same every time. He was right. John's pretty cool."

THE REVIEWS FOR *Halfway To Sanity* in September were surprisingly favourable considering everything – certainly in the Ramones home town: *Billboard* criticised Sire for not releasing 'Go Lil' Camaro Go' as a single, *New York Post* claimed it was another great album . . . but the English press was more muted. Indeed, despite another 11-date tour of the UK, it was as if the Ramones had disappeared off the map . . . one bad album could be forgiven, but two? The British music press isn't as fickle as people claim, just *choosy*.

"These albums didn't sound right without some more of Joey's songs to balance out Dee Dee's," explained fan Mark Bannister. "There was no equilibrium. At the Brixton Academy in October 1987 they seemed to be going through the motions and I was pretty pissed off. Didn't even buy a T-shirt! The following summer, the Ramones played at Brixton again, but I went to The Damned's reunion show instead as I only had enough money for one gig. I felt a bit guilty . . ."

Still, there were plenty of enthusiasts around: at a sold out Paris show, riot police tear-gassed rock-throwing fans [a distant echo of Johnny at Beatles concerts, perhaps?] who weren't allowed to join the 2,000 inside; in November, the Ramones were banned from playing at Boston University, the authorities fearing the "rowdiness, destructiveness and drug use" that the music was supposed to encourage. The University's Program Council held an anti-censorship rally in response at Marsh Plaza where Joey and Marky addressed a thousand-strong crowd. "We're here to uphold the honour of the students and the Ramones," Joey said, before pointing out that his band's shows always passed without violence.

The Ramones played 53 dates in 1987 after Marky joined – Europe and America – before ending the year with their traditional December 31 show, this time in Bayshore, LI.

Two notable records appeared around the same time.

The first was Dee Dee's solo record.

The second was Joey's wonderful Christmas song, 'Merry Christmas (I

Don't Want To Fight Tonight)', replete with sleigh bells jangling during the intro, and a suitably crisp, solid production from Jean Beauvoir, with Marky on drums. A double A-side in the UK with 'I Wanna Live', it was a shoo-in for the Christmas Number One – as perfect a pop song as even those on Phil Spector's *A Christmas Gift For You*, and sung with just as much naïve joy – that somehow failed to chart. It later turned up on *Brain Drain*.

"It's a classic Joey song in a Phil Spector vein," agrees Rey, "and it was Joey's idea to put sleigh bells on, of course. He was a Jew. It made perfect sense, because Jews wrote most of the good Christmas songs – Irving Berlin and 'White Christmas'. It was recorded at the height of summer like all good Christmas singles."

"It's a true experience," Joey told me. "It's about one Christmas Eve, one time my old girlfriend and I had a little peace to make. I always felt it cool that the Ramones should have a Christmas song because Slade had that 'Merry Christmas (Everybody)'."

WITH MARKY BACK on board, it was like old times. Except, of course, it wasn't.

Despite their public show of solidarity, and a 1988 tour schedule that took in over 100 shows in countries as disparate as Finland, America, Puerto Rico (at the World Surfing Championships, where 2,000 surfers from 64 countries congregated), Japan and England, the band were barely talking to each other and turning in workhorse performances. It was a bleak period, but still the tour ploughed relentlessly on – "Ramones Non-Stop World Tour", as the roadies' T-shirts once read. It really did feel that if they stopped even for a second now, they'd break up. Marky might've cleaned up, but Joey was still drinking heavily and God alone knows what world Dee Dee was in. Johnny, of course, left as soon as the job was done: you don't hang around with your workmates after the day is over.

One of the bright spots was the release in May of the long overdue Ramones Greatest (Non) Hits – the 30-track *Ramones Mania*, packaged with the usual cavalier disregard for logic or indeed planning. The songs pretty much picked themselves – tons from the first four albums, hardly anything from the Eighties – but the running order was non-chronological, and the handful of "rare" tracks seemed to be included only to infuriate real fans looking for new material. There was no 'Slug', no alternate demos of the first album, no outtakes from anything – just a few single versions ('Sheena', 'Needles And Pins', 'Howling At The Moon'), a previously unreleased "stereo" mix of 'Rock'N'Roll High School' and a couple of B-sides.

Still, it did serve as a timely reminder of how great the Ramones *used* to be, and gained the band their first gold record – 14 years after they'd started. "That's my first and only gold record of the Ramones to date," sighs cover designer George DuBose. "I know they got gold records in Brazil and Holland, but I never got the plaques."

'I Wanna Be Sedated' was reissued in America, backed with a slightly ridiculous 'Ramones On 45 Mega-Mix' which segued 'Sedated' and several other Ramones oldies with the "Hey Ho Let's Go" chant *over a disco beat* – an irony that presumably wasn't lost on the band or management or record company. One hopes. A video was shot, centred around the Ramones sitting at a breakfast table eating breakfast and reading comic books and looking bored (especially Johnny!) while a cast of circus and pantomime freaks rush around them in manic confusion.

An even more perplexing compilation appeared shortly afterwards, *End Of The Decade* – a collection of six UK 12-inch singles from 1984–1987, plus T-shirt and poster in a limited edition box set of 2,500. It was an odd choice of era.

On August 26, the Ramones appeared at England's annual Reading Festival, supporting Iggy Pop and The Smithereens. However, this was before the festival became fashionable (which happened in the Nineties, with the onset of grunge and Nirvana), so they played to the usual crowd of die-hard metal fans and the media-alienated. Two months later, they travelled across to Japan, to play a week of shows in front of some of their most fanatical supporters, not that the American band would've necessarily guessed it by the reaction.

"You would find some situations that would be so under control," explains Arturo. "They were like sterile, like in Japan. They got used to it after a few years, but at the beginning the kids thought it was rude and impolite to make noise. So they would clap a little bit after the song, and then it would be dead silence. Afterwards, they'd leave straight away – no encore. We'd be like, 'Oh god, what's going on?' That's too much control. It killed the energy."

Joey and Marky made an appearance in the video to Bobby Brown's theme song for *Ghostbusters II*. Joey, acting as a street musician, played the tuba while Marky collected the money – other guest stars included Grace Jones, Christopher Reeve and Donald Trump. "I think the producers wanted us there," Marky explains, "because it was New York and the Ramones are synonymous with the city." The singer also made cameos in the black and white Canadian road movie *Road Kill*, centred around a girl named Ramona, and on a single from funk king George Clinton.

Other bands the Ramones played with in 1988 included The Dickies, Grandmaster Flash (on what must have been a strange Buffalo bill), fellow Seventies "punks" The Stranglers and hard-rockin' British outfit The Godfathers. In LA, when da bruddas played the John Anson Ford Theatre, they attracted complaints when 'I Wanna Be Sedated' drowned out 'Alexander's Ragtime Band' at the Hollywood Bowl across the street, where a birthday celebration for Irving Berlin was taking place. "It was our way of saying, 'Happy Birthday Irving'," claimed Joey.

Of course, the Ramones finished the year with another New Year's Eve show – this time at NYC's legendary Irving Plaza venue.

Fourteenth year, same as the last.

25

The Search For The Hit

How motivated were the Ramones by their search for a hit?

"It was almost a blessing they never got one – things would've been so different if they'd had a hit in '78. Bands like Blondie had hits, they made millions and lost millions and got all messed up. Also, the public would've known them as a one hit wonder instead of a great, consistent group. If you have a big hit, afterwards you could feel like a failure. It meant the Ramones remained hungry throughout their career – what makes people go to work is the fact they need that paycheck.

"Joey always thought the new single might be the one. The other guys weren't as optimistic – Johnny would be in the background rolling his eyes. They were a little bitter about it. There are about 20 songs from the first four albums that would be hits in today's climate. It's so obvious to release 'Blitzkrieg Bop' now it's chanted at sporting events all over the world" – Daniel Rey

"America's music industry lacks vision. If they were English they'd be Gods. They were too smart for the record company business, with the exception of Seymour Stein. The US music industry really disrespected my favourite band. You can't measure the Ramones' impact in banal measures like market shares" – Donna Gaines

"What's great about the Ramones' legacy is that it's not based on something as ephemeral as a radio hit. They had the last laugh because they ended up making history and being loved. They didn't have the hits that meant that 10–20 years later, you'd be going, 'Oh god, I'm really embarrassed I liked that.' The memories aren't cheapened. The Ramones ended up having a quality of success that you can equate with The Beatles, the Stones and The Who, without ever having a hit single. When, in fact, all they made were hit singles.

"That goes back to where they came from – the notion of the 45 and the Bay City Rollers thing, and 'Blitzkrieg Bop'. The Ramones were a pop band but they were not making mere pop music the way a lot of people like to define it. They made the ultimate pop music and it was so ultimate that it was ultimately too big and too dirty for radio. It was too real. In a sense the radio station for the Ramones hasn't been invented yet. But once it is, they can play Ramones songs all day, every day. All killer, no filler" – David Fricke

"Ramones wanted a hit record, they wanted success. They wanted to be rock stars. I don't know if they ever became rock stars, but they sure became legends. They never sold out, the legendary Ramones. Everybody loves them" – Ed Stasium

"If everyone you spoke to says they own a Ramones album or two or three or 10 – why do they only have one gold record? We could never figure that out. Programme directors at radio stations ignored their music in droves. It wasn't ever a matter of consciously writing hits. They wrote, and everything was great. It was up to the people at the record label to decide which song to put out as a single. I was never aware of Joey or anyone else sitting down, saying, 'I'm going to write a hit.' When I worked with Kiss they would frequently say that. Because the Ramones were always there, people felt they could cut corners, not bother with a budget for them. It was very DIY, and it remained that way. The Ramones used their friends to do everything – art direction, photography, design . . . That's why they referred to everyone they worked with as part of the family" – Ida Langsam

"It's frustrating. It still remains that way, but I have to remind myself that I got farther than I ever thought I would when I bought my first guitar. I'm retired and I don't have to work anymore. I have to remind myself of that because otherwise you can sit there and think, 'I didn't make it.' When you're an athlete, you win the championship and you know you've succeeded. Music is hard. How do you know whether you've succeeded or not? Is it whether you've influenced people? OK, great . . . but what if you didn't sell records? Because you sold records, does that mean you've succeeded, really, if you haven't influenced anybody and they all think you're a lousy band? I don't know. There's no real defined way of 'succeeding' " – Johnny Ramone

"The English are more accepting of different things, the taste is broader and they weren't shocked by the sound. In America, they hated the Ramones – even though people like Ozzy Osbourne and Alice Cooper were far worse behaved. Patti Smith pissed on the stage, while the Ramones did nothing except play great shows, and kept trying, and trying, but got labelled black sheep. The radio wouldn't play them . . . and wouldn't play them . . . and wouldn't play them. I still can't believe they were treated that way" – Linda Stein

"Every song we made, we tried to hope it was a hit, but we weren't conscious about it. We didn't feel it was necessary. We had our fan base. We thought, 'Fuck it, if the radio doesn't play it.' Case in point, Phil Spector. The closest we got to a hit was Number 50 in America, and Number Seven or Eight in England, but we didn't care at that point – we just wanted to make decent albums" – Marky Ramone

26

All Screwed Up

"I QUIT DRUGS *and alcohol in 1988," says Joan Tarshis, "and Joey quit pretty much everything by the end of 1989 – I remember him calling me on New Year's Eve and saying people were shoving coke in his face. He didn't know how to refuse it without appearing a snob. I told him to tell the people he'd, 'Love to do the coke but it hurts my nose. Maybe next time.' I also warned him that if he did coke, he'd probably drink. He probably did snort the coke that night, but the next New Year's Eve we went from club to club but never had a drink, hanging out with Blondie and Joan Jett.*

"He got straight because he wanted to. He came to a realisation it wasn't healthy for him, mentally or physically. One time in the Cat Club, he was sitting at a table with three or four girls and Mickey [Leigh] – I don't know how much Chivas he'd polished off, but he was horizontal when I next saw him. I don't think he was an alcoholic. He never had to go to AA. He just stopped – like he did with his smoking. He was very proud of it. We'd celebrate our festivals of sobriety together.

"Joey had a dark sense of humour – pitch-black, very silly, we'd have a lot of in-things we'd do for each other. He'd always go 'Jo-o-o-o-o-an'. I'd be smoking in his apartment and he wanted me to lean out the window, and somehow it got to be the God window, so he'd be like if you wanna have a cigarette, go to the God window. Then the God window developed into 'Go to de window' à la The Beatles in Help. *It was little things like that I miss the most. He liked a sharp comeback. People didn't realise, because they didn't have patience, how intelligent he was. I could never spell: I would ask him to spell words, and in his two-inch big handwriting he would tell me. Because of the way he spoke and how he measured his words, ignorant people didn't realise how sharp he was. He was totally knowledgeable about everything in music, but outside of that he could come up with a one-liner.*

"He was very fragile. He was frail. I would look at his ankles and say, 'I could break your ankle like a pencil.' We had a big fight once, in '89. We both threw something at each other. I was so pissed off I called the cops – and they came up to the apartment. He was not the tidiest of people: there'd be 50 or so CDs on the floor, sleeves all over the place. Plus, he had a souvenir towel on the floor from the

Bates motel that looked like it was full of dried blood. So the cops looked at the apartment and the bloody towel, and said, 'Wow you must have had a very big fight. Where does it hurt?' They were like, 'Did you just do this?' They thought maybe we'd thrown everything in the house at each other.

"So we kind of didn't speak to each other after that, and then, a few months later, Dick Manitoba said, 'I have an idea. Why don't you buy a hammer and put a little card in with it saying, "If I ever get out of line again, hit me with this"?' Joey called me immediately and said, 'I'm keeping that hammer in a holster for when I'm with you.' "

(Interview with author, 2002)

"IN THE EIGHTIES, I was starting to party too much," Joey told Jaan Uhelszki for *Mojo* in 1999. "I got into certain drugs late. In the Seventies everybody was doing cocaine, and it didn't do anything for me. Then I broke up with this girl, and for some reason I could get high on cocaine, and then I started to like it. Then my next girlfriend liked it, too. There was this producer we used, who had a chemist who mixed drugs for him, all kinds of weirdo drugs that made you feel like you were walking on the moon. Beer was my drug of choice, my beverage of choice. I liked hanging out, having a few beers with friends. Then I fell hard on that [girl] and started developing a liking for Chivas, and things started getting a little too heavy.

"Then I had a freak accident," he continued, "where I walked off a high stage [January 1990]. I was very high. The stage was very high. I thought I could just step off it. So I hurt myself really bad. I had torn ligaments in my ankle. And that's what ended it. It happened three days before a Ramone tour, so I got hell for it, because I was in a cast up to my knee. What it did was make me see the light. It wasn't that I had a drinking problem, because I really didn't. I was always good about stopping things like that. I'd take breaks from time-to-time. I'd take three weeks off.

"It was almost as if things happened for a reason. Sometimes you're so busy in your life, you're unaware something is happening to you, and it takes a higher power to make you see. And the way you see is by having a fucked-up accident. I think that higher power was trying to tell me something. Having that accident changed everything for me. I was 39, about to turn 40, and I decided that I didn't want to look like shit at 40 from doing stuff. So I stopped before I turned 40."

IN MARCH 1989, Dee Dee released his solo album *Standing In The Spotlight* (Sire/Red Eye) under the name Dee Dee King. On it, he raps to a hard rock backing supplied by pals like Marc Bell, Daniel Rey and Chris Stein (who plays guitar on the autobiographical 'German Kid', backing vocals by Debbie Harry). Harry also sings back-up on 'Mashed Potato Time' – a fun melding of the Dee Dee Sharp 1962 hit with 'The Monster Mash' and a lyric that borders on the absurd. Even the sax break is like something taken from John Waters' record hop revival film *Hairspray*.

The album, despite being roundly ridiculed – probably because Dee Dee's voice sounds like a cartoon moose – possesses a vitality and warmth markedly lacking from Ramones albums in the late Eighties. It's clear the bassist is having a ball – freed from Johnny's restrictive regime, he sings with a joyful, warped humour. Ramones hadn't sounded this innocent since *Rocket To Russia*.

As fan Mark Prindle pointed out, "He has no clue, and that's why the album is so entertaining. You honestly cannot listen to it without furrowing your brow and asking aloud to a passer-by, 'He thought this was *good*?' "

"We got a bunch of these silly rap songs together," says producer Rey, "and much to my surprise, Dee Dee decided to make it an album. Someone once rated the worst albums of the year for a fanzine and said, 'I would include Dee Dee's album but we're only including albums recorded in English.' I thought that was funny."

It's slightly unfair, too. *Standing In The Spotlight* contains more good songs than the previous two Ramones albums put together – the hangover-laden '2 Much 2 Drink' (a shambolic cross between *The Prince Of Bel-Air* and, more obviously, the Beastie Boys' 'Fight For Your Right To Party'),* the cutesy-pie Sixties-style ballad 'Baby Doll' (Dee Dee's pet name for his wife Vera), 'Commotion In The Ocean' (where the surf meets the rap, B-52's style), 'The Crusher' (old school thrash), 'Brooklyn Babe' (a slightly more obnoxious cousin of 'Genius Of Love').

"As my alter ego, King is able to do a lot of things I've always wanted," explained Dee Dee on a press release at the time. "On 'The Crusher', he becomes a professional wrestler. In 'Commotion In The Ocean', he goes to California and becomes a surfer, and in 'German Kid', he actually raps in German. But what was the most exciting to me was the chance to be really romantic on rap ballads like 'Baby Doll'. I think people have always seen me as a very hard-edged guy. Actually, love is the most interesting

* Beastie Boys sampled 'Suzy Is A Headbanger' on 'High Plains Drifter' on 1989's *Paul's Boutique*.

thing I can think of to write and sing about. Maybe some Ramones fans will be shocked at the sentiments coming out of Dee Dee King's mouth, but that's just another part of who I am and how I feel."

In interviews, Dee Dee drew parallels between punk and rap music: believing both to be the "rebellious music of the streets", overlooking that one belonged to a white tradition, and the other black. Not that it means either race shouldn't cross over – rock music is littered with incidences of white musicians drawing from a black heritage – just that it's odd when one race copies another's mannerisms wholesale. Like Dee Dee, and the white rock-rappers that followed him in the Nineties, such as House Of Pain, Kid Rock and Limp Bizkit, did.

It didn't matter, though.

Unwittingly, Dee Dee had rediscovered one of the golden rules of pop – one that far too many bands lose sight of – that it's meant to be FUN. It is not supposed to be taken seriously, cure the world's ills. It's a throwaway medium, digested one second, forgotten the next . . . until you rediscover it down the back of the sofa several years on, and it brings you renewed joy.

The Ramones had *never* been serious early on: indeed, they were on a mission to bring the humour and passion back into rock'n'roll, fighting a rearguard battle to save it from pretentious, humourless bands like ELP and Genesis. Now they'd become precisely as dour and serious as those they once reviled: and, even worse, some of the band treated music as routine – not something to be excited over at all.

It's odd that it took a disposable novelty record from their errant bassist to put things into context. Not that anyone noticed at the time.

"That solo album was a big shock," says Ida Langsam. "Ramones fans weren't ready to accept it. What do you do with a white punk kid from Queens trying to rap? It got the strangest response. It bombed. I gave a huge slew of them away when I moved office and now I hear they're worth a load of money."

It wasn't really a rap album: more a collection of rock and Fifties pop songs, with a little novelty rapping thrown in – but because of the way Dee Dee dressed, it was marketed that way.

"Had he been 20 years younger," says Arturo now, "and without any attachments to any other band, he would've achieved what Kid Rock achieved. He was too advanced in another direction. It seemed ridiculous for *Dee Dee Ramone* to do that. It was confusing, even downright insulting to some fans. Rap was looked on as the enemy. Artistically, he had the right instincts – but once you've chosen your path as an artist, you can't deviate too much. Your audience won't allow you. Especially hardcore audiences."

THE RAMONES PLAYED their usual run of dates in the first half of 1989.

In January, da bruddas toured America, ending with a couple of shows at NYC's The Ritz on 27 and 28. In February, the band went across to Spain for a week, before heading back to the East Coast in April – and then setting their sights on Italy during the first two weeks of May. Athens followed (although whether it was in Greece or Georgia, their schedule doesn't say: one suspects it's the former – why would any travelling rock band play Georgia for four nights running?) and then the West Coast, plus a date in Tijuana, Mexico on June 23.

"That was wild," Joey told Tarshis. "There was a lot of real heavy slam dancing and stage diving. It's right across the border from San Diego where the drinkin' age is 21, and Mexico has no drinkin' age. So all the kids like to go across the border to Happy Land!"

Unsurprisingly, Arturo's memories of 22 years of touring all merge into one after a while, but the lighting technician does have fond memories of some of the countries they visited during the Eighties: "We were really big in Spain for a while," he recalls. "It was a little different, touring Spain. Once you got away from the big cities, uh, the Spaniards were the only crew that would stop everything come lunch or dinner-time . . .

"Not siesta, eating. They would sit down and have a meal with wine, and lots of food. They wouldn't do anything on the fly – because if you open the doors two hours late, it doesn't matter." He laughs. "It's expected! Once we were somewhere in the south, and we were supposed to open the doors at eight, and they opened at 11! It was no big deal.

"The Brazilians were the same. In Brazil, I gave up right away. It was impossible. They're such a cool people, so happy and well natured. You just couldn't get mad at them, because you knew it was impossible for them to even think about being on time. With the Spaniards, I did get mad a few times. I couldn't believe they could be so unprofessional. But it's a way of life. The Italians were like that, but they got better – and the food was so good you forgave them for everything."

IT'S SPLITTING HAIRS, but *Brain Drain*, the Ramones' final studio album for Sire is easily the best of the dreadful late Eighties run.

The balance, at least, was back.

Joey, bolstered by the addition of ex-Dictator Andy Shernoff to his writing team, contributed six songs, Dee Dee the same number –

including the excellent single 'Pet Sematary' (co-written with Daniel Rey). The lyrics, written for a film adaptation of the Stephen King novel of the same name, are among his most mature: "Under the arc of a weather stain boards/Ancient goblins, and warlords" – chilling, and evocative of the Sleepy Hollow graveyard* where the video was set. Popular legend has it that Dee Dee wrote the song to order, in 10 minutes, while the horror author was sitting in the next room.

"Stephen King's a big Ramones fan," Joey told me that year. "He contacted us directly and asked us to write the title track." The band had recently signed with Chrysalis in Europe, and the singer seemed happy: "They're doing a fucking great job," he said. "We did the video on the first night of the full moon with all our friends – the Cycle Sluts, Daniel Rey, Cheetah Crome (ex-Dead Boys), Debbie Harry and Chris Stein. They dug a real gravesite for us and we were buried alive. We drove up in a hearse, and the driver said, 'You guys are the first live cargo I've delivered.'

"The next day we were playing Buffalo, New York and our equipment truck exploded on the highway. It totally melted. We were lucky because these state troopers were going by, they were fans, and they helped the crew unload the equipment – I'm sure the crew would have let it burn. It held up traffic for hours. While the truck was burning it went into a hillside . . . There were a lot of weird things that happened round that period."

Joey's singing voice had gone back to normal: perhaps because he was taking more care over his own songs. Certainly, numbers like the slow-fuse bubblegum gem 'All Screwed Up' (co-written by Shernoff, Marky unusually, Joey and Daniel), and the cover of Freddy Cannon's 1962 teen dream hit 'Palisades Park' with all its hot dog stands, had a vigour and charm that had been lacking for some considerable time.

"It's fun to do covers, if it's the right one," Joey explained. "We'd be driving to the show in Philly or somewhere, listening to the oldies station, and we'd hear 'Palisades Park'. So we did that, real fast."

Dee Dee/Daniel Rey's 'I Believe In Miracles' is an upbeat, optimistic, hard-edged opening song, the minimal guitar solo barely sounding out of place – "Life's bleak," said Joey. "So what? Some people are really into that black, morbid Gothic music. That's not what I want to do with the Ramones."

Even the thrash tracks ('Zero Zero UFO', the speed metal 'Ignorance Is

* Burial place of the Rockefellers: made famous by the writings of Ichabod Crane.

Bliss') sound less forced, more natural. Joey told Tarshis that 'Ignorance' was about the disintegration of humanity: "It's about waking up before it's irreversible," he said. "It came about when I was asked to do the Rain Forest Benefit."

Some fans didn't like the new album at all – George Tabb thinks *Brain Drain* sounds awful, "like it was being piped through tin cans. Was that the guy with the Mohawk who did that? Or was it the Motorhead producer guy?"

It was the "Motorhead producer guy", Bill Laswell. Laswell had also worked with PiL and Iggy Pop, and was a world music aficionado. He produced all of *Brain Drain*, with the exception of 'Merry Christmas' (included presumably to keep costs down). Personally, I feel Laswell did a fine job – or maybe he had better material.

Although the Dee Dee/Joey/Daniel Rey-penned 'Don't Bust My Chops' sounds worryingly vindictive – directed towards a former girlfriend, with lines like "Dirty mouth/Is all I can bear/Get out of here bitch/'Cos you're nowhere" – there are more than enough fine melodies to rectify the situation. Both of Joey's 'Can't Get You Outta My Mind' and 'Come Back, Baby' are heartstring-tuggers with vocal performances to match. Laswell also managed to make the guitar sound less workmanlike, and more sympathetic – thanks, no doubt, to "musical coordinator" Daniel Rey, and also Artie Smith and Robert Musso (additional guitars).

"When I went to Sorcerer Sound Studios to talk about the sleeve," designer George DuBose recalls, "Monte told me I'd have to wait until there was a break in the recording, and then I'd have to sneak through the control room without Bill Laswell seeing me because not even the group were allowed in while he was working. So I'm playing pool with Monte upstairs, and I hear some bass lines. I look down out of the glass and there's some guy playing bass – 'Who's that, Monte?' 'Oh, that's Daniel Rey. He's just putting down some bass.' So we continue playing pool, and half-an-hour later I hear some guitar and I look out and . . . 'Who's that guy?' 'Oh, that's Daniel playing guitar.' Then Monte closes the blinds, and says, 'I think you've seen enough.' "

"That's a song with a real positive outlook," Joey told me about 'I Believe In Miracles'. "It's about having faith in yourself, not giving up." During the song's video, loads of slogans and band names are flashed across the screen around live footage of the band: silence = death: You Only Live Once, Here Comes Trouble, The New York Dolls, Motorhead, *Viva Las Vegas*, The Shangri-Las, *I Was A Teenage Zombie*, What's Your Sign?, The Heartbreakers, Howie Klein, Lisa Robinson, AC/DC, Sonic

Youth, Dead Kennedys, Agnostic Front, DOA . . . an insight into what kept the Ramones' world turning.

For the cover, the Ramones used a haunting Matt Mahurin painting. The band name is thick and blocky, the album title splattered blood. "We're fascinated by the bizarre," said Joey. "Everyone has their fascinations. With some people it's cars, with others, it's museums and art. With us, it's a little of everything – cars, freaks, fine art.

"We saw the original poster for *Pet Sematary* that was rejected by Paramount Pictures," the singer told me, "and fell in love with it. The day before the artwork was to be finalised, Paramount decided because we liked it so much they were going to use it for Europe. So I got on the phone to the artist in LA and asked him to do something similar. He did a great job."

Brain Drain was released in May 1989, promoted among the media by surgical caps. Press reaction was, as ever, varied. New York Shock DJ Howard Stern picked 'Pet Sematary' as his song of the year – but looking at Howard, with his Joey-style long hair, and height, and denim jeans, it didn't come as much of a surprise. *Stereo Review* gave a nod to Dee Dee's "boot-stomping crypto-metal" and Joey's pop sensibilities; *Melody Maker* wrote that "[it] isn't just *another* Ramones album. It has at least two moments of sublime glory, the teen angst ballads 'All Screwed Up' and 'Come Back, Baby', and one moment of heart-stopping Spector kitsch, 'Merry Christmas'." *NME* said it was "one good reason why God gave man guitars".

'Pet Sematary' failed to chart, but it seemed things were looking up once more for the Ramones. Dee Dee was happier than he'd been in years, and was keen to quash any rumours over a potential solo career: "I am NOT leaving the Ramones," he was overheard telling someone on the phone. "How many times do I have to say that?"

Then, in July, Johnny got a call from the band's management office: "Dee Dee's leaving."

27

Touring, Part 6

"I NEVER STOPPED enjoying it. They did 2,263 shows. I only missed two of those."

Wow.

"Once, we were going to Canada, and they didn't like my ID so they didn't let me go through. The other time, me and the guitar roadie and the drum roadie spent the night in jail. We were going to Maryland to the first show of the tour, in a rented car. I was in the back sleeping. They got pulled over because they were speeding and the cops found dope on them. So we got taken to jail.

"We toured almost all year round. The only time we stopped was when they were recording. Or, later on, if Joey was sick, but we never had to cancel a . . . oh yeah, a couple of times, towards the end, we had to cancel a couple of European tours, or delay them. We toured constantly. They enjoyed it, you know."

I can imagine.

"Yeah."

What a great thing to do. How big was the road crew?

"The permanent road crew here in the United States was the sound man, the monitor man, the guitar man, drum roadie, myself as lighting director, and my assistant. So there were six of us. That was it. When we toured overseas, there were just five – sound, monitors, drum, guitars and myself. Oh, and here in the States we also had the guy that drove the truck. When we did big tours in Europe, we'd hire local crew. We ended up using Germans, more than anyone else."

Why was that?

"We were big in Germany, especially during the Eighties. The largest crew we had at one point was 40 people, including cooks. That was for a German tour. And, uh, we'd take them to other countries as well, like Austria and Switzerland, or the Netherlands. Otherwise, it would be a local crew. Even later on."

Were there any special things you'd do with the lights during the show?

"Flash them a lot! I was one of the first to use a lot of white light. When we started playing at the Whiskey in LA, I had to ask Pete, the house lighting guy, to take out a lot of gels. He would complain, 'Arturo, why do you want so much white light?' He thought it wasn't cool. He later became Van Halen's lighting director, and I once saw him use, like, 300 white lights [laughs]. The only band I knew who used white light so much was The Who. I used a lot of light on the audience, because they're a big part of the show. At the big shows now, especially the televised ones, there's more light in the room than on the stage, or just as much.

"Also, there were certain patterns people associated with the Ramones. You know, the red, white and blue at the beginning of the show, the intro with the parallel beams. Some people say they were real fascist. I think of the silhouettes, the shadows. That's my favourite Ramones look."

(Author's interview with Arturo Vega, Ramones creative director)

28

'I Don't Wanna Be A Pinhead No More'

TELL ME ABOUT the events leading up to Dee Dee's departure.

"We'd been on tour all year, starting January 1. We did a big tour of Japan, Spain, Italy and Greece. Everything was right. The band was tighter and closer than we'd ever been. Everything was very exciting. We got to do the 'Pet Sematary' track, and the album with Bill Laswell . . . When the film came out, it was the Number One box office film in America and Scandinavia, Number Seven in England, and the track was doing real good. We did a real heavy saturation tour of the West Coast – California, Northwest, Vancouver, Canada, Mexico . . . The album went Top 40 in Germany . . . Everything was fine, except for me. I've been having problems with my foot, so the last three or four months I've been hanging out at the hospital.

"When the album was coming out, the doctors told me to take six weeks off and have an operation. I said, 'There's no way. I don't want to see the album bomb.' My doctor was cool, he understood about my profession, but this other doctor scared the shit out of me. He said, 'It only takes 12 hours for the infection to spread from your foot to your heart and you'll be a dead man.' So I was a nervous wreck. Not nervous, but I'd think about it all the time. After the shows, I'd go to the hotel and take it easy.

"So we did the tour and everything was fine, but Dee Dee's been pursuing an active sideline with this rap stuff. They were getting a lot of offers, I guess, and he was going out with this girl, even though he was married . . . so he wanted to divorce his wife. We figured Dee Dee was having a midlife crisis and needed a break – he'd been married 12 years. He needed to sow his oats, which was fine. At least he was getting rid of all his frustrations and was happy for the first time in a long while. It was even helping us, in a funny way.

"I do projects on the side, too. I like to create theme nights and situations, expose new artists. When I'm not doing something creative, I fall into these ruts. I'm not the type of guy who can sit home and watch TV. So I was working with this band called Tribe 375 [Mickey Leigh's band]. They were going to be on this bill at the New Music Seminar at the Downtown. Two days before the Seminar, the

Downtown shut down, so I found this great space on East 4th St and started setting a show up. I figured there should be a rock'n'roll happy hour – Tacos and beer for a buck – to get people down early. So I had seven, eight bands – the cream of new artists, Cycle Sluts From Hell, Tribe, Dee Dee Ramone's new band Sprocket, the Waldoes [Walter Lure, ex-Heartbreakers] and a few other people. Arturo Vega was doing the lights for everybody. It was a real strong bill.

"So Dee Dee went on and did five songs, and everything was fine. The next day, he freaked out, complaining that I sabotaged the sound and quit the band. I became the scapegoat for Dee Dee leaving. They blamed me, blamed the Cycle Sluts too, for sabotaging Dee Dee. It was sick. Then there was an article in the Village Voice *a week later about how we fucked Dee Dee. It was a load of bullshit.*

"It was a lot of aggravation dealing with Dee Dee. He thought he was a rock god genius and nobody could do without him. He wanted to write all the songs for the band, he wanted to be in total control of the band, which was a real joke. When he quit, I felt real weird. Things were going real good, there were no problems. It felt like losing a close family member, like when somebody dies you feel hollowness. I couldn't come to terms with the fact he'd left. Marc kept telling me . . .

"What happened was, we didn't get on our knees and ask Dee Dee back. We auditioned like 70 bass players. We didn't want a name person. We tried to get a recommendation. Names came up like Paul Simonon [The Clash]. We didn't want that. We wanted an unknown so the band would be fresh. This kid is new. He's never played with anyone before. He's 23. He joined the Marines when he was 18. He's a great bass player. He has that street look. He has that Dee Dee-ness about him but he's fresh and totally enthusiastic. He's a nice kid. No airs, no ego shit.

"Now I hear Dee Dee is bad-mouthing us every chance he gets. Dee Dee's got straight, and he was saying he had to leave otherwise he'd go off his sobriety, making it seem like we're all a bunch of fuck-ups when it was Marc who got him straight in the first place. He tells people that the Ramones are breaking up, that we're all doing drugs, and everyone surrounding us is doing drugs too. That's how things are. We're excited. The band's never sounded better. You can hear the bass now. I don't think I've heard the bass for years.

"I don't feel upset anymore. I feel excited about this kid, going to England and playing with him. People won't miss Dee Dee. We're stronger than ever. Everything's locked in. Things are finally happening for the Ramones now."

How long has this guy been practising with the Ramones?

"A good week. Dee Dee's got his own band now. He wants to be a rapper and move to the South Bronx. I think Dee Dee wants to be a black man." Joey chuckles meanly. "I don't see it. To me, rap music is an expression of the ghetto

and hard times. Dee Dee's never had it that hard. I don't hate Dee Dee, though. He's a gifted guy and a talented songwriter."

Were there clashes between various Ramones over what direction you should take?

"No. We don't discuss let's go this way or that way. We just do what we feel."

For example, Dee Dee sang more on the last few albums.

"Dee Dee's come more into his own in the last few years. I wrote most of the early albums. I never got credit but that was an agreement we had. Then John and me had a falling out, and that's when Dee Dee took over. Now everything's cool. A lot of people say, 'Do you write the ballads?' and that's not true. I'm maybe a bit sentimental but I write the hard stuff too."

Won't fans take Dee Dee's departure as the beginning of the end?

"No, because it's a new beginning again. I don't want to say 'again'. These are exciting times. Speaking personally, I'm not weary but . . . I don't know. The writing's going to fall more on me now. I feel good. I'm not worried about it. I'm excited about it. Our appetite couldn't be any stronger than it is right now. There's always been a hunger to the Ramones. People might wonder how we can still be so hungry after being around so long, but we're not like the others. It shows in our performance. We never turned into Whitesnake.

"Chris came highly recommended by the bass player in Tribe 375. He was the first person we saw, and John really liked him. Then I went into hospital for surgery. They worked with him three or four times, and set up all these other auditions, and Chris was the last one to come down. He never showed up. So Monte, our tour manger, contacted his house, and about an hour earlier the MPs had come and put him in shackles, in handcuffs, and taken him to West Virginia to this army base, shaved his head and threw him in the brig. He was jailed for seven days. It's crazy. After auditioning 70 bass players we finally find the one we want, and he's fucking in the stockade. A couple of weeks later, we got word he'll be out in a week. We're hoping it works out, because otherwise we'll have to take Dee Dee back . . . and no one wants to take Dee Dee back!

"Chris is perfect. The way he and John look is *perfect – the same way him and Dee Dee were the gunners in early English reviews. He's perfect for height, weight, image and attitude. He holds the bass real low, like Dee Dee used to. We're going to call him CJ. We didn't want to do anything that wasn't genuine. That stuff's in the past . . . It's a different band now. It's real."*

(Author's interview with Joey Ramone, 1989)

IN HIS BOOK *Poison Heart*, Dee Dee lists several complaints against his former band – that Johnny was making too many musical decisions for a person who wasn't a songwriter, that the management would call him every morning on tour at 6 am asking for new songs (sounds exaggerated), that someone else would be in his room doing coke for four hours, saying how miserable they were and how they wanted to quit (Joey, almost certainly).

"It got on my nerves," he wrote. "Johnny just criticised everything. It seemed to be his way of having fun. It was tough recording *Brain Drain* because everyone took their shit out on me. It drove me away – I didn't even end up playing on the album." This time, unlike with *End Of The Century*, one gets the impression Dee Dee was probably telling the truth. "It amazed me people could keep believing in that happy family image of the Ramones. Everybody in the band had problems: girlfriend problems, money problems, mental problems."

Dee Dee claimed he'd been sober for a few years, even though he was constantly throwing up from the cocktail of Stellazine, Buzzbar and Trofennial anti-depressants he was taking to counter the sobriety. In Jim Bessman's *An American Band*, his ex-wife Vera verified his story: "He's been straight for a long time [but] he was being sober for me and everybody else, not for himself. Everybody said he was going through a midlife crisis early. It was total insecurity. I thought he'd snap out of it early . . . When we met he was making $100 a week and had a $100-a-day habit. But I never knew he was a junkie. It was more mental than anything else. He suffered mood swings, depressions. Sometimes he'd get violent, but we'd always work it out."

Vera reported that Dee Dee suffered heavily from paranoia and had an obsessive personality: at one point, he was wearing eight watches at once, another time he wanted to get two new tattoos every day. He was covered in tattoos: scorpions, a heart saying "Mother" and "Vera and Dee Dee", another one boasting the slogan *Too Tough To Die* atop a picture of a horned, pitchfork-wielding devil, Mickey Mouse proclaiming 'Let's Dance' and one for his "Baby Doll".

"Dee Dee is either a manic depressive or suffers from multiple personality disorder," thinks video director George Seminara.* "Cool Dee Dee, grumpy Dee Dee, angry Dee Dee – they are all different manifestations of the same personality, but they're so dramatic. He doesn't seem to have a grip on what constitutes reality. He's done tons of songs, written two or three books, creates art. The lack of success causes the depressive form. Why hasn't he had more?"

The final straw for the bassist came when the Ramones played with

* All interviews were conducted before Dee Dee's death.

Murphy's Law in Santa Clara, CA on July 4. There was trouble and the support act's singer Jimmy Gestapo threatened to kick Johnny Ramone's ass: "[He] said John would never be safe in New York," Dee Dee wrote. "I wondered if that meant the rest of the Ramones as well. I was worried."

So after the flight back to New York, he bailed out.

Murphy's Law were the purest embodiment of NYC hardcore. They *killed* live. They toured with da bruddas for years. "The Ramones were supportive of everybody in NYC," says George Seminara, "any good honest and true punk band. But Murphy's Law would spit on stage. Johnny hated that. He didn't want to stand in Jimmy Gestapo's spit on his sneakers.

"Joey got sick on that tour," Seminara continues. "He had circulatory problems because he suffered from Marfan's Syndrome, the same as Abraham Lincoln. That's what caused his elongated shape, and gave his skin that slightly plastic look. He injured his foot and ended up in hospital. Halfway through, Johnny wanted to boot Murphy's Law off the tour, but he had to back down because Joey had promised them the remaining dates."

"Dee Dee quit because he wanted to be a rap star," says Marky. "That's his choice. When I rejoined the band, I'd take him to these meetings where we'd listen to people talk what they went through – and he listened. But he stopped after a few meetings, and ended up smoking pot. He didn't have a drink in his hand anymore – but he got into all these other shitty drugs. It was the same thing with Joey for a while."

Johnny blamed the female element in the equation, as he had done with Richie a few years earlier: "I never really knew what went on in his head," he said. "He'd left his wife a month before – that was a bad sign. But I never thought he'd ever quit."

"I was sick and tired of the little boy look – the bowl haircut and the motorcycle jacket," Dee Dee wrote in *Spin* that year. "Four middle-aged men trying to be teenage juveniles. I was just getting sick of playing in a revival act. I used to dress down like that when I thought I was a worthless piece of shit. Those guys were a bunch of bums. Joey never took a shower. He stunk.

"I knew I was leaving in that last California tour," he wrote, vitriol pouring out of him after years of toeing the party line. "I think they're happy because the Ramones are always happy when someone leaves. It adds new life to the group and then they can go round saying, 'We're faster' . . ."

After he left the Ramones, Dee Dee travelled to Paris where he hung out with fellow ex (and practising) junkies, Johnny Thunders and ex-Dead Boys singer Stiv Bators, and tried to form a band, The Whores Of Babylon – a sad scene. When his chums died within six months of one another, the wandering Ramone came over to England where he tried to start a metal band, with the help of Gloria Nicholl (among others) but was too paranoid and fucked-up on blow to get it together.

"Dee Dee was funny," recalls Ida Langsam, "but not like a comic. His brain was always going a thousand miles an hour, and sometimes you felt you weren't on the same planet as him. You'd bump into him on the street, and he'd talk to you like you'd been talking for the last two hours and you were supposed to know what page you were on. He was the heartthrob? I suppose. The kind of female fans the Ramones attracted were always a little odd. I only saw him being married into the band."

Dee Dee stayed in England for six months, before returning to New York, and forming several bands, including The Spikey Tops with bassist Carla Olla (formerly of all-girl hardcore outfit PMS). In the autumn of 1990, he was busted for possession of marijuana at Washington Square Park. Two weeks later it was alleged he'd been thrown out of a nightclub for doing drugs. In 1992, he formed the punk rock Chinese Dragons, with his cropped hair grown out.

All the while, though, he stayed in touch – writing songs for the remaining Ramones albums. He had to. Who else was the band going to call upon? Johnny?

DEE DEE'S BOOK said he had Ramones escape fantasies.

"That's true – you mean just getting out of the Ramones? Yeah he did."

Well, yeah.

"He's the type that doesn't like to be . . . I mean, he was controlled but he needed it. He's a genius and sometimes geniuses . . . there's a line of insanity and they can ride that line. He wavers around that craziness but he's a great songwriter. He's terrific. But he needed the structure in the Ramones. John – he had a structure. 'Dee Dee – this is what we're wearing.' You know? And all those years it built up and he wanted to get away, and he did. He did this rap thing. He showed up at one tour, the last couple of shows, wearing a gold chain and sweat pants. They freaked out like, 'What are you, nuts? Get it off. This is not the Ramones.' He didn't like that and that's why he left. He went off to do his own thing. OK – fine. At the end, he wasn't into it, and you could tell. Thank God CJ came along because he gave them another 10 years. They all had to suck their stomachs in to keep up with him. It was great."

Yeah – which is why they got him in, presumably.

"Yes. Dee Dee was fading out, and he was dragging them down. If they hadn't found anybody, that probably would have been the end at that time."

(Author's interview with Monte Melnick)

SO TELL ME about CJ . . .

"CJ was an infusion of fresh blood into the band. He was the best thing that could have happened at the time. I don't mean anything against Dee Dee but . . . he was very unhappy. He continued to write for the band, so we got the best of both worlds."

Exactly, it wasn't like he disappeared.

"CJ made the band look good, young and fresh, and we didn't have the problems that Dee Dee was creating. Everybody was affected by it. The last time we were in England on a tour – Monte called me in the middle of the night to tell me he had to go out because somebody had to watch Dee Dee."

Was that when Dee Dee met his second wife, Barbara? How is she?

"She's really cute. He met her in Argentina. She's great. A little too young, but very much in tune with Dee Dee."

Big Ramones fan?

"Very big fan, but a smart one. They have been very happy in spite of the age difference, or maybe because of it. But so far, so good."

Do you think she was influential in his decision to leave the Ramones?

"Not at all. No, he didn't meet her until much later."

But he met someone else around that time?

"At the time Dee Dee left the band, he decided to leave, in his words, everybody who was telling him how to live his life. He meant his wife, the psychiatrist, and the band. He wanted to break away from history and he did. He had this beautiful young girlfriend. I don't even remember her name. She was a momentary thing."

Was her name Brijitte?

"Yeah, it was."

She was in NY Loose. They were a good band. I hung out with them a few times.

"Yeah, that's who Dee Dee was with at the time he left the band. She was very beautiful. He didn't meet Barbara until the mid-Nineties."

(Author's interview with Arturo Vega)

"I GOT TO KNOW Dee Dee around 1989," says Brijitte West. "He was leaving the Ramones and he really needed a friend. He wanted a little more than that, and I was like, 'You're a little bit older than me.' It wasn't easy to be Dee Dee's friend especially when he called me up at work one day and said he had a shotgun to his mouth and if I didn't come home he'd shoot himself. I called Chris Stein and asked him if he was serious, he was like, 'No, it's just Dee Dee.' That was what was so sad, he was a legend, but he didn't have the respect of his peers – a lot of it was probably his own fault, he'd done a lot of people harm, he had a very quick temper and he could lay into you. I felt he was a sad individual.

"I don't really know why he left the Ramones," she continues. "He was going through some sort of midlife crisis. He'd left his wife. He was going through a lot of changes and because he'd decided to leave, he was being alienated from his friends and he started hanging round the East Village a lot. He'd been in Long Island, and all of a sudden Dee Dee appears on the scene. I was one of the people he latched onto as one of his new friends. It was one-sided, all about him. We used to go and hang out at Arturo's loft – he was definitely someone who still loved Dee Dee.

"I only knew him for a year."

"WHEN DEE DEE quit, I got a call from John saying, 'Dee Dee's gone, we need a new bass player.' I thought about it and I said, 'Me.' He was like, 'George – you play guitar.' I'm like, 'It's only two strings difference, John.' He was like, 'Alright, give it a shot.' So I auditioned for them . . ."

I get the impression they chose the person who looked most like Dee Dee.

"I looked like Dee Dee – when I walked in there, I had the black spiked hair and sunglasses. I did the voice and everything. Except Marky kept complaining, 'Upstrokes – you can't do upstrokes, that's cheating.' OK – no upstrokes. I wasn't a kid, though. I was in my mid-twenties and they said I was too old – despite the fact I was 10, 12 years younger than Johnny Ramone. They probably figured I wouldn't obey orders. And I heard the money was shit and . . . you aren't going to last unless you're a kid. But the Ramones are the greatest rock'n'roll band and I would have loved it.

"They put an ad in the Village Voice, *'World-class touring punk band looking for bassist', and you had all these people coming to audition – girls, boys, black people, white people, Asian people . . . All that racist bullshit about the Ramones is nonsense. During the whole time, John kept telling me, 'Dee Dee's going to come back – we're just doing this to make Dee Dee come back.' Monte was like, 'This is his family, he's got nothing – he'll come back.' They were wrong."*

He probably would have come back eventually.

"I think so too."

(Author's interview with George Tabb)

CJ RAMONE WAS born Christopher Joseph Ward on October 8, 1965 in Queens – he moved to Deer Park, Long Island when he was about 10.

"When I lived in Queens, it was a real mixed race neighbourhood," he says. "We were about the only white family on the block. There were a lot of Latinos and Philippinos, but because it was integrated, it had a real neighbourhood feel. Everyone knew each other. Long Island was much more blue-collar, very white. The lower your income, the closer to a minority neighbourhood you lived. The first girlfriend I brought home was black. My parents didn't understand why – but who else could I have dated?"

CJ started playing bass at age 13, when his parents bought him one as a reward for finishing Eighth Grade. "When I was young, I played drums but they must've been too noisy," he laughs, "because I came home one day and they were gone." He grew up listening to classic rock (Beatles, Creedence Clearwater Revival, Neil Young) and also newer, harder rock bands such as the new wave of British heavy metal, Judas Priest and Iron Maiden. It was 1980 when CJ met a crazy blonde girl who introduced him to both his first joint and the Ramones' first album: "I don't know if it was the weed, my raging hormones, or if the planets lined up just right but I was hooked," he says. "I'd heard of 'punk' before, but I didn't get it at all. Now suddenly it all made sense."

When he got to high school, CJ got into more of the early punk bands – The Clash, Sex Pistols, The Damned. "I really liked Blondie," he says, "and John Lydon's PiL, but not so much the California hardcore stuff, although I liked The Dickies and Dead Kennedys. I was a huge Minor Threat fan, too – I totally respect Ian MacKaye for everything he's done up to Fugazi, because they're the ultimate DIY band."

Seeking an outlet for his "honest to goodness teen angst", CJ started playing with heavy metal musicians and, with Axe Attack, recorded two albums for the British Heavy Metal America label: "It was impossible to put together a punk rock band, being from a blue-collar town," he explains. Still, his three role models were Paul Simonon, Sid Vicious and Dee Dee Ramone.

"I liked the Ramones because of the incredible amount of energy that came off stage – the choreography, and of course the songs. The show was non-stop. Joey had a real strong presence, and Dee Dee and Johnny were in constant motion . . . it was incredible.

"So, nine years later after I first heard them," he continues, "I get a call to go audition for the Ramones. I figured it'd be a neat story to tell my grandkids one day, so I went." He got the call at 3 pm, with instructions to be there at six. The studio was an hour-and-a-half drive from his Long Island home. CJ had one hour to learn some Ramones songs. "I was the first one to audition. It felt like I was going to meet Elvis. I hadn't played bass in a while, and never used a pick before. But they said I was OK and I should come back next week. In the real early photographs I've got a bandana around my head 'cause they'd just shaved it. I was a week out of jail."

CJ was technically both a marine and AWOL when he auditioned, awaiting a promised discharge because of family illness (his mother was stricken with lupus) and financial troubles (his dad lost his job as a military aircraft worker when the factory closed down). On top of that, he'd contracted Rocky Mountain spotted fever from a tick bite while at boot camp in Paris Island, South Carolina, and had been hospitalised with a 106-degree fever – so bad, that at one stage his vital signs failed. The Marines agreed that CJ had cause for an honourable discharge – but kept dragging their feet as to when it would happen. He was ordered to Japan, but visited his sister in Hollywood instead – a court martial followed at Camp Pendleton CA, where it was again agreed he should be discharged . . . once again, it didn't happen. So CJ returned to NYC, and stayed in touch . . .

Johnny decided he liked him immediately, but then he and Marky went through the charade of auditioning another 40 (by Marky's reckoning) bassists.

"He shook hands," recalled Johnny, "and all I could do was hope I didn't have to shake hands with everyone who came down to try out – I didn't want to go home with a cold. But he was great. I knew immediately. Marky and our road manager kept saying: 'Nah. He's not good. He's young. He's inexperienced. He's got a mohawk. He plays with his fingers.' That didn't matter. All that mattered was the image and that's what no one could understand. Joey didn't even come down. I thought, 'Great. Less interference.' "

CJ contradicts this version of events, saying Joey turned up halfway through the second try-out of 'I Wanna Be Sedated': "It was crazy," he says. "The feeling I had held true the whole time I was with the Ramones. It's a weird feeling to be in a band you idolised throughout your youth. A lot of times you're torn, you're in business with them and seeing sides of them you'd never see otherwise. It was a surreal situation, especially because I only went down there to meet them. I never imagined I would pass the audition."

"The whole process of them auditioning was weird," recalls Ida Langsam. "It was almost like a garage band looking for a new member. There was an ad in the *Village Voice*. They held auditions for three days.

When Limp Bizkit needed a new member a few years later, they did a huge search on MTV, and they were videotaping all these people auditioning – and some of those people were getting in magazines. The Ramones were on the same level as Limp Bizkit. It boggles the mind. Everything about the Ramones was a bit weird."

Indeed. Take CJ's arrival into the band: upon phoning the Marines to let them know he'd got the Ramones' job, and would be leaving the country soon, he was promptly thrown into the brig again. The whole mess eventually got sorted out, but not before giving the Ramones' newest member some tense moments.

One reason Johnny preferred CJ was because of his military experience. CJ, too, found life in the Ramones similar to the Marines: "Musically, Ramones stuff is very regimented – a lot like military life," he says. "It takes a good amount of concentration to play upwards of 30 songs that all sound the same and get them right. Then there was the uniform – sneakers, jeans, T-shirt and leather jacket. Johnny developed a lot of his leadership qualities when he was in military school. He was pretty rigid on how we ran things. It was a big part of why the Ramones were able to have a 22-year career. I really respect him for it. Maybe he could've made it easier on others, but he knew what he was doing . . ."

Were you on a wage? Can you tell me how much?

"I don't think I should," he laughs.

In the *Anthology* sleeve-notes, Johnny describes how he drilled CJ on stage presence: "We had a mirror in front of us in the rehearsal room. I'd say, 'CJ, face there. Don't look at Marc. Look in the mirror. When you see me go forward, you go forward. Get your bass down below your waist. Get your legs spread apart. Look forward, play forward.' I always hated it, when bands played to each other."

"He didn't actually teach me how to stand," chuckles CJ, "but he did try to give me pointers. I didn't need them. I knew the choreography already."

THE NEW BASSIST'S debut as a Ramone came during a Jerry Lewis telethon for muscular dystrophy on Labour Day, September 4. Sammy Davis Jr. introduced the band (from another studio). Johnny was typically critical: "It was really bad," he snorted. "[CJ's] finger was cut up after one song, he was moving around. But he was fine for the second show."

That happened in Leicester on September 30, at the start of a two-week British tour. It wasn't the easiest of starts: "I had a lot of problems with people because they wanted to see Dee Dee," admits CJ. "I got spit on constantly. I got pelted with shit. It was brutal but I knew I would win them over eventually because I was confident in my abilities and knew no one would ruin it. At my first show I went on for the encore covered in shit and sweat and I pulled my T-shirt off and Johnny fucking reamed me for it. 'You don't see us taking our shirts off,' he yelled, but for me it was a matter of hygiene, and obviously I was also caught up in the emotion. I had some fucked up shit done to me on stage, but it wasn't anything I couldn't handle."

Reports from the following night, in Liverpool, seemed to prove Johnny right in his maxim that professionalism mattered above everything: "I've never seen them better," drooled critic Dave Galbraith, "because I've never seen them tighter, more in control."

CJ started taping up his fingers because he was playing so hard he'd break the strings – and as a set of bass strings was $25, it meant he could waste $100 a week (four shows) on strings alone. "At the start," he says in *Ramones: An American Band*, "I'd leave chunks of skin on the bass and short out the pick-up with blood because I'd be bleeding so heavily. One time I broke a fingernail halfway down."

"CJ was good and enthusiastic," recalls Mark Bannister who saw one of the Ramones' Brixton Academy shows in '89 with The Almighty in support, "although I didn't see the point of him singing 'Wart Hog'. Later, I found out many people didn't realise Dee Dee [who was pictured in the advertisements and on the tickets] had left the group."

A tour of Australia and New Zealand followed, before the band returned to a newly reunited Germany – their first date in Offenbach on November 22 occurred shortly after the fall of the Berlin Wall.

"It was wild," recalls the new bassist. "We were at the wall one day with MTV and there was a small hole the size of a basketball, and there were two guards standing on the other side. They offered to sell me a belt buckle and a military hat, and I bought them off them and shook their hands through the wall. It was so weird to be part of a situation where you're part of history. We were one of the first bands to play in East Germany after the wall came down. The place we played was a factory where they built submarines for the Nazis. They'd emptied everything by that point – the crowd was crazy, dancing perhaps a little more violently than in the West. Anybody with an East German passport got in half-price."

Almost everyone agreed the addition of CJ had given the Ramones a fresh infusion of blood – literally. Dee Dee's departure was far from being the final nail in the coffin: in fact, it had the opposite effect. Now, the Ramones could continue touring for several more years, Johnny secure in the knowledge that with Marky sober, Joey on the way and Dee Dee departed, there would be no more fuck-ups to mess with his new, streamlined model.

The fact that the Ramones had lost their principal songwriter and in the process made the transition from actual band to tribute band (complete with one fan playing bass and another producing) seemed to escape everyone. That's not to denigrate the contributions of CJ and Daniel – both real enthusiasts and talented musicians, and Christ alone knows the Ramones couldn't have continued without them, but . . . maybe they shouldn't have continued? Hard as it was to imagine life without the Ramones, surely no one wanted to see them turn into a self-parody?

Thoughts like those were heresy. Especially when there were another 130 or so dates to look forward to the following year.

29

Joey Speaks

Extracts from an interview conducted with Joey Ramone by the author in early September 1989 . . .

. . . I WAS READING an interview with a band in a West Coast fanzine, talking about a Ramones bootleg that traces the development of your voice between '76 and '89.

"Oh yeah. Well, my voice has changed a lot. In my head . . . I always knew what I wanted to shoot for, achieve. I'm really into the improvisational, the abstract. I admire singers that have character in their voices, who kill me with their passion and raw emotion and excitement. Iggy always did that to me. He had that dirt there. It was like a knife stuck in your guts and twisted. He was fucking wild, but it was always primal, you could feel that sensitivity and raw emotion and energy, and that's how I want to make other people feel it too. Most singers are so sterile."

I think people pick up on the energy of the Ramones and sometimes miss your voice.

"I've noticed that," Joey laughs. "People are just too narrow-minded. They're not seeing what the Ramones are about. I don't believe in pigeonholing. Nothing has to be like anything. You make it."

You've done some cartooning for magazines . . .

"I used to. I lost interest. I still DJ, and I'm into new artists nights, and creating parties and situations. I've discovered a couple of new bands recently, and I'm shopping around, trying to get them deals. I got an offer doing A&R for Island Records. I got an offer doing publicity for Public Eye. There's a band I'm going to see tonight, New Breed, these black kids from New Jersey, they're fucking amazing. I'll play you a couple of tracks. It's like a total freedom thing. It's hard rock but it's got essences of funk, blues and jazz. Matter of fact, I was over at CBGBs earlier, and I heard these people mixing a tape and it sounded real good. So I went over to the kid and he gave me his number."

A few years back, around the time of *Pleasant Dreams*, there were rumours going round that you were going to do a solo album.

"Yeah. I'm working on it right now. I'm taking my time. I want to work with a lot of different producers. I've put a band together – Daniel Rey on guitar, Andy Shernoff on bass from The Dictators, Marc Bell on drums. It might have some guests too, but I'm more interested in having a strong band than guests. It'll be a rock'n'roll record, but with lots of different feelings and emotions. I want to take each song at a time. I don't want to just mark out an album. I want to make every song special. I have one ballad that really captures the isolation. It's called 'Waiting For That Railroad To Go Home'. I had an idea a long time ago of doing a duo between Axl [Rose, Guns N' Roses singer and Ramones fan] and me, covering a Righteous Brothers song. I spoke to him recently when he was in New York and he was into it. I figured I'd be Bill Medley and he'd be Bobby Hatfield 'cos he's got the real high voice. I have a song in mind but I think I've said too much already."

Author's note: Later, Joey played me a few homemade demos, and they sounded superb. One was a country-esque number, a ballad – the other had elements of doo wop: neither incorporated any elements of hardcore. If anyone reading this has tapes, please get in touch! They totally should be released.

"OUR AUDIENCE HAS never been as broad as it is now. Our fans like all kinds of music. From the beginning, kids would come up and say, 'Are you guys into The Grateful Dead?' Our audience right now is the new generation of kids. We're like the big bang. What was the question?"

Do you feel weird playing to kids half your age?

"No. They're really young, diehard fans. A lot of them have heard early Ramones and a lot of them just the recent stuff. It's kind of weird, but it's nice. The cool thing is that all the bands around are fans of us. You see shirts on all kinds of people: Axl Rose in Guns N' Roses, Metallica, Anthrax – all the high-energy metal bands . . . and then all the bands from the past, college kids. With us, you can be into jazz and the Ramones, blues and the Ramones, that's the way it should be."

Did you ever imagine you'd make over 12 albums?

"Nah. You just want to play a show. It's natural, one step at a time. I remember John saying, 'We should make one album so we have one album for ourselves.' This is what I always wanted to be doing since I was 13. I've always known. It was music."

FAVOURITE ALBUMS

Brain Drain: "That's a real high. It was really exciting working with Bill Laswell. Every song is great, yet every song is different. It's very strong in substance and execution."

Fun House: "I love The Stooges. Iggy's one of my all-time heroes. The fact he's so primal and responds to what he feels. He's very much the animal. The exciting stuff really gets you going and then the heavy, hard, emotional songs cut right through ya."

No Remorse: "I love Motorhead. They're really exciting and genuine. I probably like the Fast Eddie formation a little more, but I like the new Motorhead as well."

The Slider: "It's my favourite T. Rex album. I get into people who are unique and innovative and have colour. That's why I love Marc Bolan. There was something so mystical about him, his singing voice, his manner. His songs really move ya, they're so moving and dark."

A Quick One: "I saw The Who in New York in '67. They blew me away with the aggression, and Townshend was so visual, and Keith Moon. Their personalities, the songs, they were just great. It was a total release. The Who were my first big favourite band after The Beatles."

The Kinks: "One of my all-time favourites. Like The Who, they were a major influence."

Alice Cooper: "When Alice first came out he was sort of a hero, except that I thought he was really that sick. When I found out it was a put-on, he wasn't a true necrophiliac, I was very upset. I'm happy that he's back and doing well."

AC/DC: "One of my all-time favourite bands. They're fucking great. Like Motorhead and the Ramones, they've always stuck to their initial intentions and beliefs, and they never let you down. They're so dark and moody and intense. I really admired Bon Scott a lot, but I like the new guy too – he reminds me of Noddy Holder [Slade singer]."

Buzzcocks: "In the early days of punk, on the English side, The Sex Pistols were great but I liked the Buzzcocks better. They dealt more with feelings and events and relations and situations that nobody would discuss. I always admired Pete Shelley. 'What Do I Get?' They're amusing, but they deal with topics we can all relate to."

The Rolling Stones: "The Stones were dark and a little more realistic than The Beatles. It was always 'It's All Over Now', not 'She Came Back'. She didn't come back. I liked the way they were against the system and didn't want to conform."

30

Going Loco

"THE RAMONES WERE equally great at art and business and that was reflected in the John and Joey thing. It was genius marketing on the part of John. They could have been a flash-in-the-pan band but they weren't. John said, 'We keep our uniforms. We keep this identity going. We don't talk to the media about our bickering.' He was very strict about that and he was right. No one really knew about the Ramones fighting until Joey died. Johnny made sure. This is a family matter. It was the Mafia mentality. It worked. Dee Dee could do his rap thing and wear gold chains, but with the Ramones he had to wear the Ramones outfit. Joey wore a flowery shirt with a Holly Beth Vincent – fine, but with the Ramones he came out in black."

I remember being shocked by that Joey and Holly cover.

"Joey looks like a hippy. John was smart enough to say, 'Fine, solo record, I don't care what you guys do – you can be a rapper, you can be a hippy. But you come back and you're a Ramone.' If the Ramones had changed their costumes, changed their music or tried to experiment beyond what they did – and the live shows never changed – they would have dropped off the face of the earth."

You're right, of course.

"That was John's vision of what the Ramones were – and that's what made it work just as much as Joey's creative vision. Joey was the kind of guy who would never tell you that your band sucks. He's too nice. He was the artist's artist and Johnny was the businessman's businessman. Johnny was doing a lot for the punk rock scene, just not in an artistic way. It was more like, 'Hey, you're a band from Boston – no one's ever heard of you. We're coming up that way, why don't you guys open up for us?"

(Author's interview with George Tabb)

ON JANUARY 17, 1990, Joey injured his ankle coming off stage at Wetlands, NYC after a guest appearance with Raging Slab. The next round of Ramones dates were cancelled, as he recuperated in hospital: during his stay, the singer listened to Howard Stern's morning radio show and devoured news reports about Tiananmen Square – reinforcing his sense of injustice. "People have had it with oppression and they want a democracy," he told journalist Rob Cassatto from his hospital bed. "Even though the government really cut down the students, in the end the students will win because they're the future." The singer stopped eating meat, shocked by PETA pamphlets.

Joey had already taken part in a panel discussion about Tipper Gore's infamous music censorship group, the PMRC [Parents' Music Resource Centre] alongside Marky and rap stars Run DMC. "I'm proud of America," he explained in August '89, "but I just wonder about where we're heading. Everything is so fuckin' conservative, with the right-wing Moral Majority. They've always picked on rock'n'roll right from its inception, with record burning and calling it 'devil's music'. The ignorance of it all is sickening."

The singer also participated in benefits for the rain forest, the homeless, AIDS, the environment . . . in between organising a few more parties, recording with The Mystics and appearing on TV with his mother. The latter event took place on a 'Heavy Metal Moms' segment of *Geraldo*, where Charlotte sang a verse from 'I Wanna Be Sedated' and 'Beat On The Brat'.

The Ramones also appeared in another Canadian movie, the Bill Fishman-directed *Car 54*, where they performed 'I Believe In Miracles' in a club. Marky, meanwhile, was starting to amass backstage and onstage footage of the Ramones – later to be released as *Ramones Around The World*.

In June, *All The Stuff (And More) Volume One* was released (followed up the next year by *All The Stuff (And More) Volume Two*) – not a greatest hits package, despite the title, but a pairing of *Ramones/Ramones Leave Home* on one CD. 'Carbona Not Glue' was still banned, so 'Sheena' was again substituted – but at least there were a few demos, including 'I Can't Be' and 'I Don't Wanna Be Learned'.

In what one assumes could only have been a moment of confusion on the part of executive producer Howie Klein, the two live tracks tacked onto the album's end, 'California Sun' and 'I Don't Wanna Walk Around With You' aren't drawn from the *Live At The Roxy* versions used on the B-side of 'I Remember You' – but from *It's Alive*. It's a sad example of the disregard the Ramones were held in: why bother to include those songs if they weren't from the single? On the second compilation (*Rocket To Russia/Road To Ruin*), 'Slug' crawled into the light of day.

Another Ramones-related 1990 release was much better thought out:

the video compilation *Lifestyles Of The Ramones*, directed by George Seminara – with guest interviews from fans like Debbie Harry, Tina and Chris from Talking Heads, and Anthrax, plus the odd baseball pitcher (New York Yankee, Dave Righetti, who seemed somewhat nonplussed at his inclusion).* Seymour Stein spoke of his enthusiasm for the group, undiminished by the years. Little Steven pointed out that "really good rock'n'roll is very simple and to maintain that simplicity record after record is actually very difficult".

"I've known Joey since 1972," Seminara says. "I was 12 and he was 22. My parents used to hang out at Max's Kansas City where they had a happy hour, two drinks for the price of one, with free chilli and rice. I still have fond memories of those chickpeas . . . One day Joey Ramone walked in. I'd never seen a guy who looked like that, all glammed up like David Bowie in a Fun House mirror. So I went to get a better look. He noticed me and invited me to sit next to him at the bar. We talked about music, cool bands and great records. He left a big impression on me."

A few years later, Seminara started attending shows at CBGBs, where they'd stamp his hand with a "nobooze foryouz" underage stamp. "I was a fan. The visceral quality of punk rock is what attracted me, and the intelligence of the music, especially for my class of '76–'82, the early hardcore period. I proposed at a Bad Brains concert where they were burning Reagan in effigy. I came out the pit and said, 'Let's get hitched.' Nineteen years later, I'm still married."

Later, he shot videos for [early Ramones video director] Bill Fishman, and directed an Agnostic Front video at CBs in front of the entire NYC hardcore community. Joey liked it and called him up: Seminara thought it was someone making fun of him and promptly hung up.

"Seymour called me up," he laughs, "and asked me if I was crazy. My first job was 'I Believe In Miracles', that's where I first got a glimpse of the animosity between Johnny and Joey. I have a hard time keeping my mouth shut, so I ran foul of him. People like Daniel Rey have the ability to walk the line, but I can't. Working with Bill, I saw how Johnny hated wasting time, so I limited the band's interaction.

* The Ramones were seasoned autograph signers, but the session they undertook at Tower Records, NYC Downtown to promote the video's release in September was unusual, even by their standards. Among the usual loafers and Doc Marten's boots, the band were handed a human skull, a black leather Yarmulke, electric guitars and limbs. "At least they were attached to human bodies," Joey laughed. "In Europe, one fan pulled off his artificial leg and had us sign the prosthesis."

"Some of the videos were not as great as I'd like them to be, but if you can't get the band to work with you, what can you do?" Seminara asks. "Their desire to work was limited, so often I'd choose the other stuff after they'd left. We had Liv Tyler when she was 14, Bebe Beull, The BoDeans, The Dictators. I didn't think we ever spent more than $10,000 on one video – maybe $15,000 on the one with four cameramen and me travelling around Europe. Some of them were quite dark because they came from that whole Fifties EC comic book culture that life sucks and then you die that also permeates the entire punk rock aesthetic. No other band has celebrated such horrific concepts as lobotomies. Their subject matter was pretty gruesome.

Seminara's understanding of the necessity for financial restraint impressed the guitarist: "Johnny told me I was his favourite director, because I could get him in and out within an hour," George laughs. "The best video I ever did was 'Blitzkrieg Bop' for the *It's Alive* reissue. We shot concert footage in Belgium, and in Germany where bored fascists came along and tried to storm the stage with Iggy. We focused on stuff I thought the fans would like – people hanging out backstage, and the real hardcore fans like the guy in Europe who dressed and acted like Johnny so well he often got into shows as him."

Speak to George for a few minutes, and it's obvious which side of the Joey/Johnny divide he falls into: "Johnny's a difficult guy," he says, "and I think I know why. Early on, Johnny and Tommy were in a band together, but they were banned from playing colleges after he'd made a girl fall and cut herself. Time went by and he wanted his own band. So he and Tommy put together the Ramones, with Dee Dee as the singer, Joey on drums and Johnny the boss. They wanted to play fast and loud and be melodic and appeal to kids like them – be normal, because rock had got to be so mystical, so special, so boring . . .

"So Dee Dee was going to be the singer, and he was easy to control – he had his drug problems, you could make him do what you want. The problem was, Dee Dee couldn't play and sing at the same time – it took him till the mid-Eighties to do that, even though he had his heart set on it, that's where the '1-2-3-4' came from – but Joey could, so they promoted him to front man. But Joey's a very smart guy and had his own agenda. So Johnny's band turned into Joey and Johnny's thing. Throughout the Ramones career, Johnny would threaten to fire Joey, and get a proper singer in."

This last part of George Seminara's theory would explain the otherwise mind-boggling decision by the band (and management) to have fan CJ sing tracks on the final three Ramones albums, and have him substitute for Joey on the Ramones' final *Top Of The Pops* appearance in 1996. Johnny was grooming the bassist as an eventual successor to Joey: one that he could (finally) control.

"EVERY TIME JOEY walked around New York, people would recognise him.

"One night we were in St Mark's Place, starving, and a guy my height – 5′ 3″ – started talking to Joey. The guy was so nervous, stammering over his words, he wanted to give Joey some tapes, and he must have spoken to him for 15 minutes. I was starving so I thought I'd be bad cop, wrap it up. The kid took the hint, and as he left, he said, 'Thank you buddy man.' He obviously thought buddy was too informal so he changed it to man. We didn't want to start laughing in front of him, but we intuitively knew: 'buddy man' became something we'd play around with.

"I took him to a screening of Waterworld, *and he was so bored by it his head tucked down and he fell asleep. I was like, 'You look like the Concorde with your head tucked down. Go back to sleep.' When he walked out, he remarked,* 'Waterworld? *They should have called it* Water Main.*'*

"Joey was a very generous person unlike Johnny who has the first dime he ever made – except Johnny loved to shop at Bal Duchi's very excellent and smallish grocery store in the Village (Sixth Ave between Eighth and Ninth). Johnny would go there and come out with two giant shopping bags with their green logo on. He'll eat that really expensive food but would only pay for one breast implant [Joan isn't being literal here, just drawing a simile]. There's something about him that's granite, they could put his face on Mount Rushmore and it would fit right in.

"Joey formed a political band, The Resistance, to play at rallies . . . he played during the first Clinton primaries, supporting Jerry Brown – 'Fascists don't suck, they screw.' I added a line: 'They go to church on Sunday/They'll prey on you on Monday.' I was like, 'I'll never come up with anything that clever again.' Joey was like, 'That's great. What d'ya do – go over to the God Window to get that line?' "

(Author's interview with Joan Tarshis, journalist)

THE RAMONES' SCHEDULE for 1990 bordered on the brutal: a whole slew of dates in Scandinavia during March, any number of shows back at home during the first five months, a major festival in Lorelei, Germany on June 23. CJ, aware of his strange position in the band, hung around with the road crew – throwing footballs, playing stickball.

On June 28, the Ramones teamed up with fellow ex-CBGBs punks Debbie Harry, Tom Tom Club and Jerry Harrison, for the seven-week

Escape From New York nostalgia tour, starting in Columbia, MD. The bands flipped a coin to decide who was going to headline that night, and the tour drew very respectable crowds – between 5,000 and 10,000 fans each night, with 25,000 in Austin.

"There's some of us here today that still fuckin' remembuh rock'n'roll radio," Joey shouted by way of an intro. Not CJ, though. He was too young to recall the days the Ramones were now constantly referring back to, attacking anything new or out of the ordinary, a sad reflection on their own state of mind.

"Instead of learning from Bon Jovi or New Kids On The Block, the way they once learned from The Ohio Express and The Trashmen," critic Chuck Eddy wrote, "all the Ramones can do now is dismiss today's teenyboppers as kids who 'don't know anything about real music and who just get suckered in by the radio' (according to Johnny) or who 'buy records just because they like how the band looks' (according to CJ)."

As opposed to the Ramones, who chose their new bassist because of . . . er . . . the way he looked.

"These nice guys are missing the joke, missing what's fun," Eddy continued, "pretending the world has stopped turning. Discussing the contradictions inherent in the Ramones on CD, Marky says: 'You can't fight progress.' These days punk rock is trying its damnedest to do just that."

Carla Olla played guitar with Deborah Harry on the tour: "We played a lot of outdoor places, amusement parks," she says. "It was like travelling around with a big family, in a caravan of bands. One time, Debbie and me were cracking up because we were sitting in my room and Joey was upstairs, warming up. We could hear him through the air vent. First of all, we thought it was funny that the Ramones singer needed to warm up – so we started to imitate his scales, 'Hey hey hey, ho ho ho ho,' on the floor cracking up. Then I realised he really had improved his voice over the years.

"We got to be friends on that tour – it took a while because I couldn't understand him: he was so far away, so tall and he mumbles. The first time we had a good conversation was when I kneeled up on a chair and spoke to him. Until then it was like, 'Hey, how ya doin'?' I could talk to him about just about anything – politics, music, he was a smart guy and interested with it."

Joey was supportive of Carla's bands – The Trashaholics, Shiny Mama, her old speed metal band PMS, even Dee Dee's Spikey Tops. "He was one of the only guys that supported women in music," she says. "Joey just liked what he liked. He didn't care if men or women were playing it, he was picky about his taste and if he liked it, he'd be on MTV talking about it."

On one occasion, Joey played with Joan Jett, Dee Dee and Daniel Rey at a benefit for women called *Rock For Choice*.

The Ramones played Japan in September (before yet *another* European tour, this time including Yugoslavia) where fans followed them everywhere: in hotel lobbies, on the road, on the bullet train, showering the musicians with gifts. "It felt like the second coming of The Beatles," Joey commented.

"Japan and its people are totally different from the US – except for McDonald's," CJ told *Ramones Ramones* fanzine. "But there were things I didn't understand. I had to wear a long-sleeved shirt so my tattoos wouldn't show, and we weren't allowed to bring girls back to our rooms, yet you can buy a fifth of whiskey from a vending machine."

CJ showed himself to be as adept as Marky and Dee Dee at getting into mischief: "I went skinny dipping in the hotel pool in Austin, TX, at around 5 am with the guys from Trouble," he recalled, "and we were busted by hotel security. The guard said, 'I was going to kick you all out, but since you're all naked I better let you stay in.'"

The bassist was also known to hurl water bombs from the top of open topped buses at unsuspecting passers-by.

In Birmingham, AL, the band played an 1800s iron mill, while in Wilmington DC, Julia Roberts and (then beau) Keifer Sutherland stopped by, the duck-faced one taking time out to admire CJ's tattoos and have them explained to her.

Tons of musicians in hoary old (albeit popular) metal bands could be seen sporting Ramones shirts in photo shoots – Skid Row, Wrathchild, The Cult, Anthrax, Def Leppard, LA Guns, Megadeth, Alice Cooper, Georgia Satellites, Poison – in a form of belated recognition. Motorhead, about the only decent band among that number (alongside Metallica, who were Lemmy's blueprint for rock, updated and given an MTV-friendly sheen), even released a tribute song to da bruddas in 1991, 'R.A.M.O.N.E.S.' – a track that Joey called "the ultimate honour, like having John Lennon write a song for you."

'Blitzkrieg Bop' got used in a Bud Light commercial: "It has the rhythm and the beat we were looking for," explained producer Fred Smith. "The [Ramones] are representative of today's generation." If that's not mainstream recognition, it's hard to know what is.

Actually, there were far cooler musicians that rated and dug the Ramones – from Sonic Youth (who covered 'Beat On The Brat') to

The Wedding Present to Seattle bands like Nirvana, Soundgarden and Mudhoney – but their support wasn't so noticed. The other bands sold more records.*

That situation was shortly about to change . . .

"I HAVE A DIFFERENT take on grunge to most people. Grunge was like the compact disc, this incredible jolt that revitalised the music business but in the long run fucking killed it, because digital transferring of music means that your catalogues will be rendered useless at some point. I always heard grunge as heavy metal music. I never liked it when music took that metal turn and Black Sabbath and Deep Purple came along, beyond their first couple of records."

OK.

"As soon as metal became popular it morphed into the enemy. That stuff – Journey, the hair bands – kept the music I loved off American radio. It fucking killed punk rock here, and the Ramones were blackballed. I was a promotion guy back then and I fucking quit to go back to school to become an electrical engineer. But I loved music so much, I couldn't afford to buy everything I wanted, so I had to go back and interface with all these radio people. I hated them. They were destroying music as a part of American culture – and they succeeded!

"The alternative radio format was a rival to, and more successful than, the rock radio format for a while. But then it became infested with grunge, and back came all those people who kept the Ramones off the radio in the Seventies to get their hands into this format and turn it into a male knucklehead, testosterone, metal-driven thing. Every time I would go see these bands like Soundgarden – this was just metal music. What does anybody think is great about this?"

To me, there are two sorts of grunge – grunge, as it started, and fashion catwalk, MTV grunge like Silverchair and Bush.

"That's what morphed into the metal crap."

* Sonic Youth were an incredible noise-pop NYC band that started in the early Eighties, influenced by the attitudes of early "art loft" punks like the Ramones, James Chance and Patti Smith. They would ram screwdrivers under guitar strings, and saw their instruments on the edge of the stage. Acknowledged as the forerunners of Nirvana, and everyone that followed, the Youth always gave Joey Ramone maximum respect. The Ramones actually perform a couple of songs in the 1992 Sonic Youth movie, *1991: The Year Punk Broke*, alongside Nirvana and Dinosaur Jr, filmed on the European festival circuit. The title sardonically refers to the success of Nirvana – 15 years after the Ramones invented the form, and The Sex Pistols stormed the UK.

The Wedding Present were a band from the North of England, renowned for their heartfelt lyrics, and maniacally strummed guitars. They once released and deleted a single a week every month for 12 months, just so they could make the UK Top 40 12 times in a year, and get into the record books. Mudhoney are a damn fine live band, in The Stooges mould.

As a Ramones fan, I found it incredibly insulting that Eddie Vedder should induct them into the Rock'N'Roll Hall Of Fame [It happened in 2002, at Johnny's behest] because . . . Eddie Vedder is the enemy. Pearl Jam are Journey. There's no difference. I don't understand why Eddie Vedder – or Bono even – would be going, 'Oh the Ramones are the greatest band ever.' If that's the case, why aren't they making good music?

"That's a logical question. Whom did you just liken Pearl Jam to?"

Journey.

"Journey. OK. There's room for everybody. Stone Gossard [Pearl Jam guitarist] is a lovely guy. I wouldn't begrudge his creative output because of my taste."

Of course.

"Early Pearl Jam has a dark, Doors-ish sound, so I don't quite see how that relates to the helium vocals of Journey, but . . . I understand how you connected those dots. Interestingly, the heavy metal crowd accepted the Ramones, even before grunge. The Ramones had a unique thing about them – their records and live shows were two completely different, fantastic experiences. Live, it was like being in front of a jet engine for an hour and 10 minutes. The Ramones had some lowest common denominator of loudness that touches hard rock and metal fans. I'd rather Eddie Vedder and the Green Day people and Bono and everybody be honest about revering that the Ramones had a lot to do with why they all have careers than not."

Fair enough.

(Author's interview with Kevin Patrick, record executive, 2002)

LATE IN 1991, Soundgarden asked Joey to introduce the Seattle band during their opening set with Guns N' Roses at Madison Square Garden.

It was a public acknowledgement of the Ramones' legacy – and led to an unlikely alignment of the two bands for the remainder of the Ramones career.* Unlikely? Sure. Soundgarden sounded similar to Black Sabbath, and hadn't the Ramones been bottled off stage in the Seventies by the parents of the same fans who now came to cheer Joey on? Once punk was opposed to heavy metal: now it seemed that the two genres suffered from similar myopic vision, and were prepared to join forces to battle the new enemy – rap, hip-hop, the new dance scene sprawling from the UK's garages and warehouses, anything that looked ahead, in fact.

This isn't to denigrate the 'garden – a fine band, and with far more enlightened, liberal attitudes than their predecessors – just to point out the rich irony of the situation.

* Soundgarden covered 'I Can't Give You Anything' on the B-side of their 1992 single 'Outshined'.

Many fans viewed the embracing of the Ramones by the grunge bands – and vice versa – as a betrayal of all da bruddas had once stood for. Sure, when Nirvana came along in the early Nineties they were a breath of fresh air, a momentary return to the idea of rock music as live music, that it was possible to create with intelligence and wit and soul. But what about all the bands that followed, and got claimed as "grunge" – Pearl Jam, Silverchair, Bush, Garbage, Stone Temple Pilots, Saw Doctors, Temple Of The Dog (and far worse)? You squinted, and it was impossible to tell them apart from the reviled Seventies hair bands that punk – and most particularly the Ramones – was supposed to have done away with.

Yet, to a musician they claimed punk as their heritage, and gave the Ramones props. It was like a big college frat party: "Hey, we're all rockers under the skin." But the Ramones – and Nirvana – were originally a POP band, with their sensibilities firmly in tune with the classic two-minute melodies of Sixties radio. NOT METAL WHATSOEVER, despite Johnny's best bandwagon-jumping attempts with speed-metal and hardcore punk: except of course that the Ramones (and Nirvana) played on stage with more passion and vigour and POWER than a thousand crappy metal bands. Also, Kurt Cobain and Joey Ramone were clearly in touch with their feminine sides: a fact that lifted them far above the clichéd posturing of a thousand Axl Roses, Sebastian Bachs and Bonos.*

Post-Nirvana, post-1991 (*The Year Punk Broke*) and the success of *Nevermind*, punk became massive in America. The fact that it was a punk that had little or nothing to do with the Ramones' origins, the fact that it was a punk that followed suffocatingly restrictive rules didn't seem to matter. As Patrick pointed out, the Ramones live were a very different force to the Ramones in the studio – and by this point, the Ramones didn't even exist in the studio. Bands like Green Day, Rancid and Blink182 took the Ramones sound and changed it subtly – lost the hard edge and weird lyrics about lobotomies, and were rewarded with sales in the millions.

It was enough to make a band turn full-on bitter.

"The Ramones were as shocked as anybody when these bands started getting popular," says Daniel Rey. "Fifteen years after they'd started it all, they'd settled into being a cult group – having a limited audience and believing that it was limited, and then all of a sudden Green Day sells nine million albums. Johnny was happy because it gave their genre a little

* Cobain slipped in a tribute to Joey on the "Hey! Wait!" chorus in *In Utero*'s 'Heart-Shaped Box', a clever reversal of "Wait! Now!" from 'I Just Want To Have Something To Do'.

boost. Joey was pissed off at first, but after a while he got a kick out of it because they cited the Ramones as a main influence."

There was a real minimal artistry to what the Ramones first did – the simple lyrics, repeated over and over, the thousands of tunes hidden within three chords. The bands that followed in the Nineties, none of them had that. (Nirvana had something, but it wasn't that.) It was no wonder the mass audience never understood the Ramones.

"Kurt Cobain was a major talent," says Tommy, "and there hadn't been a talent of his calibre for a long time. I don't know if I consider them a band. The connection is that obviously he was very influenced by punk, so when he became a big seller the world finally went, 'Oh, punk rock can sell.' His feel and anger was punk, but not necessarily the music."

Addicted To Noise website: "What is your opinion of the new band Silverchair?"

Joey: "Hype."

THE RAMONES' THIRD year with CJ on board was typically busy: no albums to get in the way of touring, the band went around the world in 1991 – Australia (January), Tokyo (February), Spain (March), America and Argentina (April), Brazil (May), America (June), Italy and Switzerland (July), Canada and the European festivals (August), month off (September), America (October), Europe again (November) and, finally, Britain and America (December).

During the South American leg 15,000 people turned up to see the Ramones in Buenos Aires, pumped up by promoters who also owned the country's radio stations: "We couldn't leave our hotel because of the fans," Joey said. "They're very passionate people. They want a piece of your flesh as a souvenir – literally. After the plane landed and we were walking to the terminal, we looked up to find the viewing deck filled with fans chanting, 'Hey ho, let's go!' "

Another 20,000 saw da bruddas over three nights in Brazil.

In Canada, Joey and CJ went down to see the Lollapalooza travelling rock circus (featuring Jane's Addiction, Siouxsie & The Banshees and Living Colour) on a night off. They walked through the back and were recognised by the crowd, who gave them a standing ovation. When asked why the Ramones weren't on the tour, Jane's Addiction singer Perry Farrell replied, "I have too much respect for you. You should be headlining."

"When we first started Hole there were several Ramones fans in the band," writes their guitarist Eric Erlandson. "At some point, Courtney

[Love, singer] decided we were going to be a Ramones-free band, probably in reaction to [all-female rock band] L7's brand of bubblegum punk pop. So, she fired any member caught chewing gum on stage or wearing filthy Converse sneakers." He's not being entirely serious here. "Kind of like when John Lydon fired Glen Matlock for listening to The Beatles. Our old bass player suggested that we cover 'Carbona Not Glue' and the next day she disappeared. I still don't know what happened to her. I learned quickly to keep my Ramones fetish under wraps, sneaking a song here and there in my car on the way to practise. I saw them live once in the early Nineties but all I can remember is Johnny's shark stare, Perry Farrell standing in front of me headbanging for the entire two-hour show, and realising that I would never be able to play guitar like that. They were an incredible band. I still love them. But please don't tell anyone."

In Brussels, the Ramones headlined Pukkelpop, above Sonic Youth, Nirvana and J Mascis' turbulent, windswept and LOUD Dinosaur Jr. In Scandinavia, the band performed on ice hockey rinks – "Ramones on ice".

Clearly what was required now was a great live album, one that reflected the passion and power of the Ramones on stage, something along the lines of *It's Alive*, 13 years on. One that would show the young pretenders the original punks still had it.

What we got was *Loco Live*, released on October 21, 1991 – "33 classic thrash tracks in 67 minutes," the advert ran, giving the game away. Thrash? From the blurred live photograph on the front – is that a wig Marky's wearing? – to the distortion on Joey's voice, 10 times too loud and sounding like he's in another auditorium entirely, this is a shoddy, careless, poorly executed package. How dare the record company mention it in the same breath as *It's Alive*, one of the greatest live albums of all time? How did it take both Adam Yellin *and* John A. Markovich to completely fuck up the Ramones' sound at NYC's Electric Lady Studios? The crowd noise may well have been recorded in Barcelona (March 11/12, 1991), but it's the only genuine passion on the album.

Loco Live stinks to high heaven. It was an insult to everything the band once stood for. If ever proof existed that the Ramones were going through the motions, this was it. Since when did Joey swear on stage? Since when did he give up singing halfway through 'Sheena' because the song is being tackled too fast?

"It sounds terrible," sighs CJ Ramone. "Sonically, it's unbelievably horrid and, of course, it was the first record I played on with them. I wasn't happy with it at all. It's probably the worst Ramones record ever made. It wasn't our fault, though. We were forced to work with a producer who had no idea of what the Ramones should sound like, and besides that Marky overdubbed all of his hi-hat and cymbal tracks and stayed in the studio during the mixing to make sure his drum tracks were louder than everything else.

For some reason, the American and British versions of the CD vary: different covers and track listings. (The UK release includes 'Too Tough To Die', 'Don't Bust My Chops', 'Palisades Park', and 'Love Kills', but omits 'I Just Want To Have Something To Do', 'Havana Affair', and 'I Don't Wanna Go Down To The Basement'. The US version does the opposite.)

"I have no idea why they let it go," he adds. "It's too bad, because the show itself was pretty strong. Oh God, I don't know what they did to it. It came out super, super flat sounding . . ."

Marky, on the other hand, rather likes it: "*Loco Live* was a great fast live album," he told me. "It was more my drum sound."

If *Loco Live* sounds like a contractual obligation – an album released to honour a previous agreement – that's 'cos it was. The deal with Warner Bros./Sire was coming to an end once more – and this time it wasn't going to be renewed. There was a feeling, justified, that the label had given up on the Ramones after 15 years of steady, but hardly world-shattering, sales. The Ramones were working on songs for their next studio album, but Kurfirst Management had an ulterior motive in making sure Sire wouldn't be the recipient.

At the end of 1991, the Ramones left their first American record label, and signed to the new Radioactive imprint, run by . . . Gary Kurfirst. Usually, record labels are directly opposed to management, and vice versa (one is always trying to screw the other). Was it a wise career move, to have both management and label as one and the same?

The Ramones clearly thought so.

31

Touring, Part 7

"By the time I got into the band, they had their routine down. They'd already done their partying and seen most everything. I never felt I was on the same level as the other Ramones. My background is so blue collar [working class] it was easier to hang around with guys on the crew. I travelled with them more. I was wild, young and rambunctious. It was nice being able to rage night after night, sow my wild oats.

"The road crew was part of the whole dysfunctional family, all characters in their own right. The guitar tech Rick was a maniacal control freak, a pot-smoking wild man from Louisiana. The rest of the crew were from Youngstown, Ohio – redneck-ish Ohio boys with a great sense of humour. They were a real pleasure to hang out with. There was Moon who sold T-shirts – he'd met the band early on in their career, and they kept him around because he was such a nut, unpredictable. He eventually moved to CA.

"Then there was Arturo – lighting designer, in charge of artwork, T-shirt design, an artist and legend in his own right. The Ramones were born out of his loft, and signed their first record contract and wrote a good part of the songs there. He was a real influence on Joey and Dee Dee's lives.

"The road crew are a separate entity from the band. They don't get as much credit as they should. But the crew – and Arturo, in particular – had a lot to do with the length of the Ramones' career, and its quality. It may sound ridiculous and I don't know if Joey, Johnny, Dee Dee and Marky would agree. For example, one time the father of our soundman and monitor man – who were brothers – died when we were overseas. They realised that by the time they got back they wouldn't make the funeral so they decided to go through with the tour. That was above and way beyond anything expected of them.

"Monte should have worn an Everlast shirt. [Everlast are famous for making punching bags for boxers.] He got beat up for everything, and very rarely got credit for anything. He juggled the job of being our manager and Joey's personal assistant and coordinating concerts even though we had a booking agent, and he did it day after day. Monte did a lot of the shit work, like keeping ex-girlfriends and people who'd become a drain on the band out of the backstage area – a lot of people expected to come backstage, and sometimes when you're tired, it's difficult to deal with. You don't want to spend your first 10 minutes coming off stage making small talk, even with major fans."

What did your routine on tour involve?

"We'd come down for breakfast, walk around the local shopping area, do a soundcheck . . . everything was very organised. If you don't have a routine, you get bored very quickly. I was so young and thrilled with everything I would go out drinking till six and be able to play the next night – but I wasn't infallible. One time in Canada I got alcohol poisoning and threw up on stage two nights in a row. I couldn't move. For the most part, I kept up pretty well."

(Author's interview with CJ Ramone, 2002)

32

Strength To Endure

On December 29, 1991, the Ramones played a show at The Ritz in New York, where they previewed songs from their new album *Mondo Bizarro*. The band had been working on new material as far back as 1990: Marky (who, post-Dee Dee, now contributed to the songwriting, despite earlier doubts over his ability) had a work in progress called 'Rat Race' while Joey had written 'There's Gotta Be More To Life Than This', depressed by what he called "the most miserable Christmas of my life".

Neither song saw the light of day, but the first Ramones studio album in three years – recorded on analog equipment at Magic Shop and Baby Monster in NYC, starting January 20 – was far better than *Loco Live* had led many to expect. Ed (*Road To Ruin*) Stasium was back, only slightly hampered by the management's insistence that the band be given a commercial alt-rock jangle sound.

"I'd moved to LA in 1989," Stasium recalls, "and it was there I first saw them with CJ. I was impressed at the renewed energy. They were tight, really good, the best I'd ever heard them play – so I told Gary I wanted to produce the next record. At the time, I was flavour of the month because of my work with The Smithereens and Living Colour, so they listened to me. I tried to make a Ramones record for the Nineties."

Johnny wanted to call the album *Condemned To Live* – obviously, the guitarist still had a decent sense of black humour – or *Mondo Deprovados*, but it was felt that it would be too difficult for Americans to pronounce. So it got shortened.

Dee Dee might have left, but he was still contributing some great songs – he has three collaborations with Daniel Rey on *Mondo Bizarro*: the inspirational and desperately sad single, 'Poison Heart', 'Main Man' and upbeat 'Strength To Endure'. The latter two were given to CJ to sing – his voice was OK, but it was sure no Joey.

"It didn't matter who sang them," CJ explains, "because they're great songs."

"['Strength To Endure'] is about living life on life's terms," Dee Dee told *Boston Rock*. "We've got a responsibility to the younger generation. The other day I saw an ad for Metallica that said 'Alcoholica'. I don't think it's good," he stated, sounding like your parents, "for bands to encourage people to drink."

"I think everybody has had a time," Marky told a German magazine, "maybe in a relationship, maybe because of somebody's death, or maybe because of some personal self-doubt, where they need the strength to endure. It's that strength that tastes so bitter. Dee Dee would've needed this strength when he decided to leave the band."

There was still rancour: Dee Dee claimed the Ramones were refusing to pay him until he signed a piece of paper giving up his right to the name Dee Dee Ramone: he later wrote in his book *Poison Heart* that he was forced by the management to sell the publishing rights to his songs on *Mondo Bizarro* in exchange for a few thousand dollars so he could hire a lawyer to get out of jail [the Washington Square Park drug bust].

Whatever the truth, 'Poison Heart' is easily the finest song the Ramones recorded during the Nineties: Joey's voice soulful and understanding on lines like "I just want to walk right out of this world/'Cause everybody has a poison heart", the guitars chiming in melodic counterpoint.

"We tracked the album in a tiny cheap room in New York," Stasium says, "and mixed it in East Hill. Daniel may have written some of the songs, and played some guitar – he was always around." Daniel indeed wrote some songs, the three with Dee Dee, and two more with Joey, 'Tomorrow She Goes Away' (a likeable, traditional power pop Ramones number), and the obviously derivative 'Heidi Is A Headcase" (one more indication of the Ramones' growing self-parody). Other musicians credited include Living Colour guitarist Vernon Reid (another Kurfirst client), Andy Shernoff, of course (he co-wrote the lovely Fifties acoustic number 'I Won't Let It Happen' with Joey), Flo & Eddie, ex-The Turtles (harmonies on 'Poison Heart'), and The Psychedelic Furs' Joe McGinty (horrible keyboards on the pointless Doors cover 'Take It As It Comes').

"I was in a clothes store one day," Johnny said, "and I heard [the Doors song] come on a tape and thought it sounded like a good song for the Ramones. Usually, I don't like the way we do covers, but this one came out good."

Reid played an equally horrible guitar solo on Joey's otherwise fun romp 'Cabbies On Crack', a song inspired by a hellish taxi ride from his manager's office . . . taxi ride! Jeez. The Ramones *were* out of touch with their fans.

As self-referencing as 'Heidi' is, it's nowhere near as bad as the final song on the album, 'Rock'N'Roll High Sch . . .' – sorry – 'Touring'. Sure, it's a raucous singalong, a tribute to The Beach Boys' Sixties summer parties and endless lines of Holiday Inns, but it had also been written 14 years before – even if the Wilson steals weren't as blatant first time round, and the original didn't lift entire lines from other songs ('Rockaway Beach', 'California Girls'). Oddly, the song is so shameless in its self-plagiarism, it nearly works: "Well, we've been to London and we've been to LA," Joey gleefully sings over surfing guitars and sweet Turtles backing harmonies, "Spain, New Zealand and the USA . . ."

It's not so surprising then, that the band originally demo-ed the song in 1981, around the time of *Pleasant Dreams*. It was a Ramones reject given a new lease of life. Another demo recorded round then, 'I Can't Get You Out Of My Mind', turned up on 1989's *Brain Drain*. Clearly the Ramones believed in recycling.

The guitars on Marky Ramone/Skinny Bones' 'The Job That Ate My Brain' and 'Anxiety' sound suspiciously like outtakes from the third Buzzcocks album – fine, but another sign of the band's artistic sterility that one could place the steals: before, it was all part of the Ramones sound.

WHAT KIND OF stuff would amuse Joey?

"He had the sickest sense of humour – not like bathroom humour, but twisted. He would give you a birthday card or a Christmas card that would always have . . . not an off-colour joke, but twisted, like Mad *magazine. He loved to laugh."*

Yeah – he was very much into health food, wasn't he, in the Nineties?

"Yeah, he would go through these periods . . . there was this juice bar on 11th and Second that he used to go to all the time. He would go through these periods of juicing, but then he would go through these periods of Ben And Jerry's."

OK.

"He would get really into the health thing and eat at Angelica's, which is like a real super healthy kind of place."

He liked his sushi as well, didn't he?

"He loved sushi. There was this really trendy sushi restaurant we'd go to occasionally – it was one of those places where you needed to drop a name to make a reservation and you needed to make a reservation a month in advance. He'd always decide three hours before where we needed to go, of course, so I'd call and say, 'I'm calling from Joey Ramone's office, we'd like a table.' Once, the reservation guy said, 'Mr Ramone likes to sit at such and such a table,' and I was like, 'I know, I'm always with him,' you know? We also used to eat at a Polish diner just around the corner, almost every morning. We'd have pancakes and oatmeal. He did eat

pretty healthy. He would occasionally offer to cook for me but I never took him up on the offer."

What did he offer to cook?

"Eggs."

Eggs?

"Yeah. As I say, we'd go out to breakfast a lot."

(Author's interview with Rachel Felder, journalist)

THE MOST INTERESTING song on *Mondo Bizarro* is 'Censorshit'.

In September 1991, the Ramones wrote an article for *Musician*, detailing their opposition to the PMRC-led move to censor the record industry by placing stickers on albums warning parents of offensive content: "Teenagers want to listen to music. It's part of growing up and experiencing things. You can't take that away from them. Kids like rock'n'roll, baseball, Burger King and going to concerts. . . . They don't want repression to start happening here, because [this] is how it starts. Certain freedoms are taken away and then you have revolt."

Marky and Joey also took part in *Rock The Vote* panels: so another protest song was on the cards. 'Censorshit' is far more direct (and nastier) than 'Bonzo Goes To Bitburg' though, which couched its message in dark humour. "Ah, Tipper come on," Joey sneers. "Ain't you been getting it on?" The tune is pure Ramones – angry, motivated, great drums; unfortunate that the words, which would've made a great article, get in the song's way. Nonetheless, it was a welcome sign that there was passion in the old workhorse still.

CJ, being a Ramones fan – and thus more in tune with what made the band great than the other members – found the experience of recording *Mondo Bizarro* trying: "I'm not knocking Ed's abilities," he says, "because he was great to work with. He did what they wanted, made them sound mainstream. But I prefer my rock more lo-fi, garage. It was a little slick.

"They thought it was their real shot, a serious breakthrough," he continues. "It was very frustrating. It's like the last show in LA – why the fuck would you make the final Ramones show a star-studded event? The fans don't want that. No disrespect to any of the people who got up on stage, but . . . I tried so many times to get the guys to understand that all they needed to do was to be themselves. If they continued to be the Ramones, instead of chasing their own tails, they couldn't miss. Eventually the world would catch up . . ."

"FOR ME, JOEY RAMONE was a performer who embodied both diffidence and

grandiosity. Here was a man who was simultaneously awkward, eyes hidden by his hair, and also larger than life. This contradiction seemed to be an ideal metaphor for my own relationship to performing. Part of me wanted to own the stage while the other part of me remained uncomfortable with such power.

"The song ['I Wanna Be Your Joey Ramone' from Call The Doctor, *Chainsaw 1995] was partially about this duality but also about stepping into someone else's shoes (in this case Joey's) as a means of exploring your own fears and dreams. When Sleater-Kinney first began, it felt that the only way to get a sense of rock'n'-roll was to experience it vicariously, at least that was the message coming to us from the outside world. The song has us stepping into a male rock performer's shoes and by doing this we get a glimpse of the absurdity, the privilege, and the decadence that we didn't feel was inherently afforded to us. More than anything the song pays homage to Joey Ramone. The Ramones were one of my favourite bands when I was a teenager and their legacy remains invaluable to me. They were one of the first bands wherein I felt compelled to buy all of their albums (and by doing so turned me into a hopeless completist when it came to music later on). Their music had an energy that I had never experienced before; it was forward moving and relentless, but it was also melodic.*

"Sadly, I never met Joey Ramone. He used the song on his cable access show a few times. Merely knowing he had heard of Sleater-Kinney always felt like a certain privilege."

(Email from Carrie Brownstein, Sleater-Kinney, 2002)

THE COVER TO *Mondo Bizarro* is another DuBose production: the four members were shot in Mylar to look as if they're dissolving in a psychedelic Fun House mirror. DuBose came up with the concept after being inspired by the work of Ira Cohen – most notably, the sleeve to *The Twelve Dreams Of Dr. Sardonicus* by West Coast band Spirit. Mylar is a plastic material developed by DuPont.

"In 1970, my Florida girlfriend showed me the record, shot by her ex in NYC," he says. "I was very impressed by the melting images of wizards dressed in multi-coloured costumes, so I started experimenting with the form. You can see it on the floor of the photograph on the first (*sic*) B-52's album sleeve."

When the Ramones contacted DuBose, he showed Johnny, CJ and Marky the concept and they thought it was cool. "Then I had to deal with Joey," DuBose recalls. "He rarely went to rehearsals. I called him up and he was like, 'George, you can do the design, but I want to use this other photographer who does these melting shots.' I was like, 'Ira Cohen? I've been taking shots like this since 1970.'

"Joey was concerned that if I did this," he explains, "Ira would think he'd given me the idea. So we arranged a meeting. There was this grumpy 70-year-old guy with his pictures of Janis and Jimi . . . So I showed him my photos, and he got a little friendlier. I asked him, 'What can I do to make you happy' – he was like, why don't I come along to the photo session, smoke a joint and give you my blessing. Monte didn't allow joints, so I offered to buy one of his Jimi Hendrix prints instead and Joey bought one, too. I gave him a huge credit so everyone would know who I was ripping off."

". . . THE GUY WOULD eat sushi, the guy would go to the movies. We saw Schindler's List *together and we were stunned – we sat and talked for three hours. We couldn't just separate and go home, the way you normally do after seeing a movie. We'd play tapes together, normal stuff, watch videos."*

What kind of food would you eat?

"He was totally into sushi. I'd say about 75 per cent of the meals we ate together were sushi – pretty close to that, honestly. He took me for some of my best sushi meals ever. There were some neighbourhood places that he liked. Hasaki on 9th Street was his main sushi place and he also loved Bond Street, which wasn't a traditional sushi style. He'd go to Japan a lot so he had good sushi knowledge."

What did he like about Japan?

"He got a great response over there. He liked the tours. He would always bring back souvenirs – monsters and dragons."

Like the Godzilla kind of stuff?

"Yeah. In Japan, it's part of their culture to give presents to their favourite artists."

What records would you listen to together?

"Mostly Sixties British stuff. He would sometimes come back from Japan with videos – he loved The Animals. All the early stuff, the documentaries you couldn't get in America from the BBC. They were probably bootlegs, I don't know. Always British videos – The Who, Wizzard. He had a real big video collection."

Right. What was in there apart from music?

"It was mostly music actually."

(Author's interview with Andy Shernoff)

THE REACTION TO *Mondo Bizarro* when it appeared in September 1992 was cautiously optimistic. "It may not be the best Ramones' album ever," the *Orlando Sentinel* wrote, "but it's certainly the best in a long while." (It was their first in a long while. In the three years between 1976 and 1979, they'd released four studio albums, one double live album, and written side one of a soundtrack.) "They're the fuckin' Buddy Holly of their generation," stated Lemmy. "What can you say now – they're the same people in different jeans." "They ain't really musicians," Peter Easton explained in a *Glasgow Herald* review of their show in December at Glasgow Barrowlands, echoing distant times. "This is performance art."

In May, the same month *Loco Live* was released in America, Donna Weinbrecht won a gold medal in mogul skiing at the Albertville French Olympics – dancing to 'Rock'N'Roll High School'. Debbie Harry had written the sleeve-notes to *Loco Live*, so Joey repaid the favour by singing a duet with her on 'Standing In My Way' for her *Debravation* album. (It got released in '93 on a limited edition single only.)

The singer also performed at a couple of presidential rallies for Jerry Brown, fronting a band comprised of Marky, Skinny Bones and Andy Shernoff. "Joey did many different things like that," CJ recalls, "and if he asked me, I'd take part in it. I wouldn't always support the cause, but I'd go along to support him because I knew it was important to him. I'm kind of apolitical for the most part. I always felt that was more up to the British bands."

The band's schedule (North America in January; Europe in March and May) during 1992 was interrupted by a few accidents: Joey was looking increasingly frail, and had to go into hospital for laser surgery for a hole in his retina – and CJ was in a motorcycle crash in a Long Island rally and broke his wrist. The latter incident happened in between two festivals in Hummijkrvi, Finland (19/6) and Alsdorf, Germany (27/6).

"I was in excruciating pain," CJ remembers, "and so they brought in someone from the hospital to give me a shot in the armpit. Trouble was, he used too much and my hand went dead. I couldn't even keep it on the neck of the bass – and then some missile hit me on the hand and made it even worse. Just then a barrier collapsed and the show got called, thank God . . ."

"Uh, things were a little late at the Bizarre Festival," says Arturo. Other bands performing included The Pogues and EMF. "They said do the show, it's only for 40 minutes, and then you'll be OK. But things started running late and people were getting crushed against the barricade. So we had to stop the show. And, uh, it took them half-an-hour to get things back in order. CJ's injection was supposed to be short-term and he started getting really bad. His hand just blew up. That's the only time the Ramones never came back to the stage. They had to rush him to the hospital.

"That's like almost a cancellation," he laughs. "But it wasn't their fault. They were gonna perform anyway."

CJ's injury resulted in a Spanish tour being postponed.

In August, the band returned to South America, this time playing Chile and Mexico City alongside their regular haunts. "That was crazy," recalls CJ. "Absolutely maniacal, rabid fans, wild. In Mexico City, you see real poverty . . . but the kids appreciate rock music so much."

"When we went through the metal detectors at the airport [in Argentina]," Joey recalled in *Ramones Ramones*, "the guards stopped us just so they could get our autographs." For the five days the band stayed in Buenos Aires' Hotel Panamerica, 500 fans camped out front. In scenes reminiscent of The Beatles' *A Hard Day's Night*, fans got hold of Johnny and started pulling on his hair. Later, at a TV studio, a riot broke out between fans and police: "They busted doors and windows, and the lobby was covered with broken glass," Joey stated.

On their way back from another interview, fans parked a truck in the middle of the street so the Ramones were forced to stop.

"The band wanted to go to Mexico City for years," says Arturo. "The original offer was for a bullring. There are two in Mexico City and we were offered the smaller one. When the authorities realised who was coming to perform, they said we weren't allowed to because they knew what kind of people would be there – hardcore working class, the poorest of the poor. So they took the permit away. We ended up playing part of the Olympic swimming pool complex.

"All day long, I'm jumping on and off the stage . . . show time comes, and they realise there are no steps to get on stage." He laughs. "So the band had to climb down from the balcony. It was ridiculous. But things like that happened."

Just prior to the South American tour, Samuel Bayer directed a video for 'Poison Heart' at a reservoir water pumping station in Central Park – Bayer was best known as the man responsible for Nirvana's 'Smells Like Teen Spirit' video, the rather tacky MTV-championed promo that helped the Aberdeen band go stellar.

The commercial magic didn't translate.

Johnny took its failure with his usual grace: "Nirvana are mediocre," he said, "rap's unspeakable. Rock'n'roll is possibly dead. Some days I feel like I'm in another world." He also had little time for future pal Eddie Vedder: "I don't see nothin' there," he snarled. "The guy sings good, but I don't like the stupid outfits they wear . . . always walking around with shorts on. There was a time when you had an image and looked cool on stage. Now you gotta go up there and look a dork."

Other places played included Asia in September, and a two-month tour of America (with Social Distortion) including three nights at the Hollywood Palladium. Robbie Krieger from The Doors got up on stage on one of the nights, fitting in perfectly with the new-look "tribute" Ramones – it was no longer deemed necessary to hold the sanctity of the Ramones gang intact. Some fans, however, noticed.

"I don't know if he could tell one song from another," says Daniel Rey, who was at the show. "Joey introduced him, CJ gave the count, and he missed the first few chords because he was more of a California guy. As soon as it was done, he turned to the band to look for the 'thank you', and they just went '1-2-3-4', and he stood there like a scared deer and ran off the stage. The only other time someone else played with them was at the farewell concert, when everyone got up. I didn't go to that one. I went to see their last show in New York instead. That's how I wanted to remember them, without all the fanfare."

In Detroit, the band stayed at the same hotel as President Bush: "It really screwed up my morning swim," Joey laughed. "One point, Monte was loading the van and a secret service guy came up behind him and told him to drop the bags and walk away without looking back. It was the President."

More dates in Europe followed in December, with Terrorvision as UK support: "They told us to turn the music down in our dressing room once and wouldn't allow us to soundcheck while they were eating," says bassist Leigh Marklew. "But there were no rock'n'roll incidents. Also, they had a barney when one of them pissed in the toilet backstage and it didn't flush. Our illusions were shattered. CJ was nice, but he wasn't no Dee Dee. Maybe Dee Dee was the rock'n'roll Ramone."

Too Tough To Die – the mid-Eighties Ramones line-up featuring the almost anonymous Richie Ramone; clockwise, from top left: Richie, Joey, Johnny and Dee Dee. (George Du Bose/*LFI*)

Ex-Blondie drummer Clem Burke, who undertook a brief tour of duty with the Ramones in 1987. *(Camera Press)*

Richie Ramone, who drummed with the group from 1983 to 1987. He played 400 shows, appeared on two albums and in several videos – yet no-one close to the Ramones will talk about him. *(Pictorial Press)*

The Ramones uncharacteristically out of uniform, soundchecking just prior to Dee Dee quitting. *(Gai Terrell/Redferns)*

The Ramones with new recruit, ex-marine CJ, circa 1989; left to right: Marky, Johnny, Joey and CJ. (*Robert Knight/Redferns*)

Joey in the john at CBGBs. "Joey would say his three favourite things in the world were having a dump, having sex, and being on stage with the Ramones," says George Seminara. *(Ebet Roberts/Redferns)*

Celebrating their 2,000th show in Tokyo, February, 1994. CJ: "At the end, I threw my T-shirts and sweat bands off the stage and mooned the crowd." (*Bob Gruen/Star File*)

Joey with his mother, Charlotte Lesher, in CBGBs, May 1994 - Joey's 43rd birthday. "I knew they all had that little anger in them," said Charlotte of the Ramones, "and I thought it was a great release for him to get it all out of his system." (*Bob Gruen/Star File*)

Dee Dee in 1990. "He's a genius and sometimes geniuses… there's a line of insanity and they can ride that line. He wavers around that craziness but he's a great songwriter. He's terrific. But he needed the structure in the Ramones." – Monte Melnick. *(Steve Eichner/WireImage.com)*

Dee Dee, Johnny, Tommy and Marky after being inducted into the Rock and Roll Hall of Fame, NYC, March 18, 2002. (Ed Betz/*Associated Press*)

Mickey Leigh, Joey's brother, performing with The Bullys during the tribute show held for Dee Dee at New York's Continental, July 2, 2002. (Richard Drew/*Associated Press*)

Fans mourn Joey at the shrine set up outside CBGBs after his death on April 15, 2001. "Everyone who met him went away feeling they had made a real connection," said Ramones PR Ida Langsom.
(*Robert Spencer/Associated Press*)

33

Influence Of The Ramones

"This is classical music for future generations. Brian Wilson, the Ramones, people will be listening to it in a 100 years' time, and talking about it in the same breath as Beethoven. It may sound ridiculous now, but this is the way it's going." – Captain Sensible

"They spawned most of the late Seventies punk rock music. That was the model: chords and no solos, and really dumb lyrics. They inspired many illiterates out there to start a band – and so they were huge, way beyond The Dictators or any of their peers. They were the ones who told all the idiots it was OK to be in a rock band. Before that, all the people in rock bands were rich people and models, but they brought rock back to what it used to be like when it was raw and aggressive. And they caused thousands of kids to emulate them, to pick up a guitar, learn one chord and dive headfirst off the stage." – Don Fleming

"The Ramones legacy is vast. You can see it flowing into speed metal and hardcore and softcore: it can't be known at this time. I wouldn't say hip-hop and techno, but I would certainly say it informed noise, hardcore, softcore, Riot Grrrl . . . Sleater-Kinney would not be possible without the Ramones. Nirvana without the Ramones would not be possible, even with the Black Sabbath and Led Zeppelin influences." – Donna Gaines

"Apart from the usual, that it gave a lot more people the right to try even though they weren't perfect musicians, the Ramones gave a lot of bands the approval to be themselves without fear." – Janis Schacht

"The Ramones probably had a bigger influence than any other band in history – here it is 25 years later and there are still bands trying to sound like them. The Beatles are very influential, without them there wouldn't be a Ramones. But 25 years on, you don't go to every club in NYC and hear a band like The Beatles. Every heavy metal band, even rap bands, every hardcore band were very influenced by punk – and the Ramones put that on the map. It's astonishing that a band that never had a radio hit or a gold record turned out to be the most influential band in the history of rock. Punk rock refuses to die." – John Holmstrom

"Ramones influenced just everybody, even U2." – Rodney Bingenheimer

"There are five or 10 bands in the entire rock era that have had a massive influence, and the Ramones are one of them. England is known for producing great bands: The Beatles, the Stones, The Who, The Clash, The Smiths – while America is known for great solo artists: Bruce Springsteen, Patti Smith. It makes sense because US history is all about the cult of the individual. So who are the great US bands? Do you count The Beach Boys, or are they a glorified solo project? The Ramones are at the top of a very short list of Great American Bands that include The Velvet Underground, Sonic Youth, and maybe The Byrds and Funkadelic." – Slim Moon

"Every taxi driver in New York will mention the Ramones, and worldwide too, even more so. I was down in Brazil and I checked into a hotel, and the guy asked me for my autograph. In Japan and Spain and Germany, the universal language is Ramones. I've met people who have learnt to speak English using the Ramones. It's simple, repetitive and you can sing along to it, it's a learning tool." – Daniel Rey

34

Out Of Time

IT WAS 1993's collection of psychedelic Sixties cover versions, *Acid Eaters* (released October 11), that convinced most fans that the Ramones' time really was up.

Clearly, they no longer had a say – or no longer had any interest in having a say – in their own musical direction. The album was hacked out at Baby Monster in an attempt to cash in on the interest Stasium's excellent production job on *Mondo Bizarro* had generated. Kurfirst had been impressed at the reaction to the (very ordinary) Doors cover, and thought it'd be a good idea to put out an EP of covers. It snowballed from there to what amounted to expensive karaoke.

The whole exercise reeked of cynicism: from the inclusion of porn star Traci Lords (another Kurfirst client)* on the Jefferson Airplane cover 'Somebody To Love' to the absolutely dire Rolling Stones' cover, 'Out Of Time'. (Sebastian Bach from Skid Row sings back-up: he was invited because he'd given the Ramones gold records after 'Psychotherapy' was used as a B-side to one of his band's singles. Nice that he was nice and everything, but not necessarily the best of reasons to have someone involved.)

Band-members weren't allowed in the studio while the celebrities were present, and the production from Scott Hackwith is about as unsympathetic as the Ramones ever received (even including *Loco Live*) – turning da bruddas hallmark wall of noise into a jangling alt-rock college radio band. Scott who? He was the singer with Dig, a rather dull early Nineties Californian pop-grunge outfit, who also happened to be on Radioactive.

Not even the presence of Pete Townshend on backing vocals on the workmanlike run-through of The Who's 'Substitute' could save matters. To add insult to injury, CJ was allowed to sing three songs ('Journey To

* Lords cannot sing – even if she had previously guested on the Manic Street Preachers' 'Little Baby Nothing' after the Welsh band tried, and failed, to get Kylie Minogue.

The Center Of The Mind', 'The Shape Of Things To Come', and 'My Back Pages') – and turned in a better vocal performance than Joey. At least it sounds like he cares. He was actually asked to sing on a fourth, 'When I Was Young' but Joey put his foot down.

John Fogerty, Bob Dylan, The Troggs . . . all these bands and more found their work desecrated by a band that were once the finest in the world. It's hard to know who's more at fault: the person whose original idea it was to record an album of covers, the producer with all the soft rock frills, Johnny for buggering off out of the studio as soon as time permitted, Joey for going along with it all. The album title is from an obscure Sixties movie.

"It was kind of weird," says Daniel Rey with typical understatement. Again, Rey was called in to play guitar. "Traci Lords was a friend of Johnny's. He was a fan of her work. I didn't really work with her. I believe she may have had a short-lived career as a disco queen. I didn't meet Pete. Joey was there for that – it was a big thrill for him."

"I was very nervous when [Pete Townshend] came down because I'd never met him before," said Joey.

"It should have been an EP," says CJ bluntly. "And that's a fact. Some of the songs on there are totally pointless – the Jefferson Airplane song we did, oh Lord. Even the porn star there couldn't save the song. It was just horrible, horrible. I haven't listened to any of them for so long, I couldn't even call the names of the songs."

Joe McGinty smothered the sound with keyboards again: the Ramones' opposition to such "inauthentic" instruments long forgotten.

The Love cover, '7 And 7 Is' just about survives with dignity intact; as does the album's opener, 'Journey To The Centre Of The Mind' . . . but CJ sings the latter, and CJ was not in any shape or form the Ramones singer. It was like asking – er, a Ramones fan to take over the role of Ramones singer while the Ramones singer sat by and did nothing.

One can only speculate that Johnny's pragmatism was running rampant at this point, and that artistic concerns were not allowed to intrude whatsoever. The logic the guitarist had earlier applied to using Daniel Rey – why waste time playing a guitar part that took 20 minutes to record if Daniel could play it in five – he applied to Joey's vocals now. Joey took a notoriously long time recording – so why not get the youngster in to sing his parts if he took less time? The fact that Joey's voice was about the only recognisable part of the Ramones left escaped him: or perhaps he didn't care. Fans came to the live shows, the album would sell the same whatever the band did, why bother knocking yourself out?

It's interesting to note that one of Joey's most accomplished vocal performances was on the Holly & The Italians single – where, for once, he didn't have time restrictions placed upon him; see also his 1994 Godfather Of Soul project on 'Rockaway Beach (On The Beach)' with General Johnson, ex-Chairman Of The Board.

Even the Jan & Dean cover, 'Surf City' – a song that the old Ramones could have rattled off in their sleep – sounds lacklustre. "We used to play this one live about 14 years ago," Joey reported. "It was out on some bootlegs so we thought we'd make it official." Shame they didn't record it back then.

"Everyone now seems to be driven by the buck, the dollar," Joey wrote in the fanzine *Ramones Ramones*, without the slightest trace of irony. "We're still in it for the excitement. A lot of people are putting out covers – I hear Duran Duran are going to do one, but it'll be a travesty. Most bands butcher songs, some songs are perfection and out of respect you don't do them." What, like '7 And 7 Is', and 'Substitute' and 'Surf City'? Poor, sweet, naïve Joey.

The sleeve was a rather ugly approximation of acid-fuelled Sixties art: "Gary Kurfirst liked to buy the paintings to use as covers," explains DuBose, "and keep the artwork."

THE REACTION WAS suitably fawning (past a certain stage of bands' careers, you'll always be able to find jaded critics willing to give anything a good review): "*Acid Eaters* is a loud and proud peek at the Ramones' record collection," wrote the *People* reviewer without the slightest sense of shame, "and further proof that by keeping the pretence level nonexistent, they remain one of the coolest bands around."

Real fans weren't so impressed, however: "I always bought tickets for the shows, even though I could've guest listed it," explains Lindsay Hutton. "I felt it was totally worth the money. The last time I ever saw John I'd done a bad review of *Acid Eaters* in my magazine where I called it Odour Eaters, and he took great offence. So I asked him, 'How many people have covered "7 And 7 Is"?' Joe wanted to do 'See My Baby Jive'. I would have much preferred that. That's the difference between Joe's taste and what people considered classic rock. It was the same night Joe was involved in playing on the Die Toten Hosen record: fun, but very stupid. Die Toten Hosen were like Hanoi Rocks playing punk rock with that German sense of humour."

It was unfortunate that at a stage in their careers when the Ramones were finally achieving the recognition they deserved, they'd turned into a watered-down version of themselves. The long-awaited official Ramones biography appeared – Jim Bessman's *Ramones: An American Band* (St Martins Press). Despite it being little more than a collection of enthusiastic and descriptive reports from an obvious fan that toed the party line and failed to play up either Arturo Vega or Monte Melnick's immense contributions to the band, certain members were displeased.

Bessman had unwittingly exposed a few cracks in the Ramones Myth.

"Joey and Johnny ended up having the biggest hatred towards each other," explains John Holmstrom. "Remember the Jim Bessman book that was written about them? The layouts would be up in the office and Joey would go in and see the pictures. He would pick out all the pictures of Johnny and replace them with pictures of him. Then Johnny would go up to the office. He'd take down all the pictures of Joey and replace them all with pictures of him. Then Joey would go back up there. It would go back and forth like this. Jim told me he was sued, all the money he made from writing the book was taken away in a lawsuit – over the lyrics."

This is unverified but if true it was peculiar indeed, not least because the opening page credits "Jim Bessman in association with the Ramones".

On March 18, 1993, the Ramones achieved the ultimate accolade by appearing in the Rosebud episode in season five of *The Simpsons*, performing 'Happy Birthday Mr Burns' to the miserable, grasping nuclear power plant owner.

"I had the best line: 'Go to hell you old bastard,'" recalls CJ. "At that point, I could've retired. Lemmy had mentioned me in a song and I got to curse on primetime TV with The Simpsons and just a little while later I played on stage with Robbie Krieger from The Doors. [The episode was recorded in 1992.] *The Simpsons* is the only intelligent thing on TV."

Amen to that.

STILL THE INEXORABLE Ramones touring machine rolled on.

In January '93, the band travelled to Japan, where Joey enjoyed more sushi, and the band also ate at the Hard Rock Café in Osaka, feted by the restaurant's owner into giving the place some guitar-picks and drumsticks. A lot of American and Australian servicemen attended. "They'd be the ones with the big mouths," Joey explained. "I'd have to tell them to shut the fuck up. They kept chanting 'Beat on the brat, beat on the brat'. Japan is its own planet, the way New York City is – I love the fans, they're totally supportive and loyal and dedicated and fanatical. And the food!"

The ace Western-infatuated female pop band Shonen Knife came to see a Ramones show in Osaka – when the Knife played CBGBs, the first thing their singer said when she came out was, "This stage. Ramones."

The band did a few dates in Europe in the middle of the year, but it was becoming clear Joey's health wasn't too good, and that necessitated cancelling the odd show. Then came another bout of frenzied appearances in the Ramones' home-from-home, South America, in June. In 20 years of touring, the pace had barely slackened.

"The crowds were out of control in South America," recalls CJ. "You couldn't leave your hotel, couldn't walk along the street, each Ramone had a bodyguard assigned to him . . . If I'm honest, what I liked most about South America was the women – they're beautiful, unbelievable. I loved the whole attitude. Poverty is so huge, and the kids who don't have money appreciate everything so much. Rock'n'roll never died over there, not like it did here, especially on the East Coast where there aren't that many kids into punk rock or rock'n'roll, it's all hip-hop and R&B crap like that.

"One time I was out in a car with some kids, driving crazily, and we almost wrecked a couple of times. They were laughing about it and I was thinking, 'We have a show tomorrow, you can't get me killed.' We were so loved."

In August, the band played festivals in Europe.

In September, the band played North America.

In December, the band played Europe again – this time with the Superbang '93 festival tour (loosely based on Lollapalooza), starring the Ramones, English goths The Sisters Of Mercy, Daniel Rey's old bandmate from Shrapnel, Dave Wyndrof and his full-on metal band Monster Magnet, and others.

Like most of the bands the Ramones now played with, The Sisters Of Mercy were confirmed fans: "I've only ever collected five autographs which is quite sad," said singer Andrew Eldritch. "Four were the Ramones and the fifth was [corny British DJ] Tony Blackburn."

Obviously, on tours like these, the rider was very important. The Ramones had worked out what they required years before: "We'd have a vegetable tray," remembers CJ, "sometimes a cold cut tray, beer, soda, chips, cookies . . . I tried to get cigarettes added but they wouldn't. I tried to get Jack Daniel's added, but they wouldn't. A pizza . . . some juice . . . nothing out of the ordinary. We actually ate the pizza after the show," he laughs, after I remind him that it used to be a Ramones pre-show ritual. "They got more practical as the years went on, and realised if they ate pizza after the show, they wouldn't have to stop to get food, just for gas. Everything became a matter of practicality."

"We'd have Yoo Hoo," Marky says seriously. "Johnny liked Yoo Hoo a lot. I like it too. Beside that, Pepsi and American beer like Budweiser and Miller . . . It was a very simple rider really. They never sold Yoo Hoo in Europe, anyway. Juices, water, always bottled water, some beer. Johnny had a beer after the show and that was about it."

Still the inexorable Ramones touring machine rolled on.

. . . *SO WHEN DID you first encounter the Ramones?*

"It was probably in '76 or '77. I saw the ads for the first Ramones album and bought Ramones Leave Home *when I was 16 – I got the version with 'Carbona' on. I was learning how to play guitar then. The first band I had did all these original songs, and the rest were by the Pistols and the Ramones – 'Pinhead', 'I Don't Care'. I liked the fact it was the fastest guitar I'd ever heard – no solos, fast chords, straightforward heavy riffs. I liked the wit in the lyrics, anything from neo-Nazis to the KKK to chainsaws. The lyrics could be taken on many different levels – really move you, songs about love, naïve way to see the world, cartoon-y or over-the-top schlock. It was great getting drunk and blasting the Ramones with your friends. By the end of the night everyone would be singing along."*

What would you say the Ramones' influence on music has been?

"Being the original punk rock band, they had a strong influence on labels and musicians coming up in the late Seventies and early Eighties – SST with Black Flag, and Dischord with Minor Threat, the independent US punk rock bands. Kiss say they influenced a thousand bands but it's not true, not really. They made people aspire to pick up the guitar, but very few people wanted to sound like Kiss – they were a reference, those three mid-tempo chords, they were easy. The Ramones were like a challenge, can I play that fast? Most Kiss fans bought a guitar and left it in the garage. Most Ramones fans bought guitars and made a record. The Kiss fan now is in his mid-forties and his friends come over and he shows them the guitar on display in his bedroom, still shiny, the strings probably not even changed. The Ramones fan's guitar is well-worn with beer stains on it, and stickers."

Do you think the Ramones had an influence on grunge?

"Certainly. You don't hear it as much with Soundgarden but you can with Nirvana. But we did a few Ramones covers – 'Can't Give You Anything' off Rocket To Russia. *They were part of our inspiration and influence – and they inspired Pearl Jam, too. Of all the bands I ever played with, the Ramones were my heroes – that's why we befriended them."*

What were they like as people?

"Joey and Marky are quiet, CJ is ebullient, and Johnny is contemplative – I really like the fact he's into baseball, because that was my love before rock'n'roll. Johnny is very serious when he talks about baseball and politics. He definitely likes a good discussion."

Kim laughs.

"Joey is a very friendly guy, but very quiet. There are two kinds of singers, those that are introverted and save their voice until they're on stage, and the monkey boys like David Lee Roth who jump everywhere and can't shut up. Dee Dee was a friendly, amiable guy, too. Johnny and CJ were the most outgoing. They were pretty much regular guys, no weird rock star egos. I got in a few heated discussions on politics with Johnny, even though I tried to avoid it. You don't want to cause friction. He has strong opinions, and he won't back down. That's a good quality."

(Author's interview with Kim Thayil, Soundgarden guitarist, 2002)

IN JANUARY 1994, the Ramones joined the Big Day Out road show in Australia. That year's line-up was particularly notable, featuring bands like Kim and Kelley Deal's chain-smoking Breeders, Soundgarden, indie-pop darlings Pavement and Billy Corgan's risible Smashing Pumpkins – plus fine Australian acts such as the Sixties-influenced You Am I and Ramones near-clones The Hard Ons.

"At the Big Day Out," recalls Thayil, "they'd have these characters they call the clowns. Their job is to run around, make merry and get the crowd involved in everything. So, in the middle of the Ramones set, these guys started surfing the crowd on a giant inflatable shark. They went across the photo pit and were hoisted up onto a dolly – and ran right across the front of the stage, obscuring the Ramones briefly, trying to be funny."

Kim chuckles at the thought of what happened next.

"Rick, the guitar tech for the Ramones," he continues, "ran over and hit this clown guy square in the face. It was the coolest image – this regular road crew brother decking the clown, like, 'Motherfucker, they don't do that jerky shit while we're on stage.' The Ramones were definitely like a little gang, and the people around them took pride in being with them – we called Rick, Ricky Ramone."

Joey found it hard-going in places, however: "Some days it was 100 degrees," he explained. "It was kind of tough going on in leather jackets during the day."

Other members didn't mind so much.

"I'm not a big fan of festival tours, but that was probably the most fun I had on the road – aside from Lollapalooza," says CJ. "It was the first time I'd hung out with other musicians, and when you meet people who understand how you are, everyone cuts loose. The girls from The Breeders, the guys from Soundgarden . . . It was an incredible amount of fun. I was considering moving to Australia at one point . . ."

In February, the Ramones hit Japan again – just in time for their

2,000th show in Tokyo. "Soundgarden are coming down," Joey revealed beforehand. "And then, for 2001: The Space Odyssey Show, Smashing Pumpkins are gonna come. As for myself, Bob Dylan is playing at the Budokan – it'll be my first Dylan show."

"At the end, I threw my T-shirts and sweat bands off the stage and mooned the crowd," laughs CJ. "That was probably the most special show. We may have done a couple of extra songs. They had some pretty weird food over there. The weirder it is, the more I want to try it. There was one bar decorated by HR Geiger, and it had a bottle of alcohol with a gutted dead lizard in it. Of course I had to try it, and the guy was like, 'It isn't for sale.' There were scales floating in it. I did a couple of shots for free. It was supposed to do something for your virility.

"I don't know if it did . . ." He laughs again. "You'd have to hunt down one of the girls I was with on that tour."

In March, the band was back in San Francisco and Dallas.

On April 8, 1994, Kurt Cobain died. The Nirvana singer was (indirectly) the single biggest reason for the Ramones' renewed success back at home and in Europe, and his suicide shocked the Ramones as much as anyone.

"People like us because the Ramones have brought the fun back to music," Joey told Jaan Uhelszki for the *Addicted To Noise* website in '94. "We were called stupid for that, but rock'n'roll was always about having fun, not being some serious stiff. Now they all know that less is more.

"Like now you have those bands like Green Day, Offspring, Hole, Nirvana and Soundgarden. A lot of them are really great, and a lot of them stink. Kurt Cobain was real, and it is a loss because he wore his heart on his sleeve. Also, they were a great band [and] they were fun. When I saw Nirvana *Unplugged*, I was blown away by their version of that Bowie song, 'The Man Who Sold The World', which I always loved. It was so dark and lush with the cello. I got to meet those guys recently at an awards party thrown by R.E.M. Dave Grohl seems like the nicest guy, and the bass player is real nice too, but quiet. He's big. He towers over me."

"That's scary," remarked Uhelszki. "How tall are you? 6′ 3?"

"Yeah, 6′ 3," Joey replied. "Sometimes I fluctuate and become 6′ 4. You know how bridges expand in the summer? Heat makes me expand."

In May, the Ramones returned to South America.

In August, they played several shows in Canada. The opening act was the dreadful MTV-friendly Live – a rock band who'd clearly got their stage act together by watching every last clichéd and commercial move on TV, and patently unsuited as a Ramones support. No matter, the Ramones were big-time. There was no place anymore for great hardcore supports like Murphy's Law or even New York's trashy all-girl Lunachicks. Also, Live were on Radioactive.

In September and October, it was the turn of London (Brixton Academy) and Europe. By this point, every Ramones date was expected to be their last. No one thought the band could continue for much longer. Hadn't Johnny said on several occasions the band were going to split up once they'd served 20 years? And hadn't they started in 1974? The fact that this could be the last chance to see a touring institution play live spurred the fans on. In the same way The Rolling Stones were playing to the largest crowds of their career despite being 20 years past their prime (at least), it didn't matter to a teenage Ramones fan or their nostalgic parents who remembered punk from the first time round that the band were a pale imitation of former glories – they wanted to witness living history.

After all, it's not in many tribute bands that you can see two – three, if you like – original members.

In November, the band returned to South America again, this time part of the Acid Chaos tour, with awesome death metal Brazilian band Sepultura (who rocked as hard as even Motorhead in their prime).

"Think The Beatles at Shea Stadium," wrote Uhelszki. "Think The Rolling Stones in Las Vegas. Because that is exactly the kind of pandemonium the Ramones generate when they sell out the 50,000 seat soccer stadiums in Brazil and Argentina."

"This year has probably been our busiest for touring," stated Joey, almost without exaggeration. "We did South America three times this year. We're massive over there. The kids over there are very passionate and they love the Ramones in a way that people used to grasp onto The Beatles. It's that kind of passion and love and admiration and loyalty and devotion. It's like we're a new religion. We do especially well in Portuguese and Spanish speaking countries."

The South Americans called the band Los Ramones, pronounced Ramon-es.

"They sing these football chants and change all the words to 'Ah, ah Ramon-es'," said Joey, awestruck at the fever his band engendered. "It means a feeling that grows strong. The three biggest bands in Argentina are Guns N' Roses, Metallica and the Ramones. We've been there six times."

DEE DEE RAMONE wasn't having too good a time of it, though.

In 1991, he'd played briefly with NYC scum rocker GG Allin (the now dead musician used to throw his own excrement into the audience) on a session that later got released as the *Murder Junkies Rehearsals*, and formed a series of punk bands, the rap direction long forgotten. (Actually, to say Dee Dee ever went "rap" is misleading: *Standing In The Spotlight* is hard rock crossed with novelty.)

"The meanings behind some of his Spikey Tops songs were pretty evident," says Carla Olla, who played bass in the band. "Like 'What About Me?' and 'Why Me?' . . . a lot of it was about not being in the Ramones any more. He was upset about that. He used to quit all the time and they just took him up on it once. He never expected not to be in the band. He would've expected them to call him up, apologise, and everything would be fine . . . but I guess you can only do that for 20 years."

Dee Dee moved back to New York from London on August 28, 1992. "I was trying to hide it, but I was crying," he wrote poignantly in *Poison Heart*. "I think I was crying because I realised I was almost 40 years old and had no home – nowhere to go." Still trying to escape the drugs and his past, he moved to Holland, where he claimed he didn't make a single friend in two years: "To make things worse," he wrote, "the Ramones were still together. They even did a live show on MTV while I was living in Amsterdam. They looked horrible on MTV – so old, tired and angry. It was hard to get that Ramones stamp off your head for some reason. Even my new girlfriend Barbara was a big Ramones fan. She named all her toy dolls and animals Dee Dee when she was in Buenos Aires."

"It was really fun to play with him," Olla continues. "He's got so much energy it's impossible not to have a good time on stage with him. Dee Dee is great, he's just really high maintenance – he needs somebody to do everything for him. He's brilliant at writing songs. He turfs them out really fast. He was a very emotional guy. One of the venues had a bathroom for a dressing room and I didn't want to hang out there, so I went to another bar. He got mad because he'd been there for two hours by himself, so he started throwing beer bottles at my head. That was the end of that band. His only source of income would've been writing songs for the Ramones – that, and royalties."

The bassist continued releasing records on whatever label would take him – 'What About Me' came out as a seven-inch on American Gothic in '93, recorded by his post-Spikey Tops band, The Chinese Dragons, the full-length 'I Hate Freaks Like You' (Rough Trade, 1994) recorded with ICLC (Inter Celestial Light Commune), based in Holland. Sadly, half the songs he now wrote were old Ramones songs with slightly different lyrics or titles. He no longer had the quality control that someone like Daniel or Johnny once supplied. Also, his old band was creaming off his best songs.

In 1997, *Zonked* appeared, featuring guest appearances from Joey Ramone and Lux Interior (The Cramps), with Daniel Rey on guitar, Marky Ramone on drums, and on bass and backing vocals . . . his new wife, Barbara Zampini.

The couple first met in Argentina on November 4, 1994 – he was 42, she was 16. "I freaked out," she told Ramones fan Jari-Pekka Laition after a Ramainz show in Sweden, 2000. "I couldn't stop shaking. I couldn't believe all that was happening to me. Dee Dee was like a god for me. I was such a huge Ramones fan. I couldn't understand when Dee Dee wanted to hang with me." Barbara first listened to the Ramones when she was 12 (a year after Dee Dee left the band). "I didn't think it was possible to meet them, 'cause there was 50,000 people looking for the Ramones in Argentina." The couple married on September 12, 1996.

"This has been a so long tour," she said at the interview's end (speech as reported). "Dee Dee wants be a lot alone also. Dee Dee is a very alone person. He likes to be alone. Sometimes he looks to be lost and far away."

35

We're Outta Here!

"JOHNNY RAMONE WAS the enforcer, and said, 'Let's stick to this plan,' OK? And he was right, but boy it was a drag. We just had to learn to relax, that woulda helped us. The problem was it wasn't that we had a formula, we had a formula but we weren't allowed to use it. All that was considered a burden or excess baggage or undesirable things to put on the album [was thrown away] but there were like 20 different opinions on what we should do – producers, record companies, managers, individual band members, and it all came back to me. Boy, y'know, so it taught me how to write, that's the one thing it did. But it wasn't fun anymore 'cos it was humiliating and painful to always feel this amount of rejection, and nobody else could come up with anything else and for every 10 songs I'd write, they'd choose one and put me through the mill."

It's really rare for the non-creative band member to be the leader.

"I was just too dysfunctional to lead a band. I'm an artist, of whatever kind, and of course I'm not gonna be overly concerned with reality all the time – worrying about equipment getting to the club, 'n' all. My thing is to write the songs for the band . . . but I was really well taken care of, and I always have been. A lot of it maybe I brought upon myself."

It must've been hard for you, being in the middle. Originally, Johnny's your friend and you were a friend of Joey's, and those guys don't even speak to each other.

". . . and Marc! None of 'em! That's why they make me so nervous because you get paranoid around 'em, y'know? If we were like a week in the van – whoa! You might have to pull over and two of us might go at each other, which is ridiculous at our age but that's how we would be."

Have you ever had a fight with them?

"Yeah, everybody's fought in that band."

Blood?

"Yeah. It was really pretty bad, and John is a very tough person, and so is Marc Bell."

(Dee Dee Ramone interviewed by Mark Bannister, 1994)

We're Outta Here!

THE RAMONES PLAYED regularly through 1995.

It was obvious that, sooner rather than later, da bruddas were going to call it a day: despite the growing veneration they attracted in countries like Brazil, Argentina and Japan – and even back at home, in the wake of the respect afforded to them via young pretenders like Rancid, Offspring and Green Day – they couldn't translate their burgeoning popularity into record sales. It was the usual Catch 22 situation: the more famous a band gets and the more of an institution it becomes, the less anyone's interested in new material. Johnny understood that – which is why Ramones sets over the years would draw the majority of their content from the first three albums, and three – maybe four – tracks from whatever album had just been released.

Crowds knew what to expect from a Ramones show: the pinhead with the "Gabba Gabba Hey" sign, the "1-2-3-4", the relentless barrage of vaguely tuneful hard rock songs, the guitarists at the front like twin gunners, Joey hunched over the microphone like a giant praying mantis, Marky hammering up a storm at the back, 'Blitzkrieg Bop', 'Sheena', 'Teenage Lobotomy', 'Rockaway Beach' . . . you could never accuse Johnny of not putting the fans' interests first. The Ramones appreciated their fans, more than most bands. They'd never had any hits. They'd never had much radio airplay . . . their 22-year career was kept afloat almost entirely by their live audience.

"As far as my favourite songs to perform live," Johnny told Maggie St Thomas in 2001, "most of the songs we did live were my favourite. If they weren't, I would have gotten rid of them. I learned very early on to try to never let your fans down. It is the fans that have given me a lot of my happiness . . ."

Perhaps CJ was right, all the Ramones needed was to be themselves on record – but no one cared anymore. If you were a fan, what were you going to play: *Rocket To Russia* or *Brain Drain*, *Ramones* or *Mondo Bizarro*? Maybe the Ramones didn't know what "being themselves" meant: they had the uniform, the well-oiled touring machine and the loud, fast guitars . . . on stage they knew their business inside out. Studios didn't interest them – and anyone who's ever been inside a recording studio will sympathise with Johnny's determination to record as fast as possible: they're deathly dull places to performers, the antithesis of rock'n'roll.

So the Ramones toured in 1995 like it was 1985 or 1978 again, only in bigger venues, and sometimes more exotic locations . . . Oslo, Amsterdam, six nights in Buenos Aires, six nights in Tokyo, Salem, Salisbury, Nagoya, Sapporo, Sweden, Belgium . . .

"We saw Dee Dee when we were in Amsterdam," Joey told journalist James Bonisteel, before talking about new bands. "My favourite is Hole because Courtney Love is totally unpredictable, spontaneous, and primal. She's her own person and I like her music. It's genuine. And I always did like Nirvana and Soundgarden."

Dee Dee also liked Hole: "I'm writing with a sense of humour," he told Mark Bannister. "It's not a parody of the Ramones. My own private world, and a lot of these ideas I got from the [first] Hole album *Pretty On The Inside*. I started analysing punk rock, the rules and regulations from that album, and it's like 'everyone made me that way'. I'm writing the truth about my current situation, and there's a little anger that comes in a spurt about the Ramones. I go, 'Dirty bastards/Get out of my way/Freaks of nature/Gabba Gabba Hey' [from 'We're A Creepy Family'] – and that's a goof. They'd laugh, too – but they can't come up with that sort of mentality."

The Ramones tour of Europe took in the usual mid-summer festival season, including a date with Offspring and NOFX in Belgium on June 24; while in London, they headlined two nights at the (relatively small) Astoria Theatre. Pete Gofton, drummer with post-Riot Grrrl pop band Kenickie, was one of the many musicians who supported the Ramones that year: "Not only did they kick arse," he recalls, "but they were very nice, especially Joey. They had a smoke-free environment backstage, and did a few 'Hey ho let's go' vocal warm-ups before they went on."

Now that most of the fire and pizzazz and fervour had gone, mainstream America embraced the band – the Ramones played a variety of TV shows in '95, including *Howard Stern*, *David Letterman*, *The Tonight Show* and the *MTV Movie Awards*.

Helped by journalist Joan Tarshis, Joey started writing for the Addicted To Noise website – over the next few years he conducted a series of interviews with punk bands like Offspring and Rancid wherein politics and music were discussed. And tour stories: "Our drummer eats bugs for money," he told Offspring singer Dexter Holland. "It's rough singing and drinking Yoo Hoo," he revealed, after Holland queried him about a Ramones rider that included 10 cases of the sickly-sweet drink, "because of all the mucus. I had to give up drinking Yoo Hoo. It's a sticky situation."

On May 1, while watching ESPN in a hotel lobby in Raleigh, NC, Johnny announced to fan Rick Johnson he was thinking of retiring. "We want to go out while we're still good," the guitarist explained. "I don't want to be up there not being able to play as well as before so we're going to stop. We'll play the places we want to go to again – Europe, Japan, South America – then play some shows in New York, and that's it."

"My name is Donna Gaines. I grew up in the surfing town of Rockaway Beach, Queens where I hung out, sniffed glue, and ate at pizza places. I became a Ramones fan in the early Eighties – being suburban we don't catch on so fast. Everyone has their own favourite Ramone. I was a fan of Dee Dee, and when I went to graduate school, I wore Converse sneakers and my hair like his every day. In 1996, I wrote an article for The Village Voice *called* Ramones: A Love Story. *The next week, at a show at the Continental, Joey held up a copy of the paper and dedicated 'Now I Wanna Sniff Some Glue' to 'Doctor Donna Gaines and* The Village Voice *because this is the best fucking thing ever written about my band'.*

Can you describe the individual members for me?

"Marky, I knew from the Voidoids. He's one of New York's best ever drummers – Maureen Tucker [Velvet Underground] had retired and Clem Burke [Blondie] had moved to California, but we had Marc. His father Peter Bell is a highly regarded arbitrator lawyer in labour, so I knew of him via doctor friends . . .

"I was scared of meeting Johnny. Everyone told me Johnny was mean, but he wasn't – he's really nice and professional, shows up exactly on time, answers everything you want. He was wearing a T-shirt saying 'Kill A Commie For Mommy' to try and freak me out, being the reporter for The Village Voice *– I was like, dude, I belong to NRA, my dad is a Pat Buchanan supporter, I do this for fun. I asked him to sign an autograph for a nine-year-old kid with dialysis, and he said sure. I found him to be a perfect gentleman. I was afraid, he's so feral when playing guitar."*

I can imagine.

"Then I met Joey, the lead singer. I thought I had a special bond with him – maybe even a girlie crush, not sexual. I'd heard he loved doo wop and girl group stuff, so I made him a tape to try and manipulate him and get him to cover all the songs I loved, Chantelles, Ronettes, Shangri-La's, Frankie Lymon. Because I was so nervous, I went and got a piece of pizza beforehand – it's the holy sacrament of the Ramones. But when I got there he opened the door and it was like a mystical experience. He put me at ease right away.

"He'd become a rock star, and I'd turned into an attractive woman; but when I was a kid I was fat on diet pills when I was eight, with three fathers and an unpleasant home life . . . and he'd had some of that too. We'd both conquered some of our demons, but we had scars. We had a trust that cut through the bullshit. There were many people much closer, I wasn't up there with Arturo and Daniel Rey, but I was there in his heart. He was very kind, generous and supportive to me

– he helped me to get sober. He helped me over a broken heart. We could talk about family stuff, growing up, love stuff. A year later, I found out how sick he was – he didn't tell anyone.

"Every summer, I would come out to East Hampton for surfing, and he would visit. We'd see bands, go to the beach and hang out with his family, his dad and Nancy. His dad [Noel Hyman] died six months before him. He was devastated. He said, 'Donna, that was my whole life.' They were very close.

"CJ, I love. He's the most normal one, which is not saying much. He's my homeboy. He has three sisters, like hairdressers, all gorgeous and rock'n'roll and everyone falls in love with them. He's from Long Island, and loves tattoos and bikes, and is younger than the Ramones, and he was crucial into segueing them into the latter-day fan base. He's very family-orientated, libertarian. He is a righteous dude. He was cleaning out the mess at the World Trade Centre. Joey's liberal. Johnny is right wing, bordering on fascist. Dee Dee is fixated on Germany with his mother. CJ's politics are more like mine: we like guns, hate the government, we're populist, don't like Democrats any more than Republicans – we hate them all. We're right wing rock'n'roll bohemian outlaws, like Hell's Angels. Johnny's more hegemonic."

What about Dee Dee . . .?

"I met him at the Chelsea Hotel. We had a lot in common because of our paramilitary upbringing, and we both had dachshunds growing up. Dee Dee is childlike and utterly brilliant. He is the genius of the Ramones, the nuclear core of the Ramones. That's not to take away anything of the intensity of the chemistry of those involved – Marky, Johnny and Joey are very intense, and Tommy is the guardian angel, but Dee Dee is the centrifugal force. I'm a Dee Dee loyalist, even though Joey and CJ are more my buds. It's retarded. The whole thing is retarded. It's the Ramones."

(Author's interview with Doctor Donna Gaines, sociologist, 2002)

THE RAMONES DECIDED to put out one last album, Johnny declaring that if it didn't sell enough copies, the band would break up. In the same year, Joey was diagnosed with (incurable) lymphatic cancer. The singer had been poorly, and in and out of hospital most of his adult life, but he always firmly believed he would get better.

In a bitter irony, the Ramone who most embodied the spirit of the eternal teenager was now faced by the stark reality of his own mortality.

And, of course, he kept his illness a secret – to have behaved in any other way would have been un-Ramonelike.

The first song on *¡Adios Amigos!* is a Tom Waits cover 'I Don't Wanna Grow Up' (another "don't wanna" song!) taken at a typically fast

Ramones pace. It's a defiant opening, a straightforward denial of the facts: in the outside world, the Ramones grew up a long time ago. It's also a great cover, a thousand miles away from 1993's *Acid Eaters*: Joey's rich baritone coming into its own, and the guitars as turbulent, hard-edged and harmonic as any fan could desire.

" 'I Don't Want To Grow Up' was an isolationist variation on the Peter Pan dream of eternal youth," wrote David Fricke in the *Anthology* sleeve-notes, "a prayer to be taken away from war-torn matrimony, suck-city television, a world in mad, black flux. The Ramones saw plenty of themselves in there: 'I don't wanna be filled with doubt/I don't wanna be a good boy scout/I don't wanna have to learn to count/I don't wanna have the biggest amount/I don't wanna grow up.' Right down to the wire, in a career that defied expectation, misconception, and pitfalls, with a music so simple and pure that anybody could make it (and many soon did), the Ramones proved that if there was no such thing as eternal youth, there was a kind of eternal life – if you could be bothered to fight for it."

The reason *¡Adios Amigos!* sounds better than anyone expected after *Acid Eaters* is because of the production. Too late, the Ramones had been given the producer they deserved – Daniel Rey. He did a fine job at Baby Monster Studios, bringing back some of the spirit of earlier albums.

Even so, the album is decidedly up and down.

For a start (and perhaps this was because of Joey's illness rather than any ulterior motives), CJ sings lead on four songs (including a version of 'The Crusher', dredged up from Dee Dee's previously ridiculed *Standing In The Spotlight* album). Dee Dee himself sang on one (the overtly Stooges-sounding 'Born To Die In Berlin'), for reasons that didn't need to be explained to any Ramones fan . . . it was the final song on the final album, and he should have been there all along. The bass on the 'I Love You' cover, meanwhile, sounds about as un-Ramones as it ever got.

Dee Dee and Daniel both played a major part in the making of *¡Adios Amigos!*: they co-wrote five songs, Dee Dee teaming up with ICLC's John Carco on a sixth ('Berlin'). Each time, they almost brought to life the old Ramones – if they didn't get there, it wasn't for want of trying. 'Makin' Monsters For My Friends' (a track lifted from Dee Dee's then-current album) and 'The Crusher' bubble with good-natured humour, while 'Cretin Family' isn't a lame rehash of old lyrics that its title suggests, but a smart poke at the Ramones Myth from one of its main participants.

"Cretin family/Cretin family/Everyone's against me," Dee Dee wrote in a direct reversal of the old "We accept you/We accept you/One of us".

Now Dee Dee was claiming that, far from being a home for all creeps, misfits and outsiders, the Ramones were turning into an exclusive club, part of the mainstream. The song also has fine vocals from CJ. (Although – sorry – he's still no Joey Ramone.)

'Take The Pain Away' is probably the truest indication of Dee Dee's state of mind, with its lines "I am running away from myself/There's too many demons around here now".

The album's stand-out is the single 'Life's A Gas' – its title (and chorus) might have been the cheekiest steal [from T. Rex, duh] since George Harrison borrowed 'He's So Fine' for 'My Sweet Lord', but Joey turns in a poignant vocal *tour de force* over suitably chiming Rey guitars that absolves the song of all crimes.

Joey's other contribution, the pure early Sixties girl group pop of 'She Talks To Rainbows' (the song was later rightly covered by Ronnie Spector) is almost as great – a lovely singalong lullaby that would've fitted right in on *Pleasant Dreams*. "It was my first metaphysical composition," Joey told *Making Music* in August 1985. "I was hanging out at Daniel's house and there was a big electrical storm coming in and I . . . received this song. At first I wasn't sure it was meant for me – maybe it was meant for David Byrne or someone. But no, it was meant for me. And I was very pleased."

Unfortunately, these songs are offset by Marky Ramone/Skinny Bones' rather ordinary 'Have A Nice Day' (where the drums are mixed far too loud), and CJ's fine, but completely non-Ramones, 'Scattergun' and 'Got A Lot To Say'. Indeed, with his vocals on the former, da bruddas sound exactly like a Seattle grunge band. It's also a shame that the cover to the final Ramones album is the worst in their entire history: another Kurfirst-commissioned painting, this one shows – er – two dinosaurs wearing sombreros. And that's it. The band with the most perfect image in the history of rock – an image so perfect that they didn't deviate from it once in 22 years, and would send members home if they turned up wearing anything different – sign off with a cover that shows two dinosaurs wearing Mexican hats.

They're not even particularly cute dinosaurs.

THE PRESS REACTION was sympathetic when the album appeared in July.

"The commercial revival of punk rock seems to have revitalised the band," wrote *Stereo Review*. "The Ramones are back sounding like the Ra-mones. And make no mistake, *¡Adios Amigos!* sounds *exactly* like the Ra-mones."

"If *¡Adios Amigos!* is to be the Ramones' last," wrote *Rolling Stone* critic Matt Diehl, "at least they're going out with a bang. The album contains some of their angriest, most powerful material in years, reflecting the alienation of wizened outsiders rather than the snotty adolescent rebellion that had become a Ramones cliché."

"It was kind of weak," CJ says now. "It wasn't as good as it could have been. Probably what happened was everyone knew retirement was coming up and things got through which wouldn't usually have done . . . I realise now that the band cared, but they were in a position where some things were more important – bills need to be paid. I wish I'd started writing songs a little sooner, because I was real happy with the two I contributed. I felt they were closer to original Ramones songs than almost anything else."

Johnny declared it to be the finest Ramones album since *Too Tough To Die*, but was also determined it would be the last: "You see famous bands like The Who and The Rolling Stones, they go on and on and they're so far past their prime," he sneered in *Making Music*. "These people can't deal with life without the attention. If you had mandatory retirement for rock'n'rollers over 40, you'd have a lot of people committing suicide.

"Did The Who have any intentions of still playing in their forties," he asked, overlooking the fact that his own 40th birthday had come and gone several years previously, "with Pete Townshend getting up there with an acoustic guitar and another guitar player playing behind him?" Unlike the Ramones, of course, where Daniel only played lead on the albums. "It's pathetic," he continued. "Early punk rock was aware of that. I just want to deal with life without being in a rock'n'roll band."

"We don't want to overstay our welcome," Joey commented, the man who lived for rock'n'roll. His next comment is more telling. "Actually, music is my salvation – it excites me like nothing else."

"Johnny never thought the Ramones would be big," explains video director George Seminara, "so he settled on making a living. Johnny ensured that it would be a good living, probably better than many bands with hit records. The Ramones were very smart. They owned everything, and made a shit load of cash on T-shirts and drum sticks. Johnny's fatalistic attitude stymied their career, though. He was happy playing the same five songs even though the venues got bigger and bigger. He ran a really rough ship, for a couple of years they were playing over 300 shows [not quite – Ed] . . . these are guys in their forties, remember, and Johnny was older than Joey. I'm almost 41. I couldn't do it their way – it would have to be like U2 in a private helicopter, or frozen cryogenically like the Stones. At least they're not playing every damn night, getting in a van with four guys who can't stand each other, driving for 10–12 hours."

"I don't need to sell as many records as Madonna to be happy," explained Joey. "We tour all year round. Touring is our livelihood. We enjoy it, but it's gruelling. Twenty-one years with the clan takes a toll on you. I'm tired of travelling all the time. Someone should ask us on Lollapalooza so we can have a nice high-profile tour . . ."

¡Adios Amigos! spent two weeks in the charts.

It was too little too late. After an elongated farewell tour that lasted most of 1995, the band split . . . only for Soundgarden to offer them a slot on the sixth Lollapalooza festival.

. . . WHAT'S AMAZING IS that it wasn't even commonly known until the last few years that Johnny and Joey didn't speak.

"It didn't need to be known, that's why. It's pretty impressive they were able to keep it that discreet for so long, because it suggests – or shows – they understood they were stronger as a whole than apart. That whatever divisions there were, the band had to go on. And that this was all they had, that they'd invested so much in it that to stop now would have been like throwing away those first five, eight, 10 years of hard work and bullshit and insults, literally insults. Going out on tour, opening for Black Sabbath and having shit thrown at you. It's crazy enough that someone put that bill together. Actually, it was kind of genius, when you consider how close they were in their own way. But if you put that much into it, you look at where you are and you go, 'Do I just quit? Or do I keep going? Do I set that goal and not stop?' The Ramones represent the truth of the fact that you're never too old to rock'n'roll as long as you believe in what you're doing, and you can do it with a purity and conviction. The age of your band is irrelevant. Rock'n'roll is not for the young. It's for people who refuse not to give a shit."

That's the beauty of them doing that Tom Waits cover.

"Yeah, 'I Don't Want To Grow Up'. Perfect! They started by celebrating the most absurd aspects of teenage life. Sniffing glue, chasing girls around Queens, going to the beach. They took all that stuff and showed how timeless the basic content and emotions in those songs were – and yet to do it with such joy and to do it with such force, it's such exaltation. Who hasn't wanted to beat on some guy with a bat because they're a pain in the ass?"

(Author's interview with David Fricke, 2002)

THE ROUND OF farewell dates was relentless.

Over the course of just 10 days in November '95, the Ramones played Louisville, Cincinnati, Cleveland, Muskegon, Saginaw, Hamilton, Verdun,

Lewiston – on some, they suffered the indignity of opening for upstarts Pearl Jam and also White Zombie. The band saw the situation differently: these bands had sold millions of albums. Their respect was the recognition the Ramones had always sought from the mainstream.

After 22 years, they'd won through.

"Our popularity remained pretty much the same throughout," Johnny clarified in *Scram*. "We made more money each year. And there was no question of slipping in popularity. You start off, and I know from watching other bands, you're gonna do what you do in a five year period. That's it. You go on more than five years and you're just treading water. You're very dumb if you don't see that. The Beatles were there from '64 to '69. Where've The Rolling Stones gone since Brian Jones has left the band? They've gotten bigger. David Bowie might've gotten bigger, but what has he done that's any good since, say, *Aladdin Sane*? Say *Diamond Dogs*. Maybe it's his last decent album."

"I flew through New Orleans," recalls Kevin Patrick. "It was one of the first shows into this five or six date run with Pearl Jam. They invited Joey to come onstage and do 'Sonic Reducer' [Dead Boys song], which ended up on a Pearl Jam Christmas single. It was there that Eddie started to forge his friendship with the band. He eventually became very friendly, and still is, with John. Eddie would've been happy to be friends with any of the Ramones – he loved them.

"Something that surprised me about John," Kevin adds, "is that when he relocated to LA after the band broke up, he became very star-struck. He loves hanging around with famous rock musicians and film people. I even say to him, 'Johnny – you've turned into such a groupie.' "

The final London show took place on February 3, 1996, at Brixton Academy, after a couple of shows in Italy had been cancelled at the start of a month-long European tour due to Joey's worsening health.

Then it was back to the States, for a round of shows with The Independents that culminated in three nights in New York City – including two at the relatively tiny Coney Island High. Fans and friends of the band felt this was probably it, the Ramones were surely going to sign off in the city that right from the earliest days had nurtured and supported them, when everyone else was averting their faces.

"The Ramones were very much of the period of when America and the rest of the world was looking to NYC for inspiration," says Ida Langsam. "Those of us who live here forget how influential New York is. Anything that happens in the rest of the world you can find in New York – politics, fashion, music, commerce. The early photos of the Ramones in the subway are so perfect. I live in Forest Hills, and I know the High School they went to, and the block they used to hang out on. I didn't know them from that neighbourhood, but the subway is the train that I ride back and forth every day. It's a very comforting image, the idea they could live down the street from me. I think that's how everyone felt. They were very regular guys, and it made people feel very comfortable with and around them."

The Ramones' New York fans had reckoned without the pull of the band's fanatical South American support, though – and the lure of the almighty dollar. So, in March, they went back there one last time for three shows in Sao Paulo, plus one in Rio de Janeiro and one at Buenos Aires' River Plate Stadium (with old allies and friends Motorhead and Iggy Pop). . . .

So *another* farewell tour needed to be arranged: Indianapolis, Chicago, Kalamazoo, Detroit, Cleveland, Allentown, Pittsburgh, Rochester and Albany . . . two more nights at Coney Island High . . . Little Rock, Memphis, Atlanta, Birmingham – and *then* the final tour started. CJ, however, had already arranged to travel across America on his Harley-Davidson a long time before the offer to play Lollapalooza came in. Instead, he travelled from show to show on his bike.

"We had an agreement," remarks CJ, "that I would be fined a week's pay if I missed a show. I didn't. I'm not sure anyone ever had money docked. Johnny might have threatened it a couple of times, just to keep people in focus.

"I refused to do it at first," he continues, "because in 1992, I'd said that in the summer of '96 I would be going cross country on my bike. Plus, we were supposed to be retiring in February. Then I thought these poor bastards had never been given the credit they deserve or made to feel they were part of anything. I thought it was a good opportunity for them to meet the biggest bands of the day [Rancid, Metallica, Soundgarden, Screaming Trees] and see the influence they'd had – and I was right. When Johnny, Joey and Marky started hanging out with these guys, they realised, 'My god, we gave birth to virtually the entire rock'n'roll scene in the US.'

"It was a good way to be sent off," he continues, "knowing there were a lot of people who really did know how good they were – and it had nothing to do with radio play or sales. In spite of the entire media industry, the Ramones grew, flourished and fucking conquered the entire music industry under their own power. They fucking outlived everybody."

CJ fulfilled a personal ambition when he was asked to play 'Ty Cobb' [named after a famous US baseball player] on stage with Soundgarden: "They gave me the tape 15 minutes before we went on," he remembers, "so I ran out to my friend's pick-up truck – I only had my bike – and learnt the song. It was a great experience."

"I knew it was coming to an end," says Marky. "I wanted to breathe and start playing with my own band. I already wrote a whole album before the Ramones broke up, but I would never have a band while they were together. CJ had his own band and I thought that was very disrespectful. Joey too, but that's his own business. When band-members start forming their own groups, you can tell there's something wrong."

DIDN'T SOUNDGARDEN ASK the Ramones to come on tour?

"It was their initiative. Metallica had to approve, but it was because of Soundgarden that the Ramones got on the bill."

Hadn't the Ramones retired by that point?

"No, Johnny never set a specific date at all. Joey was sick already. We didn't know. He didn't tell us, but he was saying we had to stop. And then everybody else – well, Johnny, at least – agreed that it was enough. It was supposed to end in Argentina, on March 16 at the River Plate soccer stadium. Right before that, the offer to do Lollapalooza came, so they told the Argentinians, and they said fine, but you have to come back and do the last show here. But when we were on Lollapalooza, Joey was saying, 'No way, no way, no way.' They showed up with sacks of letters from fans saying they have to come back. And, uh, they made all kinds of offers to the band [rumoured to be in the vicinity of one million dollars for one last tour] but Joey said no. [It was rumoured he refused because he knew how much it upset Johnny, to have the money sitting there, untouched.] Everybody got kind of mad. We didn't know he was sick."

What was the final Ramones show like?

"Well, it was a fucking rush, because it was supposed to happen in another venue. And that day it got changed. Maybe it affected the film crew more than anybody else. It didn't affect us that much. We were used to that, showing up at a venue and doing the show. Usually, I had good relationships with lighting crews at different venues around the world, and on that day especially they helped any way they could. Like I said before, everybody loved working with the Ramones because we were such a professional show."

(Author's interview with Arturo Vega)

THE RAMONES PLAYED their final concert at Hollywood Palace, LA on August 6, 1996 with a few guest stars lending support and grabbing their share of the Ramones limelight: "First off," says CJ bluntly, "doing it on the West Coast in LA was ludicrous, a real slap in the face for NYC. We were touted as the epitome of the New York music scene . . ."

"I wanted to do the job the best I could do," recalls Marky. "The last day was goodbye, good luck and take care. I did the show, got interviewed and went back to New York. That was it."

Of course, the show was recorded for posterity.

It was later released as a video/CD package on Eagle. Surprisingly, *We're Outta Here!* is rather presentable, despite having another cover that failed to feature the band – this time, a decent rip-off of legendary hot rod artist Big "Daddy" Roth's cartoon style. The inner CD booklet featured photos of the guest stars – Soundgarden, Eddie Vedder, Lemmy Kilmister, Rancid, Dee Dee Ramone – unfortunately mainly larger than the band themselves. Minor quibbles aside . . .

The nearly two-hour-long video contains footage of the Ramones dating back to 1974 and on the road in the Eighties, plus interviews with fans like Jello Biafra, *The Simpsons* appearance, and some right-wing comments from Johnny. Producer Daniel Rey did a knockout job on the actual CD – cover versions of Saturday Morning Kids' TV themes ('Spiderman') and Dave Clark Five songs (a duet on 'Any Way You Want It' that unaccountably closes the show) aside. It's not in the same ballpark as *It's Alive*, of course – but it's a fine send-off nonetheless, the sound tight and tough, and Joey's voice tuneful and in control.

Almost as good, but considerably shorter, is the Ed Stasium-produced *Greatest Hits Live* (Radioactive, 1996), recorded in New York – although whether Ramones' fans needed two live albums, just a couple of years after the previous one, is questionable. Irritatingly enough, for Ramones completists, *Greatest Hits Live* contains two previously unreleased studio tracks – the Ramones' own version of the Motorhead tribute, 'R.A.M.O.N.E.S.', sung by CJ, and the Dave Clark song. Who knows what contractual obligations the Ramones were filling by releasing that?

A POPULAR RAMONES MYTH has it that after Johnny played his very final chord with the Ramones, he ran off stage and handed his Mosrite to Eddie Vedder saying, "Here, take it. I don't need it any more." A touching story, and there's only one thing wrong with it. It runs contrary to Johnny's value system to give something away. Also, it was Daniel Rey that Johnny handed the Mosrite over to, in 1997 – in exchange for a substantial sum of money.

"I have Johnny's main guitar, the white Mosrite," confirms the producer. "When I was working with them, I told Johnny if he ever wants to sell his guitar, sell it to me. He said, 'OK, when I retire, I don't want to keep that thing.' Then when he retired he called me and asked me if I was serious, and I said hell yeah. Eddie Vedder wanted it, and a few other people wanted it, so obviously the price went up. But I also told John that if he ever needed it, it would still be in the family.

"Did it cost much?" Daniel laughs, and stops to consider his answer. "Well, put it this way . . . I had to sell about 10 guitars to buy it – and I'm a collector."

"DID DANIEL TELL you about the guitar, the Mosrite? Do you know Johnny wants to buy it back?'

He does?

"Johnny sold it cheap. He was like, 'I'm selling my equipment. I've sold half the stuff to Eddie Vedder, I've sold half to other people.' "

That's not what Daniel says. He said it cost a fair amount . . . oh, I see what you're saying.

"Most of those guys don't live in the real rock'n'roll world because I am telling you, that guitar is worth easily 20 or 30 times what Daniel paid for it, or more. It's Thor's hammer."

I can't believe I didn't ask Daniel to show it to me.

"I played that guitar a lot. It's a great guitar. Piece of shit – feels like a piece of balsawood, it's lighter than hell, but it's the hammer of the gods and Johnny sold it for what I consider relatively cheaply to Daniel Rey and now, of course, he wants it back. Japanese buyers, anyone in the world is going to want that guitar. And now the Ramones are in the Rock'N'Roll Hall Of Fame? Please – that's the guitar. They need that guitar. That's the guitar that started punk rock."

It's not the guitar.

"Well, no, there was the blue one and there was the . . ."

The original guitars were stolen.

"Yeah, and I know where to."

You do?

"You live in New York long enough – this shit turns up. But it's the guitar in Rock'N'Roll High School. *It's the guitar that people saw. It's the Johnny Ramone guitar."*

(Author's interview with George Tabb)

"THE RAMONES WEREN'T the most likeable people, but we were fun too. We weren't a vindictive, hateful band. We always tried to get people enjoying themselves. There is a lot of hate today and the Ramones are more necessary than ever. Even in music – the hip-hop and the rap – it's such shit. There's no rhyme. There are no choruses. It's just bullshit fake thumping drum machine crap. There's so much hate and uptightness and shootings – enough already. When's it going to end? It's going to get to the point where we'll all end up killing each other and there won't be anyone left on the planet, you know?

"The Ramones fought and bickered and argued, but so did a lot of other bands. We were family. We were closer than a family was. We were brothers – brothers fight. They make movies out of it. That's how it is. But we had some decent values, you know?"

(Author's interview with Marky Ramone, 2002)

36

Ramones: An American Band

"THE RAMONES MAY very well be THE classic American rock band. There are a lot of great American bands of every era – Gene Vincent & The Bluecats, The Grateful Dead from 1966 through whatever year you want to pick. But the Ramones are THE classic American rock band because everything we recognise as being great about American music was boiled down to its clean and unmistakable essence in what they did.

"Now that I've lived here for the past 20 years, as far as I'm concerned, New York is the classic American city because we have everything that is spread around everywhere else. The Ramones were exactly the same way. You can find elements of what they were in Cleveland, even in 1975, with the stuff that the Pere Ubu guys were doing, and The Dead Boys, you go to Iggy Pop and the MC5 up in Detroit, and The Doors, to an extent, in LA in '67. You can talk about any of that stuff, but it all came together and was balled up in a perfect undeniable bullet in what the Ramones did. And they were all of it at once without any of the extra stuff that makes it come undone.

"Having hits and being heard are not exactly the same thing. The Ramones did not get on the radio because radio was scared, they didn't understand, and by the time . . . It would've been interesting to see if the Ramones would have got on the radio in 1966, because if you think of the garage punk records that were hits then, 'Talk Talk' by The Music Machine, 'I Had Too Much To Dream Last Night' by The Electric Prunes, some of the stuff they covered on that covers album [*Acid Eaters*], the Ramones were not making music that extreme. It's just that the end result was almost like white light. Everything just boiled down . . . like the Velvets, you know? There's the real precedent, The Velvet Underground. A band that had taken out all the blues influences and cut the music and the songs and the voice down to a pure New York heart. They had more of an art thing going on than the Ramones did, but they didn't get on the radio either.

"The Ramones had to work for a living. They were a real touring band. The Ramones took their thing to each person individually through the years and that's why we're talking about them now, whereas . . . How much time are we going to spend talking about Journey and Styx?" – David Fricke

"Sure, they're an American band. One of the greatest American rock'n'-roll bands ever, and important – a big influence on music and the industry and culture. Music wise, they helped promote a very heavy important revolution. It was like the reverse of The Day The Music Died when Buddy Holly died, Elvis went into the army, Gene Vincent screwed up and Eddie Cochran died, and then we got Frankie Avalon and the guys with the sweaters and stuff. So we went into this bland pop period, and then the Ramones blew the roof off the sucker.

"The Ramones had a cultural effect like The Beatles on *Ed Sullivan* – the culture expanded and exploded. It really helped to rip open some new possibilities as to whether the music industry knew what to put out or not, because that generation of A&R got caught off guard –18 months after saying they'd never sign that sort of music, they were all coming to the clubs trying to sign anything without having a clue what the music was about because it had become trendy. That influenced alt-radio and that, in turn, influenced culture. Their mode of dress, also, brought in a rustic, underplayed James Dean look – as opposed to the hippie look. The only American bands we have that intense are The Beach Boys and The Doors. The Ramones are part of that trio." – David Kessel

"They're the most American band ever. It's their love of pop culture, their understanding of Americana, their organic intellectual *par excellence*." – Donna Gaines

"The Ramones are uniquely American in the way Americans have this 'I can do it' concept in the face of adversity – 'I can become a sex God even if I look like Joey Ramone'. What was he thinking? How did he even think he could become a lead singer?" – George Seminara

"Oh yeah, we are. Like The Beatles are an English band, and the Stones are an English band, and Cream are an English band. We are an American band. Exactly. We love the country. It has a lot of faults, it's still a great country and we'll always stick by it. There are a lot of things that need to be corrected, but the US has helped a lot of countries too. Whether it's military or monetary. And then there are things that I disagree with, but that's my right as an American. That's why we have the right to vote and the right to air our opinions. People died for that right too.

"The Ramones couldn't have come from anywhere else except from New York – the excitement, the attitudes, the street noises, the bars, the drugs – the fast lane of it all. You live in New York you become a fast-paced maniac. That's the whole thing." – Marky Ramone

ADDENDA 1

Don't Worry About Me

"IF YOU LOOK at most Ramones fans, you'll find that most of them come from dysfunctional families like me. I could never be a part of the jocks because I was 4' 11 in the 11th grade. I could never be one of the freaks because I didn't take that many drugs. I could never be one of the preppies because I didn't have the money or the clothes. I couldn't be part of this gang, that gang – but there was always the Ramones.

"That's why I'd wear a different Ramones shirt every day of the week. No matter what town I was in – if my parents went somewhere like Lake Tahoe, if some girl was wearing a Ramones shirt, I would say 'hi' to her and she'd say 'hi' and you have a friend. My first band, Roach Motel, started because I met other guys with Ramones shirts. All my friends in college? Ramones shirts.

"That was the best thing the Ramones did. They gave a lot of people a sense of identity. They helped a lot of us kids identify with something and kept us alive. They sang the suicidal lyrics for us so we didn't have to really go and off ourselves. Songs like 'Here Today, Gone Tomorrow' – you heard the real pain and lived vicariously through that. Maybe if it wasn't the Ramones, it would have been something else, but no – they came at the exact right time and helped a lot of people, especially me."

(Interview with George Tabb, Ramones fan)

"JOEY WOULD SAY his three favourite things in the world were having a dump, having sex, and being on stage with the Ramones," laughs George Seminara.

After the Ramones split in 1996, their music began to get more and more recognition – perhaps it was easier to fete a band whose recorded output could no longer further tarnish the image. Or maybe it was a case of, you don't know what you've got until it's gone. Everyone assumed that the Ramones would be around forever: one of life's constants, like *The Simpsons* and the new football season. Suddenly, they were gone. It was like losing one of the family.

Tribute bands and tribute albums sprang up around the world – Ne Luumäet, Screeching Weasel, The Vindictives, Acid Eaters from Holland, The Cabrones from Florida, the Gabba Gabba Heys from California, The Rämouns from Germany, Carbona Not Glue from Scotland, The Joeys from Australia, The Cretins from Sweden.

Green Day called kids up to play 'Blitzkrieg Bop' on stage with them, taking for granted that everyone knows the Ramones. 'Blitzkrieg Bop' was also played between innings at World Series games: Ramones achieving Bay City Rollers status, 25 years on. And Joey himself was recognised wherever he went.

"We went to LA together for *The Drew Carey Show*," says journalist and friend Rachel Felder. "He hadn't been there since the band broke up. It didn't dawn on me what the effect of walking down Melrose with Joey would be. It was unbelievable. People were screaming out of cars. Another time, we went to see Blondie play a reunion show at a theatre at the back of Madison Square Garden. He got like a standing ovation just walking to his seat.

"Joey loved popcorn," she continues. "The challenge was that he'd want to eat popcorn and then have dinner. We got to the premiere of one of his movies late, and then there was the popcorn, and then there was who was going to pay for the popcorn, and then we sat down. And all I could think was, 'How would you feel if Joey Ramone sat in front of you? There goes the view . . .'

"He loved movies," she adds, "smart-ass mainstream comedy movies like *Analyse This* and *Meet The Parents*. We would never see art house films – just mainstream Hollywood things. He was into his coffee. His apartment was a mess but there would always be the good coffee beans and the good coffee maker."

The feuds between the ex-Ramones didn't diminish. In fact, they increased. There was a hilarious Howard Stern show where Marky phoned to harangue Joey for allegedly calling him a drunk. Marky referred to Joey's obsessive/compulsive disorder – which was supposed to be a secret – and Joey suggested that Marky was mad with him because he'd curtailed his income by breaking up the Ramones. It was classic brutal dysfunctional family stuff. Marky hit back by asking Joey if the Prozac was kicking in, so Joey started telling Howard how everyone at Lollapalooza would laugh at Marky behind his back because he wore a hairpiece. Marky countered by saying everyone made fun of Joey because he was fat. "Well, you know," said Joey. "Weight is something you can always lose, but hair, you can't get back." It was very spiteful and childish, and highly entertaining for everyone except the two combatants: Stern was in shock half the time, but that didn't stop him from airing the row.

"There was a lot of animosity between Joey and Marky," George Seminara confirms, "because Johnny had convinced everyone that Joey was lying about his sickness, and that Joey was doing everyone out of a lot of money by faking it."

Rumours started to fly around about Joey's sexuality, as the singer remained unmarried: "There was a rumour last year that Joey was gay," says Seminara, "and Arturo was his lover. That wasn't true. Basically, I think he was so burned by the whole Linda incident, he felt real fear in committing himself.

"He was a big fan of fun, cool stuff – monster movies, science fiction, *Jurassic Park*, the Disney movies, he was well in touch with his inner child," the video director continues. "He was also a really good guy, prone to being taken advantage of. People would come to stay in his other apartment. After a few days, he'd want to be left alone but he wouldn't be and then he'd get mad. All the years of being on the road made him appreciate that private alone time. He was a big Internet guy, too."

"Joey was a lot like me," laughs Handsome Dick Manitoba. "He had a bachelor pad, stuff all over the place, pieces of paper, written notes. He went to Japan and had a lot of Japanese toys and knick-knacks. It was a real messy, lived in, fun house.

"We talked about food, movies, rock'n'roll, girls, life . . ." The Dictators singer says. "He'd tell me things that were wrong or bothering him physically, little ailments. He was a very proud guy. I wrote [on The Dictators' website], 'Joey was a sickly guy but he never defined himself by his disease.' We would loosen up to each other. It was funny, these two New York Jewish rock guys going, 'Listen, I got this pain here . . .' – that's very bad for your image, you know? But I felt safe telling Joey."

"DEE DEE DOES what I call punk fiction," explains Arturo. "But to him, it's true. Once I was at the Chelsea Hotel with him, right before *Chelsea Horror Hotel* came out [2000]. We'd been reading it and I was amazed at how fantastic the dialogue was. The scenes were so surrealistic, so insane. Then we walked out of the hotel, and he started acting and saying the same things I'd just read, but this time it was reality."

Whereas 1997's *Poison Heart*, Dee Dee's sad and entertaining account of life with, before and after the Ramones, is "faction" – half-fact, half-fiction – *Chelsea Horror Hotel* is complete fiction, framed by a real setting. Its depictions of drugs, bodily fluids and violence are further coloured by scenes like the one where Dee Dee shoots up with the ghosts of Sid Vicious, Johnny Thunders and Stiv Bators.

"It's a very eerie place," he told *Boston Phoenix* about his favourite hotel. (It's also where Nancy Spungen's body was discovered.) "Just the architecture alone is conducive to mystery. The chaos of living on 23rd Street is a story in itself."

"I met him one day while he wasn't in the band anymore," recalled Johnny. "Went by the Chelsea Hotel. About four kids stop us along the way and ask him what he's doing now. Each person he talks to, he gives a totally different story. He had an appendix scar on his stomach. While he was in the band if anybody would ask him he'd tell a story. A knife fight . . . every time a different story."

"I could've killed him," says Monte, referring to made-up tales of drunken debauchery involving the tour manager in *Poison Heart.*

"People ask me so many times, 'How can you talk to Dee Dee after the things he said about you?' " says Arturo. "It makes me laugh. If people are stupid enough to believe it's true, then it's their problem. Dee Dee's great. He's a genius. He's the real thing."

Dee Dee was a talented painter, too: at Arturo's apartment, I saw several pieces of block art created by the Ramone dealing with his confusion and split personalities. His drawing is scrawled, scratchy, his use of colour and line vivid. He has a cartoon-y, naïve approach to art.

"This piece existed before Dee Dee touched it," explained Arturo, showing me one of the works. "It's one of my minimalist paintings. Once Dee Dee touches it, I call it minimal nihilism. It all started because I sent him a piece of canvas once that was like this, divided into segments and this whole painting, he created it in one square. He reacted to the black and white, the opposites. Then I said he would have to do it again in a more presentable format. So I sent him the canvases with a polythene seal and this is what he did with it – he turned it into a T-shirt. That's Danny Fields. And this is him complaining about me whining, making him do things."

Chelsea Horror Hotel is illustrated with Dee Dee's own drugged-out *Fear And Loathing* style paintings: "At the time, that's how I perceived New York – blood and grease on the sidewalk, with a disco downstairs in front of my window," he stated bluntly. ". . . And every couple of nights, people would have a bad fight, and the stabbings, over girls. I wanted to get my dog shoes to wear, y'know?"

"Of the three Ramones I spoke with," suggests writer Michael Hill, "Joey's head is just a mess, is just like a blob of feeling, like 'I'm so happy,

I'm so excited, that was amazing'; Tommy would say, 'Let us put this in the context of music, art, fashion, culture, this is what it meant'; and then there was Dee Dee – 'I was dressed like a pirate and I went down to this place and I met these chicks and I bought some drugs and . . . oh my God'."

WHAT ARE YOU doing at the moment?

"I'm working on this project called Uncle Monk, which is combining bluegrass instruments and some ideas from old-time music with modern music, trying to make it as acoustic as possible but adding some electronic things as well. I'm actually doing the third version of this now – I did two other versions, which I didn't care for. Hopefully by next Spring I'll have something I'm pleased with. I'm also on the lookout to do some production work."

That's good. I would imagine that you're probably something of a perfectionist?

"Oh yeah."

Where does that come from?

"I just don't think it's worth putting out something unless it's good."

(Author's interview with Tommy Ramone, 2002)

JOHNNY CONTENTED HIMSELF with his baseball and movie memorabilia, and his new friends in LA. He moved to California the same year that the Ramones split up.

In February 1999, he made a rare public appearance on stage with Pearl Jam, playing on their cover of 'The KKK Took My Baby Away': "I was nervous. I was never nervous in the Ramones because I knew the crowd liked us," he said, "but playing for Pearl Jam's audience . . . I didn't know. Jim Carrey was on the side of the stage, and he kept making jokes and making faces. That helped a little bit."

"I'm perfectly content with retirement," he told Jeff Niesel in 2001. "In the summer, I'll watch the Yankees game every day. I'll watch a movie or two. I go out to dinner just about every night with my wife. I either have friends over and watch a movie, or go over to a friend's house and watch a movie. I do a lot of movie watching. I'll sit by the pool. Friends will ask me, 'Why don't you come and play here or there?' I got so spoiled with the reaction the Ramones got, and anything less than that would not be as good."

"John had a huge baseball card collection," says George Tabb. "Every time there would be a baseball convention, he'd be there with his cards. He had a humungous set – he finally sold it for lots of money, and he now has the world's largest collection of celebrity autographs. He showed me some of this stuff. He has all these autographs of famous people going back to the Thirties and Forties. He sends movie stars letters saying, 'My name is Johnny Ramone – can you please send me an autograph? I would love to add it to my collection,' and he gets them. Every actor you can think of, everybody. He's totally into collecting. What's funny now is that he's hanging out with Nicholas Cage or whatever."

Yeah, but what does he do?

"He seems to be having a great time," replies Tabb, "living in California."

After the Ramones split, Johnny stated that, given the choice between rock and baseball as a career, he'd have chosen baseball – if he could've had a 22-year career. And he'd have cut his hair to do it. "I think people in baseball are better remembered," he explained, revealing a deep-rooted insecurity. "They always go on talking about those guys. You are never forgotten in the baseball world. I don't know about music . . ."

"JOEY WAS THE most open, emotionally and spiritually. He was liberal in his thinking and philosophy, and seemed to genuinely like meeting the fans. He gave freely of himself, and was extremely unpretentious. He was almost always willing to give interviews, and was surprisingly approachable. More often than not, he would invite the writer up to his apartment to conduct the interview, or give me permission to give out his home phone number so they could call him directly. He was just a regular guy, walking around the streets of NYC. Truck drivers would yell out greetings when they recognised him, people would stop him on the street – he would talk to them all. He welcomed receiving tapes from new bands and was genuinely interested in developing new talent. He loved music and being around it. He was diligent and conscientious, especially after he became sober all those years ago. Sometimes his illness would take its toll and he would be too tired to do interviews but he never blew anyone off, he was always upfront with me about it and would ask me to reschedule if an interview had been planned. Everyone who met him went away feeling they had made a real connection.

"John was more guarded, more private, harder to get close to. He was protective of his privacy, and never gave out his phone number or home address. To reach John I always had to call the management office, even after nine years of being the band's press agent. John was mysterious – you never knew what he was doing when he wasn't with the band. He seemed to always have something else that kept him busy but never discussed what that might be – if there were interviews to do, he would schedule very specific times he would be available and then wanted to keep them short and as brief as possible.

"Whereas Joey might spend an hour with one writer, John wanted to do three

interviews in the same one-hour space, keeping each one down to 20 minutes. He was very succinct. There were no frills about him. He seemed to always be serious and business-like. If Joey's stance was to the left, John's politics and emotions seemed to be to the right. I rarely saw John smile or laugh. That's not to say he didn't, but it seemed he was more comfortable around guys – he is a guy's guy, into macho pleasures like baseball and such. I never knew him to nurture new bands or go to clubs to hear new music. He always struck me as very set in his opinions and very adamant in his conservative outlook."

(Author's interview with Ida Langsam, PR)

AND SO THE RAMONES' story draws to a close . . .

Unlike The Beatles, there would not be countless years of reunion rumours – on December 30, 2000 Joey injured his hip, slipping on an icy sidewalk outside his apartment on the Lower East Side after hosting a show at the Continental featuring Mickey Leigh's Rattlers, The Independents and The Misfits. Joey performed a set of Ramones covers that night.

"The Continental Divide sucks, in my opinion," says Michael Hill, who was writing a piece for *Mojo* on the Ramones. (It opened with a description of the scene at the club.) "It was a terribly cold night. There was ice everywhere."

"I took Phil Spector's daughter Nicole to see him play," recalls Don Fleming, "and introduced them. He was really excited to meet her. She knew a lot of Ramones stuff, mostly her dad's."

The fall briefly forced Joey off the medication that was controlling his cancer so that he could be operated on. "When he broke his hip, he was in the Altercocker [Yiddish for grumpy old person] ward," says George Seminara. "He was by far the youngest guy there. Here were all these chubby balding old guys complaining about breaking their hips, with a rock star. They found common ground by talking about jazz vocalists from the Thirties and Forties. He was only out for a few days in February and returned to the cancer ward. He never left."

The following March, Joey went into hospital again for more treatment, but sadly it didn't take. His body couldn't handle the chemo medication. "They were using masses of steroids," Seminara says. The singer never went home again. The fact that Joey had lived for eight years with non-Hodgkin's Lymphoma may yet prove to be beneficial to other sufferers, however – the normal life expectancy is three years.

"I used to read him *Harry Potter*, but we never finished it," Seminara recalls. "I even got it for him on tape, but he couldn't concentrate because he'd want to ask questions and the book kept going. His fans knew he was ill. I read him fan mail – there was this giant card from a South California high school that the teacher got all the kids to sign: 'We know you're going to beat this'."

At 2.40 pm on Easter Sunday, April 15, 2001, in the New York Presbyterian Hospital, Joey Ramone passed away. He was just under five weeks short of his 50th birthday.

"He didn't know he was going to die until the day before," says George. "That's when they finally told him. He gave up and died 18, 19 hours later. He wouldn't let them put a feeding tube in for fear it would hurt his vocal chords. He died while listening to a U2 song ['In A Little While']. He said he wanted to hear it. Halfway through, he closed his eyes, and by the song's end he was dead. I cried like a baby.

"He was surrounded by family and friends," he adds. "It was quite the loving situation, who wouldn't want to die like that? In the last few months of his life, Joey and his real life brother Mickey Leigh became close for the first time since they were children. Joey told me that he really loved having his brother at the hospital. All the shit between them was over, and Joey could just love the doting affection thrown on him by Mickey."

Bono, U2's singer, had been confirmed as a major fan years before (his band passed their first TV audition by playing three Ramones covers). That night, U2 played two songs dedicated to Joey – 'Amazing Grace' and an acoustic rendition of 'I Remember You' at the Rose Garden, in Portland, Oregon. "I told the people, 'I want to talk to you about Joey Ramone . . .' and the whole crowd went up in this roar," Bono recalled with awe. The crowd, unasked, sang along with every note. "Then," he added, "I said Joey Ramone had passed away that day. The roar stopped right there. The place went silent."

Music channel VH1 screened a Billy Idol *Behind The Music* special the evening the news was announced.

"My favourite album is *Too Tough To Die*," says Joan Tarshis. "I loved the album so much Joey gave me his T-shirt from it. When he died, I was wearing it to feel close to him. I knew about his lymphoma for years, and about his death – my own God Window. His inability to get a new pair of glasses was probably the reason he fell, and that started the snowball but he was like, 'I like to keep the world a little blurry.' "

"His funeral was the saddest . . ." Handsome Dick trails off. "I mean, all funerals are sad inherently. This funeral, for some reason, when I looked around the gravesite and I saw Joan Jett and Debbie Harry and all these rock stars just hugging and sobbing . . . It was the graduation class of '77 all standing at the gravesite because this amazing human being . . . I get chills thinking about it. In a world of sadness, it was particularly sad."

"When Joey passed away, it was a shock," says Marky. "I saw him at the hospital once – the nurse picked him up and put him in a wheelchair, a black woman, and the guy was 6′ 6 and what did he weigh? Like 110 lbs and she just wheeled him away. I was standing – I had to go to the right, they went that way, and that was the last I saw of him. I remember it was snowy out, I parked my car and on the way home I realised I'm not going to see the guy again. I guess everyone thought that, because lymphoma – it's fucking cancer. You go to chemotherapy and you hope that something will come along, a new discovery or invention that will cure the situation. That's why, I guess, it was shocking because . . . I don't know – the Ramones have a mystique about them."

Johnny didn't call Joey before he passed away. Instead, he called Arturo Vega every couple of days: "It didn't really sink in until I got home and there was like 20 messages," the guitarist said. "After a week of that, I felt very depressed."

"LAST WEEK I WENT to see my beloved Yankees play at the Stadium. The 'Hey Ho, Let's Go' chant started in order to rile up the fans. I felt so proud that MY BOY, Joey Ramone, was blaring out of the loudspeakers, at MY shrine. But I felt so sad that I could no longer call him to tell him how proud I was! I just sat there, looked at my girlfriend and said, 'OH MAN, JOEY!!!' " – Handsome Dick Manitoba

"BEFORE JOEY DIED," says George Seminara, "we promised him three things.

"One: He wanted to be in the Rock'N'Roll Hall Of Fame, first pass, because he never felt the band's legacy would be respected until their peers accepted them. The trouble was that the Ramones were way too good at their concept. It was a concept that was created and implemented with such perfection you couldn't tell whether it was art or real life. These guys lived it 24 hours a day. They always looked like they were in costume because that's what they wore. Joey would never look natural in a suit or tie.

"Two: We promised him a huge 50th birthday party, because each year we'd have a big birthday bash – always with a vast array of interesting people. One time, Jonathan Richman played an acoustic set at 7 pm – early because Jonathan was skittish about loud noises. Another time, it would be Joey singing with the original Stooges. It was the same with the Christmas parties. I would be the punk rock Santa Claus and have people sit on my lap and ask them what they wanted, and they'd say something like, 'I want a really clean bag of heroin so I can shoot up and not worry about overdosing.'

"Three: That his solo album would go gold. It's selling pretty strongly – stronger than the last four or five Ramones albums, but I don't know if it will sell half-a-million. I hope so, because the beneficiary will be the Lymphoma Foundation. We're going to put out the Birthday Bash on DVD in the fall, and all the benefits will go to the foundation. Joey was good for pretty much any cause – the Jerry Brown Campaign, Stop Spousal Abuse, Planned Parenthood, Neutering Straight Cats . . . He was an easy touch."

A MINI-WAR NEARLY broke out at Joey's 50th Birthday Bash on May 19, 2001.

One side accused Mickey of trying to front the Ramones by himself. The other side accused the Ramones of selling the memory of Joey short by requesting guest vocalists like Eddie Vedder, Rob Zombie and Joe Strummer. Johnny was nervous at the idea of playing live again. Charlotte Lesher had requested the band play only instrumentals so the audience could sing along, but somehow Arturo Vega got the message muddled. Maybe. To an outsider, it was all very tedious and all very sad.

"John was hesitant to come and even play Joey's thing," says Kevin Patrick, who stayed close to both Johnny and Joey. "John told me, 'I'm just intimidated to play.' He hadn't done it for five years. He said originally they were asked whether they'd like to do one song, an instrumental – the unattended mic with the spotlight on it. John thought it was cheesy, which is fair enough. But even if they did do that, he wasn't in shape. You don't run the marathon and take five years off, and then run it and win again, you know?"

In the end, Cheap Trick, Blondie, The Independents, Mickey Leigh's Stop, Bellevue and The Damned played at the Bash . . . but no Ramones. Still, two pinheads did jump out of a huge cake, triggering a massive food fight.

"Decisions are made by the band," Johnny explained. "I find it ridiculous that anyone has to be consulted. It should always be just the band – if I die, I don't expect anyone to call up my wife to make a Ramones decision. Why do I have to discuss a Ramones performance with his brother and his mother?"

One has sympathy with Johnny, but only in the entertainment industry would work colleagues expect to take precedence over family.

JOEY'S LONG-AWAITED solo album *Don't Worry About Me* was released by Sanctuary Records on February 19, 2002 – 21 years after the idea was first mooted.

"Over the previous 10 years," its producer Daniel Rey says, "whenever a song wasn't right for the Ramones, Joey would say, 'I'll take it for my solo album,' and we'd begin making demos. In '97, we started to do it for real. The Ramones were coming to a close. Over the next two years, Joey would come in here [Daniel's 4th Avenue home studio] and sing. Right before he got sick, the recording was finished. We mixed it after he passed."

It's a fine send-off. The opening song, a tear-stained Ramones-style version of Louis Armstrong's 'What A Wonderful World' (a song that celebrates the minutiae of life like none other) is particularly resonant: how couldn't it be, listening to the lymphoma-diagnosed Ramone sing lines like, "I see babies cry/I watch them grow/They'll learn more than I'll ever know"? The next few tracks – the upbeat, pleasantly silly 'Mr Punchy', featuring Captain Sensible of The Damned on guest vocals (plus Welsh singer/fan Helen Love, and Veronica Kofman, president of the UK British Ramones fan club) and 'Stop Thinking About It' (co-written by Andy Shernoff) – are also fine.

"Joey wasn't really a good guitar player so sometimes he couldn't hit the right chord," explains Shernoff. "He'd sing me something and then try to play it, and I'd be like, 'Oh, you mean like this?' and he'd be like, 'Yeah.' Or he'd have a song and would need a bridge. I helped him with 'Stop Thinking About It'. We were going into the studio the next day and he hadn't finished the lyrics. I wrote two pages of rhymes, and he was looking at them in this weird kind of hunched over way – then he took the phrases and put the song together in a different form."

Then there's the catchy 'Maria Bartiromo', a song written for one of Joey's main crushes, a financial TV reporter: "Joey was just so damn open when he spoke to you," says Jaan Uhelszki. "The fact he didn't talk to Johnny, the fact he thought Drew Barrymore and Courtney Love were fetching. Joey would watch *Money Talk* on CNN during the day, and read the *Wall Street Journal*. He had a broker, was into technical stocks and AOL and made quite a killing. He had a huge crush on Maria Bartiromo, because she was savvy – he didn't just go for pretty faces."

"He was obsessed with the stock market," confirms Rachel Felder, "to the extent that, when he broke his hip, he found a bright spot in sitting alone in bed in the hospital: he could watch the stock-trading TV shows all day. He was super-bright but because he spoke in the heavy Queens accent and wasn't the most articulate guy on the planet, people missed it."

"Joey was a fairly successful day trader," George Seminara adds. "He would watch all the markets worldwide. He gave me a couple of tips, one worked out and two didn't but only because I was inexperienced to the world of stocks and bonds. Joey, like Johnny, was also a good businessman, but he had the soul of an artist and that would get in his way."

Other songs are equally as good – 'Venting (It's A Different World Today)' where Joey unashamedly sounds like your parents letting off steam about the kids of today; the acoustic, sweet 'Searching For Something', which continues the lineage of travelling fans first started with 'The Return Of Jackie And Judy'; the simple and undeniably sad 'I Got Knocked Down (But I'll Get Up)' – "Sitting in my hospital bed/I, I want life/I want my life," Joey sings plaintively. "It really sucks."

The final track, 'Don't Worry About Me' – classic Fifties Joey Ramone beach party pop – simply melts your heart. You'd need to be made of granite to resist its final message. (The song was written several years before, but that's beside the point.)

Overall, however, the album is oddly unsatisfying. It's not that it isn't any good (it is), but some of us were expecting something a little . . . *different*.

"I heard some of his earlier demos," says George Tabb, "and that's what I thought this album would be like. Doo wop, some country – even acoustic numbers. And then he comes out and does a Ramones album. Not only is it a Ramones album – but the same frickin' people who played on the last five Ramones album played on it [Daniel, Marky, Andy Shernoff]. So it was another Ramones album. The shock was on me. It's a good one, at that. Maybe Joey grew into the Ramones, maybe the Ramones grew into Joey, I don't know."

Certainly, *Don't Worry About Me* proves beyond a doubt that Joey was as vital an artistic force as Dee Dee in the Ramones, and that he could've existed without Johnny, too – at least, in the studio. But we're greedy. We want more.

"He needed a push to get going," says Daniel. "He'd always be like, 'I don't want to come over today.' So I'd have to say, 'Just come over, we'll hang out, have coffee.' I'd start playing his demos and all of a sudden he'd get creative."

"I think Joey liked it because it was less stressful than the Ramones,"

Shernoff suggests. "He didn't call me because I was the greatest bass player in the world – he just felt comfortable around me, same with Daniel."

"We did the LP in New Jersey," says Marky. "It took me one day to do the seven tracks I'm on. I had other commitments so I couldn't finish it. We would do the basic tracks, and Joey would do a scratch vocal with the track so I'd have something to follow. I got out of there 6.30 in the morning, it was March or April, the sun was coming up, everyone was going to work and I was going home. The mood was great. It was good to see Joey out and we let bygones be bygones. There was a lot of kissing and hugging and how you doing."

Other contributors include Mickey Leigh (backing vocals and guitar on the title track), and Joe McGinty with his usual swath of keyboards. Frank Funaro (Cracker) drummed on the four tracks that Marky wasn't on, except on the misplaced Stooges cover '1969' (the Ramones and The Stooges never did go well together, despite the bracketing) recorded a few years earlier with two Misfits. George Seminara took the cover photo (Arturo Vega took an alternate version), and George DuBose designed the package. Charlotte Lesher and Mickey were executive producers. Joey wrote, or co-wrote, nine of the songs present.

It was the entire family, almost.

"For Joey," states Arturo, "everything was going to have a happy ending. He was certain he was going to beat his cancer. He was used to being in and out of hospital. To him, this was just another obstacle. He felt he was going to overcome it, but you could also tell by the songs that he was feeling down and doubtful and crazy. Sometimes he used to call and say the medication was making him feel he was going insane. It was really tough, but he felt he was going to come out the other end. And that's what makes the album so great.

"The album is a triumph," states his old flatmate. "That album is a victory in itself. That album is the ultimate statement about having that conviction that no matter what you go through, no matter how low and painful and desperate your situation may be, everything is going to be alright."

NEW YORK, 16/11/01 — It's official. The corner of East Second Street and the Bowery in the East Village, just a few steps from legendary punk haven CBGBs, will be known as Joey Ramone Place, after a request for an honorary street sign was approved by the local community board on Thursday.

THE RAMONES' INDUCTION into the Rock'N'Roll Hall Of Fame on March 18, 2002 – screened by major Ramones fans, VH1 – did not pass without controversy.

First: there were the seating arrangements. Johnny refused to be placed at the same table as Mickey Leigh and Charlotte Lesher. They requested to be seated next to Tommy. Joey's family were supposed to go up and collect an award on his behalf, but no one prompted Charlotte – the usual stuff.

Next: there was the thorny problem of who actually qualified as a Ramone. CJ – despite having played with the band for eight years and three studio albums – wasn't a real Ramone, not according to the event's organisers. They wouldn't even grant him a ticket. This made Johnny furious: "CJ was our ambassador," he told *Village Voice*'s Bill Werde. "We would just sit in the dressing rooms and not talk to anyone because we didn't think anyone cared about us. And all of a sudden Soundgarden wanted us to tour with them, and White Zombie, and Pearl Jam. I felt [CJ] was more important than Marc. Marc is a great drummer, but CJ is a front man."

This in turn made Marky understandably upset – he made a couple of catty comments about Johnny playing on stage with another guitarist behind a curtain, and then immediately withdrew them.

Then there was the choice of the person to give the keynote speech. Johnny wanted, and got, Eddie Vedder – but Pearl Jam's music has nothing in common with the Ramones. There were far better candidates for the job. More famous ones, even – if that's what mattered. Even Bono would've been preferable: Vedder made reference to Mohawks in his speech, when it was common knowledge that the Ramones never sported a Mohawk haircut in their entire career.

Still, it wasn't like any of the industry glitterati sitting in their $2,500 seats at the Waldorf-Astoria would have known any different.

Then, of course, there was Dee Dee – still determined not to toe the party line. He refused to wear his leathers when he walked up to accept his award. Strike one for the individual. Actually, it was a shame – if ever there was a time when the uniform was applicable, it was then. Still, all awards ceremonies suck – right, kids? Here were the Ramones accepting acknowledgement – 28 years after they first started, and six years after they'd split, and a year after their singer had *died* – from an industry that had actively done its best at every turn to thwart them. Why seek recognition from such people?

"Britney Spears is in the Hall Of Fame, isn't she?" asks original *Punk*, John Holmstrom pointedly.

"Anything that makes people happy is fine," says PR Ida Langsam, diplomatically. "I heard that Joey knew before he passed away that he was going to be inducted, and it really made him happy, so that's good."

"Joey always felt rock'n'roll was a valid art form, and should be recognised," explains Daniel Rey. "He would say, 'Yeah, it would be cool if we got inducted the first year.' "

"I donated my Ramones sneakers to the Rock'N'Roll Hall Of Fame," laughed Marky. "And they did not smell good, I can tell you that."

"I SAW THIS INCREDIBLE quote from Seymour a few days after Joey passed away.

"He said, 'A band like the Ramones don't come along once in a lifetime, they come along once.' That's it. Hence it's just the characters, the look, the different physical styles, the writing mentality and the craziness that led up to those kinds of songs from Dee Dee and Joey – and the athletic stamina that they developed as a live band. Johnny Ramone is the greatest guitar player ever. I don't care about the flash stuff. Hendrix, all these people . . . I know they're fantastic but no one is as good as Johnny Ramone. He has the sound and the style. It can't be imitated." – Kevin Patrick

IT WAS WHILE I was finishing my research for this book that I heard about Dee Dee's death – British PR Penny Brignell phoned me with the news. I was holding at the time for Seymour Stein, former Sire record boss – the man who'd given so much support to the Ramones over the years. He offered to do an interview anyway, but neither of us felt in the mood to continue. I took a note of the time. It was 6.15 pm, Thursday June 6 – the unconscious body of Dee Dee Ramone had been found by his wife Barbara at 8.25 pm PT the night before, and pronounced dead at the scene by fire department paramedics who arrived 15 minutes later.

Drug paraphernalia was noted at the scene, including a single syringe on the kitchen counter.

"Dee Dee played the previous Saturday in LA," says Rodney Bingenheimer, "at a Club Make Up 'Tribute To Punk' evening. There were lots of Ramones T-shirts there. Dee Dee looked great; black leather jacket, T-shirt, black jeans, right off an album cover. He had his Ramones hair back – perfect black hair. Pleasant Gayman, one of the original punk rock girls, was the MC. She introduced Dee Dee, said he was her idol – and she bowed down and literally kissed his feet. Dee Dee went '1-2-3-4', and went into 'Chinese Rocks'. Then he did 'Blitzkrieg Bop' and a few more Ramones songs. He had the whole audience going . . ."

"It's not a shock," Seymour told me as he confirmed the news. "It's very sad, though. I'm very strained right now. These things hit me the hardest when I go to sleep at night. I hope I'll be able to sleep tonight, but sometimes it's very hard . . . I knew Joey the best, but in some personal ways I was very close to Dee Dee. It wasn't a shock, but very, very sad. I tell you one thing: he looked very good at the Hall Of Fame. I chatted to him about his paintings."

It was sad. Checking out his official website, and his self-penned fanzine *Takin' Dope* that he'd posted up there, Dee Dee seemed very depressed following both the deaths of his father and Joey: "I took a lot of walks in the woods and let myself cry," he wrote. "I was upset because I would never get to see these guys ever again and that the only way I could resolve the problems I had with them was to pray for them to forgive me and for myself to forgive them. But I can't seem to get over that it's over, it's painful. Some people I met at a book signing told me that when Joey died they felt that their youth died. I know how they feel. The Ramones kept us all young. . . .

"When I saw the Twin Towers blow up in New York on TV," he added, "I freaked and I cried. I'm sad sad sad for New York."

Dee Dee's mother attended his funeral, somewhat to the surprise of many of his friends – he'd told them she was dead.

"JOEY ACCEPTED DEE DEE on the level that he was on. It's always very difficult to accept junkies, because you know you can't rely upon them and that they aren't in control, and you always forget it if you aren't a junkie yourself. Joey understood that, which was cool – he probably thought it was a drag, but he didn't get moralistic about it, and didn't try to put him down.

"Dee Dee lived a very full life. He wrote like 20 records, two books, played 3,000 gigs, had his artwork, married a couple of times, travelled constantly – he did an awful lot in his 50 years . . . those guys were good at getting money from what they did. He lived this triangular lifestyle in Amsterdam, Brazil and at the Chelsea Hotel in New York. He always looked grand to me. He was very careful not to get in trouble with drugs. If people started approaching him too much he'd leave and fly on to the next city. I don't know why he chose LA to live in [Dee Dee moved there in 1999, according to Daniel] because it's a deadly city – it's a good place if you have a lot to do, but if you don't then you can easily fall into a malaise because everything's so far apart. It can lead very often to taking drugs. You start getting angst-y, what are you going to do? It's been a death trap for a lot of rock stars.

"It happens, former junkies misjudging how much dope they can handle after they've stopped for a while. You'd have thought Dee Dee, of all people, would

have had the experience not to make that mistake. Unfortunately, the amount of time it takes to make rock'n'roll is very short, so you have this creative person sitting around doing nothing. Dee Dee had a fast mind. He'd get bored. Some people know how to handle life when they don't have to do anything – aristocrats are very good at it. Dee Dee never had that worked out. He wasn't going to go skiing in the winter. He wasn't going to buy a yacht. He was a rock star sitting around a city having nothing to do. This is a great failing in our culture, that we have a lot of artists sitting around needing attention. It's such a pity."

(Author's interview with Victor Bockris (Keith Richards and Blondie biographer) a week after Dee Dee's death)

I ACTUALLY SPOKE TO Dee Dee just four days before he died, on the Sunday. Someone had anonymously passed me his phone number – and fortified by folk like Marky Ramone and Arturo Vega advising me to give him a try (journalists, despite what you read, don't like to call people cold: like anyone, we prefer an introduction) and to use their names if need be, I called. Both Daniel and Arturo had warned me that the bassist had good and bad days.

"Maybe you'll be lucky," Arturo said.

I wasn't.

"Hey wussup?" went a familiar voice on the other end, like I was an old friend he'd just resumed a conversation with: "Whass happening, man?" He seemed confused, not entirely orientated. I explained the situation to him – I was doing a book on the Ramones, and as he was a totally integral part of the story, I wanted to talk with him. "Yeah?" he said, and listened for a few seconds more.

"Nah man," he decided. "I don't want to do that."

And that was that.

ADDENDA 2

. . . And The Beat Goes On

JOEY WORKED WITH many artists over the years.

When I showed up to interview the singer in NYC in '89, I was also recording a single for Sub Pop ('Do Nuts') under my stage alias of The Legend!, that coincidentally included an a cappella version of 'Rockaway Beach'. Upon learning my plans, Joey volunteered to come down and sing harmony. He never showed, but spent 15 minutes apologising on the phone.

Artists he did sing with (or for), however, included the following . . .

Mickey Leigh – Joey and his brother sang backing vocals on The Seclusions' 'Shape Of Things To Come' (Fuzz International, 1983). The pair also sang together on Mickey's band, The Rattlers' 'On The Beach' (Rasto, 1979) – the song later turned up on their joint project, Sibling Rivalry's three-track single 'In A Family Way' (Alternative Tentacles, 1994). There was the Sun City apartheid single from 1985 . . .

Dead Boys – Joey and Dee Dee sang backing vocals on the Ohio scuzz rockers' second album *We Have Come For Your Children* (Sire, 1978).

The White Trash Debutantes – background vocals on the NYC trash band's 'I Wanna Party', B-side of 'Crawl For It' (Desperate Attempt, 1992).

Die Toten Hosen – duet on 'Blitzkrieg Bop' with Campino, singer of phenomenally successful stadium-filling German punks, from *The Nightmare Continues* EP (Virgin, 1992). Joey also sang on several numbers on the Hosen's 1991 album *Learning English Part One* – Johnny Thunders also contributed, four days before his death.

John Cage – Joey contributed the strange, spoken-word piece 'The Wonderful Widow Of Eighteen Springs' to *Caged/Uncaged* in 1993.

Spacemaid – Joey does the DJ intro part to the British band's version of 'Do You Remember Rock'N'Roll Radio?' (Big Star single, 1996).

Dee Dee Ramone – Joey sings lead vocals on 'I'm Seeing UFOs' (Blackout, 1997). The track later got reissued on *Zonked/Ain't It Fun.*

Lolita No 18 – the Japanese band managed what I failed to achieve, by having Joey sing the chorus to their version of 'Rockaway Beach', *Fubo Love NY* (Sister, 1998).

Furious George – Joey sings on 'Gilligan' from their 1997 album *Gets A Record!*

"We had to go to his apartment because he was sick," recalls Furious George guitarist George Tabb. "Not that we knew it then. We digitally edited him in later. But Joey decided he wanted to add more, and came down to the sessions with 50 kids singing backup. He wanted to meet everybody. So all these kids got to sing with Joey. He was such a sweetheart."

AND THE LIST goes on . . . most particularly with Native American band Blackfire and The Independents, two bands Joey was working with up to his death.

"Joey was a fan of Blackfire," says producer Don Fleming. The Ramones singer sang backing vocals on two tracks on their 2001 album *One Nation Under.* "He was extremely coherent, and a real workaholic. It surprised me how much of a perfectionist he was over his vocals. He also made great comments on other things on the record, like he had a producer's ear. He wanted to come back and work on it more."

It was CJ who'd been responsible for turning Joey on to Native American music in the first place. "My dad is part-Iroquois," the ex-Ramones bassist explains, "but I never made that much of it, especially back then when people were jumping on the bandwagon. I had friends from the Big Mountain reservation in Arizona, in a family band called Blackfire – two brothers – and Joey ended up developing a respect for them and their lifestyle, which borders on the traditional. In fact, when the medical treatments he was going through weren't working, they tried to get him out there because their dad is a very successful medicine man. By that point, however, he was so sick and he'd already chosen his course . . ."

Joey co-produced The Independents' second album, 2001's *Back From The Grave*, with Daniel Rey: "I met CJ Ramone in Myrtle Beach SC," singer Evil Presley said, "at a casino that was next to where they were playing that night. We hung out after the next two shows and became great friends. He got us on tour with the Ramones for *Acid Eaters*. We got along great so he offered to manage the band. Joey became my best friend. We had like a father and son relationship."

"Chris [Snipes aka Presley]," explains CJ, "was probably the person who took care of Joey on a daily basis, more than anyone else. He'd be turning him over, making sure he didn't get bedsores, looking out for him with the hospital staff. [Chris cancelled a tour to look after Joey.] He really stuck with him till the end."

ONE HIGHLIGHT OF JOEY's collaborative work – alongside the Holly & The Italians duet – was The Godchildren Of Soul (featuring former Chairman Of The Board singer General Johnson)'s quite fantastic, thoroughly Sixties version of 'Rockaway Beach/On The Beach' (Rhino, 1994). If ever proof was needed that the Ramones wrote classic pop singles, here it was. Joey's vocals are outasite!

Equally great, and in a similar vein, are The Nutley Brass' horn-filled, upbeat interpretations of several Ramones classics on *The Ramones Songbook As Played By The Nutley Brass* – well worth checking out. Other recent albums by Ramonetures (the songs of the Ramones interpreted in The Ventures' surf guitar instrumental style) and the near-legendary Gabba (Abba songs done in a Ramones style) also prove the versatility of da bruddas sound.

Other cover versions and tributes of note include Sonic Youth's 1987 medley of Ramones songs on their 'Master Dik' (Blast First) 12-inch, Ronnie Spector's New Wave, synth-driven version of 'Here Today, Gone Tomorrow' on *Siren* (Red Shadow, 1980), Per Gessie's touching 'I Wanna Be Your Boyfriend', The Dictators' 'I Just Wanna Have Something To Do', Thee Headcoatees' 'Swallow My Pride' (*Sisters Of Suave*) . . . and anything involving The Donnas, Screeching Weasel, The Queers, Sator and Shebang. All these acts grasped that a lot of what made the Ramones so memorable was their POP element.

Welsh singer Helen Love – who sang with Joey on her own Damaged Goods seven-inch 'Punk Boy' (later to show up on the 1997 singles compilation *Radio Hits 1*) – understood this better than most.

"The Ramones were the greatest band in the world ever," she writes. "They were The Archies, The Bay City Rollers, The Beach Boys and The Who all rolled up into one magic two-minute pop explosion. They burst my heart when I first heard 'Rockaway Beach', I jumped around my bedroom punching the air, '1-2-3-4, let's GO'. I was Joey Ramone, I was the leader, and they changed my world. 'Joey Ramoney' was written to say cheers to the TALL man for changing this girl's life.

"Joey got sent a copy of our single from Veronica from the Ramones fan club who'd heard it on Mark Radcliffe," she continues, "and he loved it. A few weeks later and he's ringing me up at home. He set up our first ever gig in The Continental, New York City. He arranged everything and he let us stay with him for a week in his apartment. We had a fantastic time, it was all quite unbelievable, but there we were in Joey's place in New York City, with him telling us that he played our album to Howard Stern who loves it, and Debbie (Harry) loves it too. It was a great time.

"The fact Joey took such time and trouble over a little band from Swansea, Wales just goes to show what a great guy he was, generous, gentle, funny and COOOOOL. He was a POP man, knew his music history, knew a tune when he heard one, no bullshit, just verse, chorus key change end, BOOOOOM, two minutes, if not less, super-fast POW, next song please . . . 1-2-3-4 . . . Phil Spector was no mug. Send the rest of the band home, I don't need 'em, all I need is Joey Ramone, that's how great he was.

"If you want a record to sing from the rooftops, to drive into the ocean, to smoke your first fag to, or get your first love bite, then *It's Alive* on the stereo and I'm there and I LOVE IT. That's what the Ramones mean to me."

MY FAVOURITE JOEY collaboration is undoubtedly the 1999 Kill Rock Stars Ronnie Spector single, 'She Talks To Rainbows' – Joey co-produced the former Ronettes singer, with Daniel Rey, duets with her on the sumptuous 'Bye Bye Baby' and does background vocals on the touching Johnny Thunders cover 'You Can't Put Your Arms Around A Memory'.

"The day he played [the original demo] for me," said Joey's mother Charlotte Lesher, "I swear tears came to my eyes. I love the way he sings it. I really think that's a beautiful song."

The backing is sensitive, and sparse (for Ronnie). She hasn't sounded this great since she left Phil, and the Joey/Ronnie duet is simply heartbreaking. The two other songs, Brian Wilson's 'Don't Worry Baby', and a slightly over the top live version of the Ronettes' 'I Wish I Never Saw The Sunshine', are almost as good. Joey and Daniel were working on a solo Ronnie Spector album right up to the moment of Joey's death – and man, it's great. Keith Richards guests on a few numbers.

"Joey was always a big fan of Ronnie's," says Daniel. "He's got a lot of Ronnie in his voice. You can definitely hear it. So it was a mutual admiration thing. We used to go and see Ronnie's Christmas Show at the Bottom Line, and one year Joey got up and did 'Baby, I Love You' with her. Ronnie had no deal going on or anything, so Joey was like, 'Come and do some of my songs.' We knew it wasn't going to be a big money maker. She was the original bad girl, the Courtney Love of 1963."

Better voice, though.

"She was a hell of a lot sexier, too."

DEE DEE ALSO continued releasing records up to his death in 2002.

Following the demise of the Ramones, he formed the Ramones tribute band, the Ramainz (formerly The Remains) with his wife Barbara on bass, Marky and initially CJ . . . indeed, you could argue that this version of the Ramones was almost as authentic as the last official line-up – except that, as a vocalist, Dee Dee was no Joey and, on guitar he was certainly no Johnny either.

"Dee Dee was always my favourite Ramone," CJ explained, "and I couldn't pass up the opportunity to play with my idol. It was just for fun and I don't think we'll do it again." CJ didn't appear on *Zonked*, the 1997 album whose main highlights occurred when Barbara started singing in her robotic voice, threatening other girls to "stay away from my chico". A couple of the songs are too close to the Ramones for comfort – 'Why Is Everybody Always Against Germany' draws on 'Today Your Love . . .' and 'It's A Long Way Back . . .' both lyrically and musically. But Daniel was there to lend support with guitar, so it sounded OK anyway.

"His wife is amazing," exclaims Donna Gaines. "She's like a teenage Dee Dee, a female Dee Dee playing bass. She's gorgeous, and is idolised everywhere by young rocker women who read *Rocker Girl*. She writes songs, sings and is crazy about Dee Dee – and he's crazy about her."

The Ramainz put out a negligible collection of Ramones covers, *Live In NYC* in 1999 – although they did at least have the grace to slow down the frenetic speed of latter-day Ramones. The following year's *Hop Around* (Corazong) is simply sad: Dee Dee barely rewriting song titles as he cannibalised his own back catalogue – 'I Don't Wanna Die In The Basement', 'Mental Patient', 'Now I Wanna Be Sedated', '38th & 8ths' . . . *Greatest And Latest*, also from 2000, is just as bad. Chris Spedding produced the last two albums. It was ironic: the former Sex Pistols producer famously hated *Rocket To Russia*.

"I met Johnny on the street in LA when he was with his girlfriend,"

Dee Dee told *Live Daily*'s Alexa Williamson in 2000, "and he said he wants to record another Ramones album. He asked me if I would work with Daniel Rey, and I said no. He also asked me if I'd play on the album but I said no, I think CJ should. However, I told him I'd be happy to give them some songs. I'm not sure how serious he is about a new album, and I'm not sure if Joey's voice is up to it; it's a little worn out."

"THE RAMAINZ WERE me and Dee Dee deciding we wanted to have some fun after the Ramones broke up," explains Marky. "That's all it was – him, his wife and me doing Ramones songs. The Intruders was my band. I wrote all the songs. We toured, we did some good shows, we made two albums and that's all I wanted to do. I was happy with that. Then I met some other people who wanted me to play on their albums, like The Speedkings. So I did just that."

Marky Ramone And The Intruders released a brace of records – 1996's self-titled album, 1999's *The Answer To Your Problems* (produced by Lars Fredrickson of Rancid, with a guest spot from Joan Jett). The Speedkings put out *No If's, And's And But's* in 2001, and more recently Marky's been drumming with horror punks The Misfits.

"[The Speedkings] are faster," Marky reveals, "more about girls and sex, cars, gasoline and oil. The realities of women and guys, and what they really lust for. I like to build and race cars. I like to make their engines bigger and their transmissions more powerful and grease them up and take a stock car and beef it up a little, make it street legal.

"I like to collect Fifties sci-fi posters, from the monster science fiction era. I like to do what everyone else does, watch videos, go out to eat, go out to clubs – which is a little hard to do these days because a lot of people recognise you because the clubs are inhabited by Ramones fans. They're the only ones I'd want to go to anyway."

"Also, I do a lot of speaking engagements. Spoken word stuff about the punk scene now, then, everything. I have a slide show and video projector. It's about 90 minutes long. A lot of curiosity seekers turn up – young punks, old punks, historians in the music business. I do question and answer for half-an-hour, then I sign autographs and go home."

CJ'S HARD ROCK outfit Los Gusanos also released several records during the Nineties, some while the Ramones were still going. He now sings and plays bass in Bad Chopper (formerly Warm Jets).

JOHNNY has retired.

Selected Discography 1976–2001

(all UK/US pressings unless otherwise stated)

SINGLES

Blitzkrieg Bop/Havana Affair
7/76 (UK); Sire 6078 601

I Remember You/California Sun (Live)/I Don't Wanna Walk Around With You (Live)
2/77 (UK); Sire 6078 603

Sheena Is A Punk Rocker/Commando/I Don't Care
5/77 (UK); Sire RAM 001 (6078 606)

Sheena Is A Punk Rocker/Commando/I Don't Care (12″ single)
5/77 (UK); Sire RAM 001 (6078 606) 12,000 copies only

Swallow My Pride/Pinhead/Let's Dance (live)
8/77 (UK); Sire 6078 607

Rockaway Beach/Teenage Lobotomy/Beat On The Brat
11/77 (UK); Sire 6078 611

Rockaway Beach/Teenage Lobotomy/Beat On The Brat (12″ single)
11/77 (UK); Sire 6078 611

Do You Wanna Dance?/It's A Long Way Back To Germany/Cretin Hop
3/78 (UK); Sire 6078 615

Don't Come Close/I Don't Want You
9/78 (UK); Sire SRE 1031

Don't Come Close/I Don't Want You (12″ single)
9/78 (UK, yellow and red vinyl); Sire SRE 1031

She's The One/I Wanna Be Sedated
1/79 (UK); Sire SIR 4009

Rock'N'Roll High School/Rockaway Beach (live)/Sheena Is A Punk Rocker (live)
9/79 (UK); Sire SIR 4021

Baby, I Love You/High Risk Insurance
1/80 (UK); Sire SIR 4031

Do You Remember Rock'N'Roll Radio?/I Want You Around
4/80 (UK); Sire SIR 4037

I Wanna Be Sedated/The Return Of Jackie And Judy
8/80 (UK); RSO 70 (2090 512) (from *Times Square* soundtrack)

MELTDOWN WITH THE RAMONES (EP)
I Just Want To Have Something To Do/Here Today, Gone Tomorrow/I Wanna Be Your Boyfriend/Questioningly/We Want The Airwaves
11/80 (UK); Sire SREP 1

We Want The Airwaves/You Sound Like You're Sick
7/81 (UK); Sire SIR 4051

She's A Sensation/All Quiet On The Eastern Front
10/81 (UK); Sire SIR 4052

Time Has Come Today/Psycho Therapy
6/83 (UK); Sire W 9606

Time Has Come Today/Psycho Therapy/Baby, I Love You/Don't Come Close (12″ single)
6/83 (UK); Sire 9606T

Howling At The Moon (Sha-La-La)/Smash You
2/85 (UK); Beggars Banquet BEG 128

Howling At The Moon (Sha-La-La)/Smash You/Street Fighting Man (12″ single)
2/85 (UK); Beggars Banquet BEG 128T

Chasing The Night/Howling At The Moon/Smash You/Street Fighting Man (7″ double pack)
3/85 (UK); Beggars Banquet BEG 128D

Chasing The Night/ Howling At The Moon (Sha-La-La)/Smash You/Street Fighting Man (12″ p/s)
3/85 (UK); Beggars Banquet BEG 128 TP

Bonzo Goes To Bitburg/Daytime Dilemma
6/85 (UK); Beggars Banquet BEG 140

Bonzo Goes To Bitburg/Daytime Dilemma/Go Home Annie
6/85 (UK); Beggars Banquet BEG 140T

Somebody Put Something In My Drink/ Something To Believe In
4/86 (UK); Beggars Banquet BEG 157

Somebody Put Something In My Drink/Something To Believe In/ Can't Say Anything Nice
4/86 (UK); Beggars Banquet BEG 157T

Crummy Stuff/She Belongs To Me
7/86 (UK); Beggars Banquet BEG 167

Crummy Stuff/She Belongs To Me/I Don't Want To Live This Life
7/86 (UK); Beggars Banquet BEG 167T

Real Cool Time/Life Goes On
9/87 (UK); Beggars Banquet BEG 198

Real Cool Time/Life Goes On/Indian Giver
9/87 (UK); Beggars Banquet BEG 198T

I Wanna Live/Merry Christmas (I Don't Wanna Fight Tonight)
11/87 (UK); Beggars Banquet BEG 201

I Wanna Live/Merry Christmas (I Don't Wanna Fight Tonight)
11/87 (UK); Beggars Banquet BEG 201T

Pet Sematary/All Screwed Up
9/89 (UK); Chrysalis CHS 3423

Pet Sematary/All Screwed Up/Zero Zero UFO
9/89 (UK); Chrysalis CHS12 3423

Sheena Is A Punk Rocker/Baby, I Love You
1990 (UK); Old Gold OG9909

Poison Heart/Censorshit
1992 (UK); Chrysalis

Poison Heart/Sheena Is A Punk Rocker (recorded live BBC Scotland, 1991)/
Rockaway Beach (recorded live BBC Scotland, 1991)
1992 (UK); Chrysalis CHS 3917

Poison Heart/Rock'N'Roll Radio (recorded live BBC Scotland, 1991)/Chinese Rocks
(recorded live BBC Scotland, 1991)
1992 (UK); Chrysalis CHS 3917

Carbona Not Glue/I Can't Be (Sub Pop)/Substitute
1994 (UK); Chrysalis

END OF THE DECADE
1990 (UK); Beggars Banquet (Box-set with 6 × 12″s, T-shirt, postcards, poster, 2,500 only)

Poison Heart/Chinese Rock/Sheena Is A Punk Rocker (live)/Rockaway Beach (live)
(12″ single)
1992 (UK); Chrysalis 0496 3 23917 66 (yellow vinyl); Chrysalis CDCHSS 3917

ALBUMS

THE RAMONES
7/76 (UK) Sire 9103 253; (US) Sire SR6020
Blitzkrieg Bop/Beat On The Brat/Judy Is A Punk/I Wanna Be Your Boyfriend/
Chain Saw/Now I Wanna Sniff Some Glue/I Don't Wanna Go Down To The Basement/
Loudmouth/Havana Affair/Listen To My Heart/53rd & 3rd/Let's Dance/I Don't Wanna
Walk Around With You/Today Your Love, Tomorrow The World

RAMONES LEAVE HOME
4/77 (UK) Sire/Warner 9103 254; (US) Sire SA 7528
Glad To See You Go/Gimme Gimme Shock Treatment/I Remember You/Oh Oh I Love
Her So/Carbona Not Glue*/Suzy Is A Headbanger/Pinhead/Now I Wanna Be A Good

* Track was deleted and replaced by 'Babysitter' in the UK and 'Sheena Is A Punk Rocker' in the US.

Boy/Swallow My Pride/What's Your Game/California Sun/Commando/You're Gonna Kill That Girl/You Should Never Have Opened That Door

ROCKET TO RUSSIA
12/77 (UK) Sire/Warner 9103 255-2; (US) Sire SR6042
Cretin Hop/Rockaway Beach/Here Today, Gone Tomorrow/Locket Love/I Don't Care/Sheena Is A Punk Rocker/We're A Happy Family/Teenage Lobotomy/Do You Wanna Dance?/I Wanna Be Well/I Can't Give You Anything/Ramona/Surfin' Bird/Why Is It Always This Way?

ROAD TO RUIN
9/78 Sire/Warner SRK 6063
I Just Want To Have Something To Do/I Wanted Everything/Don't Come Close/I Don't Want You/Needles And Pins/I'm Against It/I Wanna Be Sedated/Go Mental/Questioningly/She's The One/Bad Brain/It's A Long Way Back
All songs written by The Ramones expect 'Needles And Pins' (Bono/Nitzsche)

IT'S ALIVE
4/79 (UK) Sire/Warner SRK 2-6074 (double album)
Rockaway Beach/Teenage Lobotomy/Blitzkrieg Bop/I Wanna Be Well/Glad To See You Go/Gimme Gimme Shock Treatment/You're Gonna Kill That Girl/I Don't Care/Sheena Is A Punk Rocker/Havana Affair/Commando/Here Today, Gone Tomorrow/Surfin' Bird/Cretin Hop/Listen to My Heart/California Sun/I Don't Wanna Walk Around With You/Pinhead/Do You Wanna Dance?/Chainsaw/Today Your Love, Tomorrow the World/I Wanna Be A Good Boy/Judy Is A Punk/Suzy Is A Headbanger/Let's Dance/Oh Oh I Love Her So/Now I Wanna Sniff Some Glue/We're A Happy Family

END OF THE CENTURY
1/80 Sire SRK 6077
Do You Remember Rock'N'Roll Radio?/I'm Affected/Danny Says/Chinese Rock/The Return Of Jackie And Judy/Let's Go/Baby, I Love You/I Can't Make It On Time/This Ain't Havana/Rock'N'Roll High School/All The Way/High Risk Insurance

PLEASANT DREAMS
7/81 Sire SRK 3571
We Want The Airwaves/All's Quiet On The Eastern Front/The KKK Took My Baby Away/Don't Go/You Sound Like You're Sick/It's Not My Place (In The 9 To 5 World)/She's A Sensation/7-11/You Didn't Mean Anything To Me/Come On Now/This Business Is Killing Me/Sitting In My Room

SUBTERRANEAN JUNGLE
4/83 (UK); Sire 9 23800-1; (US) Sire 7 23800-1
Little Bit O' Soul/I Need Your Love/Outsider/What'd Ya Do?/Highest Trails Above/Somebody Like Me/Psycho Therapy/Time Has Come Today/My-My Kind Of A Girl/In The Park/Time Bomb/Everytime I Eat Vegetables It Makes Me Think Of You

TOO TOUGH TO DIE
1/85 (UK) Beggars Banquet BEGA 59; (US) Sire/Warner 7 25817-1
Mama's Boy/I'm Not Afraid Of Life/Too Tough To Die/Durango 95/Wart Hog/Danger Zone/Chasing The Night/Howling At The Moon/Daytime Dilemma (Dangers Of Love)/Planet Earth 1988/Human Kind/Endless Vacation/No Go

Selected Discography

ANIMAL BOY
7/86 (UK) Beggars Banquet BEGA 70; (US) Sire 7 25433-1/7 25433-2
Somebody Put Something In My Drink/Animal Boy/Love Kills/Apeman Hop/ She Belongs To Me/Crummy Stuff/My Brain Is Hanging Upside Down (Bonzo Goes To Bitburg)/ Mental Hell/Eat That Rat/Freak Of Nature/Hair Of The Dog/Something To Believe In

HALFWAY TO SANITY
10/87 (UK) Beggars Banquet BEGA 89; Beggars Banquet BEGA 89CD; (US) Sire 9 25641-1/9 25641-2
I Wanna Live/Bop 'Til You Drop/Garden Of Serenity/Weasel Face/Go Lil' Camaro Go/ I Know Better Now/Death Of Me/I Lost My Mind/A Real Cool Time/I'm Not Jesus/ Bye Bye Baby/Worm Man

BRAIN DRAIN
8/89 (UK) Chrysalis CHR 1725; Chrysalis CCD 1725; (US) Sire 7 25905-1/9 25905-2
I Believe In Miracles/Zero Zero UFO/Don't Bust My Chops/Punishment Fits The Crime/ All Screwed Up/Palisades Park/Pet Sematary/Learn To Listen/Can't Get You Outta My Mind/Ignorance Is Bliss/Come Back, Baby/Merry Christmas (I Don't Want To Fight Tonight)

LOCO LIVE
10/91 (UK) Chrysalis CCD 1901
The Good, The Bad And The Ugly/Durango 95/Teenage Lobotomy/Psycho Therapy/ Blitzkrieg Bop/Rock'N'Roll High School/I Wanna Be Sedated/The KKK Took My Baby Away/I Wanna Live/Bonzo Goes To Bitburg/Too Tough To Die/Sheena Is A Punk Rocker/Rockaway Beach/Pet Sematary/Don't Bust My Chops/Palisades Park/Mama's Boy/ Animal Boy/Wart Hog/Surfin' Bird/Cretin Hop/I Don't Wanna Walk Around With You/ Today Your Love, Tomorrow The World/Pinhead/Somebody Put Something In My Drink/ Beat On The Brat/Judy Is A Punk/Chinese Rocks/Love Kills/Ignorance Is Bliss

LOCO LIVE
10/91 (US) Sire/Warner 9 26650-2
The Good, The Bad And The Ugly/Durango 95/Teenage Lobotomy/Psycho Therapy/ Blitzkrieg Bop/Do You Remember Rock'N'Roll Radio?/I Believe In Miracles/Gimme Gimme Shock Treatment/Rock'N'Roll High School/I Wanna Be Sedated/The KKK Took My Baby Away/I Wanna Live/My Brain Is Hanging Upside Down (Bonzo Goes To Bitburg)/Chinese Rocks/Sheena Is A Punk Rocker/Rockaway Beach/Pet Sematary/ Carbona Not Glue/Judy Is A Punk/Mama's Boy/Animal Boy/Wart Hog/Surfin' Bird/ Cretin Hop/I Don't Wanna Walk Around With You/Today Your Love, Tomorrow The World/Pinhead/Somebody Put Something In My Drink/Beat On The Brat/Ignorance Is Bliss/I Just Want To Have Something To Do/Havana Affair/I Don't Wanna Go Down To The Basement

MONDO BIZARRO
1992 (UK) Chrysalis 3 21960 2
1992 (US) Radioactive RAR-10615/RARD-10615
Censorshit/The Job That Ate My Brain/Poison Heart/Anxiety/Strength To Endure/ It's Gonna Be Alright/Take It As It Comes/Main Man/Tomorrow She Goes Away/ I Won't Let It Happen/Cabbies On Crack/Heidi Is A Headcase/Touring

ACID EATERS
1993 (UK) Chrysalis CHR 6052/CD CHR 6052
Journey To The Center Of The Mind/Substitute/Out Of Time/The Shape Of Things To Come/Somebody To Love/When I Was Young/7 And 7 Is/My Back Pages/ Can't Seem To Make You Mine/Have You Ever Seen The Rain/I Can't Control Myself/ Surf City (+ Surfin' Safari on Japanese edition)

¡ADIOS AMIGOS!
1995 (UK) Chrysalis CHR 6104
1995 (US) Radioactive RARD-11273
I Don't Wanna Grow Up/Makin' Monsters For My Friend/It's Not For Me To Know/ The Crusher/Life's A Gas/Take The Pain Away/I Love You/Cretin Family/Have A Nice Day/Scattergun/Got A Lot To Say/She Talks To Rainbows/Born To Die In Berlin ('Spiderman' is hidden track on US LP pressing; 'R.A.M.O.N.E.S.' is bonus track on Japan pressing.)

GREATEST HITS LIVE
1996 (UK) Radioactive RARD-11459-1
(US) Radioactive RARD-11459-2
Durango 95/Blitzkrieg Bop/Do You Remember Rock'N'Roll Radio?/I Wanna Be Sedated/Spider Man/I Don't Want To Grow Up/Sheena Is A Punk Rocker/Rockaway Beach/Strength To Endure/Cretin Family/Do You Wanna Dance?/We're A Happy Family/ The Crusher/53rd & 3rd/Beat On The Brat/Pet Sematary/R.A.M.O.N.E.S. (New studio track, originally performed by Motorhead on their album *1916*)/Any Way You Want It (New studio track. Originally performed by the Dave Clark Five.)

WE'RE OUTTA HERE!
11/97 (UK) Eagle EDLEAG007-2
(US) Radioactive RARD-11555
This live album documents the Ramones' final concert at The Palace in Hollywood, California, on August 6, 1996.
Durango 95/Teenage Lobotomy/Psycho Therapy/Blitzkrieg Bop/Do You Remember Rock'N'Roll Radio?/I Believe In Miracles/Gimme Gimme Shock Treatment/Rock 'N' Roll High School/I Wanna Be Sedated/Spider Man/The KKK Took My Baby Away/ I Just Want To Have Something To Do/Commando/Sheena Is A Punk Rocker/ Rockaway Beach/Pet Sematary/The Crusher/Love Kills (with Dee Dee Ramone)/ Do You Wanna Dance?/Somebody Put Something In My Drink/I Don't Want You/ Wart Hog/Cretin Hop/R.A.M.O.N.E.S. (with Lemmy from Motorhead)/Today Your Love, Tomorrow The World/Pinhead/53rd & 3rd (with Tim Armstrong and Lars Fredrikson of Rancid)/Listen To Your Heart/We're A Happy Family/Chinese Rocks (with Ben Shepard of Soundgarden)/Beat On The Brat/Any Way You Want It (with Eddie Vedder of Pearl Jam)

COMPILATIONS & REISSUES

RAMONES MANIA
6/88 (UK) Sire 925 709-2 (double album); (CD) Sire 925709 2
I Wanna Be Sedated/Teenage Lobotomy/Do You Remember Rock'N'Roll Radio?/ Gimme Gimme Shock Treatment/Beat On The Brat/Sheena Is A Punk Rocker/ I Wanna Live/Pinhead/Blitzkrieg Bop/Cretin Hop/Rockaway Beach/Commando/

I Wanna Be Your Boyfriend/Mama's Boy/Bop 'Til You Drop/We're A Happy Family/
Bonzo Goes To Bitburg/Outsider/Psycho Therapy/Wart Hog/Animal Boy/
Needles And Pins/Howling At The Moon (Sha-La-La)/Somebody Put Something In
My Drink/We Want The Airwaves/Chinese Rock/I Just Wanna Have Something To Do/
The KKK Took My Baby Away/Indian Giver (previously available only as a B-side)/
Rock'N'Roll High School

ALL THE STUFF (AND MORE) VOL. 1
8/90 Sire CD 759926204
Repackage of RAMONES and LEAVE HOME albums with bonus tracks:
I Don't Wanna Be Learned/I Don't Be Tamed/I Can't Be/Babysitter/California Sun (Live)/
I Don't Wanna Walk Around With You (Live)

ALL THE STUFF (AND MORE) VOL. 2
Repackage of ROCKET TO RUSSIA and ROAD TO RUIN albums with bonus tracks:
Slug/I Want You Around/I Don't Want To Live This Life (Anymore)/Yea, Yea

RAMONES
2001 Rhino
Remastered version of original album with previously unissued bonus tracks:
I Wanna Be Your Boyfriend (Demo)/Judy Is A Punk (Demo)/I Don't Care (Demo)/
I Can't Be (Demo)/Now I Wanna Sniff Some Glue (Demo)/I Don't Wanna Be Learned/
I Don't Wanna Be Tamed (Demo)/You Should Never Have Opened That Door (Demo)/
Blitzkreig Bop (Single-version)

LEAVE HOME
2001 Rhino
Remastered version of original album with previously unissued bonus tracks:
Babysitter (Studio) and Loudmouth/Beat On The Brat/Blitzkrieg Bop/I Remember You/
Glad To See You Go/Chain Saw/53rd & 3rd/I Wanna Be Your Boyfriend/Havana Affair/
Listen To My Heart/California Sun/Judy Is A Punk/I Don't Wanna Walk Around
With You/Today Your Love, Tomorrow The World/Now I Wanna Sniff Some Glue/
Let's Dance (all live Roxy Club, Hollywood, CA, 8/12/76)

ROCKET TO RUSSIA
2001 Rhino
Remastered version of original album with previously unissued bonus tracks:
Needles And Pins (Early Version)/Slug (Demo)/It's A Long Way Back To Germany (UK
B-side)/I Don't Care (Single Version)/Sheena Is A Punk Rocker (Single Version)

ROAD TO RUIN
2001 Rhino
Remastered version of original album with previously unissued bonus tracks:
I Want You Around (Ed Stasium version)/Rock'N'Roll High School (Ed Stasium
version)/Blitzkrieg Bop - Teenage Lobotomy - California Sun – Pinhead - She's The One
(medley, live at the Roxy, Hollywood)/Come Back, She Cried a.k.a I Walk Out
(Demo Version/Yea, Yea (Demo Version)

END OF THE CENTURY
2001 Rhino
Remastered version of original album with previously unissued bonus tracks:

I Want You Around (Soundtrack version)/Danny Says (Demo)/I'm Affected (Demo)/Please Don't Leave (Demo)/All The Way (Demo)/Do You Remember Rock'N'Roll Radio? (Demo)

PLEASANT DREAMS
2001 Rhino
Remastered version of original album with previously unissued bonus tracks:
Touring (1981 version)/I Can't Get You Out Of My Mind/Chop Suey (Alternate Version)/Sleeping Troubles (Demo)/Kicks To Try (Demo)/I'm Not The Answer (Demo)/Stares In This Town (Demo)

SUBTERRANEAN JUNGLE
2001 Rhino
Remastered version of original album with previously unissued bonus tracks:
Indian Giver (Original Mix)/New Girl In Town/No One To Blame (Demo)/Roots Of Hatred (Demo)/Bumming Along (Demo)/Unhappy Girl (Demo)/My-My Kind Of Girl (Acoustic Demo)

TOO TOUGH TO DIE
2001 Rhino
Remastered version of original album with previously unissued bonus tracks:
Street Fighting Man/Smash You (UK single)/Howling At The Moon (Sha-La-La) (Demo)/Planet Earth 1988 (Dee Dee vocal version)/Daytime Dilemma (Dangers Of Love) (Demo)/Endless Vacation (Demo)/Danger Zone (Dee Dee vocal version)/Out Of Here/Mama's Boy (Demo)/Pass This Way/Too Tough To Die (Dee Dee vocal version)/No Go (Demo)

ANTHOLOGY
May 2001
Warners CD 8122735572
Disc 1: Blitzkrieg Bop, Beat On The Brat/Judy Is A Punk/I Wanna Be Your Boyfriend/53rd & 3rd/Now I Wanna Sniff Some Glue/Glad To See You Go/Gimme Gimme Shock Treatment/I Remember You/California Sun/Commando/Swallow My Pride/Carbona Not Glue/Pinhead/Sheena Is A Punk Rocker/Cretin Hop/Rockaway Beach/Here Today, Gone Tomorrow/Teenage Lobotomy/ Surfin' Bird/I Don't Care/I Just Want To Have Something To Do/I Wanna Be Sedated/Don't Come Close/She's The One/Needles And Pins/Rock'N'Roll High School/I Want You Around/Do You Remember Rock'N'Roll Radio?/Chinese Rocks/Danny Says/Baby, I Love You
Disc 2: The KKK Took My Baby Away/She's A Sensation/It's Not My Place (In The 9 To 5 World)/We Want The Airwaves/Psycho Therapy/Howling At The Moon (Sha-La-La)/Mama's Boy/Daytime Dilemma (Dangers Of Love)/I'm Not Afraid Of Life/Too Tough To Die/Endless Vacation/My Brain Is Hanging Upside Down/Somebody Put Something In My Drink/Something To Believe In/I Don't Want To Live This Life (Anymore)/I Wanna Live/Garden Of Serenity/Merry Christmas (I Don't Wanna Fight Tonight)/Pet Sematary/I Believe In Miracles/Tomorrow She Goes Away/Poison Heart/I Don't Wanna Grow Up/She Talks To Rainbows/R.A.M.O.N.E.S.